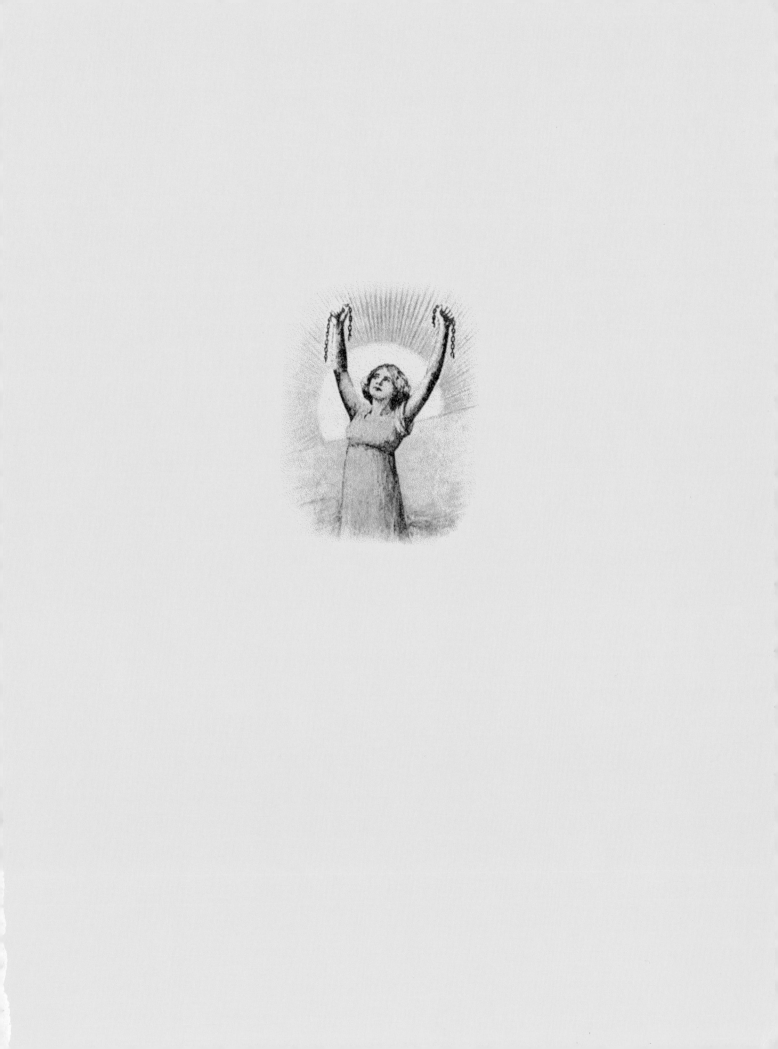

WINNING THE VOTE

WINNING

AMERICAN GRAPHIC PRESS

THE VOTE

THE TRIUMPH OF THE AMERICAN WOMAN SUFFRAGE MOVEMENT

ROBERT P. J. COONEY, JR.

in collaboration with the
National Women's History Project

ISBN 0-9770095-0-5   Cloth
ISBN 0-9770095-1-3   Special Edition
Library of Congress Control Number: 2005904560

Published and distributed by
American Graphic Press
P. O. Box 8403
Santa Cruz, CA 95061

Available from the
National Women's History Project
3343 Industrial Drive, Suite 4
Santa Rosa, CA 95403
(707) 636-2888, Fax (707) 636-2909
www.nwhp.org

Dustjacket and book design by Robert Cooney Graphic Design.
Composition by Scott Perry at Archetype Typography, Berkeley, CA.
Printed in Canada.

Dustjacket cover and title page photograph courtesy of the New Jersey
Historical Society.
Cover emblem by Nina Allender courtesy of the National Woman's Party.
Frontispiece courtesy of the Sophia Smith Collection, Smith College.
Photographic credits begin on page 463.

for Margaret

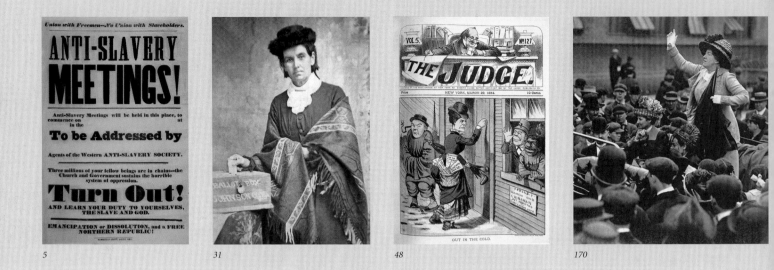

5   31   48   170

Contents

289   260   345   456

THE VOTE

Acknowledgments

Since beginning my research for this book in the early 1990s, I have encountered people who have gone out of their way to help. I want to express to each of them my deepest appreciation for their assistance, and to acknowledge their contributions to making this book a reality. I have been blessed and guided by forces beyond my understanding during this project, and I am grateful for having been able to do this work.

Just after I started this book I found *Women's History Sources,* a wonderful reference work that lists manuscript collections in universities, museums, and institutions related to woman suffrage and individual suffragists. It guided my years of research and correspondence with public and private sources nationwide.

I have relied on the work of many historians, biographers, journalists, and suffragists themselves in compiling this account. Their books and articles are listed in the bibliography. I encourage readers to make use of these resources to gain a fuller picture of this multi-faceted movement.

I benefited greatly from the individuals in the institutions listed in the photo credits – and many not listed – who helped me search for and reproduce images from their collections. I especially want to thank Marie-Helen Gold and Jacalyn Blume at the Schlesinger Library, Edith Mayo and Lisa Kathleen Graddy at the Smithsonian Institution, the staff of the Sophia Smith Collection, Dorothy Ferrell Gevinson and Jennifer Spencer at the National Woman's Party, and Sheridan Harvey, Janet Ruth, Maja Keech, the photoduplication staff, and many other helpful souls at the Library of Congress. I also want to acknowledge the friendly assistance of Heather March-Rumion at Corbis, Susanna Steisel and Ken Burns at Florentine Films, Coline Jenkins-Shalin at the Elizabeth Cady Stanton Foundation,

Ann Forfreedom, Rachel Sweeney, and suffrage collectors Frank Corbeil, Ronnie Lapinsky, and Dr. Danny Crew.

Throughout this process Molly Murphy MacGregor and her colleagues at the National Women's History Project have been of enormous help. Molly led me to many of the scholars who reviewed my manuscript, and her support and friendship have been an unfailing source of encouragement for years.

My research was accelerated when historian Amelia Fry referred me to Ruth Pollak at the educational film center. Working with Ruth to locate images for her 1995 PBS documentary, "One Woman, One Vote," allowed me to visit key sources in Chicago, Los Angeles, New York, Boston, and Washington D.C. personally, which makes all the difference. I also made extensive use of the University of California at Berkeley and the Bancroft Library nearby.

My particular thanks go to those who reviewed and commented on early drafts of this manuscript. Their advice, corrections, questions, and suggestions improved the book immensely. These women – professors, historians, writers, teachers, and other professionals – generously gave their time and shared their hard-earned expertise.

Calling on their overall knowledge of the movement, I was privileged to receive the comments of Mary Ruthsdotter, Alice Sheppard, Ann Gordon, Ellen DuBois, Bonnie Eisenberg, Edith Mayo, Linda Wharton, Dorothy Bristol, and Margaret Zierdt. A.T. Birmingham-Young offered help with style questions as well, as did my friend Elizabeth Whitney. Anne Derousie, Sally Roesch Wagner, and Judith Wellman were of particular help with specific historical periods. I also appreciated the responses of Ann Lewis, Doris Weatherford, Joan Meacham, Ruth Pollak,

Holding hands on a windy Saturday afternoon, suffragists in New York City marched up Fifth Avenue during the great Banner Parade on October 23, 1915.

and Molly Murphy MacGregor. Mistakes are solely mine, and readers are encouraged to respond with corrections and any leads to additional material.

While recognizing my early teachers, I also want to acknowledge the influence of the Institute for the Study of Nonviolence, which was located in Palo Alto, California. There, in the early 1970s, I learned to appreciate grassroots, non-governmental social change efforts like the woman suffrage movement. Not only was I immersed in the discussion and practice of Gandhian nonviolence, but I was also surrounded by charismatic organizers and outspoken women activists passionate about ending war. The experience helped me understand the dynamics of a national political movement. Fellow staff members, and Institute founders Joan Baez, Ira Sandperl, and Roy Keppler, led me to the work of nonviolent theorists including Gene Sharp, Barbara Deming, and George Lakey. I gratefully salute them all.

My family and friends have been an abiding source of strength and reassurance. My sister Ellen Cooney was the first to read the manuscript. My father and late mother, Hildegarde Bramman Cooney, enthusiastically and financially supported my work, as did my stepson, Gabriel Stern. Joan and Paul

Virgo, Art Rogers, Nancy Adess, Suzanne d'Coney, Bob Fitch, Armon Stover, and many other friends and colleagues helped in a multitude of ways.

I could not imagine going through this process without my wife Margaret Fendall Cooney by my side. Her love and encouragement were there throughout the long journey, and she helped ground, guide, and support me in countless ways. Not surprisingly, her energetic relative, Gertrude Fendall, was one of the women jailed for equal suffrage.

During the final months of production I depended on the skill and patience of Scott Perry, who put all the words and pictures together, and his partner Dickie Magidoff at Archetype Typography in Berkeley. They helped me realize my vision for this book and contributed substantially to its final quality. I also appreciated the assistance of Duncan McCallum at Spectrum Books and Ralph Hamm at Friesens Printing. Vito Victor reviewed and edited the final manuscript, and Jannie Dresser did a fine job compiling the index.

Thank you all for your invaluable help making this book, and this history, come alive.

Robert P. J. Cooney, Jr.
July 4, 2005

Introduction

THE WOMAN SUFFRAGE MOVEMENT wrote a remarkable chapter in American history. Over a period spanning 70 years, the suffrage cause involved hundreds of thousands of Americans and resulted in the enfranchisement of half the population. This is a central part of our heritage and it offers a spectacular example of the drive for democracy and self-determination that lie at the heart of the American experience.

From the late 1840s, well before the American Civil War, to 1920, just after World War I, American women were involved in a great struggle for their own independence. During this long period, most women were without a direct political voice: They could not vote, hold office, or participate as fully in society as men. In response, a growing number of women organized themselves to pursue their own rights, particularly the right to vote.

The story of how women attained the franchise, and entered into the American governing structure, is a tribute to their passion for independence and their commitment to full participation in the national community. In an extraordinary time, which included slavery, civil war, epidemic, economic depression, and political corruption, suffragists held true to their vision of democratic, nonviolent change. They overcame, or maneuvered around, every obstacle in their way. Gaining the support of male voters and legislators across the country, women validated America's ideals at a critical time in history and gave substance to the dream of a government of the people, by the people, and for the people.

THIS BOOK IS DESIGNED to fill a large gap in our understanding of American history. Not many people are aware of the woman suffrage movement. Few have leaned how women organized politically and rewrote the law of the land to guarantee their rights. The first two decades of the 20th century are a critical period that has been strangely overlooked. Yet these are the years in which suffragists accelerated their efforts and won a conclusive victory.

There is no shortage of material. Vivid photographs and eyewitness accounts of this tumultuous time survive, and they drive the chronology that follows.

Why is this movement so little known? One legitimate reason, certainly, is the complexity of its history. Suffragists faced their powerful and entrenched opponents with an often-confusing assortment of overlapping strategies and simultaneous actions at both the state and the national levels. During the early 20th century alone there were 40 separate referendum campaigns in 26 states. This was in addition to local petition drives, national demonstrations, and hunger strikes in prison. Nationally there were two and sometimes three major women's associations competing for leadership, often with important differences in emphasis and sharp disagreements over tactics. Suffragists were active in nearly all of the 48 states for up to five decades. No wonder the movement has defied easy interpretation.

Suffragists used – and in some cases originated – approaches that reflected a blend of traditional and progressive strategies. Their ability to experiment with specific methods, improving some and abandoning others, attests to their strategic flexibility, an important element in their success. That some women remained loyal to high standards of respectability and decorum, while others adopted more aggressive and often

A final generation of suffragists called for the vote
during the 1913 county fair in Mineola, Long Island, New York.

bitterly controversial stands, shows both the diversity of the participants and the extreme difficulty of their task. All of this, however, has made their story a difficult one to tell.

There may be a deeper reason why we know so little about the popular history of this struggle. In the early years of the movement, male historians were focused on the male legislators, executives, and judges who were obviously destined to control national affairs. There was little interest in women trying to win their own enfranchisement. The result was that, in historian Eleanor Flexner's words, the extraordinarily difficult achievement of winning the vote for women was essentially forgotten "since those who ought to have included it in the history of this country simply obliterated the whole story."

After the 19th amendment was ratified, it may have become difficult for men to admit that women had been systematically excluded for so long, and that they once had to plead with their own fathers, husbands, and sons for the rights that men took for granted. Women's exclusion was ignored because it had been a flaw in our image of us as a nation; it contradicted our stated values. Suffragists called it a "blot on the escutcheon," a stain on our national honor.

Thus a student could read some American histories and never realize that over one half of the adults in our democracy were denied any political voice in its operation for the first 150 years of its existence. Nor would one learn that determined women worked for decades to overcome a fierce and well-funded opposition. Yet the history of their campaign engages some of our most cherished national values. From its ideological origins in the drive to abolish slavery, through its later alliances with the labor movement and the national government during the First World War, woman suffrage was always identified with the passion for liberty that fuels American patriotism.

The struggle was also consistent with our nation's long-standing conservative antipathy to class warfare and violent revolutionary upheaval. Woman suffrage became that rarity: a massive social transformation achieved largely without bloodshed and without creating new and lasting schisms in the population. Perhaps nonviolence originally became a commitment because of the proportionately large number of Quakers in the early woman's rights leadership. But it was adopted later as a strategy by deliberate and informed choice. American suffragists rejected violence and threats; theirs was a revolution that aimed at converting their opponents, winning legal protection, and transforming society to include women as equal participants with men. Suffragists understood that justice and reconciliation were their goals, and that the enemy was not men per se, but the discriminatory and prejudicial treatments long sanctioned by male-dominated society.

The first step, of course, was to make women aware of public affairs and to enlist them as participants. It was here that the struggle against slavery was of paramount importance. The authors of the *History of Woman Suffrage* (1881) credit that movement with enlisting women for the first time in a cause with national scope. Their period prose evokes the era vividly:

"The ranks of the Abolitionists were composed of the most eloquent orators, the ablest logicians, men and women of the purest moral character and best minds of the nation. They were usually spoken of in the early days as 'an illiterate, ill-mannered, poverty-stricken, crazy set of long-haired Abolitionists,' While the fact is, some of the most splendid specimens of manhood and womanhood, in physical appearance, in culture, refinement, and knowledge of polite life, were found among the early Abolitionists . . .

"In the early Anti-Slavery conventions, the broad principles of human rights were so exhaustively discussed, justice, liberty and equality so clearly taught, that the women who crowded to listen readily learned the lesson of freedom for themselves, and early began to take part in the debates and business affairs of all associations. Woman not only felt every pulsation of man's heart for freedom, and by her enthusiasm inspired the glowing eloquence that maintained him through the struggle, but earnestly advocated with her own lips human freedom and equality."

In the decades that followed the Civil War it was the cause of woman's rights that similarly impressed another generation of women and men. The issue of suffrage was by no means the only challenge that women faced. Their development was obstructed by widespread discrimination in a society that championed education, employment, and enfranchisement for men but had long denied those rights to women. By the early 20th century, we can see the results of what the *History of Woman Suffrage* authors called "the great uprising of women out of the lethargy of the past."

Politics was the key. When Carrie Chapman Catt tried to explain why it had taken so long for women's rights to be recognized, she chose one word: politics. It was not an antagonistic, uneducated, or indifferent public that blocked equal suffrage, she and Nettie Shuler claimed in their 1923 book, *Woman Suffrage and Politics*, "it was the control of public sentiment, the deflecting and the thwarting of public sentiment, through the trading and the trickery, the buying and selling of American politics." It was ongoing, short-term political expediency –

more concerned with power than gender – that refused to recognize women's democratic rights.

Suffragists learned political organizing out of necessity in order to fashion an effective grassroots reform movement. Their later successes show how well they learned. Unenfranchised women became influential forces in states like New York, Illinois, Massachusetts, and Texas, and pressed their claim with sophistication and success. Their political strategies, including their coalitions to defeat opponents in the various legislatures and Congress, spoke to male politicians in ways they could no longer ignore. In this regard, the dynamics of the suffrage movement hold important lessons for modern political reformers. The evolving strategies suffragists used at different times, and the nonviolent tactics they employed, all merit closer analysis. Their actions underscored both the complicated problems they repeatedly faced, and their remarkable ability to find creative solutions to them.

Some men immediately saw the justice of "the cause," as it came to be known. Other men – and women – never did. In some cases they actively worked against women voting. Opponents of both sexes tried to brand woman suffrage as a gender-challenging and tradition-breaking reform, but it was the economic power of the male business world that gave anti-suffrage efforts their muscle.

The story of men's conversion is a key aspect of suffrage history. Ultimately, suffragists persuaded enough men – voters, but especially legislators – of the justice of their cause to win the support they needed. While not the driving force in the movement, male involvement and approval were central to all the state electoral drives as well as the lobbying campaigns in Congress and the legislatures. Besides the women profiled in this book, there were many male heroes in the equal suffrage movement.

In addition to its historical importance, the suffrage movement is full of wonderful stories. It has adventure, daring, heroism, defeat, recovery, and ultimate triumph. There is the love of justice and the passion for liberty throughout, with eloquent words infused with raw truth and intense conviction. There are also conflicts, philosophical and strategic disagreements, personal rivalries, ambition and betrayal. The whole range of human emotions – from despair to elation – is present, linked not only to personal issues but also to the universal quest for freedom. No writer or editor could ask for richer material.

The cause united an enormously diverse array of people, not just in the electorate but also among suffragists themselves. The families and the friendships that bound these women together were extremely important in keeping the movement alive and focused. The links were often direct, since daughters of suffragists often followed in their mother's and father's footsteps, sometimes engaging three generations. Other connections evolved as the movement grew and more women were drawn to the work. Their friendships and voluntary partnerships formed the basis for what became a national movement.

One cannot but respect the women who rose to the task. Their courage, resolve, and sense of self set them apart from other women of their time. Their stories brim with life – pioneer life, early life in the national capital, life on the Kansas prairie, and life in the mansions, tenements and precincts of New York City. Their personal memories and experiences help place the cause in its human context.

After winning the vote in 1920, a new generation of women revitalized society with the women's liberation movement in 1970. But today much work remains to be done. The obstacles women have long faced have not entirely disappeared, and true equality has not yet been realized. Women are gaining positions of real economic and political power, and as they do, the story of winning women's rights becomes even more timely and significant.

Recognizing and honoring the struggle of women 100 years ago reminds us of their vision, persistence, and sacrifice. Women's drive for political freedom helped shape the history of our country and remains a noble heritage in which we can take enormous pride. For, as many participants and supporters at the time realized, the achievement of American suffragists represented the triumph of American democracy and in a world of conflict and division, that triumph remains a shining hope.

A Note on Terminology: The most common abbreviations used are: NAWSA (National American Woman Suffrage Association), NWP (National Woman's Party), CU (Congressional Union), and WCTU (Woman's Christian Temperance Union). Period terminology, such as "disfranchisement," has been retained for consistency. The label "suffragette" is reserved for the British militants; "suffragist" is the term most American activists used. Woman suffrage, and woman's rights, were also the accepted phrases.

Leslie's

THE PEOPLE'S WEEKLY

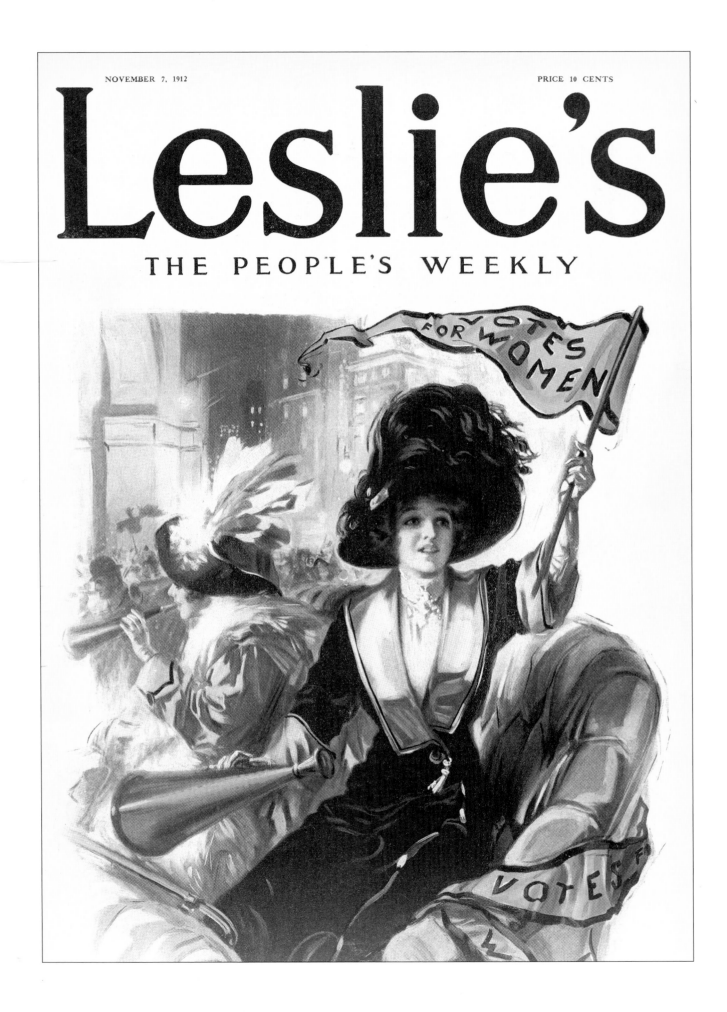

Chapter 1: 1800-1865

Raising the Call for Woman's Rights

THE DEMAND by American women for the right to vote emerged during the anti-slavery campaigns of the 1830s and 1840s. While individual women had spoken out for equal rights for decades, and had acted bravely on their beliefs, the ability to organize women effectively took years to develop.

In the early 19th century women were generally limited to family, children, and domestic duties, with few opportunities for education or decent employment. Women were rarely allowed to speak publicly and were expected to be silent supporters of their fathers, husbands, and male family members. Nonetheless, a few notable figures during the colonial years made a strong case for greater rights for women. Others have undoubtedly been forgotten.

One was Margaret Brent, born in England about 1601, whose courage and sound judgment were widely acknowledged in the Maryland colony. In 1648 she demanded her right as a property owner to vote in the colonial assembly, but her request was denied by the all-male body. After an impassioned protest, she left Maryland for Virginia.

Patriotic women during the Revolutionary War period

Margaret Brent's early argument before the Maryland Assembly was commemorated by this plaque in Historic St. Mary's City.

took risks to win independence, fully conscious of their own legally inferior status. Abigail Adams, the wife and mother of U.S. presidents, is renowned for her advice to her statesman husband John in 1776:

"In the new code of laws which I suppose it will be necessary for you to make, I desire you would remember the ladies and be more favorable to them than your ancestors. Do not put such unlimited power into the hands of husbands. Remember all men would be tyrants if they could. If particular care and attention are not paid to the ladies, we are determined to foment a rebellion and will not hold ourselves bound to

obey any laws in which we have no voice or representation." Her husband responded with amusement noting, "We know better than to repeal our masculine system."

The work of several intellectual women from abroad greatly influenced many Americans in the years following the Revolution. These included Mary Wollstonecraft in England as well as Frances Wright, Ernestine Rose, and Harriet Martineau. Several male lecturers and writers also championed the ideal of women's equality and inspired more organized activity for woman's rights in the U.S. as the young country established itself.

Making an enthusiastic appeal, two stylish suffragists cheered an election day crowd in this 1912 illustration (facing page) on the cover of *Leslie's* magazine. Campaigning for the vote had gone on for over sixty years by the time this issue of *Leslie's* appeared and women were still trying to win enfranchisement at both the state and national levels. Few such public displays as parades or street speaking occurred in the U.S. during the more discreet and circumspect 19th century, but the passion, courage, and vitality of women in the suffrage movement were evident throughout its long history. A wide array of buttons and badges (below) broadcast their demand during the early 20th century.

Losing the Vote After the Revolution

AFTER THE Revolution of 1776 former colonies, now states, rewrote their constitutions to clearly define voting requirements. Male lawmakers generally restricted the electorate to other white male citizens who met certain property and residency requirements.

In New Jersey, however, probably reflecting the state's Quaker influence, the 1776 constitution defined voters as "all inhabitants" and some women, Black and white, apparently voted in the state until male legislators disfranchised them in 1807. Women denounced the move as illegal

and petitioned the legislature without success. New York and other states had already limited voting to men and most new states and territories followed suit.

Women were excluded from or segregated within nearly all colonial institutions. In the mid-1830s, when

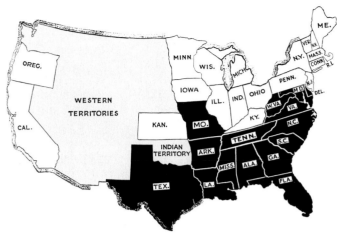

Slavery Divides a Growing Nation and Compels Women's Involvement

BETWEEN 1820 and 1860 slavery in the United States grew to include over four million Black men, women, and children constituting a substantial portion of the young country's population. Slavery supporters violently defended the institution, attacking abolitionists, disrupting meetings, and raiding anti-slavery offices to silence the opposition.

Foremost among the women who first spoke out against slavery were Angelina and Sarah Grimke of South Carolina who left their well-established, slave-holding family and resettled in Philadelphia. There they lectured to anti-slavery meetings in the late 1830s despite harsh criticism from clergymen. Challenged on account of their sex, the Grimke sisters added a defense of a woman's right to speak to their appeals for abolition.

Their courageous example encouraged other women to speak out for both abolition and woman's rights. As historian Eleanor Flexner noted, "It was in the abolition movement that women first learned to organize, to hold public meetings, to conduct petition campaigns. As abolitionists they first won the right to speak in public, and began to evolve a philosophy of their place in society and of their basic rights." Working to end slavery, women launched their own drive for equality.

Above: The extent of slavery in 1860. Below: A pro-slavery mob destroying an abolitionist printing press.

organized efforts mounted for the complete abolition of slavery, few women were active in the newly formed anti-slavery societies. Those who publicly denounced slavery were condemned for going beyond women's domestic "sphere." But this criticism led them to reflect on their own condition as women and to compare their legal status with that of the slave. This led individual women to speak out bravely in defense of their own rights as women and, slowly, to organize.

Above: Women voted in New Jersey until 1807.

Abby Kelley Foster played a central role in the American abolition movement. Born on a rural Massachusetts farm and raised a Quaker, Foster was 28 when she began to lecture in 1838. For over 15 years she toured the northeast and midwest calling for the abolition of slavery before mostly hostile audiences. She bravely faced ridicule, rocks, and rotten fruit hurled at her because of both her opposition to slavery and her gender. Foster became a legendary organizer and outstanding fundraiser who spoke at several early woman's rights conventions. Her example inspired many future leaders including Lucy Stone, who later wrote of Foster that "the movement for the equal rights for women began directly and emphatically with her."

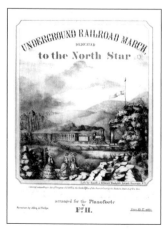

Courageous Women Speak Out Against Slavery

THE INHUMAN horror of the slave trade, which included the breakup of families and the buying and selling of women and children, lit the passions of Black and white abolitionists in the 1830s. However, in opposing slavery they challenged a deeply-entrenched and staunchly-defended national institution with strong economic, religious, and cultural ties. Many citizens including clergymen unquestioningly supported slavery and barely considered the subjection of women and reacted strongly when either practice was challenged.

Anti-slavery agents traveled and spoke extensively, facing sometimes violent attacks, but they gradually built up an active and influential following. From the 1830s on, abolitionists organized meetings, circulated petitions, published tracts, boycotted the products of slave labor, and helped individual slaves escape through the legendary "Underground Railroad" of safe houses, memorialized in story and song (bottom left).

Many of the women who first publicly opposed slavery were members of the Society of Friends, or Quakers. Quaker belief held that men and women were equals, and in religious meetings women could speak as freely as men and so gained experience denied most other women of the time. The example of Quakers led the way for a larger outcry against slavery and later against the oppressive treatment of women.

Above: An enslaved woman and child on the auction block. Below: An 1851 petition.

CIRCULATE THE PETITION

NO MORE SLAVE HUNTING IN THE EMPIRE STATE.

Send up long lists of signatures early in January, addressed to some reliable member of the Legislature, or to Lydia Mott, Anti-Slavery Office, Albany, N. Y.

☞ Orders for blank Petitions, Tracts for gratuitous distribution, also letters relative to lectures, and those containing contributions to the cause, should be addressed to the General Agent, LYDIA MOTT, Anti-Slavery Office, Albany, N. Y.

☞ The Fourth Annual New York State Anti-Slavery Convention will be held at Albany, the first Tuesday and Wednesday of February, 1861

PETITION.

To the Honorable Senate and Assembly of the State of New York :

The undersigned, citizens of   State of New York, respectfully ask you to put an end to SLAVE HUNTING, in New York, by enacting that no person, who has been held as a slave, shall be delivered up by any officer or court, State or federal, within this State, to any one claiming him on the ground that he owes "service or labor" to such claimant, by the laws of one of the Slave States of this Union.

"Thou shalt NOT deliver unto his master the servant which is escaped from his master unto thee: *he shall dwell with thee, even among you in that place which he shall choose in one of thy gates, WHERE IT LIKETH HIM BEST: thou shalt not oppress him.*"—DEUT. xxiii, 15 and 16.

NAMES.	NAMES.

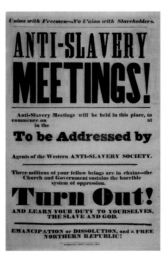

Lucy Stone, a Massachusetts farmer's daughter, was one of the first women to lecture publicly for woman's rights. Stone worked as a teacher to pay for her own education, graduating from Oberlin in 1847 at the age of 30, and then touring widely as an anti-slavery lecturer. She soon began speaking for woman's rights explaining, "I was a woman before I was an abolitionist. I must speak for the women." When she married abolitionist Henry Blackwell in 1855 her decision to keep her own name and omit the word "obey" from the ceremony was widely publicized. Stone disarmed critics with her courage and quiet sincerity and converted many who heard or read her widely-reprinted speeches.

The life of an "abolition emissary" (above) was challenging, grueling, and often dangerous. Traveling in even severe weather to address audiences of every sort, field workers needed a deep reservoir of courage, conviction, and common sense to succeed. They were supported in the field through funds raised by anti-slavery societies and by the speakers themselves. Pre-printed posters (right) announced local meetings.

Lucretia Mott was a prominent and beloved figure in 19th century reform movements. An eloquent and self-assured Quaker minister from Nantucket, Massachusetts, she was a leader in advocating both abolition and woman's rights. The mother of six, she kept a warm and hospitable home in Philadelphia despite traveling extensively to encourage spiritual growth and "practical righteousness." Recognized as one of the leading abolitionists in America, she was chosen as a delegate to the 1840 World Anti-Slavery Convention in London. When she arrived, the all-male body refused to seat her and the other American women representatives. The experience deepened her dedication and she became an influential mentor for many future woman's rights supporters until her death in 1880. Abolitionists cast anti-slavery tokens (below) to raise money for their work.

Woman's Rights Splits the Male Anti-Slavery Movement

W OMEN RARELY participated in mixed gender organizations outside the home in the early 19th century so women who were active in abolition societies were constantly challenged. Eventually the issue led to a split in the anti-slavery movement. While leading abolitionists in the American Anti-Slavery Society, including William Lloyd Garrison and Wendell Phillips, defended the public role of women, other anti-slavery proponents charged that woman's rights were "irrelevant" and actually "injurious" to the cause and formed their own organization.

In 1840 the World Anti-Slavery Convention in London, amid enormous controversy, refused to recognize the American women as delegates. In protest, Garrison refused to participate and sat through the convention with the women delegates in the rear balcony.

By the 1840s antislavery societies existed throughout

Anti-slavery agitation often triggered violent reactions. When Black women and white women met together in Philadelphia for a second Anti-Slavery Convention of American Women in May 1838 an angry pro-slavery mob numbering over 17,000 surrounded the newly-built Pennsylvania Hall (below) and burnt it down after the meeting. Several years later, when another mob roke up an abolitionist meeting, Lucy Stone bravely entrusted her own safety to one of the men roused against her (above) and her calm appeals convinced him to round up others to hear her speak.

the northern states, particularly in areas rich with Quaker settlements. The Pennsylvania Anti-Slavery Society, an affiliate of the American Anti-Slavery Society, was formed in 1839 and its executive committee (above, in 1851) included several well-known Quakers, and Black as well as white woman's rights activists. In the front, from the left, are anti-slavery editor Oliver Johnson, Margaret Jones Burleigh, Benjamin Bacon, Society president Robert Purvis, Lucretia Mott, and James Mott.

In the rear are journalist Mary Grew, Mott's son-in-law Edward Davis, Haworth Wetherald, Abby Kimber, anti-slavery agent Miller McKim, and schoolmistress Sarah Pugh. Lucretia Mott, Grew, Kimber, and Pugh were all turned away as delegates at the 1840 World Anti-Slavery Convention in London.

Above: Distinguished Pennsylvania abolitionists.

Calling a Woman's

Iₙ ᴍɪᴅ-Jᴜʟʏ 1848 Elizabeth Cady Stanton, Lucretia Mott, Martha Coffin Wright, and Mary Ann M'Clintock met in Jane Hunt's parlor and formed a plan for a "woman's rights convention" in Seneca Falls, New York. They enthusiastically sent off a brief notice to the local newspaper. They then found themselves with just a week to create a program for the unprecedented meeting. It was Stanton, with the help of others, summarized women's overall condition of servitude and social degradation and protested against an array of unjust laws and practices.

The document boldly stated that "all men and women are created equal," then went on to describe how men held "an absolute tyranny" over women. Laws which women had no hand in writing, which were based on the "false supposition of the supremacy of man," discrimi-

East view of the village of Seneca Falls, New York.

who formulated a Declaration of Sentiments, modeled on the Declaration of Independence, which enumerated the injustices women faced in bold and revolutionary language.

A New Declaration of Independence for Women

The Declaration of Sentiments was presented for discussion at the convention's opening day in the Wesleyan Chapel on July 19, 1848. Eloquent in its outrage and indignation, the document nated against them. A woman who married became "in the eyes of the law, civilly dead." No longer a separate individual, she lost the right to own property or make contracts in her own name. An unmarried woman with property paid taxes yet had no say in how her taxes were used.

Men, the Declaration continued, monopolized profitable employment, denied women a thorough education, and thereby closed all "avenues of wealth and

James and Lucretia Mott of Philadelphia were part of the progressive wing of the Society of Friends who were condemned as heretics by the more conservative wing. Lucretia had earned a reputation as a courageous abolitionist and her husband had changed his business so as not to trade in slave-produced cotton. Both reflected ideals of gracious egalitarianism, spirituality, and equality.

When women delegates were turned away from the 1840 World Anti-Slavery Convention in London, it launched the friendship between Lucretia Mott, age 47, and 24-year-old Elizabeth Cady Stanton, on her honeymoon after recently marrying a delegate from New York. While in London the two women spent hours together, and Stanton later wrote that Mott gave her a "new-born sense of dignity and freedom." They even discussed calling a convention "to advocate the rights of women." Eight years passed before they made the idea a reality.

James Mott accompanied his wife to that 1848 Seneca Falls convention and agreed to act as chair when none of the women felt experienced enough to lead the large mixed crowd themselves. A brief notice (below) in the *Seneca County Courier* announced the historic meeting.

Women's Rights Convention.

A Convention to discuss the social, civil and religious condition and rights of Woman, will be held in the Wesleyan Chapel, at Seneca Falls, N. Y., on Wednesday and Thursday the 19th and 20th of July current, commencing at 10 o'clock ᴀ. ᴍ.

During the first day, the meeting will be exclusively for Women, which all are earnestly invited to attend. The public generally are invited to be present on the second day, when Lᴜᴄʀᴇᴛɪᴀ Mᴏᴛᴛ, of Philadelphia, and others both ladies and gentlemen, will address the Convention.

Rights Convention

distinction." Women were excluded from the ministry, were subject to a different moral code, and were constantly having their confidence and self-respect undermined.

And yet, as Stanton emphasized in a later speech, "Every allusion to the degraded and inferior position occupied by women all over the world has been met by scorn and abuse. . . . We meet ridicule, and coarse jests, freely bestowed upon those who dare assert that woman stands by the side of man, his equal, placed here by her God, to enjoy with him the beautiful earth which is her home as it is his!"

The lively two-day meeting drew some 300 people who energetically discussed the issues raised by the various speakers. Resolutions addressing key injustices were passed unanimously, including one that encouraged women to "no longer publish their degradation, by declaring themselves satisfied with their present position."

However, when Stanton proposed that women demand the vote even Lucretia Mott hesitated, fearing that so radical a measure would make the women look foolish. But with the support of abolitionist Frederick Douglass, the controversial proposal was narrowly approved – the first such organized public demand for the vote by women. The final resolutions were signed by 68 women and 32 men.

Within days, though, such a backlash of ridicule and opposition grew up that several people who had signed the document asked to have their names removed. Other participants, however, had anticipated "no small amount of misconception, misrepresentation, and ridicule" and remained steadfast in their resolve to "employ agents, circulate tracts, petition state and national legislatures, and endeavor to enlist pulpit and press in our benefit."

A Second Convention

Two weeks after the Seneca Falls convention, women in nearby Rochester, New York, organized a follow-up meeting which featured many of the same speakers and drew an enthusiastic, overflow audience. This time, despite hesitancy over such an unusual experiment, Abigail Bush chaired the meeting and woman-led meetings became the tradition thereafter.

The Rochester meeting dealt with measures in greater depth and it drew even more critical and satirical response. Lucretia Mott, however, found the interest "encouraging" and hoped the subject "will soon begin to receive the attention that its importance demands."

Seventy-two years had passed since the American Revolution. It would take another seventy-two years for women to win their own political independence. ◆

Elizabeth Cady Stanton, a judge's daughter, learned of women's subordinate legal status as a child in her father's New York law office. Determined to show she was in no way inferior to boys, she excelled at sports and academics. Married in 1840, she moved from cosmopolitan Boston in 1847 to the quiet rural town of Seneca Falls, New York, and by 1848 felt isolated and exasperated with three rambunctious sons, an often-absent husband, and a life of domestic obligations.

In mid-July she visited Lucretia Mott in nearby Waterloo. While unburdening herself with Mott and her Quaker friends Stanton returned to the idea of a convention to address the larger concerns of women. The proceedings of the historic meeting, and those of subsequent conventions, were published as pamphlets (left) and circulated widely.

Between 1842 and 1859 Stanton bore seven children but still made time to write countless letters, articles, and speeches noted for their passion and eloquence. Stanton's forceful personality and intellectual curiosity soon made her one of the most notable advocates of woman's rights in the country.

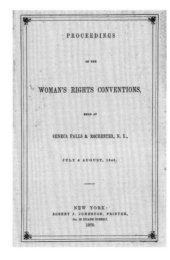

Ernestine Rose was one of the most articulate and influential of the early advocates for woman's rights in the U.S. Born in 1810, the daughter of a rabbi named Potowski, she left her native Poland at 17, rebelling against a marriage contract in which she had no say. Marrying in 1836, she moved to New York City and began to circulate petitions and lobby the legislature in support of a married women's property bill. She also spoke against slavery, in some cases directly to slave-holding southerners. Courageous, provocative, and independent-minded, Rose became one of the leading female orators of the day. Between 1850 and 1870 she addressed several legislatures and audiences in over 20 states. She called for "political, legal, and social equality with men" at the national Woman's Rights Convention in Worcester in 1850, and spoke at many subsequent meetings. She declared in 1844 that "when we hold the earth in common, and enjoy its products as equal children of one family, then there will be nothing to quarrel about."

Organizing the First National Woman's Rights Convention

Following the woman's rights meetings in New York, like-minded women in Ohio held several regional conventions in 1850 hoping to influence the state constitutional convention to consider votes for women.

In May 1850 a small group of abolitionists in Boston, including Lucy Stone and Abby Kelley Foster, met to discuss calling a national woman's rights convention. After Paulina Wright Davis did much of the planning work, the meeting was held on October 23 and 24 in Worcester, Massachusetts. The convention drew over 1,000 people from 11 states including Lucretia Mott, Frederick Douglass, Sojourner Truth, Antoinette Brown, William Lloyd Garrison, and other leading abolitionists. Davis had hoped

To answer a critical clergyman at an 1851 woman's rights convention in Akron, Ohio, Sojourner Truth (above) rose to deliver what became a legendary speech. "That man over there says women need to be helped into carriages and lifted over ditches, and to have the best place everywhere. Nobody ever helps me into carriages or over puddles, or gives me the best place – and ain't I a woman?"

The powerful dignity of the former slave turned itinerant preacher hushed the hecklers and won the audience's acclaim. Articles, lectures (below), and her widespread travels magnified her fame as a courageous advocate for equality and an eloquent defender of human rights. She lived until 1883.

that writer Margaret Fuller would take a leading role on her return from Europe but that brilliant intellectual had just drowned with her family in a shipwreck in July.

While some newspapers reported the convention objectively, others could not help fuming over such inappropriate and "unwomanly" behavior. Nonetheless, news of the meeting spread, and in England an article about it by his wife eventually led John Stuart Mill to write the widely influential book, *The Subjection of Women.*

Above: A satirical illustration from an 1859 *Harper's Weekly* showed the pious and orderly participants at one woman's rights convention being heckled and interrupted by disruptive men in the galleries.

FREE LECTURE!

SOJOURNER TRUTH,

Who has been a slave in the State of New York, and who has been a Lecturer for the last twenty-three years, whose characteristics have been so vividly portrayed by Mrs. Harriet Beecher Stowe, as the African Sybil, will deliver a lecture upon the present issues of the day,

At   On

And will give her experience as a Slave mother and religious woman. She comes highly recommended as a public speaker, having the approval of many thousands who have heard her earnest appeals, among whom are Wendell Phillips, Wm. Lloyd Garrison, and other distinguished men of the nation.

☞ At the close of her discourse she will offer for sale her photograph and a few of her choice songs.

Harriet "Hattie" Purvis Jr. (top) came from a family of reformers in Philadelphia and gave much of her adult life to the cause of woman suffrage. She later served on the boards of both the state and national suffrage associations. Frederick Douglass (above) gained international renown for his *Narrative* about his life as a slave. Publisher of the newspaper *The North Star* and the most prominent Black leader in the abolition movement, Douglass remained a fervent supporter of woman's rights until his death in 1895. Upper right: Enslaved men, women, and children on a South Carolina plantation around 1861.

Black Women Lead Early Efforts for Abolition and Woman's Rights

SEVERAL BLACK women played a significant role in the growth of early abolition societies and in the ensuing drive for woman's rights during the 1850s. Maria Stewart became the first woman to hold a lecture tour before a racially mixed audience of men and women in 1831. Her tour was celebrated as the "first female political attack on slavery."

In 1837 the Anti-Slavery Convention of American Women drew participants from several states to New York City for what historian Ann Gordon called the "first attempt to forge a political force of women." The delegates resolved that "it was the duty of woman ... to overthrow the horrible system of American slavery." A second convention in 1838 in Philadelphia (right) showed just how controversial such a meeting of Black and white abolitionist women was when a violent mob burned down their hall after the first day (see page 7).

Philadelphia abolitionists Harriet Forten Purvis and her sister Margaretta Forten were delegates to the convention who raised funds through annual anti-slavery fairs. They also helped organize the na-

Frances E. W. Harper, a prolific writer and noted abolitionist, became one of the most active Black leaders in the equal suffrage movement in the second half of the 19th century. Born in Baltimore in 1824, Harper received an exceptional education at the Watkins Institute run by her abolitionist uncle. In 1854 a volume of her anti-slavery verse was published which sold over 12,000 copies. Harper became known as the "bronze muse" and used most of the proceeds to aid fugitive slaves. She also built a reputation as an accomplished orator working for the Maine Anti-Slavery League from 1854 to 1856. "Her eloquence and intelligence astounded audiences," wrote biographer Bettye Collier-Thomas. Harper later became one of the most articulate advocates for woman's rights, racial equality, and temperance nationally. By her death in 1911 she was widely honored and praised as "a symbol of empowered and empowering womanhood."

tional woman's rights convention in 1854. Other Black abolitionists included Sarah Parker Remond, who lectured with Abby Kelley Foster and addressed the 1859 woman's rights convention, and Mary Ann Shadd Cary, who helped found and edit the *Provincial Freeman,* an anti-slavery weekly, in 1853. Cary remained an active suffragist and became an attorney 30 years later.

Early leaders attracted younger women such as Purvis' daughter Harriet "Hattie" Purvis, Jr. and Frances E. W. Harper. Both women were active with the American Equal Rights Association after the Civil War and continued working for suffrage and racial equality during the decades that followed.

Throughout their struggle for the right to vote, as historian Rosalyn Terborg-Penn has noted, Black women had to fight both racial and sexual discrimination, a condition never adequately recognized by white suffragists. For decades some Black women worked with the mainstream white movement but most directed their efforts – speaking, writing, and organizing – towards other members of the Black community.

PROCEEDINGS

OF THE

ANTI-SLAVERY CONVENTION

OF

AMERICAN WOMEN,

HELD IN

PHILADELPHIA.

May 15th, 16th, 17th and 18th, 1838.

PHILADELPHIA:
PRINTED BY MERRIHEW AND GUNN,
No. 7 Carter's Alley.
1838.

Amelia Bloomer was 30 when she attended the first woman's rights convention in 1848. Married to the anti-slavery editor of the *Seneca County Courier*, Bloomer began publishing *The Lily* in January 1849 as a temperance newspaper focused on alcohol abuse but, influenced by Elizabeth Cady Stanton, it soon emphasized "the interests of woman." Bloomer edited the popular monthly for six years before selling it to Mary Birdsall. A former teacher, Bloomer was also a talented writer and popular lecturer who later led efforts for woman's rights in Iowa and the midwest.

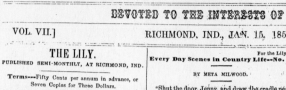

DEVOTED TO THE INTERESTS OF WOMAN.

VOL. VII.]　　　RICHMOND, IND., JAN. 15, 1855.　　　NO. 2.

THE LILY.
PUBLISHED SEMI-MONTHLY, AT RICHMOND, IND.

Terms---Fifty Cents per annum in advance, or Seven Copies for Three Dollars.

All communications designed for the paper or on business, to be addressed to

Mrs. MARY B. BIRDSALL,
Editor and Proprietor.

Mrs. AMELIA BLOOMER,
Corresponding Editor.

Written for The Lily.
MAN'S WRONGS.

Enough, there are, in these last days,
All woman's wrongs to scan:
So I, for once, will try to state
Some of the wrongs of man.

The laws fall short of being right,
So far as he's concern'd---
'Tis time he took the case in hand
To have the tables turn'd.

Too long, alone, he's meekly drudg'd
O'er matters multiplex;
Not only serving church and State,
But ev'n the weaker (?) sex.

Whose fairy, soulless, strengthless forms
Can't even cast a vote;
And also, if married, have not pow'r
To *hold* a paper note.

And sure the man doth pity need
Who's stoop'd to take a wife:
Sad wrongs are his---by law he's made
A shackl'd slave for life.

He then may toil from morn till night---
No mirth, no sport, no rest: (!)
While like a queen the wife may sit
In silks and jewels dress'd.

She need not toil---nothing is hers---
Not even her dear self;
Man must her lord and master be,
He, too, must earn the pelf.

Her actions, words, and e'en her dress,
He faithfully must guide,
What o'er she's *told* is *right* and *best*,
She may adopt with pride.

And is't her purse that must supply
The cash that she may need?
Ah! no! man, too, that load must bear;
A sufferer indeed!!

How he can still such laws endure,
And with such frail barks mate,
Is what I cannot comprehend,
I own the task too great.

Ye noble(?) men---your shackles break!
Up, to the rescue hie;
And strive for laws that shall compel
Women with you to vie.

Brave fathers, brothers, husbands, sons,
Arouse---your wrong resist---
Till mothers, sisters, daughters, wives
As equals will assist.　　　A. E.
March 18th, 1854.

☞ Suspension of specie payment became general in this country May 10th, 1837. We fear it will come again before the anniversary of that time, without the Eastern question is soon settled.

For the Lily.
Every Day Scenes in Country Life--No. 1.

BY META MILWOOD.

"Shut the door, Jenny, and draw the cradle nearer the stove. This is a hard day for the babies and little lambs. There, that will do. Now be quiet, children, and do not disturb papa in his reading. Mother is going into the kitchen to attend to the baking."

"Please leave the door open, mother, so that we can see you. It is so lonesome when pa is busy with his paper, and we must not talk for fear of disturbing him."

"I will, but you must not interrupt me unnecessarily."

"Mamma," calls out little Meta from the window, where she is watching the fast falling snowflakes, and sees with childish amusement the little whirling eddies, as the whistling wind drives them across the yard, "there is old Mr. Crampton coming down the road on his old scollop. Oh! I hope he will not stop here, the naughty old man."

"Hush, Meta," says Jenny, "perhaps he is cold and wants to warm---or maybe some one is sick, that he comes out on such a day as this. We must be kind to every one, you know, mother says:

"I know it, and ma says we must love everybody, but I can't love old Mr. Crampton; he is so cross, and scolds poor Mrs. Crampton so; and she is so kind and good, I can't believe God loves such wicked people either. There, he is coming through the gate; how cross he looks," and the little one drew near her father, as if for protection. A thundering rap on the door announced Mr. Crampton.

"Good morning," said father, handing him a chair. A blustering morning, this."

"Well it is, but I don't mind the weather when I'm out on such an errand as I'm out on this morning. You see, I'm just mad enough to keep me warm, and I'm going to W---, to see lawyer N---, I guess they'll find the old man's enough for them yet."

"Why, what's the matter now, Mr. Crampton---another neighborhood quarrel?"

"No, not exactly that. But you know that boy Thad, my wife's boy, that I kept last winter; well, he got oneasy last spring, and pertended I didn't use him well, and I treated him better than he deserved. The impudent fellow, to ask me for money to buy a pair of boots, after I'd boarded him all winter. I told him he hadn't earned his board, and he said something saucy like, and so I just choked him so as to bring him to his manners, and so he went off and said I abused him. Well, he went down to C---, and worked for old Mr. Algood, and he bragged him up and called him a good boy, I spose just to spite me. And now he's got sick, and cause I arn't willing to let my old woman go and take care on him, and leave things to go to destruction, they're going to send him back on me. I see the old man, yesterday, and he said the boy was so weak, and cried and fretted so to see his mother, he guessed he'd fetch him up in a few days to see her. I knowed what they wanted, so I told him they need not fetch

him there for me to take care of; I'd turn him out of doors.

He said he guessed I wouldn't be so cruel as to do that; but I'll let 'em see I'll not see my hard arnings go to take care of HER CHILDREN, I warnt ye. The boy's sick, and I'm glad on't---hope he'll git enough on't before he gits through."

"Well, Mr. Crampton, there is no need of getting into such a passion as this. No one can make you take care of the boy unless you choose to do so. The boy must have a residence somewhere, and if he is brought to you, and you do not feel able or willing to bear the expense of his sickness, you have only to present him as a town charge, and it becomes the duty of the trustees to see that all his expenses are paid, and charge the same to any other township where he may have gained a residence."

A gleam of fiendish triumph lighted up the countenance of the old man, and the tones of his voice moderated, as he replied:

"Do you say, Mr. ---? Well, I spected you could tell me all about it, so I just thought I'd call and ask you. After all, it seems kind o' hard not to allow my woman the privilege of taking care of the boy. If he is bad, I 'spose its natural she should think something on him. So I guess I'll jest go on and see lawyer N---, and find out zactly what steps to take, and then I'll let 'em bring him home. I'll charge 'em a good bit, I'll---"

During this colloquy, my hands had been actively employed in the process of bread making, but I seemed to be in the position of "the luckless wight, who could not make the flour take form of loaf or cake." At least my haste to accomplish the feat did not seem in the least to accelerate my progress. At last, however, it was completed, and the round loaves were duly deposited in their snug resting places beneath the cooking stove. My hands were yet in a very floury condition, but I must not wait for ablution, for Mr. Crampton might be gone, and I had a duty to perform. The old man was just buttoning his overcoat, when I made my egress into the family room. "Good morning, Mr. Crampton."

"Good morning, ma'am," and the old man bowed obsequiously.

"Please sit down, sir, I should like to ask you a few questions, if you are not in too great haste. How many years have you lived with your present wife, Mr. Crampton?"

"Seventeen years last March, ma'am, since we're married."

"Mrs. Crampton has enjoyed good health most of the time, I believe?"

"She's been pretty well the most of the time, ma'am."

"It has been well for you, as you have had so much sickness in the time. She seems an excellent nurse!"

"She can't be beat, Mrs. M---. She has saved me hundreds of dollars in doctor's bills. I don't think of callin' a doctor any more. I depend on her skill entirely."

"Yes. And she seems a hard-working woman, too. I doubt not that it is by her skill and management that you have got along so well in the world, considering all your *complaining*.

Addressing the Wider Interests of Women

CHAMPIONING DRESS reform in person as well as in print, Amelia Bloomer (left) wound up having her name associated with the new fashion she helped popularize. The "Bloomer costume," consisting of loose Turkish trousers and shorter dresses, contrasted dramatically with the long, uncomfortable, and impractical dresses then in fashion.

The Lily (above) was one of the earliest periodicals to promote dress reform and woman's rights. Although interest in the new outfit boosted circulation from 500 to 4,000, Bloomer grew concerned that the controversial fad and ensuing ridicule distracted too much attention from more serious issues.

MUSICAL TREASURY N.º 606-7. PRICE SIXPENCE.

London.

G.H. DAVIDSON, 19 PETERS HILL, SOUTH SIDE OF S.T PAUL'S.

Dress reform turned out to be a hotly contested subject when women first wore "panteletts," or bloomers, in the early 1850s. Elizabeth Smith Miller (above), daughter of a wealthy reformer and the cousin of Elizabeth Cady Stanton, introduced the looser, less hampering outfit in 1851 after a trip to Europe. Since many woman's rights leaders immediately adopted the appealing new fashion, their gatherings attracted even greater ridicule and inspired countless satirical cartoons featuring manly, cigar-smoking women wearing trousers. After persevering for several years almost all the woman's rights advocates abandoned the outfit as too distracting and controversial. "I hoped to help establish the principle of rational dress," Susan B. Anthony lamented, but "the attention of my audience was fixed upon my clothes instead of my words." Left: Sheet music cover from 1852.

A Discouraging Fight for Dress Reform

Although many considered the Bloomer costume both comfortable and practical, women wearing the outfit often drew crowds of men and boys who jeered at them when they appeared in public. Critics considered bloomers "unladylike" and felt they were immodest, inflammatory, and in violation of the Bible, which warned women against wearing that which pertains to man.

Although the novel attire came to symbolize women's growing independence, it provoked such scorn, condemnation, and ridicule that most women eventually stopped wearing it. The radical breakthrough in style did, however, influence fashions several decades later.

Paulina Wright Davis
helped organize early woman's rights meetings in the years leading up to the Civil War. Orphaned at six, Paulina Kellogg was 19 when she married abolitionist Francis Wright in 1833. She lobbied the New York legislature with Ernestine Rose for married women's property rights and lectured on women's health in the 1840s. Widowed at 32, Wright married Thomas Davis, a one-term congressman, and subsequently used her contacts and position to promote equal rights, particularly in Rhode Island. A striking figure with blond hair and blue eyes, Davis was an earnest, poised, and well-informed leader who tried to lend dignity and stability to women's early meetings. A "right good ballad" from 1853 (below) celebrated woman's cause.

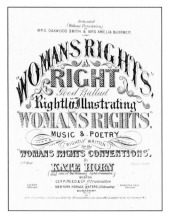

New Voices for Woman's Rights

WITH THE increase in conventions in the 1850s came new publications which amplified the discussion of woman's rights. Paulina Wright Davis began publishing a monthly newspaper entitled *The Una* (above) in February 1853 "to discuss the rights, duties, sphere, and destiny of women fully and fearlessly." *The Una* and *The Lily* were two of the earliest periodicals concerned about woman's rights and edited by women. Both featured the writings of prominent equal rights advocates and encouraged the proliferation of woman's rights meetings.

Other papers which defended women's equality included Jane Grey Swisshelm's *Saturday Visiter* in Pittsburgh, Anna McDowell's *Woman's Advocate* in Philadelphia, and Lydia Hasbrouck's *Sibyl* in Middletown, New York, which continued to promote dress reform into the 1860s. Hasbrouck herself won renown for publicly refusing to pay her local tax assessments because she had no vote in how the money was spent.

THE GREAT REPUBLICAN REFORM PARTY,
Calling on their Candidate.

Meetings and Annual Conventions Build Support for the New Movement

ALTHOUGH THEY resisted suggestions to create a formal organization, woman's rights supporters held a second national convention in Worcester, Massachusetts, in 1851 and a third one in Syracuse, New York, in 1852 where Lucretia Mott presided. This was the first convention for 32-year-old teacher Susan B. Anthony and for Matilda Joslyn Gage, a 26-year-old mother and wife of a local businessman. In 1853 over 1,500 people from eight states gathered in Cleveland for a fourth annual convention, chaired by Ohio leader Frances Dana Gage.

The movement continued to grow. Supporters in some states, like Indiana and Ohio, formed fledgling woman's rights associations. In New York, Anthony, Elizabeth Cady Stanton, and others organized the first political campaign for equal rights legislation. Women worked in 60 counties collecting 5,931 signatures on a petition calling for equal rights for women which they presented, with little immediate effect, to the state legislature.

Although widely ridiculed in the press, the demand for woman's rights was gaining national attention. An editorial cartoon from 1854 pictured an early advocate (above, second from left), clothed in exaggerated bloomers and smoking a cigar, in the company of eccentric reformers and special interests. The young suffragist demanded equality and the "right to Vote and hold Office" from Republican presidential nominee John C. Fremont.

THE EIGHTH

National Woman's-Rights Convention

WILL BE HELD IN

NEW YORK CITY,

AT MOZART HALL, 668 BROADWAY,

On Thursday and Friday, May 13 and 14, 1858,

Commencing at 10 o'clock Thursday A. M.

**Lucy Stone, Ernestine L. Rose, Wendell Phillips,
Wm. Lloyd Garrison, C. Lenox Remond,
Mary F. Davis, Caroline H. Dahl,
Rev. T. W. Higginson, Aaron
M. Powell, Frances D.
Gage, and others,**

will address the several sessions of the Convention.

We regret that so many of the noble men and women, who, in spirit, are fully with us, should have so long withheld from us, kind words of recognition and encouragement.

We earnestly ask all those who believe our claims are just, who hope and look for a higher type of womanhood in the coming generations, to assert, now, their faith in the everlasting principles of justice, that have no respect for age, sex, color, or condition. Is it too much to ask that the BRADYS, the CURTIS', the CHAPINS, the BEECHERS, and the STOWES shall cheer us by their presence at our coming Convention, or by letter make known their position in regard to this movement? Feeling assured that our cause is just, that our positions are tenable, our platform is FREE for all fair discussion.

Communications for the Convention may be addressed to SUSAN B. ANTHONY, ANTI-SLAVERY OFFICE, 138 NASSAU STREET, NEW YORK.

The Civil War Ends a Decade of Organizing for Woman's Rights

DESPITE THE remarkable work of woman's rights activists during the 1850s, political leaders as well as social institutions were very slow to change. Nonetheless, the growing woman's rights movement gradually established an identity of its own during this period when supporters actively pursued temperance and the abolition of slavery as well as reforms specifically relating to women's condition.

The right to vote was not the primary focus for most early advocates. Rather, they saw a more pressing need to extend education, open the professions, and pass legisla-

tion relating to property rights, custody of children, divorce, economic issues, and similar concerns affecting women's lives.

Supporters continued to organize national conventions annually (except for 1857) in Philadelphia, Cincinnati, and New York successively. After a tenth national convention in 1860 no others were held until after the Civil War in 1866. In several states, including New York, Massachusetts, and Ohio, women appeared before the legislatures to testify in support of equal rights legislation.

As activity and conventions multiplied, Paulina Davis re-

membered, "the discussion of principle became more general. Societies were organized, and the question was emerging from the ridicule which had enveloped it, when the war came."

Above: A satirical cartoon from *Harper's Weekly* in 1859 asked rhetorically, "Why Should We Not Vote?" From the general male perspective, the very idea of letting women take further control was plainly ridiculous. Left: The 1858 national convention featured an impressive roster of abolitionists, reformers, and woman's rights leaders.

Susan B. Anthony, the energetic daughter of a Quaker farmer in New York, was among those drawn to the emerging woman's rights movement in the early 1850s. The young teacher had just traded in her traditional gray Quaker clothing for a "daring" plaid dress when she posed (above) in 1848. Anthony, 31, found a like-minded soul mate in Elizabeth Cady Stanton, 35, when Amelia Bloomer introduced them in 1851.

Anthony became a paid

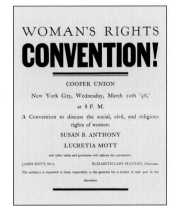

agent for the American Anti-Slavery Society in 1856, following in Lucy Stone's footsteps and similarly facing hostile mobs. But as Anthony became more devoted to the rights of women, she came to resent the "loss" of talented leaders including Stone (top left with daughter Alice) and others to the demands of marriage and children. Personal and political differences deepened the rift in their friendship over the following years.

Anthony, who remained single, appeared with Lucretia Mott at an 1856 state convention (left). "If Lucretia Mott typified the moral force of the movement, if Lucy Stone was its most gifted orator and Mrs. Stanton its outstanding philosopher," historian Eleanor Flexner wrote, "Susan Anthony was its incomparable organizer, who gave it force and direction for half a century."

Mary Livermore led relief efforts in the midwest during the Civil War and became a leading advocate of woman suffrage in the post-war years. A former teacher and mother of three married to a supportive minister, Livermore joined the Sanitary Commission in Chicago in 1861 to raise funds, gather medical supplies, and provide aid to soldiers on the western front. She toured military hospitals with co-worker Jane Hoge, assessing needs and caring for the wounded, and then wrote vivid firsthand reports. When the war ended she called a suffrage convention in Chicago in 1868 and was elected president of the resulting Illinois Woman Suffrage Association. In 1869 she began a woman's rights newspaper, *The Agitator,* and became active with the American Woman Suffrage Association. Moving to Boston, she merged her paper with *The Woman's Journal* which she edited for two years. A figure of integrity and moral authority, Livermore became a best-selling author and popular lecturer for over 20 years, her success earning her the title the "Queen of the Platform."

CALL

FOR A MEETING OF THE

LOYAL WOMEN OF THE NATION.

In this crisis of our Country's destiny, it is the duty of every citizen to consider the peculiar blessings of a republican form of goverment and decide what sacrifices of wealth and life are demanded for its defence and preservation.

The policy of the war, our whole future life, depends on a universal, clearly defined idea of the end proposed, and the immense advantages to be secured to ourselves and all mankind, by its accomplishment.

No mere party or sectional cry, no technicalities of Constitution or military law, no mottoes of craft or policy are big enough to touch the great heart of a nation in the midst of revolution. A grand idea, such as freedom or justice, is needful to kindle and sustain the fires of a high enthusiasm.

At this hour, the best word and work of every man and woman are imperatively demanded. To man, by common consent, is assigned the forum, camp and field. What is woman's legitimate work, and how she may best accomplish it, is worthy our earnest counsel one with another.

We have heard many complaints of the lack of enthusiasm among Northern Women ; but, when a mother lays her son on the altar of her country, she asks an object equal to the sacrifice. In nursing the sick and wounded, knitting socks, scraping lint, and making jellies, the bravest and best may weary if the thoughts mount not in faith to something beyond and above it all. Work is worship only when a noble purpose fills the soul.

Woman is equally interested and responsible with man in the final settlement of this problem of self-government; therefore let none stand idle spectators now. When every hour is big with destiny, and each delay but complicates our difficulties, it is high time for the daughters of the revolution, in solemn council, to unseal the last will and testament of the Fathers,—lay hold of their birthright of freedom, and keep it a sacred trust for all coming generations.

To this end, we ask the loyal Women of the Nation to meet in New York, on Thursday, the 14th of May next.

Let the Women of every State be largely represented, both by person and by letter.

There will be two sessions — The first at 10 o'clock, A. M., at the Church of the Puritans, (Dr Cheever's), Admittance Free—The second at the Cooper Institute—at 7½ o'clock, P. M., Admittance 25 cents. On behalf of the Woman's Central Committee,

ELIZABETH CADY STANTON.

N. B.—Communications relative to and for the meeting should be addressed to SUSAN B. ANTHONY, 48 Beekman St., New York.

Supporting the Abolition of Slavery as a War Aim

THE OUTBREAK of the Civil War in April 1861 caused almost all work for woman's rights to cease immediately. Two years later, as the war dragged on without clear purpose, Elizabeth Cady Stanton and Susan B. Anthony used their organizing experience to mobilize support for the proposed 13th Amendment to the Constitution abolishing slavery.

Hundreds of women from around the country responded to their 1863 Call (above) and met in New York on May 14 with Lucy Stone presiding. The convention established the Women's Loyal National League and elected Stanton president and Anthony secretary. Over the following year, 2,000 women circulated petitions while field workers traveled throughout the midwest to build support for the amendment. Anthony directed league activities from New York and sent completed petitions to the capital.

The league eventually collected nearly 400,000 signatures and provided allies in Washington D.C. with the support they needed to win passage of the 13th Amendment. Although the league disbanded in 1865, it built up an extensive network of women who were passionate about winning equal rights.

Above: The 1863 Call.

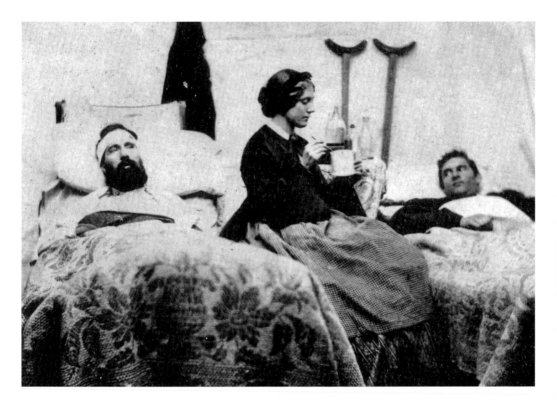

Clara Barton devoted herself to humanitarian service during the Civil War, exemplifying the dedication and contributions of tens of thousands of women during the terrible conflict. Barton was 39 when she began to help soldiers in Washington D.C. in 1860. Leaving her job at the Patent Office, she raised money, gathered needed supplies, and distributed them herself to battlefield hospitals in Maryland and Virginia. There she also nursed the wounded, comforted the dying, and helped identify the missing and the dead. Her compassion and efficiency endeared her to soldiers who referred to her as the "Angel of the Battlefield." After the war, Barton lectured widely and learned about the International Red Cross while in Europe. She founded and led the American Red Cross from 1881 to 1904, expanding its mission to include domestic relief after natural disasters. One of the most respected women in the country, Barton often voiced her support for equal rights and showed the determination and ability of women in national affairs.

Wartime Needs Displace Work for Woman's Rights

Setting aside their own affairs, women in both the north and the south took over men's work on the farms, in the factories, and elsewhere during the Civil War and gave themselves and their labor to the war effort. Women throughout the country gathered food and medical supplies, organized local aid societies, and raised millions of dollars for the war. Several hundred women, disguised as men, secretly fought as soldiers in the field.

Many women became deeply involved with the care of soldiers. Dr. Elizabeth Blackwell led the effort to organize Union relief work and to train women as army nurses. Clara Barton and others gathered needed supplies and often took them to the front themselves. Thousands of women worked with the U.S. Sanitary Commission to improve conditions in army camps while also pro-viding medical care for the sick and wounded.

After the war ended in 1865 and the 13th Amendment abolishing slavery was ratified, two other constitutional amendments were proposed to help newly-freed male slaves. The wording and, later, the interpretation of these two post-war amend-ments would become a principal focus for woman's rights supporters for much of the following decade. ◆

Above: Nurse Anne Bell was one of thousands who ministered to the wounded. Below: The U.S. Sanitary Commission helped improve Union camp conditions.

As the nation grew in the years following the Civil War, more women began to speak publicly and some toured the country (above) as lecturers. Traveling speakers were a popular source of information and entertainment for audiences in widespread cities, towns, and rural settlements before the arrival of electricity.

Elizabeth Cady Stanton, Susan B. Anthony, and other woman's rights figures had lecture bureaus organize profitable speaking tours which included addresses to a wide variety of groups, clubs, and civic organizations although not always on equal rights. Stanton claimed her lecture fees paid for her sons' college educations.

Anthony spoke throughout the west and midwest for years, encouraging women to work for equal rights in their own states as well as for a new amendment to the constitution. After a typical year, Anthony wrote in her journal,

"Thus closes 1871, a year of hard work, six months east, six months west of the Rocky Mountains; 171 lectures, 13,000 miles of travel; gross receipts, $4,318; paid on debts, $2,271. Nothing ahead but to plod on."

Searching for a Way to Win the Vote

AFTER THE Civil War ended and slavery was abolished, Congress proposed two additional amendments to the constitution. The 14th Amendment defined national citizenship and declared that former slave states could not deny voting rights to any male citizen, inserting the word "male" into the constitution for the first time. The 15th Amendment declared that voting rights could not be denied on account of race. By deliberately leaving out the word "sex," politicians refused to recognize what women called their "existing" right to vote.

The proposed amendments, which southern states were forced to ratify as a condition of surrender, proved bitterly divisive. While most abolitionists welcomed the enfranchising of former male slaves, others could not sanction legislation which dismissed women outright. "Your test of faithfulness is the negro," Elizabeth Cady Stanton told fellow abolitionists, "ours is the woman." After the two amendments were ratified, suffragists challenged their interpretation both in court and at the polls.

The lack of support in Congress both frustrated and infuriated suffrage leaders. "There is no reason, no argument, nothing but prejudice, against our demand," Susan B. Anthony told a Joint Congressional Committee in 1870, "and there is no way to break down this prejudice but to make the experiment."

Slowly, men and women in the western territories began to do just that.

In the years immediately following the war, early woman's rights supporters joined abolitionists in a new movement for equal rights. But after former male slaves were enfranchised and women were not, they turned towards the specific issue of woman suffrage. While still retaining broader aims, these early suffragists struggled to find a way to win the vote both at the national level and in the individual states and territories. They believed that the vote was the key to all the legislative changes needed to bring about progress for women.

Kansas: The First State Campaign for Equal Suffrage

IMMEDIATELY AFTER the Civil War, woman's rights supporters repeatedly met with representatives in Congress to request that women be included in any new Federal legislation. When the 14th Amendment was proposed to enfranchise only male former slaves, suffragists tried to have the wording changed to include women as well. But among those who blocked their efforts were former allies in the abolition movement who claimed that it was the "Negro's hour" and that demanding woman suffrage could jeopardize Black freedom.

Gathering for the first time since the end of the war, woman's rights supporters held their 11th national convention in New York City on May 10, 1866. Agreeing that it was time to endorse universal suffrage, delegates approved a new name, the American Equal Rights Association. It would, in Susan B. Anthony's words, "broaden our woman's rights platform and make it ... a human

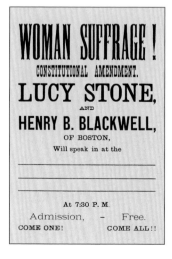

rights platform." Lucretia Mott, now 73, was elected president of the new organization which would advocate voting rights for Black men and for all women.

The following year, as association members met in New York, Lucy Stone and Henry Blackwell were in Kansas speaking and aiding local supporters during the first state drive for woman suffrage. In the fall Olympia Brown, Susan B. Anthony, and Elizabeth Cady Stanton traveled throughout the frontier state canvassing for votes with little help from men in the AERA.

Above: "Lady Lobbyists at the White House, 1866" from *Harper's Weekly.* **Left: Poster used to announce meetings.**

TRACTS published at the Office of the American Equal Rights Association:

ENFRANCHISEMENT OF WOMEN,
BY MRS. JOHN STUART MILL.

Suffrage For Women,
BY JOHN STUART MILL, M. P.

FREEDOM FOR WOMEN,
BY WENDELL PHILLIPS.

PUBLIC FUNCTION OF WOMAN,
BY THEODORE PARKER.

WOMAN AND HER WISHES,
BY COL. T. W. HIGGINSON.

RESPONSIBILITIES OF WOMEN,
BY MRS. C. I. H. NICHOLS.

Woman's Duty to Vote,
BY HENRY WARD BEECHER.

UNIVERSAL SUFFRAGE,
BY ELISABETH CADY STANTON.

The Mortality of Nations,
BY PARKER PILLSBURY.

EQUAL RIGHTS FOR WOMEN,
BY GEORGE WILLIAM CURTIS.

SHOULD WOMEN VOTE?
AFFIRMATIVE TESTIMONIALS OF SUNDRY PERSONS.
Price, per Single Copy, 10 Cents; per Hundred Copies, $5;
per Thousand Copies, $30.

GEO. FRANCIS TRAIN'S KANSAS CAMPAIGN FOR WOMAN'S SUFFRAGE.
Price 25 Cents per Copy.
Orders should be addressed to

SUSAN B. ANTHONY,
Secretary American E. R. Association.
37 PARK ROW, (Room 17), NEW YORK CITY.

Olympia Brown was a 32-year-old pastor in Massachusetts when she volunteered to campaign for woman suffrage in Kansas. A Universalist minister who kept her maiden name when she married, Brown was the first American woman to be ordained by full denominational authority. A tireless speaker, she addressed over 200 meetings (below) in Kansas between July and October 1867. In May 1868 she called together eastern supporters and formed the influential New England Woman Suffrage Association.

Several pamphlets by men promoting woman suffrage were featured in this 1868 advertisement sponsored by the American Equal Rights Association. When members mounted an active statewide drive in Kansas in 1867, the popular Hutchinson Family Singers added music from their repertoire of rousing abolition and woman's rights songs. "Both parties, the press, the pulpit, and faithless liberals" opposed the suffrage measure, in Elizabeth Cady Stanton's words, and it was defeated 19,857 to 9,070. This was the first of over 52 state referendum drives.

Elizabeth Cady Stanton (top) was 52 when she began editing *The Revolution* together with Parker Pillsbury (above), a 58-year-old minister and anti-slavery editor. Pillsbury was ridiculed by fellow editors as "Mrs. Pillsbury" for his loyal work editing the paper and composing strongly worded editorials supporting woman's rights. Susan B. Anthony, 47, took care of business as proprietor and used her le... e tours to drum ... tions. She ... sympa- ... gressman ... pies of ... tial

The Revolution.

PRINCIPLE, NOT POLICY: JUSTICE, NOT FAVORS.

VOL. I.—NO. 1. NEW YORK, WEDNESDAY, JANUARY 8, 1868. $2.00 A YEAR.

The Revolution;

THE ORGAN OF THE

NATIONAL PARTY OF NEW AMERICA.

PRINCIPLE, NOT POLICY—INDIVIDUAL RIGHTS AND RESPONSIBILITIES.

THE REVOLUTION WILL ADVOCATE:

1. IN POLITICS—Educated Suffrage, Irrespective of Sex or Color; Equal Pay to Women for Equal Work; Eight Hours Labor; Abolition of Standing Armies and Party Despotisms. Down with Politicians—Up with the People!

2. IN RELIGION—Deeper Thought; Broader Idea; Science not Superstition; Personal Purity; Love to Man as well as God.

3. IN SOCIAL LIFE.—Morality and Reform; Practical Education, not Theoretical; Facts not Fiction; Virtue not Vice; Cold Water not Alcoholic Drinks or Medicines. It will indulge in no Gross Personalities and insert no Quack or Immoral Advertisements, so common even in Religious Newspapers.

4. THE REVOLUTION proposes a new Commercial and Financial Policy. America no longer led by Europe. Gold like our Cotton and Corn for sale. Greenbacks for money. An American System of Finance. American Products and Labor Free. Foreign Manufactures Prohibited. Open doors to Artisans and Immigrants. Atlantic and Pacific Oceans for American Steamships and Shipping; or American goods in American bottoms. New York the Financial Centre of the World. Wall Street emancipated from Bank of England, or American Cash for American Bills. The Credit Foncier and Credit Mobilier System, or Capital Mobilized to Resuscitate the South and our Mining Interests, and to People the Country from Ocean to Ocean, from Omaha to San Francisco. More organized Labor, more Cotton, more Gold and Silver Bullion to sell foreigners at the highest prices. Ten millions of Naturalized Citizens DEMAND A PENNY OCEAN POSTAGE, to Strengthen the Brotherhood of Labor; and if Congress Vote One Hundred and Twenty-five Millions for a Standing Army and Freedman's Bureau, cannot they spare One Million to Educate Europe and to keep bright the chain of acquaintance and friendship between those millions and their fatherland?

Send in your Subscription. THE REVOLUTION, published weekly, will be the Great Organ of the Age.

TERMS.—Two dollars a year, in advance. Ten names ($20) entitle the sender to one copy free.

ELIZABETH CADY STANTON, } EDS.
PARKER PILLSBURY,

SUSAN B. ANTHONY,
  Proprietor and Manager.
  37 Park Row (Room 17), New York City,
To whom address all business letters.

KANSAS.

THE question of the enfranchisement of woman has already passed the court of moral discussion, and is now fairly ushered into the arena of politics, where it must remain a fixed element of debate, until party necessity shall compel its success.

With 9,000 votes in Kansas, one-third the entire vote, every politician must see that the friends of "woman's suffrage" hold the balance of power in that State to-day. And those 9,000 votes represent a principle deep in the hearts of the people, for this triumph was secured without money, without a press, without a party. With these instrumentalities now fast coming to us on all sides, the victory in Kansas is but the herald of greater victories in every State of the Union. Kansas already leads the world in her legislation for woman on questions of property, education, wages, marriage and divorce. Her best universities are open alike to boys and girls. In fact woman has a voice in the legislation of that State. She votes on all school questions and is eligible to the office of trustee. She has a voice in temperance too; no license is granted without the consent of a majority of the adult citizens, male and female, black and white. The consequence is, stone school houses are voted up in every part of the State, and rum voted down. Many of the ablest men in that State are champions of woman's cause. Governors, judges, lawyers and clergymen. Two-thirds of the press and pulpits advocate the idea, in spite of the opposition of politicians. The first Governor of Kansas, twice chosen to that office, Charles Robinson, went all through the State, speaking every day for two months in favor of woman's suffrage. In the organization of the State government, he proposed that the words "white male" should not be inserted in the Kansas constitution. All this shows that giving political rights to women is no new idea in that State. Who that has listened with tearful eyes to the deep experiences of those Kansas women, through the darkest hours of their history, does not feel that such bravery and self denial as they have shown alike in war and peace, have richly earned for them the crown of citizenship.

Opposed to this moral sentiment of the liberal minds of the State, many adverse influences were brought to bear through the entire campaign.

The action of the New York Constitutional Convention; the silence of eastern journals on the question; the opposition of abolitionists lest a demand for woman's suffrage should defeat negro suffrage; the hostility everywhere of black men themselves; some even stumping the State against woman's suffrage; the official action of both the leading parties in their conventions in Leavensworth against the proposition, with every organized Republican influ-

ence outside as well as inside the State, all combined might have made our vote comparatively a small one, had not George Francis Train gone into the State two weeks before the election and galvanized the Democrats into their duty, thus securing 9,000 votes for woman's suffrage. Some claim that we are indebted to the Republicans for this vote; but the fact that the most radical republican district, Douglass County, gave the largest vote against woman's suffrage, while Leavenworth, the Democratic district, gave the largest vote for it, fully settles that question.

In saying that Mr. Train helped to swell our vote takes nothing from the credit due all those who labored faithfully for months in that State. All praise to Olympia Brown, Lucy Stone, Susan B. Anthony, Henry B. Blackwell, and Judge Wood, who welcomed, for an idea, the hardships of travelling in a new State, fording streams, scaling rocky brinks, sleeping on the ground and eating hard tack, with the fatigue of constant speaking, in school-houses, barns, mills, depots and the open air; and especially, all praise to the glorious Hutchinson family-- John, his son Henry and daughter, Viola--who, with their own horses and carriage, made the entire circuit of the state, singing Woman's Suffrage into souls that logic could never penetrate. Having shared with them the hardships, with them I rejoice in our success.

E. C. S.

THE BALLOT—BREAD, VIRTUE, POWER.

THE REVOLUTION will contain a series of articles, beginning next week, to prove the power of the ballot in elevating the character and condition of woman. We shall show that the ballot will secure for woman equal place and equal wages in the world of work; that it will open to her the schools, colleges, professions and all the opportunities and advantages of life; that in her hand it will be a moral power to stay the tide of vice and crime and misery on every side. In the words of Bishop Simpson—

"We believe that the great vices in our large cities will never be conquered until the ballot is put in the hands of women. If the question of the danger of their sons being drawn away into drinking saloons was brought up, if the mothers had the power, they would close them; if the sisters had the power, and they saw their brothers going away to haunts of infamy, they would close those places. You may get men to trifle with purity, with virtue, with righteousness; but, thank God, the hearts of the women of our land—the mothers, wives and daughters—are too pure to make a compromise either with intemperance or licentiousness."

Thus, too, shall we purge our constitutions and statute laws from all invidious distinctions among the citizens of the States, and secure the same civil and moral code for man and woman. We will show the hundred thousand female teachers, and the millions of laboring women, that their complaints, petitions, strikes and protective unions are of no avail until they hold the ballot in their own hands; for it is the first step toward social, religious and political equality.

Launching "The Revolution"

TWO MONTHS after the Kansas campaign, Elizabeth Cady Stanton and Susan B. Anthony began publishing *The Revolution*, a weekly 16-page newspaper which championed woman's rights and a host of other radical reforms, drawing new attention to woman suffrage. Backed initially by flamboyant financier George Francis Train, the paper built an immediate reputation as a lively, informative, and controversial national forum for news and debate on issues of importance to women.

WIN THE VOTE
25

?65-1878

ANNIVERSARY

OF THE

American Equal Rights Association.

The American Equal Rights Association will hold its Anniversary in New York, Steinway Hall, Wednesday and Thursday, May 12th and 13th, and in Brooklyn, Academy of Music, on Friday, the 14th.

After a century of discussion on the rights of citizens in a republic, and the gradual extension of Suffrage, without property or educational qualifications, to all white men, the thought of the nation has turned for the last thirty years to negroes and women.

And in the enfranchisement of black men by the Fourteenth and Fifteenth Amendments to the Federal Constitution, the Congress of the United States has now virtually established on this continent an aristocracy of sex, an aristocracy hitherto unknown in the history of nations.

With every type and shade of manhood thus exalted above their heads, there never was a time when all women, rich and poor, white and black, native and foreign, should be so wide awake to the degradation of their position, and so persistent in their demands to be recognized in the government.

Woman's enfranchisement is now a practical question in England and the United States. With bills before Parliament, Congress and all our State legislatures—with such able champions as John Stuart Mill and George William Curtis, women need but speak the word to secure her political freedom to-day.

We sincerely hope that in the coming National Anniversary every State and Territory, east and west, north and south, will be represented. We invite delegates, too, from all those countries in the Old World where women are demanding their political rights.

Let there be a grand gathering in the metropolis of the nation, that Republicans and Democrats may alike understand, that with the women of this country lies a political power in the future, that both parties would do well to respect.

The following speakers from the several states are already pledged: Anna E. Dickinson, Frederick Douglass, Mary A. Livermore, Madam Anneke, Lilie Peckham, Phebe Couzens, Mrs. M. H. Brinkerhoff.

LUCRETIA MOTT, President.

Vice-Presidents.

Elizabeth Cady Stanton, New York.
Frederick Douglass, "
Henry Ward Beecher, "
Martha C. Wright, "
Frances D. Gage, "
Olympia Brown, Massachusetts,
Elizabeth B. Chase, Rhode Island,
Charles Prince, Connecticut,
Robert Purvis, Pennsylvania,
Antoinette B. Blackwell, New Jersey,
Josephine S. Griffing, Washington, D. C.,
Thomas Garrett, Delaware,
Stephen H. Camp, Ohio,
Euphemia Cochrane, Michigan,
Mary A. Livermore, Illinois,
Mrs. I. H. Sturgeon, Missouri,
Amelia Bloomer, Iowa,
Mary A. Starret, Kansas,
Virginia Penny, Kentucky.

Corresponding Secretary.
Mary E. Gage.

Recording Secretaries.
Henry B. Blackwell,
Harriet Purvis.

Treasurer.
John J. Merritt.

Executive Committee.
Lucy Stone,
Edward S. Bunker,
Elizabeth R. Tilton,
Ernestine L. Rose,
Robert J. Johnston,
Edwin A. Studwell,
Anna Cromwell Field,
Susan B. Anthony,
Theodore Tilton,
Margaret E. Winchester,
Abby Hutchinson Patton,
Oliver Johnson,
Mrs. Horace Greeley,
Abby Hopper Gibbons,
Elizabeth Smith Miller.

Communications and Contributions may be addressed to John J. Merritt, 131 William street, New York.
Newspapers friendly, please publish this call.

Equal Rights Supporters Split Over the 15th Amendment

Long-time abolition and woman's rights activists met together in May 1869 for the third anniversary meeting of the American Equal Rights Association. The 14th Amendment had been ratified in July 1868 and the 15th Amendment was under consideration in the states.

Members of the AERA remained divided over these new amendments which deliberately excluded women. Elizabeth Cady Stanton and Susan B. Anthony opposed the 15th Amendment in protest while Lucy Stone and others felt strongly that equal rights association members should at least not work against it.

An indignant Stanton railed against women having just "another class of ignorant men . . . to be their lawmakers and governors" and called support for the amendment "licking the hand that forges a new chain." Stone said she would be thankful "if *any* body can get out of that terrible pit."

Above: The Call for the 1869 convention.

Focusing on Woman Suffrage

The New York meeting in 1869 was the last for the American Equal Rights Association. Long-simmering conflicts and rivalries came to a head. Early on, abolitionist Stephen Foster of Massachusetts vehemently objected to association officers Elizabeth Cady Stanton and Susan B. Anthony arguing against the 15th Amendment and advocating "educated" suffrage (requiring literacy tests) over universal suffrage. Dominated by men, the convention refused to commit to woman suffrage, and a majority of the women withdrew.

A week later Stanton, Anthony, and supporters formed a new, women-led society specifically to secure the ballot, the National Woman Suffrage Association. In this new group were allies like Ernestine Rose and, later, Isabella Beecher Hooker, plus many women connected with *The Revolution* in New York including Paulina Wright Davis, Lillie Devereux Blake, and Matilda Joslyn Gage.

The NWSA held the Federal government responsible, rather than the states, for enfranchising women, and demanded protection for women under the constitution like former slaves received. A 16th Amendment guaranteeing women the right to vote was actually introduced by Senator Samuel C. Pomeroy of Kansas and Representative George W. Julian of Indiana. It met with little support.

Julia Ward Howe (top) became a prominent figure in the American Woman Suffrage Association after being won over by Lucy Stone. A revered American writer after her "Battle Hymn of the Republic" was published during the Civil War, Howe was also a leader in the growing women's club movement. She became a loyal contributor to *The Woman's Journal*. Abolitionist Thomas Wentworth Higginson (above) also lent his talent and reputation to *The Woman's Journal*. Higginson, a minister, author, and colonel of a Black regiment during the war, was a regular contributor along with popular authors Louisa May Alcott and Harriet Beecher Stowe.

WOMAN SUFFRAGE CALL.

The undersigned, being convinced of the necessity of an AMERICAN WOMAN SUFFRAGE ASSOCIATION, which shall embody the deliberate action of the State organizations, and shall carry with it their united weight, do hereby respectfully invite such organizations to be represented in a Delegate Convention to be held at CLEVELAND, Ohio, *November 24th* and *25th*, A.D. 1869.

The proposed basis of this Convention is as follows:

The Delegates appointed by existing State organizations shall be admitted, provided their number does not exceed, in each case, that of the Congressional delegation of the State. Should it fall short of that number, additional Delegates may be admitted from Local organizations, or from no organization whatever, provided the applicants be actual residents of the States they claim to represent. But no votes shall be counted in the Convention except of those actually admitted as Delegates.

JOHN NEAL.................Maine.	WM. H. BURLEIGH.....New-York.	SHARON TYNDALE.......Illinois.
NATHANIEL WHITE..N. Hamps're.	AARON M. POWELL.... "	J. P. WESTON............ "
ARMENIA S. WHITE.. "	ANNA C. FIELD......... "	ROBERT COLLYER........ "
WILLIAM T. SAVAGE "	GERRIT SMITH......... "	JOSEPH HAVEN........... "
JAMES HUTCHINSON, JR., Verm't.	E. S. BUNKER.......... "	MOSES COIT TYLER....Michigan.
C. W. WILLARD......... "	LUCY STONE.................N.J.	JAMES A. B. STONE.... "
WM. LLOYD GARRISON....Mass.	HENRY B. BLACKWELL..... "	LUCINDA H. STONE..... "
LYDIA MARIA CHILD....... "	JOHN GAGE................. "	AUGUSTA J. CHAPIN..Wisconsin.
DAVID LEE CHILD....... "	PORTIA GAGE............ "	H. EDDY............... "
GEORGE F. HOAR.......... "	ANTOINETTE B. BLACKWELL "	AMELIA BLOOMER..........Iowa.
JULIA WARD HOWE........ "	A. J. DAVIS............... "	
GILBERT HAVEN........... "	MARY F. DAVIS............. "	CHARLES ROBINSON......Kansas.
CAROLINE M. SEVERANCE.. "	MARY GREW........Pennsylvania.	MRS. C. I. H. NICHOLS.... "
JAMES FREEMAN CLARKE. "	ROBERT PURVIS.... "	JOHN EKIN, D.D.......... "
ABBY KELLY FOSTER...:.. "		J. P. ROOT............. "
STEPHEN S. FOSTER........ "	THOMAS GARRETT.....Delaware.	MRS. S. BURGER STEARNS.,Minn.
FRANK B. SANBORN........ "	FIELDER ISRAEL....... "	MRS. W. T. HAZARD......Missouri.
PHEBE A. HANAFORD....... "	HANNAH M. TRACY CUTLER, Ohio.	ISAAC H. STURGEON.... "
ELIZABETH B. CHACE... Rhode I.	A. J. BOYER. .. .. "	MRS. BEVERLY ALLAN... "
T. W. HIGGINSON........ "	MARY V. LONGLEY......... "	JAMES E. YEATMAN.... "
ROWLAND G. HAZARD... "	J. J. BELLVILLE............. "	MARY E. BEEDY......... "
	MIRIAM M. COLE.......... "	J. C. ORRICK............. "
H. M. ROGERS........Connecticut.	S. BOLTIN.................... "	MRS. GEORGE D. HALL... "
SETH ROGERS........ "	AMANDA WAY...........Indiana.	GUY W. WINES........Tennessee.
MARIANNA STANTON "	GEORGE W. JULIAN..... "	CHARLES J. WOODBURY "
GEORGE WM. CURTIS......N. Y.	LAURA GIDDINGS JULIAN "	MARY ATKINS LYNCH..Louisiana.
LYDIA MOTT............... "	LIZZIE M. BOYNTON...... "	GRACE GREENWOOD........D. C.
HENRY WARD BEECHER.. "	MARY A. LIVERMORE.....Illinois.	A. K. SAFFORD...........Arizona.
FRANCES D. GAGE......... "	C. B. WAITE.............. "	J. A. BREWSTER........California.
SAMUEL J. MAY............ "	MYRA BRADWELL .... "	
CELIA BURLEIGH.......... "	JAMES B. BRADWELL.... "	

In addition to the above names, the following were received too late for publication:

EDNA L. CHENEY..........Mass.	BELLE MANSFIELD.........Iowa.	MRS. ELLIOTT........Minn.
SAMUEL MAY, JR........... "	T. M. MILLS................. "	MR. A. KNIGHT .... "
	B. F. GUE .... "	HON. G. C. JONES. .....Mich.
OLIVER JOHNSON.....New-York.	HON. MR. POMEROY.......... "	HON. WM. S. FARMER....... "
WM. P. TOMLINSON... "	MRS. J. C. BURBANK.... ...Minn.	HON. T. W. FERRY.......... "
FREDERICK DOUGLAS. "	MRS. SMITH................. "	REV. J. STRAUB........... "
MRS. AUSTIN ADAMS ......Iowa.	REV. J. MARVIN............. "	S. H. BRIGHAM............. "
EDNA T. SNELL ....:.. "	CAPT. RUSSELL BLAKELY. . "	
MATTIE E. GRIFFITHS...... "		

Organizing the American Woman Suffrage Association

AFTER NEW York women created the National Woman Suffrage Association in May 1869, Boston-based woman's rights supporters asked just how "national" it really was, despite members from many states.

Lucy Stone favored a more comprehensive and more widely representative organization, with specific qualifica-

tions regarding delegate selection and voting rights. Many equal rights activists agreed with her and signed the Call (above) for a founding convention.

Meeting in Cleveland, Ohio, in late November 1869, men and women from 21 states formed the American Woman Suffrage Association and elected Boston preacher

Henry Ward Beecher president and Stone head of the executive committee. The AWSA supported a new constitutional amendment but mainly encouraged efforts for any form of suffrage for women in the states and western territories.

Above: Invitation to the 1869 national convention.

After her years as a ground-breaking woman's rights speaker, Lucy Stone (top) embraced domestic life, leaving lecturing for nearly a decade. She returned to the public eye in 1866 and, along with her husband Henry Blackwell (above), encouraged the formation of local suffrage clubs and new state associations. They helped link these together through *The Woman's Journal* and annual conventions of the American Woman Suffrage Association. Charming and enthusiastic, Blackwell was one of the few men who worked continuously to secure equal rights for women.

Starting a New Woman's Rights Journal

In January 1870 the new American Woman Suffrage Association began publishing a national weekly newspaper entitled *The Woman's Journal*. Edited by Mary Livermore for two years and thereafter by Lucy Stone and her family, the paper became a leading force in the drive for equal suffrage both nationally and internationally while steering clear of more controversial reforms.

Four months later, facing an accumulated debt of $10,000, Susan B. Anthony reluctantly sold *The Revolution* for one dollar to Laura Curtis Bullard and then worked for six years to pay off all the newspaper's creditors. *The Woman's Journal* became the respected voice of the AWSA and by 1875 had over 5,000 subscribers and readers in 39 countries.

Esther Morris was 54 when she settled in rugged Wyoming in 1869 after living in New York and Illinois. The robust pioneer, the mother of three boys, was nearly six feet tall and a known advocate of equal rights. Celebrated as the "Mother of Woman Suffrage" in Wyoming, she was actually one of several who helped the bill become law. In February 1870, just after women were enfranchised, she was appointed the country's first woman Justice of the Peace and served ably in an early test of woman's ability to hold public office. Striding forward with flowers and portfolio, this bronze statue honoring Morris (right) stands in the State Capitol Building in Cheyenne. Wyoming (below) became the first place on the continent where women could vote equally with men.

1869

Wyoming and Utah Territories Approve Woman Suffrage

JUST AFTER suffragists in the east started their new associations, surprising news came from the west. In December 1869 the newly-organized territory of Wyoming approved woman suffrage and two months later Utah followed. In the territories, unlike in the states, the governor and legislature could approve equal suffrage without a popular vote.

In Wyoming supporters of the bill, introduced by William H. Bright, claimed it would draw attention and women settlers to the new territory (population 9,000). The measure passed both Houses by a total of 12 to 6 votes "in a jocular manner as an experiment," according to one contemporary. Some Democrats hoped to embarrass the Republican governor.

Governor John A. Campbell, however, recalled being impressed by a woman's rights convention in Ohio when he was young and surprised many by signing the historic measure on December 10, 1869. The bill withstood a partisan drive for repeal by only one vote in 1871. After that, women voting became widely accepted.

In February 1870, the Utah

territorial legislature passed a similar bill, although the issue was complicated by the practice by some Mormon residents of plural marriage, or polygamy. Critics feared woman suffrage would give Mormon men greater influence than non-Mormons. The legislature's action was largely political and, in one historian's words, was "certainly not a statement of equality." Nonetheless, women voted in Utah until 1887 when they were disfranchised by Congress over the issue of polygamy.

Above: A Currier and Ives print, "The Triumph of Woman's Rights," from 1869 showed a bevy of suffrage caricatures taking over the polls. Left: D. S. Sonnesberger became the first woman to vote in Johnson County, Wyoming.

Suffragists Claim Protection Under the 14th Amendment

AFTER THE 14th Amendment was ratified, suffragists made the claim that its wording actually protected women's right to vote. The case was put forward by Francis Minor, attorney husband of Missouri suffrage leader Virginia Minor. He argued that women were U.S. citizens, that the constitution guaranteed the rights of all citizens, and that under the new amendment, states which excluded citizens from voting were in violation of the constitution. This was one of the first legal strategies developed to challenge women's political exclusion.

Suffragists came to refer to this argument as "the new departure" and lost little time putting it to the test. In No-vember 1868 over 170 women including Lucy Stone tried to vote in several towns in New Jersey, but were "courteously refused" by the male registrars. The women instead cast their votes at a table set up nearby by supporters.

There were other demonstrations made in at least ten states over the next several years. In 1870 Black women voted in some South Carolina districts and forty women, led by the elderly Grimke sisters, attempted to vote in Massachusetts. A group of seventy women was turned away in Washington D.C. in 1871. They sued but lost their appeal.

Taking the argument to the Judiciary Committee of the U.S. House of Representa-tives, New Yorker Victoria Woodhull addressed lawmakers on January 11, 1871 during a hearing arranged by Massachusetts congressman Benjamin Butler. Surprised and impressed by her presentation, Susan B. Anthony and Isabella Beecher Hooker invited Woodhull to address the convention of the National Woman Suffrage Association where she delivered a rousing and impassioned speech.

Charismatic, glamorous, and ambitious, Woodhull became closely involved with suffragists in New York but evoked the displeasure of those in Boston. Despite her inflammatory defense of "free love," Woodhull charmed suffrage leaders and gradually exerted a stronger influence.

The growing demand for woman suffrage following the 1867 Kansas campaign inspired the 1869 song, "We'll Show You When We Come to Vote" (facing page). The sheet music cover poked fun at the idea of equal suffrage by showing women voting at a ladies-only ballot box surrounded by posters promoting well-known suffragists as candidates. Background signs ridiculed both Parker Pillsbury and George Train as women. Victoria Woodhull (above) addressed congressmen in 1871.

Victoria Woodhull was one of the most notorious figures associated with the woman suffrage movement just after the Civil War. Raised with her sister Tennessee Claflin in a traveling family medicine show, Woodhull embraced spiritualism, free love, and other controversial doctrines and drew accusations of fraud, prostitution, and blackmail at an early age. Moving to New York City in 1868, Woodhull, 30, founded a brokerage firm and newspaper. Two years later, in a bold self-promotional gesture, she declared herself a candidate for president of the U.S. In late 1872 she exposed a sex scandal which implicated two well-known male figures in the woman suffrage movement. She accused popular preacher Henry Ward Beecher of having an affair with the wife of his protege, Theodore Tilton. Woodhull was briefly jailed for publicizing the accusations. In 1877 she and her sister left the country, sailing for Great Britain where each subsequently married wealthy English men.

Turned Away at the Polls

INVOKING the 14th Amendment, Victoria Woodhull attracted national publicity when she tried to vote in New York City in 1871. But like Sojourner Truth in Michigan, Abigail Scott Duniway in Oregon, and Matilda Joslyn Gage in New York, she was turned away by election offi-

The right of women to vote was already protected by the existing constitution, argued Susan B. Anthony in March 1871 (above), popularizing the case put forth by Frances Minor and Victoria Woodhull. The following year Anthony abruptly cut short her lecture tour when she heard of Woodhull's latest plan. Woodhull and her supporters were scheming to take over the National Woman Suffrage Association's convention to formally nominate her for president of the U.S. Anthony shut down the meeting before Woodhull could speak and turned her allies out. Woodhull's campaign fizzled and her influence declined, but her brief involvement left the suffrage movement tarnished with the stigma of "free love" which alienated the public and kept supporters on the defensive for years. Left: "Would-Be Voters" from *Harper's Weekly*.

cials. In 1872 Susan B. Anthony used all her persuasive powers to convince officials in Rochester, New York, to register women and pledged to pay any penalties they might face for their action. In St. Louis, Missouri, after Virginia Minor was not allowed to vote, she and her husband sued voting registrar Reese Happersett in a closely-watched test case which they pursued to the U.S. Supreme Court.

Susan B. Anthony Indicted for Voting Illegally

ON November 5, 1872, Susan B. Anthony, along with her three sisters and a dozen other women, went to the polls in Rochester, New York, and cast her vote in the presidential election. Two weeks later, they were all arrested.

Anthony was singled out, indicted (right), and put on trial on June 17, 1873 on the charge of voting illegally because she was a woman. Preparing for her trial, she spoke to potential jurors throughout the county where it was to be held asking, "Is It a Crime for a U.S. Citizen to Vote?" When the trial was moved to a new county, she and Matilda Joslyn Gage again took her case directly to the local residents.

The court proceedings drew national attention and were the center of much political maneuvering. At the outset Anthony was ruled incompetent to testify in her own behalf because she was a woman. Then, after the government presented its case, the judge instructed members of the jury to find her guilty and then dismissed them. To the amazement of the courtroom, he then pulled the already written verdict from his pocket and read it, pronouncing her guilty and fining her $100 for her crime. She replied, "May it please your honor, I shall never pay a dollar of your unjust penalty." The court did not order her imprisoned until she paid and thus denied her the opportunity to appeal.

Above: Victoria Woodhull objects to not being allowed to vote in 1871.

INDICTMENT

AGAINST SUSAN B. ANTHONY.

DISTRICT COURT OF THE UNITED STATES OF AMERICA,

IN AND FOR THE

NORTHERN DISTRICT OF NEW YORK.

At a stated session of the District Court of the United States of America, held in and for the Northern District of New York, at the City Hall, in the city of Albany, in the said Northern District of New York, on the third Tuesday of January, in the year of our Lord one thousand eight hundred and seventy-three, before the Honorable Nathan K. Hall, Judge of the said Court, assigned to keep the peace of the said United States of America, in and for the said District, and also to hear and determine divers Felonies, Misde-

THE DAILY GRAPHIC

AN ILLUSTRATED EVENING NEWSPAPER.

39 & 41 PARK PLACE.

VOL. I—NO. 81.   NEW YORK, THURSDAY, JUNE 5, 1873.   FIVE CENTS.

GRAPHIC STATUES, NO. 17—"THE WOMAN WHO DARED."

Susan B. Anthony was 52 when she faced Federal and grand jury indictments for voting illegally. She had hoped thousands of women would also vote, but there were only scattered reports of women doing so since most were turned away at registration. Although she could not appeal her Federal conviction to the U.S. Supreme Court, Virginia Minor's effort was already underway there. After her trial Anthony used some of the $1,000 donated by supporters to print up a record (below) of the whole proceedings which she distributed nationally. The male voting inspectors who registered the women were prosecuted but later pardoned by President Grant.

AN
ACCOUNT OF THE PROCEEDINGS
ON THE
TRIAL OF
SUSAN B. ANTHONY,
ON THE
Charge of Illegal Voting,
AT THE
PRESIDENTIAL ELECTION IN NOV., 1872,
AND ON THE
TRIAL OF
BEVERLY W. JONES, EDWIN T. MARSH
AND WILLIAM B. HALL,
THE INSPECTORS OF ELECTION BY WHOM HER VOTE WAS RECEIVED.

ROCHESTER, N. Y.:
DAILY DEMOCRAT AND CHRONICLE BOOK PRINT, 2 WEST MAIN ST.
1874.

Humorous caricatures and editorial cartoons like the one above kept votes for women topical and made Susan B. Anthony a suffrage symbol. Thomas Wust's illustration, from just before Anthony's 1873 trial for voting illegally, was in part a tribute to her bold action which won her the appellation, "The Woman Who Dared." In the background are satirical fantasies depicting sign-carrying women staging a political parade, ladies orating from a stage, two men tending a baby, and a female police officer standing by. At her trial, Anthony told her judge that women should "rebel against your man-made, unjust, unconstitutional forms of law." She risked a maximum penalty of three years in jail for her crime.

Lucie Wilmot Smith promoted woman suffrage in the Black press and the Black community during the late 1800s. However, like many Black women of her time, little about her life survives. Born in Kentucky in 1861, Smith was teaching by the age of 16. She continued her own education and eventually became a professional journalist and a member of the faculty at the University of Louisville. When she was 23, Smith began a children's column for the *American Baptist* and soon was directing the publication of *Our Women and Children,* a Louisville periodical. As editor of its "Women and Women's Work" department she defended equal rights and championed votes for women. Smith was a member of the Afro-American Press Convention and a frequent contributor to the *Indianapolis Freeman* and other newspapers. Her articles were often reprinted and kept women's equality and related issues before Black readers throughout the country.

Championing Woman's Rights in Print

To encourage support for equal rights legislation, suffragists formed new state associations, held meetings, circulated petitions, and also started newspapers which pressed their demand for "woman's emancipation."

In 1869 Emily Pitts-Stevens, 25, a former Illinois school teacher, founded the west's first woman suffrage paper, *The Pioneer,* in San Francisco, a year after *The Revolution.* Mary Livermore was also impressed by *The Revolution* and began *The Agitator* in Chicago, which soon merged with *The Woman's Journal.*

Abigail Scott Duniway began *The New Northwest* in Portland, Oregon, following a tour of the region with Susan B. Anthony in 1871. Duniway published the crusading weekly for sixteen years, and it played a major role building

Abigail Scott Duniway and *The New Northwest.*

support for women's equality in the Pacific northwest. Other newspapers championing woman's rights included *The Queen Bee,* published by Caroline Nichols Churchill in Colorado, *The Woman's Exponent,* edited by Emmeline B. Wells in Utah, and *Our Herald,* a weekly launched by Helen M. Gou-

gar in Indiana in 1881. Elizabeth Boynton Harbert edited *The New Era,* a suffrage paper in Illinois, in 1888 and Clara Bewick Colby began *The Woman's Tribune* in Nebraska in 1883 and published it for over twenty years.

Although chronically underfunded and often short-lived, suffrage newspapers played a key role in the movement. As historian Sherilyn Cox Bennion observed, they "articulated and refined the ideas that became the bulwarks of the suffrage cause." The papers also lent prestige, boosted morale, and "enabled suffragists to solidify a base from which to extend their efforts."

Above: Participants actively discussed woman's rights at a convention in Saratoga, New York, from an 1869 *Harper's Weekly.*

THE DAILY GRAPHIC

AN ILLUSTRATED EVENING NEWSPAPER.

39 & 41 PARK PLACE.

VOL. VIII. | All the News. Four Editions Daily | NEW YORK, THURSDAY, OCTOBER 21, 1875.—TWELVE PAGES. | $12 Per Year in Advance. Single Copies, Five Cents. | NO. 816.

REAL vs. IMAGINARY WANTS.

Misses Anthony and Dickinson and Mrs. Stanton— We hold that this gives women the right to vote. Any way, you might let us."
Chief Justice Waite—" In the opinion of the Court the XIV Amendment does not confer on women the right of suffrage."
Public Opinion— And you might add, Mr. Chief Justice, that the great question of the day is, How to improve the suffrage—not how to extend it."

Anna Dickinson overcame dire poverty to become one of the most popular lecturers in the country during the Civil War years. Raised a Quaker in Pennsylvania, Dickinson spoke out against slavery and for the rights of women while still in her teens. Encouraged by abolitionists, she began to lecture publicly. Passionate and persuasive, Dickinson enthralled her audiences with her eloquence and fervor while denouncing opponents with biting sarcasm. Her success on behalf of Republican party candidates and her staunch defense of the Union launched her nationally, and in 1864 when she was 21, she was invited to address President Lincoln and other dignitaries in the Capitol. Susan B. Anthony tried to convince her to take a leadership role in the suffrage movement. Instead she continued lecturing and took up play writing and acting before her fame faded. In 1869 *The Revolution* noted, "An illustrious individual remarks that Mrs. Stanton is the salt, Anna Dickinson the pepper, and Miss Anthony the vinegar of the Female Suffrage movement. The very elements to get the 'white male' into a nice pickle."

The U.S. Supreme Court ruled in 1875 on the suit brought by suffragist Virginia Minor and her husband after she was kept from voting. In *Minor vs. Happersett* the Court unanimously rejected the argument that the 14th Amendment protected women's voting rights, ruling that it only applied to former male slaves and affirming that voting was a matter for each state to decide. The editorial cartoon above portrayed three suffrage leaders, Susan B. Anthony, Elizabeth Cady Stanton, and Anna Dickinson, clothed in ridiculous outfits, receiving the bad news from the Chief Justice.

With that approach closed to them, suffragists had to secure a new constitutional amendment or else win over male voters in each state one by one.

UNCLE SAM'S THANKSGIVING DINNER.

Developing New Strategies During the 1870s

During the 1870s, suffragists began pursuing a variety of strategies simultaneously to advance their cause. With new journals and two new national organizations encouraging action, supporters pressured Congress, lobbied their state legislatures, and protested their status by attempting to vote.

They also tried to persuade legislators to include votes for women whenever a new state constitution was drawn up. Nebraska lawmakers included equal suffrage in a new constitution but voters rejected it in 1871. The following year the Dakota territorial legislature defeated a similar measure by only one vote.

Woman suffrage was placed on the ballot in two states, Michigan and Colorado, in the 1870s. During the 1874 drive in Michigan, Susan B. Anthony joined local activists and canvassed the state for forty days speaking

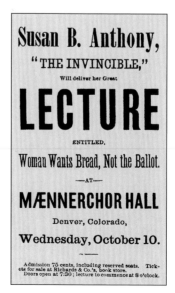

to large and enthusiastic audiences, but this second campaign for suffrage met with defeat 135,957 to 40,077.

Colorado became a state in 1876 and a vote was scheduled on equal suffrage for the following year. Local supporters together with leaders from both national associations were able to wage a modest drive. On October 2, 1877 voters defeated the measure 14,053 to 6,612.

Above: Native and foreign-born women had a place at the table in Thomas Nast's image of universal suffrage from an 1869 *Harper's Weekly*. Left: By 1877 Susan B. Anthony's persistence had earned her the title, "The Invincible."

Protesting Taxation Without Representation

THE YEAR 1873 marked not only Susan B. Anthony's trial but also the 100th anniversary of the Boston Tea Party where American colonists rebelled against excessive British taxation. Suffragists in the northeast used this and subsequent patriotic anniversaries as opportunities to protest the fact that women, like the early colonists, suffered from taxation without political representation. In December, suffragists throughout New England hosted centennial tea parties and supporters in Massachusetts held a statewide Anti-Tax Convention which drew thousands of women.

Tax Protests

Lucy Stone made one of the earliest tax protests in 1857, just two months after giving birth to her daughter Alice. Stone refused to pay the tax on her Orange County, New Jersey, home because, she wrote, "women suffer taxation, and yet have no representation, which is not only unjust to half of the adult population, but is contrary to our theory of government."

On January 22, 1858, in the winter cold, an uncomfortable constable auctioned off several of Stone's household belongings, including engravings of famous abolitionists, to pay the tax while she watched with her baby in her lap. A neighbor secretly bought and returned most of

the items to her that night. In 1874 Stephen and Abby Kelley Foster refused to pay $100 in taxes in protest and saw their farm sold as a result. They later repurchased it but for much more money.

Two elderly sisters, former abolitionists Abby and Julia Smith, also refused to pay taxes on their farm in Glastonbury, Connecticut, because they had no voice in how the money was used. The town council, however, showed what Stephen Foster called "contemptible meanness" and used the protest as an excuse to seize some of their choicest land as well as several of their Jersey cows.

Centennial Display

In 1876 Stone created a modest display honoring women's drive for equality for the Women's Pavilion at the Centennial Exposition in Philadelphia. However her small framed exhibit on "Protests of Women Against Taxation Without Representation" was hung too high and out of the way to be read. In July, members of the National Woman Suffrage Association organized a more visible protest during the centennial festivities. As Stone later noted, "They know better than we do how to make a noise." ◆

Top: Editorial cartoonist Thomas Nast satirized the New England Woman's Tea Party. Bottom: An 1873 handbill from New York.

The New York Woman's Suffrage Society.

TO THE TAX PAYING WOMEN OF NEW YORK;

SISTERS: You are earnestly requested to unite with us in

A MASS MEETING,

To be held at UNION LEAGUE THEATRE,

(26TH STREET AND MADISON AVENUE.)

On the Centennial of the "Boston Tea Party"

Tuesday Evening, Dec. 16th, 1873.

To protest against the Tyranny of Taxation Without Representation.

One hundred years ago our ancestors precipitated a rebellion by refusing to pay a tax, on Tea, imposed against their will. At the end of a century 20,000,000 of their daughters are suffering precisely the same wrong; taxation without representation; and it behooves us as their descendants to demand that the freedom for which our forefathers struggled shall be given to us also! And to demand of right that the coming Centennial of "American Independence" shall find us enfranchised, or freed from taxation and responsibility to a government which denies us personality and Citizenship.

LILLIE DEVEREUX BLAKE, Sec'y.   CLEMENCE S. LOZIER. Pres.

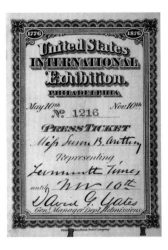

No Mood for Celebrating

By 1876, the centennial of the country's birth, suffragists had every reason to feel frustrated and disappointed. The Supreme Court had rejected their claim that women were covered by the constitution. There was little support for a new amendment in Congress. And numerous state legislatures had defeated efforts to put the measure on the ballot.

In addition, the political parties refused to include votes for women in their platforms, few male politicians were sympathetic, and male voters had defeated equal rights in Kansas and Michigan. There was little to encourage woman's rights activists during the decade following the Civil War.

By July, many suffragists felt a passionate resentment. Not only were women still largely excluded from the public sphere, but they were also being denied a role in the great national celebration. The string of patriotic events that included the Centennial Exposition in Philadelphia offered new opportunities to protest and suffragists made the most of them.

1876. PROTEST.
National Woman Suffrage Association.

To the Men of the United States in Celebration of the Nation's Centennial Birth-day, July 4th, 1876.

One century ago the walls of Independence Hall echoed to that famous "Declaration" of our Fathers, that startled the world from its old dreams of authority, and proclaimed the individual above all principalities and powers.

The revolutionary heroes of '76 asserted and re-asserted these great truths, : "All men are created free and equal, with certain inalienable rights to life, liberty, and the pursuit of happiness;"—"taxation without representation is tyranny;"—"no just government can be framed without the consent of the governed."

Such were the fundamental principles of the experiment of government they proposed to try in the new world. Such are the grand doctrines taught their sons and daughters through the century; the texts for our Fourth of July orations; the mottoes for our banners; the songs for our national music. Individual rights, individual conscience and judgment are our great American ideas, the cardinal points of our faith in church and in State, the soul of our republican government.

Through prolonged discussion, hot debate, and bloody conflict on the battle-field, the men of this generation have secured for their sex, white and black, rich and poor, native and foreign born, the liberty of self-government, and it well befits them to celebrate the centennial birth-day of such sacred rights.

But the mothers, wives and daughters of this republic have no lot nor part in this grand jubilee; they stand to-day where their fathers did when subjects of King George; "slaves" according to the definition of Benjamin Franklin, "having no voice in the laws and rulers that govern them."

Women are denied the right of self-government; the most ignorant and degraded classes of men are their rulers.

Women are denied a right of trial by a jury of their peers; men, foreign and native are their judges and jurors.

Women are taxed without representation, governed without their consent, and now Kings, Emperors and Czars from the despotisms of the old world are invited here to behold the worst form of aristocracy the sun ever shone upon, "an aristocracy of sex."

Our rulers may learn a lesson of justice from the very government they repudiated a century ago. In England women may occupy the highest political position, fill many offices, and vote on a property qualification at all municipal elections, while here the political status of the daughters of the pilgrims, is lower than that of the paupers from the old world who land on our shores to vote our taxes and governors.

In view of such degradation of one-half our people, citizens of a Republic, WE PROTEST before the assembled nations of the world against the centennial celebration, as an occasion for National rejoicing, as only through equal, impartial suffrage can a genuine republican form of government be realized.

With pride we may point the world to our magnificent domain, our numberless railroads, our boundless lakes and rivers, our vast forests, and exhaustless mines, our progress in the arts and sciences, our inventions in mechanical and agricultural implements, but in human rights how false to our theory of government we still remain.

The enfranchisement of 20,000,000 of women, is the only act of justice that in its magnanimity and magnitude is worthy the occasion you propose to celebrate, the crowning glory of the great events of the century.

NAMES.   **NAMES.**

Striking a Discordant Note at the National Centennial

Members of the National Woman Suffrage Association drew up a passionate Petition of Protest to coincide with the 100th birthday of the United States in 1876, voicing their indignation over "calling this Centennial a celebration of the Independence of *the people,* while one-half of the people are still subjects – still political slaves."

Rebuffed after asking that women be included in the official Fourth of July centennial observances, suffragists were still able to obtain several platform passes. In preparation, Anthony, Matilda Joslyn Gage, and Elizabeth Cady Stanton drafted a Woman's Declaration of Rights which called for the impeachment of "our rulers" based on their denial of rights to women.

On July 4, during a pause in the welcoming ceremony, Anthony, Gage, Lillie Devereux Blake, and Sara Andrews Spencer rose from their seats, approached the podium, and solemnly presented their Declaration to the startled chairman. The action disrupted the meeting and drew national publicity as audience members scrambled for copies of the Declaration which the women handed out as they left.

Above: The 1876 petition.
Top left: Susan B. Anthony's press ticket.

DECLARATION OF RIGHTS

OF THE

WOMEN OF THE UNITED STATES

BY THE

NATIONAL WOMAN SUFFRAGE ASSOCIATION,

JULY 4th, 1876.

WHILE the Nation is buoyant with patriotism, and all hearts are attuned to praise, it is with sorrow we come to strike the one discordant note, on this hundredth anniversary of our country's birth. When subjects of Kings, Emperors, and Czars, from the Old World, join in our National Jubilee, shall the women of the Republic refuse to lay their hands with benedictions on the nation's head? Surveying America's Exposition, surpassing in magnificence those of London, Paris, and Vienna, shall we not rejoice at the success of the youngest rival among the nations of the earth? May not our hearts, in unison with all, swell with pride at our great achievements as a people; our free speech, free press, free schools, free church, and the rapid progress we have made in material wealth, trade, commerce, and the inventive arts? And we do rejoice, in the success thus far, of our experiment of self-government. Our faith is firm and unwavering in the broad principles of human rights, proclaimed in 1776, not only as abstract truths, but as the corner stones of a republic. Yet, we cannot forget, even in this glad hour, that while all men of every race, and clime, and condition, have been invested with the full rights of citizenship, under our hospitable flag, all women still suffer the degradation of disfranchisement

The history of our country the past hundred years, has been a series of assumptions and usurpations of power over woman, in direct opposition to the principles of just government, acknowledged by the United States at its foundation, which are:

First. The natural rights of each individual.

Second. The exact equality of these rights.

Third. That these rights, when not delegated by the individual, are retained by the individual.

Fourth. That no person can exercise the rights of others without delegated authority.

Fifth. That the non-use of these rights does not destroy them.

And for the violation of these fundamental principles of our Government, we arraign our rulers on this 4th day of July, 1876,—and these are our

ARTICLES OF IMPEACHMENT.

BILLS OF ATTAINDER have been passed by the introduction of the word "male" into all the State constitutions, denying to woman the right of suffrage, and thereby making sex a crime—an exercise of power clearly forbidden in Article 1st, Sections 9th and 10th of the United States Constitution.

Writing Women into History

INSPIRED BY the national centennial, Elizabeth Cady Stanton and Susan B. Anthony (above) began soliciting material for a *History of Woman Suffrage* which would record the efforts of woman's rights activists up to that time. Together with Matilda Joslyn Gage they produced the first thick volume in 1881, covering the years 1848 to 1861, and two more volumes (below) by 1886. Despite at times favoring their own efforts over those of their rivals, the books offered an inspiring chronicle of the long, heroic drive for equality. Anthony sent copies to libraries throughout the country. Ida Husted Harper edited three later volumes, completing the monumental history.

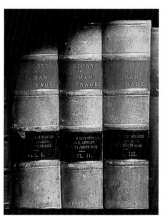

The Declaration of Rights (above), which suffragists distributed at the Centennial Exposition's July 4, 1876 ceremony, put their case for political equality clearly before the public. "From the earliest history of our country," it declared, "woman has shown equal devotion with man to the cause of freedom, and has stood firmly by his side in its defense. Together, they have made this country what it is. Women's wealth, thought and labor have cemented the stones of every monument man has reared to Liberty."

The Declaration concluded, "We declare our faith in the principles of self-government; our full equality with man in natural rights; that woman was made first for her own happiness, with the absolute right to herself – to all the opportunities and advantages life affords, for her complete development; and we deny that dogma of the centuries, incorporated in the codes of all nations – that woman was made for man – her best interests, in all cases, to be sacrificed to his will."

Asking that justice and equality "be guaranteed to us and our daughters forever," the Declaration was signed by two dozen woman's rights leaders including Lucretia Mott, Sarah Pugh, Mary Ann McClintock, Olympia Brown, and Virginia Minor.

FLOCKING FOR F
(THEY SAVED THE ANCIENT CAPITOL; THEY B

Left: **Preparing for a new assault in 1878.**

Demanding Action from Congress

SUFFRAGISTS FOLLOWED their centennial protests with a new assault on Congress, including a petition of 40,000 signatures backing their demand for a Federal suffrage amendment. In response, California Senator Aaron A. Sargent introduced what women hoped would become the 16th Amendment to the Constitution on January 10, 1878. The bill read simply: "The right of citizens of the United States to vote shall not be denied or abridged by the United States or by any State on account of sex. Congress shall have the power to enforce this article by appropriate legislation."

Ardent suffragists "besieged" the Capitol in support of the new bill in Josef Keppler's satirical 1878 illustration for *Puck,* "Flocking for Freedom" (left). Prominent among the feminist "geese" were Lucy Stone, Susan B. Anthony, Elizabeth Cady Stanton, popular lecturers Phoebe Couzins and Anna Dickinson, Isabella Beecher Hooker, Civil War veteran Dr. Mary E. Walker, and British columnist Emily Faithfull. The same bill, referred to as the 16th Amendment until the early 1900s, would be resubmitted to every session of Congress until it was passed, unchanged, as the 19th Amendment forty years later.

Women Stage a Spontaneous Revolt Against Alcohol Abuse

In December 1873 groups of women in small towns in Ohio, New York, and other states grew outraged by the unregulated sale and widespread abuse of alcohol. The women, most financially dependent on men, gathered in front of local saloons and began reciting prayers and singing hymns in an effort to shut them down. Saloonkeepers argued, doused the women with cold water, and tried to outlast them. But many saloons soon closed in the face of the spontaneous "Woman's Crusade" of temperance activists. Women in other towns quickly followed suit and temporarily shut several thousand saloons, many illegal, over the following months.

In October 1874 the national Woman's Christian Temperance Union was organized and it grew into the largest and most powerful woman's organization in the U.S. The WCTU mobilized women across the country to "temper" or moderate alcohol consumption, combat vice, and promote a broad range of social reforms including woman suffrage, which their leader, Frances Willard, astutely referred to as "the home-protection ballot."

Above: Women gathered in protest outside a Hillsboro, Ohio, saloon in 1873. Below: Pleading with a saloon-keeper. Far left: A white ribbon symbolized the purity of the home. Facing page: "Woman's Holy War" against alcohol, a Currier and Ives print from 1874.

Frances Willard, a former teacher and college dean, was 40 when she was elected president of the Woman's Christian Temperance Union in 1879. Visionary, magnetic, and persuasive, she used her oratorical and executive skills to mobilize tens of thousands of American women. Her leadership catalyzed action nationally for legislation dealing with alcohol and vice, the age of sexual consent, working and prison conditions, and other critical issues usually ignored by male politicians. In 1880 she persuaded WCTU members to endorse the controversial cause of woman suffrage. Willard, whom Susan B. Anthony once called a "general with an army of 250,000," organized a World WCTU in 1891 in part to work against the international drug trade. The widely-respected temperance leader died at 58, but her unprecedented success in harnessing the energy of women inspired suffragists to build their own national organization with similar political strength and public appeal.

New Opposition to Equal Suffrage

Under Frances Willard and her motto "Do Everything," the Woman's Christian Temperance Union organized 39 departments by 1889 to help woman in "the protection of her home." In several states the WCTU became the main organization of women and members led referenda campaigns for both the prohibition of alcohol and for woman suffrage. But temperance workers' support for equal suffrage soon led the liquor and brewing industries, and a vast web of interdependent farming, railroad, and banking interests, to vehemently oppose women voting, fearing they would back prohibition. ◆

Above: Ready to "clean up" the town, temperance workers paraded in Devil's Lake, North Dakota.

IN THE NAME OF GOD AND HUMANITY

TEMPERANCE LEAGUE

WINE & LIQUORS

RUM

BEER

WHISKY

GIN

BRANDY

PUBLISHED BY CURRIER & IVES.   ENTERED ACCORDING TO ACT OF CONGRESS IN THE YEAR 1874 BY CURRIER & IVES, IN THE OFFICE OF THE LIBRARIAN OF CONGRESS AT WASHINGTON.   125 NASSAU ST. NEW YORK.

WOMANS HOLY WAR.

Grand Charge on the Enemy's Works.

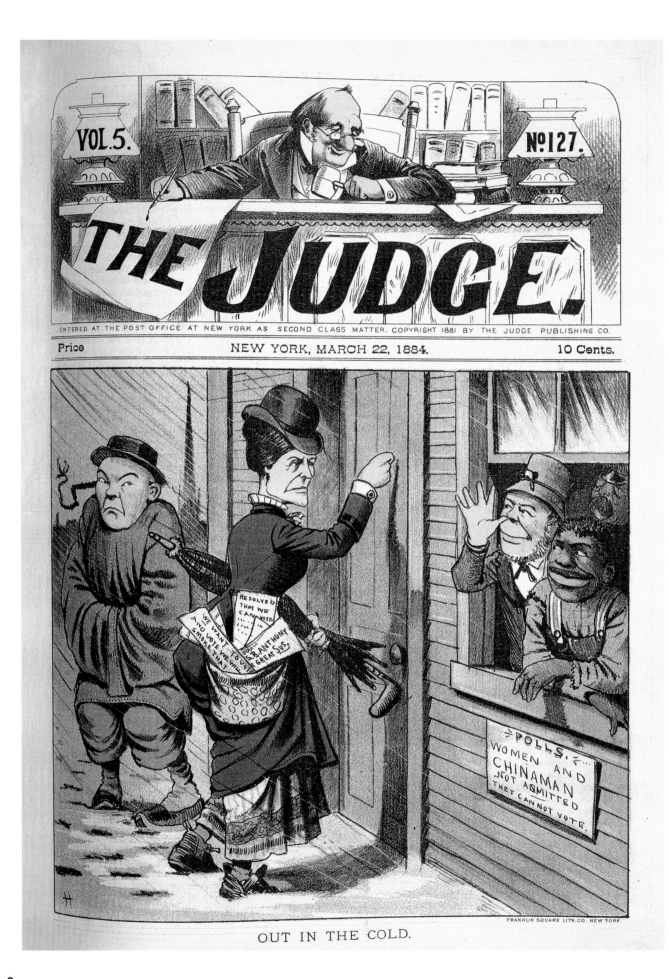

OUT IN THE COLD.

Chapter 3: 1878-1900

The First Suffrage Victories in the West

Rejected by the courts, ignored by Congress, and defeated in several states during the 1870s, suffragists struggled to sustain hope in their ultimate goal. For many women, Susan B. Anthony became an invaluable source of inspiration, displaying a confidence and optimism that were reinvigorating. Despite continual defeats and setbacks, persistence paid off with a growing suffragist presence in Washington D.C. and tangible gains in some states.

As the population grew and new states were admitted, suffragists lobbied state legislatures to have the question put to the voters. They also testified annually before congressional committees for the Federal amendment. After years of experience, suffrage leaders realized that little progress could be made without the endorsement of at least one of the major political parties. They also recognized that state legislators were often more sympathetic to women than the mass of male voters. So they undertook influencing state politicians and building up political support in addition to waging electoral campaigns whenever possible.

Real political progress was slow, however, since the

Boston women cast their ballots during a hotly contested school board election in 1888.

strongest antipathy to woman suffrage, in Anthony's view, was the fear of the various political parties that it "might be disastrous to their interests." The parties would be much more interested in women voting, she claimed, "if it was known that we could be driven to the ballot-box like a flock of sheep and

all vote for one party."

Women gradually won partial forms of suffrage, such as the right to vote for school board members, in certain states. And, after years of lobbying state legislatures and running referendum campaigns, woman suffrage finally became law in the 1890s in four western states.

Excluded from voting almost everywhere, women (as well as all Chinese) were left standing "Out in the Cold" (facing page) in Grant E. Hamilton's 1884 illustration for *Judge* magazine. A caricature of Susan B. Anthony, complete with umbrella and bowler hat, was shown knocking on the polls' door and receiving taunts from the newly arrived Irish and recently enfranchised Black men inside. In a few states women exercised partial suffrage and could vote on certain bond or school-related measures. In contrast, recent male immigrants in some midwestern states could become full voters just by declaring their intention to become citizens at a later date.

WOMEN CITIZENS
Of the UNITED STATES.

To the Republican Party in Presidential Convention Assembled, Chicago, June 2, 1880.

Seventy-six delegates from local, State and National Woman Suffrage Organizations, representing every section of the United States, are here to-day to ask you to place the following plank in your platform:

RESOLVED, that we pledge ourselves to secure women citizens in the exercise of their right to vote.

We ask you to pledge yourselves to protect the rights of one-half of the American people, and to thus carry your own principles to their logical results.

The Thirteenth Amendment of 1865, abolishing slavery, the Fourteenth Amendment of 1867, defining citizenship, and the Fifteenth Amendment of 1870, securing United States citizens in their right to vote, and your prolonged and powerful debates on all the great issues involved in our civil conflict, stand as enduring monuments to the honor of the Republican Party.

Impelled by the ever growing demand among women for a voice in the laws they are required to obey, for their rightful share in the government of this fair Republic, various State Legislatures have conceded partial suffrage to women.

But the great duty remains of securing to woman her right to have her opinions counted at the ballot-box, in the decision of all questions of public welfare.

What will you do now? You cannot live on the noble words and deeds of those who inaugurated the Republican Party. You should vie with those men in great achievements. Progress is the law of national life. You must have a new, vital issue to rouse once more the enthusiasm of the people. Our question of human rights answers this demand. The two great political parties are alike divided upon finance, free-trade, labor reform and general questions of political economy.

The essential point in which you differ from the Democratic party is National versus State Supremacy, and it is on this very issue we make our demand, and ask that our rights as United States citizens be secured by an Amendment to the National Constitution.

To carry this measure is not only your duty but your privilege. Your pledge to enfranchise ten millions of women citizens will rouse an enthusiasm which must count in the coming closely contested election. But above expediency is right, and to do justice is ever the highest political wisdom.

Appealing to Parties and Politicians to Support the Federal Suffrage Amendment

Exemplifying years of persistent effort, Elizabeth Cady Stanton (above) addressed the Senate Committee on Privileges and Elections in January 1878 in support of the newly-introduced Federal suffrage amendment. Stanton, an outstanding speaker, later wrote that she was so infuriated by the "studied inattention and contempt" of the chairman that she had to suppress the urge to hurl her manuscript at his head.

The National Woman Suffrage Association arranged for hearings during every session of Congress from 1878 on, but while several committee reports were favorable, woman suffrage came to a vote only once. It was defeated in the Senate on January 25, 1887, 34 to 16 with 25 absent. Clearly there was not nearly enough sympathy in either House to pass a constitutional amendment.

Faced with limited support in Congress, Susan B. Anthony, Lucy Stone, and other suffragists traveled extensively throughout the country encouraging state initiatives and pro-suffrage candidates, and lobbying the political parties to endorse votes for women. When suffragists attended party conventions they were often met with jeers and ridicule. Sometimes their reception was cordial, but they received little actual support. Neither political party took any substantive action nationally until the very end.

Above: Elizabeth Cady Stanton addressing senators in 1878. Top left: Seeking Republican Party support. Right: Laura De Force Gordon and Susan B. Anthony are escorted to the stage at a political convention.

Women Against Woman Suffrage

WOMEN WHO opposed equal suffrage responded to the proposed 16th Amendment with their own protest in 1886. Countering "the views of the few," they claimed that voting would lessen the influence of "intelligent and true" women.

As early as 1868 nearly 200 women from Lancaster, Massachusetts, had petitioned the legislature not to give them the vote lest it diminish "the moral influence of women." A Woman's Anti-Suffrage Association was founded in Washington D.C. around 1870. Similar opposition by women, in addition to the more organized opposition of business and political interests, met nearly every effort of suffragists. Since they were never numerous, anti-suffrage women were relatively easy for supporters to dismiss. But speaking to the press and testifying before congressional committees, these opponents bolstered the claim that most women did not want to vote.

In 1882 Mrs. Henry O. Houghton of Boston founded the Massachusetts Association Opposed to the Further Extension of Suffrage to Women. Two years later, several members announced they were sending money to Oregon to defeat the suffrage measure to counter eastern suffragists who were raising funds to support it.

Above: An early anti-suffrage argument.

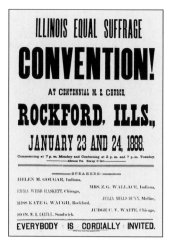

A Brief Victory in Washington

AFTER SEVERAL narrow defeats, the Washington territorial legislature finally passed a suffrage bill enfranchising the women of the territory. Governor William A. Newell signed it on November 23, 1883 and church bells rang out in celebration. In 1884 over 8,000 women voted on the same territorial questions as 42,000 men.

Three years later, however, opponents fearing prohibition filed a lawsuit contending that women were neither legal jurors nor voters. The suit was upheld by the territorial supreme court, which voided the suffrage bill on a technicality. When the legislature passed a corrected bill in 1888 it, too, was overruled. Suffragists protested in vain that the decisions were blatantly unconstitutional.

With women disfranchised, only men prepared the new constitution before Washington was admitted as a state in 1889. Constitutional convention delegates refused to include equal suffrage but were lobbied by Henry Blackwell and others to schedule a separate vote on the question.

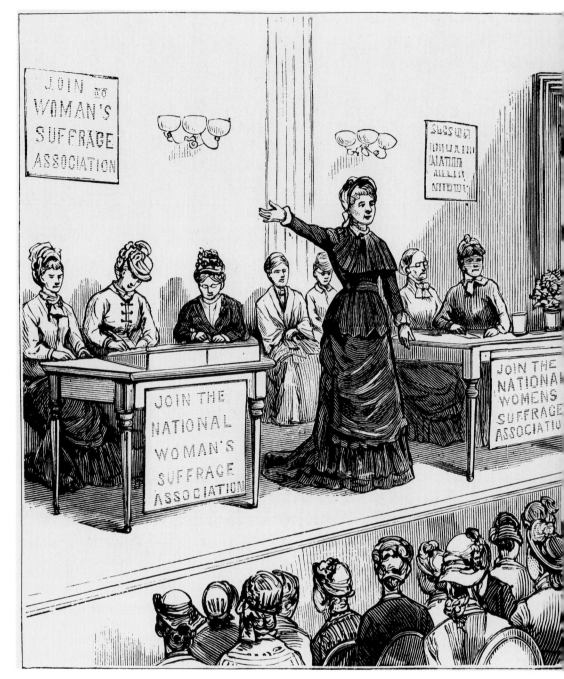

Two Approaches to Winning Enfranchisement

LIKE THE national suffrage associations, groups in states such as Illinois (top left) met regularly to share news, make plans, and boost spirits during the 1870s and 1880s. Every year the National Woman Suffrage Association convened in Washington D.C. so that members could testify before congressional hearings on the Federal amendment. The American Woman Suffrage Association met in different cities to encourage local efforts.

The American association, like Lucy Stone herself, took a more mainstream approach than the National and promoted equal suffrage separate from other controversial reforms of the day. The American emphasized state efforts for full or partial suffrage while the National encour-

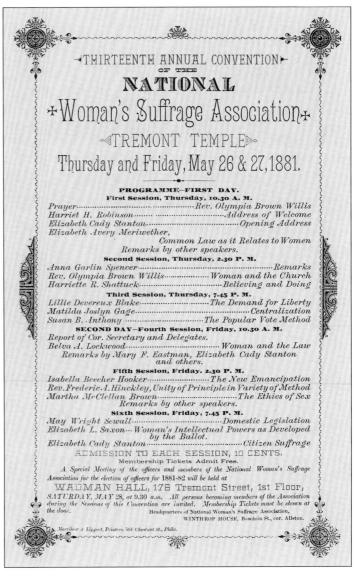

Demanding Federal Action

Unlike the American Association, the National Woman Suffrage Association was run by women only and had a general membership as well as delegates from state organizations. Susan B. Anthony and the National built up a presence in Washington D.C. to educate congressmen and lobby for Federal action. The National still supported most of the state campaigns just as the American formally endorsed the Federal amendment. But under the influence of Elizabeth Cady Stanton and Matilda Joslyn Gage, the National made its appeal for suffrage (above) in the larger context of women's rights and more controversial reforms.

Both associations nurtured political allies and struggled to stay solvent. Helping immensely was a bequest in 1886 from philanthropist Francis Jackson's daughter, Eliza Eddy of Boston, who left Anthony and Lucy Stone over $20,000 each to continue their work.

Above: Far-ranging discussions in 1881.

aged women to demand a constitutional amendment. For years attempts at unity proved unfruitful partially due to the bitter personal rivalry that grew up between Stone and her supporters and Susan B. Anthony and hers.

Some women ignored the rift and were active in both associations, working for protection at both the state and the national levels. They ar-gued that American women already *had* the right to vote since a democratic government was based on the consent of the governed.

Above: Suffragists met in Chicago in 1880 to influence delegates to the Republican National Convention. Top left: Announcing a state convention.

Belva Lockwood, born Belva Ann Bennett in New York, became a prominent attorney in Washington D.C. and an influential advocate of equal rights for women. Married and widowed twice, Lockwood raised a daughter and taught school before earning a law degree at 43 in 1873. As one of the foremost women lawyers in the capital, she testified at congressional hearings and drafted countless resolutions, bills, and petitions in support of equal suffrage. In 1879 she became the first woman lawyer admitted to practice before the U.S. Supreme Court after ushering an enabling bill through Congress herself. She also defended Cherokee interests, pursued pension claims, and worked for equal pay for equal work for women in government service. In the early 1900s she encouraged territories applying for statehood to include equal suffrage in their constitutions.

A Suffragist Runs for President

AFTER Elizabeth Cady Stanton and Susan B. Anthony encouraged women to support the Republican Party's candidate for president in 1884, attorney Belva Lockwood wrote to her friend Marietta Stow in California, "It is quite time that we had our own party, our own platform and our own nominees." In response, Stow and a small group of friends created the National Equal Rights Party and notified Lockwood that they had nominated her for president and Stow as her running mate.

Surprised yet aware of the novel idea's publicity potential, Lockwood ran a modest but dignified campaign which promoted a broad platform of progressive reforms. Although her campaign captured public attention, it also drew ridicule from the press and censure from some suffragists who saw the effort as a damaging distraction. With supporters in several western states, however, Lockwood won over 4,000 votes in 1884. She fared worse when she ran again in 1888 and grew increasingly estranged from the suffrage leadership. However the notoriety of her presidential campaign elevated her to national prominence, and she remained a popular personality on the lecture circuit for years, forcefully calling for international peace as well as equal rights.

Equal Rights Ticket.

FOR PRESIDENT,
BELVA A. LOCKWOOD.
FOR VICE-PRESIDENT,
MARIETTA L. STOW.
1884

Top: Making fun of Belva Lockwood's 1884 campaign, men in a Rahway, New Jersey, parade looked ridiculous themselves dressed in women's clothing. Above: The Equal Rights Ticket. Left: An 1886 announcement.

THE DISTINGUISHED ORATOR AND QUEEN OF THE AMERICAN BAR.

BELVA LOCKWOOD

"The Champion of Equal Civil and Political Rights."

WHO WAS NOMINATED FOR

PRESIDENT
OF THE UNITED STATES.

AT IRVING OPERA HOUSE,
WARSAW, N. Y.
Friday Evening, Nov. 26th, 1886.

ADMISSION, 25 & 50 CENTS.

Reserved Seats for sale at Whitlock & Pratt's.

HENRY L. SLAYTON, Manager.
CENTRAL MUSIC HALL,
CHICAGO.

Trying to Win an Equal Suffrage State

URING THE early 1880s suffragists waged referendum campaigns in Nebraska and Oregon after winning the approval of both state legislatures. Numerous efforts proceeded simultaneously in other states but without immediate results.

Nebraska

Suffragists in Nebraska organized a small but efficient campaign which was met with surprisingly strong opposition in 1882. The state association spent a year preparing and the contest, only the fourth suffrage referendum effort in a state, attracted workers from around the country.

Nebraska suffragists under Ada M. Bittenbender opened headquarters in Lincoln and circulated literature, sent out press information, and published both a campaign song book and a special supplement for county newspapers. Clara Bewick Colby, whom Susan B. Anthony described as "indefatigable," organized lecture tours and, along with Harriet Brooks and Rachel Foster, directed state efforts from Omaha.

Both the American and the National Woman Suffrage Associations held well-attended conventions in Omaha in September after which influential members spent several weeks assisting with the drive. Lucy Stone, Henry Blackwell, and Hannah Tracy Cutler from the American and An-

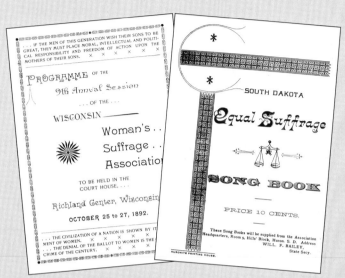

For decades suffragists across the country published a multitude of newspapers, tracts, programs, and songbooks, and tried in every way to attract popular support.

thony, Helen M. Gougar, May Wright Sewall, and Phoebe Couzins from the National were only a few of those who spoke to voters at agricultural fairs, picnics, soldiers' reunions, and other gatherings during the exciting final weeks.

The suffrage measure enjoyed the support of many prominent professionals. Most politicians, however, took pains to avoid it, and earlier promises of help by local allies failed to materialize. The measure was vehemently opposed by the Republican Party machine and the brewery industry which claimed it would lead to the "menace of prohibition." In addition, the bill had to receive a majority of the total of all the votes cast at the election to pass.

On election day, November 5, 1882, suffragists tried to create a festive mood, decorating polling places and providing men with refreshments while appealing to their sense of justice. Voters still defeated the measure 50,693 to 25,756, although suffragists charged widespread corruption, including fraudulent ballots and questionable counting, which left the true tally unknown.

After the campaign Colby began publishing a weekly newspaper, *The Woman's Tribune,* which enjoyed the support of both Anthony and Elizabeth Cady Stanton for years and came to be seen as the official organ of the National Association.

Oregon

Oregon suffragists worked for

two years to generate support for their measure, which was placed on the 1884 ballot. Led by veteran journalist Abigail Scott Duniway, local workers divided the state into districts, canvassed the main population centers, and enlisted the support of many influential civic leaders. Eastern suffragists contributed over $1,000 in donations and literature.

The women were optimistic until just before the election. Then political candidates and pledged speakers deserted the campaign while saloons and other business interests mobilized the opposition. The measure was defeated 28,176 to 11,223. Rural areas were supportive, but the Portland vote was overwhelmingly opposed.

Declaring "we were repulsed but not conquered," Duniway gave vent to her anger after the election, decrying "the ignorant, lawless, and unthinking multitude whose ballots outweigh all reason." Still, state supporters rejoiced in their "formidable" strength and pledged themselves anew to the cause.

In 1885, aiming to join the equal suffrage territories of Wyoming, Utah, and Washington, both houses of the Dakota territorial legislature passed a bill enfranchising women. However, the Federally appointed governor vetoed the measure, claiming that it might jeopardize future hopes for statehood. ◆

Encouraging Congressmen to Act

Lobbying individual legislators was a never-ending task for unenfranchised women during the late 1800s. It was particularly difficult since women had no real power and could easily be dismissed. Every year Susan B. Anthony and other leading suffragists lobbied and testified on behalf of the Federal amendment in Washington D.C. But congressmen repeatedly advised the women to take their cause to the individual states.

"We have neither the women nor the money to make the canvasses of the 38 states, school district by school district," Anthony retorted in February 1884, "to educate each individual man out of the old belief that woman was created to be his

subject." Already voters in four states had rejected their appeal despite making "the best canvass of each which was possible for a disfranchised class outside of all political help." She asked them "to lift the decision of our question from the vote of the populace to that of the legislatures."

"When you insist that we shall beg at the feet of each individual voter of every one of the states, native and foreign, Black and white, learned and ignorant, you doom us to incalculable hardships and sacrifices and to most exasperating insults and humiliations."

Congressmen were unmoved, leaving suffragists no choice but to turn to voters in each individual state.

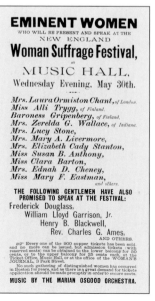

EMINENT WOMEN
WHO WILL BE PRESENT AND SPEAK AT THE
NEW ENGLAND
Woman Suffrage Festival,
AT
MUSIC HALL,
Wednesday Evening, May 30th.

Mrs. *Laura Ormiston Chant*, of London.
Miss *Alli Trygg*, of Finland.
Baroness *Gripenberg*, of Finland.
Mrs. *Zerelda G. Wallace*, of Indiana.
Mrs. *Lucy Stone*,
Mrs. *Mary A. Livermore*,
Mrs. *Elizabeth Cady Stanton*,
Miss *Susan B. Anthony*,
Miss *Clara Barton*,
Mrs. *Ednah D. Cheney*,
Miss *Mary F. Eastman*,
and others.

THE FOLLOWING GENTLEMEN HAVE ALSO
PROMISED TO SPEAK AT THE FESTIVAL:
Frederick Douglass,
William Lloyd Garrison, Jr.
Henry B. Blackwell,
Rev. Charles G. Ames,
AND OTHERS.

Every one of the 900 supper tickets has been sold and no more can be issued, but admission tickets (with reserved seats) can be obtained to the lower balcony for 50 cents, or to the upper balcony for 25 cents each, at the Ticket Office, Music Hall, or at the office of the WOMAN'S JOURNAL, 3 Park Street.

No such gathering of distinguished women has occurred in Boston for years, and as there is a great demand for tickets application should be made promptly in order to secure seats.

MUSIC BY THE MARIAN OSGOOD ORCHESTRA.

Winning Partial Suffrage in the States and Territories

Above: Practicing the art of persuasion on a congressmen. Left: Distinguished speakers appeared in Boston in 1888.

oters in Guthrie Ok. June 5th

Maria Louise Baldwin was a widely admired teacher and club woman who promoted equal rights to new generations. Born in Cambridge, Massachusetts, Baldwin began teaching at the inter-racial Agassiz Grammar School and was 33 when she was named principal in 1889. She held the post for over 30 years becoming a beloved educator and administrator. At Agassiz Baldwin supervised a dozen white teachers who taught the children of both working class parents and Harvard faculty. The president of Harvard, Charles Eliot, called her the best teacher in New England. Since Massachusetts women could vote in school board elections, Baldwin argued from experience that the vote would benefit all women. She noted that even school suffrage, "so meagre a share of voting power," had given greater leverage to Boston teachers. A popular speaker praised for her "dignity, her calmness, and beautiful voice," Baldwin was deeply involved in community affairs including The Woman's Era Club and the Robert Gould Shaw Settlement House in Boston.

IN ADDITION to a constitutional amendment and state referenda, suffragists also pursued more limited forms of voting. In several states the legislatures were persuaded to approve partial suffrage bills which allowed women to vote on specific school-related or bond measures. Although school suffrage was far less than what suffragists were aiming for, it broke the ice in offering women a political voice and helped defuse some of the mystery and prejudice surrounding women voting. Partial suffrage, however, did not usually excite or draw many women voters.

In 1887 Kansas, which had passed school suffrage in 1861, became the first state to approve municipal suffrage for women, recognizing their right to vote in local elections. Alice Stone Blackwell called it "the first large victory" the cause had won in nearly 20 years. Unfortunately, however, few states followed Kansas' lead. It was during this campaign that suffragists made the sunflower, Kansas' state flower, their chosen emblem and yellow their official color.

One unfortunate result of municipal suffrage, historian Eleanor Flexner observed, was that "women promptly aligned themselves with a political party and so became responsible to it on decisions regarding suffrage tactics." By 1900 women had won school suffrage in 23 states but had to fight constant challenges by opponents to its constitutionality.

A buggy brought the "first lady voters" (above) to the polls in Guthrie, Oklahoma, probably to vote on school issues after the state legislature approved school suffrage in 1890. Even with limited suffrage, Laura Johns reported from Kansas, "We felt our power and it was a new thrill which we experienced."

RESPECTFULLY DEDICATED TO LOYA
WHO PAVED THE WAY TO WOMAN'S ENFRANCHISEMENT IN THE PACIFIC NORTHWEST, UNITED STATES

UBJECTS OF LIBERTY

A, ANNO DOMINI ONE THOUSAND EIGHT HUNDRED EIGHTY THREE.

KURZ & ALLISON'S ART STUDIO, CHICAGO.

Setbacks in the West

THE "HONORED FACES" of men who supported women's rights in the Pacific Northwest were grouped together in this special engraving (left) commissioned by Abigail Scott Duniway and paid for with funds from the 1884 Oregon suffrage campaign. Territorial legislators in Washington had approved woman suffrage in 1883 and Oregon lawmakers had just scheduled a popular vote. Anticipating victory, Duniway wanted an illustration which paid tribute to regional and national politicians as well as stalwarts such as Henry Blackwell (bottom left) and William Lloyd Garrison (bottom center). The recognized leaders of the woman's rights movement were featured in the gallery. They are, from the left, Martha Coffin Wright, Elizabeth Cady Stanton, Lucy Stone, Frances Wright, Lucretia Mott, Elizabeth Boynton Harbert, Susan B. Anthony, and Abigail Scott Duniway. On the right are Dr. Clemence Lozier, Helen Gougar, Sarah Knox Goodrich, Mary Livermore, Mary J. Collins, Julia Ward Howe, Lillie Devereux Blake, Matilda Joslyn Gage, and Ernestine Rose. Despite real signs of progress in the region, suffragists' elation was short-lived. Oregon voters defeated the measure in June 1884, and three years later opponents overturned women's right to vote in both Washington and Utah.

Left: Western supporters.

Naomi Talbert Anderson
was considered one of the
strongest Black voices in the
woman suffrage movement
during the later 19th century.
Born free in Indiana, Naomi
Bowman was 25 when she
was encouraged to speak at
an 1869 suffrage convention
in Chicago. She declared that
God "will hear the call of
woman." She lectured in the
midwest on temperance and
woman's rights throughout
the 1870s. Widowed in 1877,
she learned hairdressing to
support her three children
but continued her public
work writing and speaking.
Remarrying and migrating
west, Anderson was active
in the 1892 suffrage cam-
paign in Kansas. Three years
later she represented Black
women in California at the
state level, lobbying the legislature for equal suffrage and
earning the praise of Susan
B. Anthony. Anderson fought
against racial prejudice and
countered discrimination
with a strong defense of
Black Americans as equal
citizens. A pioneer in the
Black women's club move-
ment, she believed that
"woman has a power
within herself."

Waging Campaigns on Both Coasts

I N THE late 1880s suffragists
waged campaigns in Wash-
ington state on the Pacific
coast and in Rhode Island on
the Atlantic coast, the first
referendum drive in the east.

Rhode Island

In 1887, after eighteen years
of effort, suffragists in Rhode
Island succeeded in winning
legislative endorsement for a
woman suffrage amendment.
The measure was passed by
two successive legislatures as
required, but then it was immediately put before the voters, leaving women little time
to organize broad support.
Susan B. Anthony considered
the effort hopeless.

Led by president Elizabeth
Buffum Chace and vice-president Rev. Frederic A. Hinckley, the state suffrage association opened headquarters
in Providence, raised over
$5,000, and sent speakers to
all the cities and towns in the
small state. In one month
suffragists organized nearly
100 meetings in churches,
halls, and parlors and distributed nearly 40,000 packets of
literature. Mary Livermore,
Henry Blackwell, Julia Ward
Howe, and other distin-
guished speakers addressed
large public meetings.

Faced with a largely hostile
press, which labeled the
measure "premature and im-
politic," suffragists bought
space in the principal newspapers for columns of pro-

suffrage arguments. Supporters also published 20,000
copies of their own news-
paper, *The Amendment,* followed by 40,000 copies of
a second edition two weeks
later.

On election day, April 6,

Woman Suffrage Convention
STATE HOUSE,
⁺PROVIDENCE, R. I.⁺

Wednesday Evening, Dec. 3d, at 7.30.
FREDERICK DOUGLASS,
MARY E. HAGGART,
FREDERIC A. HINCKLEY.

Thursday Forenoon, Dec 4th, at 10.30.
ELIZABETH B. CHACE,
HENRY B. BLACKWELL,
SUSAN B. ANTHONY,
CHAS. W. WENDTE,
MARY F. EASTMAN.

Thursday Afternoon, at 2.30.
WM. I. BOWDITCH,
WM. LLOYD GARRISON,
MARY E. HAGGART,
JOHN C. WYMAN,
FREDERICK DOUGLASS.

Thursday Evening, at 7.30.
SUSAN B. ANTHONY,
LUCY STONE,
THOMAS R. SLICER,
HENRY B. BLACKWELL.

On Thursday, Lunch served at 1 o'clock, and Supper,
at 50 Cents per plate, served at 6 o'clock.

**"Great throngs of people
filled the seats, occupied all
the standing room and overflowed into the lobbies,"
reported one participant at
this 1884 convention, held in
the Rhode Island State House.**

1887, campaign workers
stood outside the polls hoping to influence voters but
were unable to overcome
male prejudice and conservatism or the opposition of
the political parties. Rhode
Island voters rejected the
measure three to one, 21,957

to 6,889, leaving supporters
thoroughly dispirited.

Washington

After the Washington territorial supreme court disfranchised women in 1887 and
1888, male delegates to the
constitutional convention
agreed to put the question on
the 1889 ballot separate from
the new state constitution.

Unfortunately, supporters
were unprepared for the two-
and-a-half month drive and
lacked the leadership, funds,
and political support needed
for a successful effort. Clara
Colby of Washington D.C.
and Matilda Hindman of
Pennsylvania came from the
east to help the westerners.
Suffragists canvassed the rugged territory where Abigail
Scott Duniway had labored
for nearly two decades. But
the task was extremely difficult. On November 5, 1889,
male voters approved the new
state constitution but defeated equal suffrage 35,913
to 16,521.

The series of setbacks in
Washington, following de-
feats in six other states, served
as discouraging reminders
that woman suffrage faced
powerful and deep-seated opposition even where it seemed
to enjoy popular support.
Nevertheless, in several of
these states suffragists went
back to work to have the
question submitted again to
the voters. ◆

PROTEST

AGAINST THE UNJUST INTERPRETATION OF THE CONSTITUTION PRESENTED ON BEHALF OF THE WOMEN OF THE UNITED STATES BY OFFICERS OF THE NATIONAL WOMAN SUFFRAGE ASSOCIATION.

To the President of the United States, the Governors of the States, and other Federal and State Officials, on the occasion of the Constitutional Centennial in Philadelphia, September 17th, 1887.

Rejoicing as dwellers in this favored land that the noble series of celebrations in commemoration of the birth of a mighty nation have been fittingly brought to a conclusion by the ceremonies of this day, we yet cannot allow the occasion to pass without reminding you that one-half the people who obey the laws of the United States are unjustly denied all place or part in the body politic. In the midst of the pomps and glories of this celebration women are only onlookers, voiceless and unrepresented.

This denial of our chartered rights, this injustice of which we complain, is inflicted in defiance of the provisions of the Constitution you profess to honor. When we examine that instrument we find it is declared in the Preamble that it was: "Ordained and established by "The People of the United States," one-half of the people of the United States are women, yet they are allowed no voice, direct or indirect, in framing this Constitution or executing its provisions, we protest therefore that the words of the Preamble have been falsified for a hundred years.

We find it declared in Art. I, Sec. 2, That "The House of Representatives shall be composed of members chosen by the people." One-half of the people of every State are women and yet they have never been permitted to choose the members of the House of Representatives. We protest therefore that this important provision of the Constitution has been shamefully violated and that the denial to women of the right thus plainly secured to them, has been a grievous wrong.

We find that in Art. IV, Sec. 2, it is declared: " The citizens of each State shall be entitled to all the privileges and immunities of citizens of the several states." The Supreme Court of the United States has ruled that women are citizens, and yet these millions of citizens are denied the privilege of the ballot, which is throughout the land granted to male citizens and refused to female citizens. We protest therefore that in thus denying to women the exercise of the elective franchise, the fundamental rights of citizenship are withheld in defiance of a direct provision of the Constitution.

We find that in Art. IV. Sec. 4, it is declared that: "The United States shall guarantee to every state in the Union a Republican form of Government." A Republic is defined as "a state governed by representatives elected by the citizens." One-half of the citizens of every state are women; they have never been permitted to elect the officials who have held rule over them. We protest therefore that the provisions of this article have never been fulfilled, that not a solitary state in the Union has a Republican form of Government But, that on the contrary, each and every one is a despotism under which one-half the citizens are held in a condition of political slavery.

The recital of these facts is the summary of a century of injustice. We solemnly and earnestly protest against its continuance, and demand that hereafter the Constitution of these United States shall be interpreted in accordance with the simple words in which it is framed. That there shall be no longer a cruel and unwarranted discrimination against any class of our citizens, but that in the future all the people of the nation shall have an equal voice in choosing the rulers whose high mission it shall be to guide a true Republic on its course of glory.

On behalf of the National Woman Suffrage Association,

> SUSAN B. ANTHONY, N. Y.,
> *Acting President.*
> MATILDA JOSLYN GAGE, N. Y.,
> *Vice-President-at-Large.*
> RACHEL G. FOSTER, Pa.,
> *Corresponding Secretary.*
> MARY WRIGHT SEWALL, Ind.,
> *Chairman Executive Committee.*
> LILLIE DEVEREUX BLAKE, N. Y.,
> *Vice-President for New York,*
> *Chairman Presentation Committee.*

Matilda Joslyn Gage used her intellectual power and organizational talent to further woman suffrage following the Civil War. Married at 18 and the mother of four children, Gage was 26 when she spoke at her first women's rights convention in 1852. She worked with Elizabeth Cady Stanton and Susan B. Anthony for over three decades and was co-author of the first three volumes of *The History of Woman Suffrage*. A forceful writer, Gage drew up countless resolutions and petitions, and edited a monthly newsletter for the National Woman Suffrage Association, *The National Citizen and Ballot Box*, between 1878 to 1881. She co-authored with Stanton the Women's Declaration of Rights in 1876 and wrote the eloquent Protest (left) which was handed to President Grover Cleveland at the Constitutional Centennial in 1887. In later years Gage, like Stanton, focused on religion as a major force in the subjugation of women. She was, in Anthony's words, "one of the most intensely earnest, true women" in the movement, an able scholar and a valued partner.

Anna Howard Shaw was 41 and had just become a professional lecturer when she addressed the International Council of Women in 1888 and caught the attention of Susan B. Anthony. Born in England, Shaw was four when she first faced the severe hardships of frontier Michigan. Knowing she wanted to preach, she practiced speaking to the trees in the forest years before being licensed as a preacher in 1871. Refused elsewhere, she was finally ordained the Methodist Protestant Church's first woman minister. Her tremendous energy and desire to help improve women's lives led her to medical school while still a pastor. Between 1885 and 1887 she worked with Lucy Stone in Massachusetts and then led the WCTU's Franchise Department for four years. In the lecture field Shaw faced bone-chilling blizzards, hungry wolves, train wrecks, ptomaine poisoning, typhoid fever, and arson in the hall where she was speaking. She met the ordeals with good humor and a particularly strong character. After 1888 Shaw was active in most of the state campaigns, usually at Anthony's side.

Forming an International Congress of Women

THE FIRST International Woman's Rights Congress, held in Paris in 1878, included women from 13 countries including Julia Ward Howe and Mary Livermore from the U.S. Five years later women from several nations met in Liverpool and resolved to consider creating a permanent international body.

In 1888, following initial calls by Elizabeth Cady Stanton, Susan B. Anthony, and Frances Willard, women from 49 nations met together for eight days in Washington D.C. The meeting recognized the 40th anniversary of the Seneca Falls Convention and resulted in the formation of the International Council of Women.

During the meeting several foreign delegates posed

(above) with prominent members of the National Woman Suffrage Association and other organizations for a historic portrait of feminist leaders. In the front row, from the left, are: Virginia Minor, Zerelda Wallace, Laura O. Chant of Scotland, Susan B. Anthony, Isabelle Bogelot of France, Elizabeth Cady Stanton, Matilda Joslyn Gage, Alexandra Gripenberg of Finland, and Margaret Dilke of England.

Standing behind them from the left are: Rev. Ada Bowles, Elizabeth Boynton Harbert, Rev. Anna Howard Shaw, Rachel Foster, Frances Willard, Bessie Starr Keefer of Canada, and Lillie Devereux Blake directly behind Anthony. Continuing on are Sophia Magelsson Groth of Norway, Hannah Whitall Smith, Victoria Richardson, Louisa Reed Stowel, Allie Trygg of Finland, Rev. Antoinette Brown Blackwell, Alice Scatcherd of England, Elizabeth Lisle Saxon, Carolyn Merrick, May Wright Sewall, and Margaret Moore of Ireland.

Representatives from over fifty other women's groups including the American Woman Suffrage Association were also present. Delegates discussed the state of women's rights around the world but many felt that demanding the vote in their own countries was still too controversial and unrealistic. The council met again in Chicago in 1893.

Above: American suffragists posed with international guests in 1888.

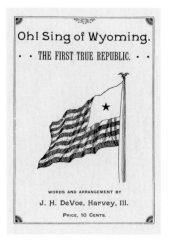

Oh! Sing of Wyoming.

· · THE FIRST TRUE REPUBLIC. · ·

WORDS AND ARRANGEMENT BY
J. H. DeVoe, Harvey, Ill.
PRICE, 10 CENTS.

Wyoming: The First "Free" State

WOMEN IN WYOMING had voted since 1869 and when the territory applied for statehood in 1889 they were determined to keep that right. In June, leading women in the region held a convention in Cheyenne and passed a resolution demanding that woman suffrage be affirmed in the new constitution. It was, and a strong majority of both male and female voters approved the new charter guaranteeing that equal suffrage would continue. Democratic congressmen in Washington D.C., however, used the suffrage clause to oppose admitting the Republican territory and heated debate extended the admission process for six months. In the midst of the battle one state legislator reputedly declared that Wyoming would stay out of the Union forever rather than abandon its women. The "Equality State" was finally admitted in 1890 and suffragists across the country celebrated the landmark victory.

Above: Sheet music hailed the only equal suffrage state with a one star flag.

FRANK LESLIE'S ILLUSTRATED NEWSPAPER

Entered according to Act of Congress, in the year 1888, by MRS. FRANK LESLIE, in the Office of the Librarian of Congress at Washington.—Entered at the Post Office, New York, N. Y., as second-class Matter.

No. 1,732.—VOL. LXVII.]   NEW YORK—FOR THE WEEK ENDING NOVEMBER 24, 1888.   [PRICE, 10 CENTS. $4.00 YEARLY. 13 WEEKS, $1.00.

WOMAN SUFFRAGE IN WYOMING TERRITORY.—SCENE AT THE POLLS IN CHEYENNE.
FROM A PHOTO, BY KIRKLAND.—SEE PAGE 233.

Women voting was part of normal life in Wyoming, as the 1888 illustration above showed. For twenty years female voters had cast their ballots responsibly, establishing a history of woman suffrage and disproving the dire predictions of opponents. Local residents were determined to maintain the tradition. Suffrage leaders welcomed the admission of Wyoming as "not only a seal of approval upon woman suffrage . . . but it makes woman a recognized factor in national politics."

Uniting Forces for the Cause of Women

TWO DECADES after suffragists bitterly divided into two groups, Lucy Stone and Susan B. Anthony met together with their aides in 1889 to plan a reconciliation between the American and the National Woman Suffrage Associations. Stone's daughter, Alice Stone Blackwell, was an important force in the union. After the aging rivals agreed to put aside past differences they settled on a new name, the National American Woman Suffrage Association, or NAWSA.

NAWSA

In February 1890 members of both associations met together in Washington D.C. to approve the merger. Although Lucy Stone was ill, the extraordinary gathering included Henry Blackwell and his daughter Alice, Elizabeth Cady Stanton and her daughter Harriot Stanton Blatch, Susan B. Anthony, Julia Ward Howe, Matilda Joslyn Gage, Robert Purvis, Mary Livermore, former American Association head William Dudley Foulke, Anna Howard Shaw, and many other workers from across the country. The merger also brought in younger admirers of both Anthony and Stone including Carrie Chapman, an enthusiastic 31-year-old delegate from Iowa.

NAWSA, keeping the delegate structure of the American, claimed member groups in nearly every state although many were barely active.

Stanton was elected president, Anthony vice-president, and Stone head of the Executive Committee. When age led Stanton and Stone to resign in 1892 Anthony was elected president.

Following the National's strategy, the association met every year in February in Washington D.C. while Congress was in session. Starting

NAWSA's new letterhead featured a sunflower in honor of earlier campaigns in Kansas and the date 1848 in honor of the first woman's rights convention in Seneca Falls.

in 1895 the annual conventions were held outside of the capital on alternating years, a move Anthony opposed as it would lessen the steady pressure on Congress. However younger women like Blackwell felt the impressive gatherings would bolster developments in various hopeful states.

Not all suffragists had faith in the new association. Some questioned its basic focus on winning suffrage in each state while others feared that it would lack flexibility and be too tame to effect real change nationally. Olympia Brown

and Clara Colby felt that more pressure should be put on the Federal government. Stanton and Gage focused on the "religious and social bondage" of women, and particularly on the ways the Bible and religious dogma promoted women's inferiority. Anthony concentrated almost exclusively on suffrage, inspiring others with her single-minded focus but exasperating friends like Stanton who believed that women should maintain broad interests to be effective voters.

South Dakota

When South Dakota applied for statehood in 1889, legislators refused to include woman suffrage in the new constitution but pledged to schedule a vote immediately after admission. In February 1890 state suffragists led by Philena Everett Johnson appealed to NAWSA for assistance and, hoping to celebrate its formation with an elec-

toral victory, the new association helped raise over $5,500. Susan B. Anthony arrived in late April and stayed until the election.

More than 400 local clubs were organized and national figures including Anthony, Shaw, Colby, Brown, Emma De Voe, Laura Johns, and Henry Blackwell made hundreds of speeches. The nine month campaign was "one of the most difficult we ever made," Shaw later recalled, as the state was suffering from desperate poverty and severe drought, and easterners drew local resentment.

Again, hoped-for allies abandoned the cause in the midst of the campaign when a new independent party reflecting farm and labor interests refused to endorse the measure. No other political party supported it, either. When Anthony spoke before the state Democratic convention she faced a group of recently arrived Russian men, who could vote, displaying large yellow badges which read, "Against Woman Suffrage and Susan B. Anthony."

On November 4, 1890 South Dakota voters defeated the measure 45,682 to 22,792, causing Shaw to write dejectedly, "The fact that our cause could be defeated by ignorant laborers new to our country was a humiliating one to accept." The arduous drive left supporters exhausted but state leaders resolved to "press fearlessly on." ◆

Alice Stone Blackwell, one of the most prominent of the second generation of suffragists, overcame a pervasive shyness to become a skilled debater and one of the most insightful advocates for woman suffrage. When Blackwell was 12 her parents, Lucy Stone and Henry Blackwell, settled in Boston where she remembered that visiting abolitionists and suffragists "used to pet me as the child of the regiment." Shortly after graduating Phi Beta Kappa from Boston University in 1881, Blackwell went to work at her parents' newspaper and over time assumed major responsibility for editing *The Woman's Journal.* She was 33 when she helped arrange the merger of the separate suffrage associations.

Woman Suffrage Leaflet.

Published Monthly by the American Woman Suffrage Association at 3 Park Street, Boston.

Vol I. Entered at the Boston Post-Office as second class matter. No. 4

Subscription, 25 cents per annum. **SEPTEMBER 15, 1888.** Extra copies, 15 cts. per 100, postpaid

A WOMAN SUFFRAGE CATECHISM.

BY LUCY STONE.

At the woman suffrage hearing before the Committee of the Massachusetts Legislature, on the 17th of February, 1885, Lucy Stone presented the following statement, with questions and answers which illustrate some phases of the movement for the equal legal and political rights of women that are not as visible now as they will be hereafter:

Gentlemen of the Committee:—We have come up to this room for many years, vainly asking for equal rights with yourselves. We have quoted the great principles on which our government is based: the Declaration of Independence and the Bill of Rights. We have found that those principles are not respected in their application to women. We have answered over and over all objections that have ever been offered against the ballot for woman. We have quoted the successful working of woman suffrage wherever it has been tried, in England, Scotland, Ontario, Nova Scotia, and in our own Western Territories, without avail. I propose now, to show the historic record the Massachusetts Legislature has made for itself, on this question, by the following questions and answers:

Question—Shall the men and women who are to obey the laws have a right to make them?

Answer—No. Only the men shall have that right.

Q.—But there must be laws that especially concern women. Who shall make those laws?

A.—Only men shall make them.

Q.—May not mothers help make the laws that settle their legal relation to their children?

A.—They shall not. The men shall have the sole right to make such laws.

Q.—May not married women help make the laws that decide what share of the property acquired by a husband and wife during marriage shall belong to the wife?

A.—They shall not.

Q.—May not a married woman help make the laws that decide how much of her property acquired before her marriage shall belong to her husband after her death?

A.—No. The men shall decide it.

Q.—Who shall make the laws that decide how much of the property of the husband shall go to the wife?

A.—The men shall make them.

Q.—Who shall make the laws that decide how, and how much, a wife may will of her own property?

A.—The men.

Q.—Who shall make the laws that decide the rights of married partners in case of marriage and divorce and alimony?

A.—The men.

Q.—By the laws the men have made, do the father and mother have an equal legal right to their children?

A.—No. The right of the father is supreme so long as he lives with his wife.

Q.—What share shall a husband have in the real estate of his wife?

A.—He shall have the use of the whole of it as long as he lives, if his wife has ever had a living child.

Q—What is his right to that property called?

A.—"The estate by the courtesy."

Q.—What share shall a wife have in the real estate of her husband?

A.—She shall have the use of one-third *after her husband's death.*

Q.—What is the right to that property called?

A.—It is commonly called "the widow's incumbrance," "dower," or "widows' thirds."

Finding a Vital Center in Boston

THE WOMAN'S JOURNAL had served as the official organ of the American Woman Suffrage Association for twenty years. After the two associations merged in 1890 it retained its independence. Suffragists around the country contributed to the popular weekly, which brought encouragement as well as news to its widespread readership. The paper, wrote Alice Stone Blackwell, "was the center of a suffrage activity that radiated out all over the country" and for many years nearly all suffrage tracts and leaflets which circulated nationally were published from its Boston office.

Above: Alice Stone Blackwell and Anna Howard Shaw preparing an issue of *The Woman's Journal.* Left: One leaflet featured Lucy Stone's 1883 testimony before the Massachusetts legislature.

Remembering "The Morning Star"

Through her writing, publishing, lecturing, and campaigning across the country, Lucy Stone devoted her life to improving women's status. The leading force in the American Woman Suffrage Association for twenty years, she gave her energy, talent, and earnings as a speaker to countless state efforts and to her historic weekly, *The Woman's Journal.* As editor and publisher with her husband Henry Blackwell, Stone made her newspaper office the hub of AWSA work nationally.

She worked continuously, despite bouts of depression and chronically poor health, to produce speeches, articles, leaflets, and printed material which helped turn public sentiment in favor of women's rights. She also traveled extensively to persuade legislators and voters of the justice of the cause.

Although modest and self-effacing, "she had a wonderful eloquence," her daughter Alice remembered. "Her zeal for woman suffrage . . . was like a fire in the bones." More conventional in her views than some reformers, her well-reasoned arguments and personal sensitivity charmed critics and won over many women including Susan B. Anthony, Julia Ward Howe, and Frances Willard. Stone believed that all forms of suffrage were effective and that women's performance with limited suffrage would help

"Where is Lucy Stone's monument, reaching upward to the stars?" exclaimed popular writer and critic H. L. Mencken after reading of her achievements.

win further progress which would finally lead to a constitutional amendment.

Personal Sacrifice

Preparing for the 1890 merger of suffrage organizations, Stone overcame personal and political disagreements for the good of the cause and essentially stepped aside when her association

united with that of her long-time rivals. Lingering differences colored Elizabeth Cady Stanton's, Matilda Joslyn Gage's, and Susan B. Anthony's version of suffrage history but Stone's lasting influence and that of her remarkable newspaper are impossible to ignore.

She was widely recognized for her courageous, pioneer-

ing work in the 1840s and for her steady leadership and dedication to the cause ever since. Her last public speech was to the International Council of Women at the Columbian Exposition in Chicago in May 1893 where a marble bust of her by Anne Whitney was on display.

By 1893, however, her energy was gone. After several bouts of illness and exhaustion she died on October 18 at the age of 75. Her last words to her daughter were, "Make the world better." Ever the pioneer, she became the first woman in Massachusetts to be cremated.

Eulogized as the "morning star" of the woman's movement for her trail-blazing work, Lucy Stone was honored as a towering figure who, despite constant opposition, remained devoted to the ideals of equal rights and true democracy. Admirers celebrated her birthday, August 13, for years.

Stone's daughter kept her memory alive, writing articles and a biography that helped to secure her place in history. Although the bold public actions of Anthony and the controversial ideas of Stanton and Gage tended to overshadow Stone's contributions, her state-oriented association formed the basis for NAWSA and her *Woman's Journal* continued to draw together the disparate but growing movement for women's enfranchisement. ◆

Carrie Chapman Catt, born Carrie Lane, graduated from Iowa State College, began teaching, and soon found herself promoted to superintendent of schools (below). Widowed at 27, she was drawn to work for woman's equality partly through Lucy Stone's influence, and joined the Iowa suffrage association in 1885, becoming an officer four years later. She married engineer George Catt, who was very supportive of her work, just months before joining the 1890 South Dakota campaign. In 1893 she was sent by NAWSA to help suffragists in Colorado where she showed a particular talent for administration, planning, and political organizing.

Quiet Determination Pays Off in Colorado

After a series of discouraging defeats in the states, expectations were low when Colorado suffragists appealed to NAWSA for help in 1893. Reorganized in 1890, state supporters saw a "golden opportunity" when the Populist Party was voted into power, and successfully lobbied the legislature to place votes for women on the 1893 ballot.

The state association under Martha Pease rechristened itself the Non-Partisan Equal Suffrage Association and sent vice-president Ellis Meredith east to seek support from NAWSA. Doubtful of success and stretched by other demands, the association nonetheless sent Carrie Catt to help organize the off-year campaign.

Local suffrage societies were formed throughout the state with special attention given to the greater Denver

area, home to a quarter of Colorado's population. Encouraged by Lucy Stone, Catt successfully appealed to Denver's wealthy society and club women. Prominent citizens volunteered as speakers and often pointed to the success of women voting in neighboring Wyoming. Suffragists produced and distributed over 150,000 leaflets and won the endorsement of newspapers and many county political party conventions.

The quiet, well-organized campaign caught the liquor trade and other opponents by surprise until just before the election. Then, in addition to rallying saloon keepers, opponents attempted last-minute ruses including deceptively written ballots and various technical challenges.

But it was too late. On election day, November 7, 1893, the measure passed 35,798 to 29,451 making Colorado the first state where men approved equal suffrage at the polls. The victory added a second star to the suffrage flag and showed supporters nationally the importance of careful organizing and strategic campaigning. In 1894 the first three women were elected to the Colorado state legislature.

Above: Women lined up to vote in Denver after winning the ballot in 1893. Inset: Flag from NAWSA's 1894 convention program.

VOL. XXXV. No. 900.   PUCK BUILDING, New York, June 6th, 1894.   PRICE 10 CENTS.
Copyright, 1894, by Keppler & Schwarzmann.

Entered at N.Y.P.O. as Second-class Mail Matter.

Puck

A SQUELCHER FOR WOMAN SUFFRAGE.

HOW CAN SHE VOTE, WHEN THE FASHIONS ARE SO WIDE, AND THE VOTING BOOTHS ARE SO NARROW?

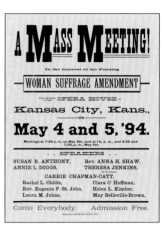

A MASS MEETING!

In the Interest of the Pending

WOMAN SUFFRAGE AMENDMENT

OPERA HOUSE

Kansas City, Kans., ON

May 4 and 5, '94.

Meetings at 7:30 p. m. on May 4th, and at 10, a. m., and 2:30 and 7:30, p. m., May 5th.

. . SPEAKERS . .

SUSAN B. ANTHONY,   Rev. ANNA H. SHAW,
ANNIE L. DIGGS,   THERESA JENKINS.
CARRIE CHAPMAN-CATT,
Rachel L. Childs,   Clara C. Hoffman,
Rev. Eugenia F. St. John,   Helen L. Kimber,
Laura M. Johns,   May Belleville-Brown.

Come Everybody.   Admission Free.

Another Try in Kansas

UNDER THE able leadership of Laura M. Johns and Populist Annie L. Diggs, members of the Kansas Equal Suffrage Association organized a particularly ambitious campaign in 1894. Susan B. Anthony, Anna Howard Shaw, Carrie Catt, and hundreds of volunteers worked for months addressing voters at gatherings throughout the vast, often desolate region. To make one engagement, Catt steered a horse-drawn wagon alone across the empty plains for four hours, finally reaching her destination by dead reckoning but shocking the local residents by her risky feat.

Notable men and women endorsed the measure but the political parties offered no support. New York suffragist Mary Peck remembered that the women faced "a mesh of political rivalries" before being "sold out by their friends for wholly imaginary political advantage." On November 7, 1894 the measure lost 130,139 to 95,302 in what Catt called a "heart-breaking defeat."

Above: A flier from the 1894 Kansas campaign.

High fashion presented yet another obstacle to women voting according to the satirical 1894 illustration above by C.J. Taylor. Women were actually encouraged to vote in Massachusetts in 1895 when a "mock referendum" asked all adult residents if women should be enfranchised. After a brief but vigorous campaign, during which suffragists were divided over supporting the non-binding poll, the measure received 187,837 negative and 108,974 positive votes. Of these women cast 861 no and 22,204 yes votes. The level of male support surprised suffragists, but opponents used the low number of women voting as proof that most women did not want to vote, discouraging progress in the state legislature for years.

Trying to Amend the State Constitution

IN ADDITION to state referendum campaigns, suffragists tried to have votes for women included whenever a state or territory drafted a new constitution, as New York did in 1894. To get the constitutional convention to submit a suffrage amendment supporters waged an ambitious and carefully planned campaign directed by Jean Brooks Greenleaf and headquartered in Susan B. Anthony's Rochester home. In six months supporters raised $10,000 and collected over 332,000 signatures plus the endorsements of 250,000 in labor unions, the Grange, and other organizations.

Meetings were held throughout the state and this rare image (left) depicts one probably held in Lily Dale, New York. Susan B. Anthony is seated in the center, Anna Howard Shaw is to the left of her, and Carrie Catt is second to the right. Local leaders and prominent supporters are seated on the decorated platform before images of women's rights pioneers and U.S presidents. A two-star banner hangs from the ceiling at right.

By the end of the suffrage drive there would be an estimated 47 efforts to influence state constitutional conventions but nearly all of them, like this one, would prove unsuccessful.

Left: Building support for equal rights in 1894.

Ida B. Wells, courageous journalist and respected leader in the Black community, was a staunch suffragist who refused to be ignored by the white-dominated movement. Born in Mississippi during the Civil War, Wells began work as a teacher at 14, educating others as she educated herself. In 1884, when she was 22, she refused to move to the Colored Section on a train and was forcibly removed. She successfully sued the railroad but the case was reversed on appeal. As editor of a Memphis newspaper in 1892, she condemned the lynching of three Black men as economically motivated. Rather than a response to Black men raping white women, she wrote, lynching was often related to racism and financial competition. What's more, white women could be attracted to Black men. Mobs ransacked and destroyed her office while she was away but she launched an influential anti-lynching campaign from New York. More outspoken than most of her contemporaries, Wells admonished white suffrage leaders for supporting racial segregation out of expediency for women's rights.

THE WOMAN-SUFFRAGE MOVEMENT IN NEW YORK CITY.

SOCIETY LEADERS SECURING SIGNATURES TO PETITIONS TO BE PRESENTED TO THE CONSTITUTIONAL CONVENTION—SCENE AT SHERRY'S. DRAWN BY B. WEST CLINEDINST.—[SEE PAGE 290.]

The drive to add woman suffrage to the New York state constitution in 1894 attracted a host of new volunteers. One group of stylish young society women (above) set up a table at Sherry's, a popular Manhattan restaurant, to collect signatures on the suffrage petition. In addition to signatures, state suffragists also collected statistics on women as taxpayers and found that women property holders outside New York City paid well over $348 million in taxes. Understandably, a growing number of women of wealth and social influence were showing interest in political equality.

"The Mother of Woman Suffrage"

WIDELY RECOGNIZED for her writing, lecture tours, and leadership in the woman's rights movement, Elizabeth Cady Stanton had become a well known national figure by the end of the century. Honorary president of NAWSA after 1892, she delivered eloquent addresses at several of its annual conventions, particularly "The Degradation of Disfranchisement" in 1891 and "The Solitude of Self" in 1892. Liberal and iconoclastic, Stanton's notoriety grew after her controversial *Woman's Bible* was published in 1895. This bold effort to analyze and reinterpret the *Bible's* passages about women drew censure from more conservative NAWSA members. Historian Alma Lutz praised Stanton's lifelong effort "to emancipate women's minds" and reported that for months after her death on October 26, 1902, "newspapers and magazines paid her tribute as the statesman of the woman's rights movement and the mother of woman suffrage."

Above: Elizabeth Cady Stanton (right) visiting Susan B. Anthony in 1891.

Elizabeth Cady Stanton (above center), traveled regularly in her later years to visit her daughter Harriot in Great Britain and her son Theodore in Paris. Harriot Stanton Blatch (above right) married Englishman William Blatch in 1882 and raised a daughter Nora (left) outside London. While abroad, Stanton interested other women in the idea of an International Council of Women and paved the way for the meetings in 1888 and 1893. She was honored on her 80th birthday in 1895 with a gathering of 6,000 at the Metropolitan Opera House in New York. Stanton continued writing letters, speeches, and articles on a wide range of subjects until her death just before her 87th birthday. The popularity of the native New Yorker was reflected in the 1899 endorsement at right.

Mrs. Elizabeth Cady Stanton

HONORARY PRESIDENT OF THE NATIONAL AMERICAN WOMAN SUFFRAGE ASSOCIATION, under date of June 10, 1899, says : —

"I have tried Fairbank's Fairy Soap and find it delightful. It leaves the skin soft and velvety, and I particularly like it because it is as free from odor as the air and sunshine. I abhor a perfumed woman. The fragrance of clean clothes and the daily bath with Fairy Soap is more to be desired than the odors of Araby the blest."

To Convince Everybody that

FAIRY SOAP

Is different from any other floating white soap—purer, more scientific and delicate, made of better materials, and by latest perfected methods, we make the following offers:

EXTRA SPECIAL—If your own grocer has not Fairy Soap on sale send us his name and address, as well as your own, and we will send you a full sized cake, absolutely free of charge.

Fairy Tales Pictures.—Send us five (5) Fairy Soap wrappers, with your name and address, and we will mail you free a beautiful picture in water colors, by the celebrated artist, Leon Moran, entitled "Fairy Tales," 17½ by 24 inches, on fine plate paper, ready for framing.

Fairy Tales Booklet.—Send us one Fairy Soap wrapper, with your name and address, and we will mail you free, a pretty book of charming Fairy stories for children, entitled "Fairy Tales," beautifully illustrated in colors. In answering this advertisement

Dept. X, The N. K. Fairbank Company

CHICAGO   ST. LOUIS   PHILADELPHIA   BALTIMORE   NEW ORLEANS
NEW YORK   BOSTON   PITTSBURG   SAN FRANCISCO

Success in Utah

I N 1895, after spending a month touring the south with Susan B. Anthony, Carrie Catt suggested that NAWSA take a more systematic approach to state work. In response, she was named head of a new Organization Committee which included directing work in the field. Also on the committee were Mary Garrett Hay from Indiana, Laura Clay from Kentucky, Emmeline B. Wells from Utah, and Annie L. Diggs from Kansas. During its first year the committee placed fourteen organizers in the field and set up 100 local clubs along with nine new state branches.

In 1896 Wells, president of the Utah suffrage association, helped lead the campaign which brought Utah into the Union as an equal suffrage state. Women in Utah had voted between 1870 and 1887 when they were disfranchised by Congress in a dispute over polygamy. The dispute resolved, the constitutional convention was successfully persuaded to include votes for women in the new constitution which male voters approved 28,618 to 2,687 making Utah the third equal suffrage state.

Idaho Votes for Woman Suffrage

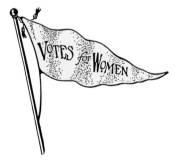

I DAHO APPLIED for statehood in 1890 without woman suffrage but five years later the Republican-controlled legislature put the question on the 1896 ballot.

In the summer of 1895, at the request of the newly organized Idaho Equal Suffrage Association, NAWSA sent Emma Smith DeVoe of Illinois to speak and help organize suffrage clubs in the state. The following year Laura Johns came from Kansas to offer assistance, followed by Carrie Catt, Mary Bradford of Colorado, and Emily Richards of Utah, who was particularly influential with Mormon voters.

National organizers helped state suffragists, led by Mrs. M. J. Whitman, lobby delegates to the political conventions and win endorsement by all the major parties in the state. Spending less than $2,500, suffragists organized by counties and then by precincts. They spoke at meetings and political rallies, distributed literature, and "made many converts" to the cause. Johns remembered traveling over "wild, dangerous, lonely roads" but finding "fine women and noble men" at each journey's end.

An advisory board of influ-

American Woman and her Political Peers.

COPYRIGHT, 1893, BY HENRIETTA BRIGGS--WALL.
MISS MARY W. MILLER, Photo.

ential citizens was particularly helpful, including *Idaho Statesman* editor William Balderston who encouraged men to persuade their wavering colleagues. The simple yet spirited campaign faced little organized opposition and most of the newspapers endorsed the measure.

On election day women stood outside the polls all day, sometimes ankle-deep in snow, to appeal to Idaho men. Voters approved the measure enfranchising women on November 3, 1896 nearly two to one, 12,126 to 6,282, making Idaho the fourth equal suffrage state. When their elec-

toral victory was challenged by opponents, suffragists mounted a successful defense before the state supreme court.

Two years later, following the lead of Colorado and Utah, voters elected three women to the state legislature and others to state and county positions. Idaho officials praised the "elevating influence" of the new women voters.

Above: Supporters of "Idaho Equality" marched in a Lewiston parade in 1896. Top left: Period cartoon. Left: Flag from suffrage newspaper.

Some May, Some May Not

IN THIS COUNTRY SOME PEOPLE *MAY* VOTE AND SOME *MAY NOT.* THOSE WHO *MAY* ARE:

White Men	Blind Men
Black Men	Lame Men
Red Men	Sick Men
Drunken Men	Rag Men
Deaf Men	Bad Men
Dumb Men	Dead Men

THOSE WHO *MAY NOT* ARE:

Minors	Lunatics
Idiots	Convicts
Women	

Henrietta Briggs-Wall of Hutchinson, Kansas, designed the classic early suffrage propaganda card above, "American Woman and Her Political Peers," just before the state campaign in 1893 and distributed it widely. Although the imaginative image depended on vulgar stereotypes, it did suggest how noble womanhood, personified by widely-respected Woman's Christian Temperance Union leader Frances Willard (center), was demeaned by the company of those who were her political equals.

"No one can fail to be impressed with the absurdity of a statutory regulation that places woman in the same legal category with the idiot, [the convict], the Indian and the insane person," Briggs-Wall noted. Most suffragists agreed. The leaflet at left made the same point with a touch of humor.

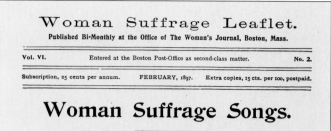

Woman Suffrage Leaflet.

Published Bi-Monthly at the Office of The Woman's Journal, Boston, Mass.

Vol. VI.   Entered at the Boston Post-Office as second-class matter.   No. 2.

Subscription, 25 cents per annum.   FEBRUARY, 1897.   Extra copies, 15 cts. per 100, postpaid.

Woman Suffrage Songs.

1. Battle Hymn of the Republic.

BY JULIA WARD HOWE.

Tune—"John Brown."

Mine eyes have seen the glory of the coming
   of the Lord,
He is trampling out the vintage where the
   grapes of wrath are stored;
He has loosed the fateful lightning of his
   terrible swift sword;
   His truth is marching on.
CHORUS—Glory, Glory, Hallelujah!
   Glory, Glory, Hallelujah!
   Glory, Glory, Hallelujah!
   His truth is marching on.

He has sounded forth the trumpet that shall
   never call retreat;
He is sifting out the hearts of men before his
   judgment-seat;
Oh, be swift, my soul, to answer him! be
   jubilant, my feet!
   Our God is marching on.—Chorus.

In the beauty of the lilies Christ was born
   across the sea,
With a glory in his bosom that transfigures
   you and me;
As he died to make men holy, let us die to
   make men free,
   While God is marching on.—Cho.

2.   Columbia's Daughters.

BY HARRIET H. ROBINSON.

Tune—"Hold the Fort."

Hark! the sound of myriad voices
   Rising in their might!
'Tis the daughters of Columbia
   Pleading for the right.
CHO.—Raise the flag and plant the standard,
   Wave the signal still;
Brothers, we must share your freedom,
   Help us, and we will.

Think it not an idle murmur,
   You who hear the cry;
'Tis a plea for human freedom,
   Hallowed liberty!—Chorus.

O our country, glorious nation,
   Greatest of them all!
Give unto thy daughters justice,
   Or thy pride will fall.—Chorus.

Great Republic! to thy watchword
   Wouldst thou faithful be,
All beneath thy starry banner
   Must alike be free.—Chorus.

3.   Woman's Crusade.

Tune—"John Brown."

The light of truth is breaking,
   On the mountain tops it gleams;
Let it flash along our valleys,
   Let it glitter on our streams,
Till all our land awakens
   In its flush of golden beams;
   Our God is marching on.
CHORUS—Glory, Glory, Hallelujah!
   Glory, Glory, Hallelujah!
   Glory, Glory, Hallelujah!
   Our God is marching on.

With a purpose strong and steady,
   In the great Jehovah's name,
We rise to snatch our kindred
   From the depths of woe and shame,
And the jubilee of freedom
   To the slaves of sin proclaim.
   Our God is marching on.—Chorus.

From morning's early watches
   Till the setting of the sun,
We will never flag nor falter,
   In the work we have begun,
Till the forts have all surrendered
   And the victory is won;
   Our God is marching on.—Chorus.

4.   The Taxation Tyranny.

Arranged from words by Gen. E. Estabrook.

Tune—"The Red, White and Blue."

To tax one who's not represented
   Is tyranny—tell if you can
Why woman should not have the ballot?
   She's taxed, just the same as a man.

King George, you remember, denied us
   The ballot, but sent us the tea,
And we, without asking a question,
   Just tumbled it into the sea.

CHORUS:

Then to justice let's ever be true,
   To each citizen render his due,
Equal rights and protection forever
   To all 'neath the Red, White and Blue!

That one man shall not rule another,
   Unless by that other's consent,
Is the principle deep underlying
   The framework of this government.

So, as woman is punished for breaking
   The laws which she cannot gainsay,
Let us give her a voice in the making,
   Or ask her no more to obey.—Chorus.

Nationally known suffragists (above), accompanied by friends and local supporters, visited California's Yosemite Valley in June 1895. From the left on horseback are Miss Crane of Wisconsin, Anna Howard Shaw, Dr. Henry A. Baker of San Diego, Susan B. Anthony, Hester A. Harland of Los Angeles, Dr. Elizabeth C. Sargent of San Francisco, and Mrs. Fisher of Chicago. Patriotic woman suffrage songs (top) became an important part of every state campaign.

Organizing to Win California

WHILE SUPPORTERS labored in Idaho in 1896, suffragists in California waged what one participant called the "best conducted, liveliest, and most enthusiastic" campaign to date. Members of the California Equal Suffrage Association, led by Ellen Clark Sargent, raised some $19,000 and, according to Anna Howard Shaw, treated visiting suffragists

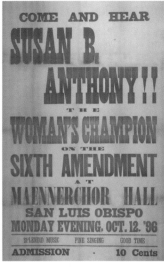

A Close Contest in the Golden State

THE CALIFORNIA suffrage campaign mobilized thousands of residents throughout the vast state in 1896. Anna Howard Shaw and other speakers covered great distances trying to reach voters in every county.

Suffragists in southern California organized by voting precinct both to reach men and to build interest among women. Dr. Mary T. Longley led the Colored Woman's Club helping to win Black support. Meetings in halls and outside factories were usually crowded and jubilant, and there was general support in the press, which Ida Husted Harper actively solicited. Suffragists won endorsements, if not active assistance, from all the major political parties except the Democrats.

Just before the election however, a "frenzy of hostility" was unleashed by urban politicians and liquor dealers. Opposition in the main cities of San Francisco and Oakland outweighed all other counties and on November 3 voters defeated the measure 137,099 to 110,355.

from the east "royally."

Shaw is pictured seated to the left of NAWSA president Susan B. Anthony (above, center) who posed with her lieutenants and several California women active in the 1896 campaign. To the left of Shaw is her long-time companion and secretary Lucy Anthony, Susan's niece. Beside her, on the far left, is volunteer Lelia S. Martin.

To the right of Susan B. Anthony sit Carrie Chapman Catt and her fellow organizer Mary Garrett Hay. Seated on the floor before them are Anthony's secretary Emma B. Sweet and office worker Mary Gorham. In the rear, from the left, are organizer Harriet May Mills from New York, office volunteers Louise Donnelly, Effie Scott Vance, Mary Donnelly, Sarah Donnelly,

and state officer Nellie Holbrook Blinn.

Anthony, 76, stayed in California almost constantly from March to November, speaking nearly every night and helping to manage the ambitious campaign from San Francisco.

Above: Suffragists active in California in 1896.
Right: Campaign poster.

Repeated Efforts to Win State Approval

Sᴜᴄᴄᴇssᴇs ɪɴ Utah and Idaho in 1896 doubled the number of equal suffrage states and encouraged supporters working throughout the country. While most other efforts were turned away, suffragists did get the measure placed on two state ballots, Washington and South Dakota, both for the second time in 1898. The campaigns ran simultaneously with the Spanish-American War which lasted from April until July.

Washington

Washington state legislators had shown themselves favorable to equal suffrage in the past, only to have their bills overturned by the territorial supreme court. In 1898, nine years after statehood, suffrage supporters worked diligently to have the question again put to the voters. This time, the suffrage bill was "delayed, defeated, pigeon-holed," according to one participant, finally passed, and then actually stolen in the legislature – with a worthless bill being substituted in its place. Finally a leading suffragist personally brought the actual legislation to the governor for his signature.

The Washington Equal Suffrage Association under Mrs. Homer M. Hill divided the state into six districts and throughout 1898 organizers held meetings, distributed literature, and collected signa-

Women were shown lining up to vote in Colorado in 1906. Illustrations like this, from the cover of *The Christian Herald*, reminded the rest of the country that equal suffrage was a fact of life in four western states.

tures on petitions of women who said they wanted to vote. An estimated 88% of those asked signed.

The state association encouraged independent efforts by other societies and circulated a booklet of testimonials from prominent citizens in the four "Free States." Funds were extremely hard to raise, however, and the association collected less than $500 for the modest campaign. Tens of thousands of leaflets were contributed by Carrie Catt

and NAWSA's Organization Committee and by Henry Blackwell at *The Woman's Journal*. The difficult campaign ended on November 5, 1898 when voters defeated woman suffrage 30,540 to 20,658, a closer margin than 1889.

South Dakota

Supporters in South Dakota also recovered from an earlier defeat and successfully persuaded the state legislature to resubmit the measure to the

voters. The second campaign was managed by Anna R. Simmons and Emma A. Cramer of the state suffrage association with the help of Laura Gregg of Kansas who NAWSA sent for two months.

Suffragists published a special campaign newspaper, the *South Dakota Messenger*, circulated literature, and tried to rally support. Voter response improved since 1890 but the measure was still narrowly defeated 22,983 to 19,698. Disappointed but undeterred, supporters began planning for a third campaign.

Federal Work Stalled

Suffragists across the country continued their work during these difficult years. Often the indifference of the public and the unrelenting efforts of the opposition were hard to overcome. War, economic depression, mass immigration, and other social changes made the country more conservative, slowing the movement's progress.

The steady lobbying in the nation's capital also diminished and the Federal suffrage amendment, while still introduced in each session of Congress, lost the immediacy and momentum which Susan B. Anthony and others had worked so hard to build. Without constant pressure, women's cause took a back seat to other legislation and the Federal amendment stalled. ◆

Mary Church Terrell articulated the needs of the Black community for over six decades and represented the deep support for women's rights among Black women. Terrell had a privileged upbringing in Memphis as the daughter of the first Black millionaire in the south. After graduating from Oberlin in 1884, she taught school then studied in Europe before returning to Washington D.C. to help other Black Americans. Brilliant, multilingual, and refined, she was 33 when she became president of the new National Association of Colored Women in 1896 and helped build it into the premier Black women's organization in the country. With the resolve and skills of a diplomat, Terrell repeatedly challenged white suffragists not to abandon their Black sisters, addressing the NAWSA convention in 1898 (left). Twenty years later she picketed the White House demanding the vote. Terrell was a lifelong activist, speaking out for equality and civil rights more pointedly as she grew older.

Women Organize in the Black Community

AFTER THE Civil War the movement among Black women for political equality continued largely separate from the white suffrage movement. Two decades after the conflict, Black women throughout the country went through a critical phase of organizing, expanding their church and social circles into a remarkable network of women's clubs and civic organizations.

Two important clubs were formed in October 1892 after women gathered in New York City to honor anti-lynching crusader Ida B. Wells. New York activists created the Woman's Loyal Union and Boston women led by Josephine St. Pierre Ruffin founded the Woman's Era Club. These and other groups focused particularly on improving conditions in Black communities where social

services were sorely needed. Members established kindergartens, nurseries, homes for the elderly and infirm, and many other critical programs.

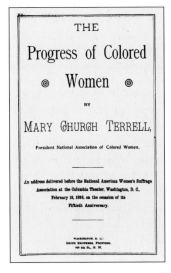

Determined to create a single strong national organization, the two largest club associations, the National Federation of Afro-American

Women and the National League of Colored Women, voted to merge in July 1896. The new National Association of Colored Women elected Mary Church Terrell as its first president and adopted the motto, "Lifting As We Climb." The coalition quickly grew in influence and encouraged thousands of members to organize support locally for equal suffrage, temperance, and other civic reforms.

"These women valued self-help, protection of women, honesty, and justice," professor Dorothy Salem observed, and they used the NACW as a "major vehicle" for reform across the country over the next four decades.

Above : Leaders of the local Women's League In Newport, Rhode Island, around 1899. Inset: Mary Church Terrell's 1898 speech to NAWSA.

Jane Addams moved into one of the poorest sections of Chicago in September 1889 and began a movement for self-help and social service whose reputation spread around the world. Following a comfortable childhood and young-adult ennui, Addams was 29 when she and Ellen Gates Starr opened Hull House to serve the neighborhood's immigrant population. A pioneer social worker and adept fundraiser, Addams attracted a host of talented individuals who worked with their neighbors for civic improvement as well as for social and industrial reform. Her insightful articles and books brought her international recognition and led President Theodore Roosevelt to call her "the most useful citizen in Chicago." Addams believed that without the vote women were "outside the real life of the world" and she served as vice president of NAWSA from 1911 to 1914. She guided Hull House, which she called "an institution attempting to learn from life itself," for over 40 years and became one of the country's leading advocates for peace, equality, public service, and international cooperation.

Clubs and Settlement Houses Offer Women New Opportunities

I N THE late 19th century women's interest in clubs and new associations grew as never before. Thousands of literary, social, and civic groups were organized in cities and towns across the country. Many of these white groups affiliated with the General Federation of Women's Clubs, which counted one million members by 1910. While most clubs initially avoided such controversial issues as equal suffrage, they exposed women to broader public concerns and offered valuable experience in working together.

In 1889 Jane Addams founded Hull House in Chicago to help some of the millions of poor immigrants crowded into urban slums. Four years later Lillian Wald established the Henry Street Settlement and Visiting Nurse Service in New York City. Offering challenging work and a seedbed for new ideas, more than four dozen settlement houses drew eager young reformers, particularly college-educated women and men from around the country, a number of whom went on to positions of leadership in government, academia, and

the newly developing field of social services.

Unlike most women's clubs, settlement houses embraced people of all backgrounds and understood the needs of workers, children, and poor families. Over time, settlement leaders brought these broader concerns to the attention of suffragists and gradually helped wage-earning women organize for the ballot themselves. Settlements and other associations played a central role in training a new generation of women to assume expanded responsibilities.

Residents and friends dined together in the Hull House Coffee House (above left) where they could discuss recent events and formulate plans for the future. Hull House brought new options for recreation to Chicago's

Near West Side when it opened the city's first public gymnasium in 1893. Supporters organized fencing classes (above) and Chicago's first women's basketball team. Settlement houses made a point of offering services

and activities for all ages. Residents taught a wide variety of classes and training programs (top) and led efforts against child labor, impure food, sweatshops, and the exploitation of women.

A Unifying Standard-Bearer

SUSAN B. ANTHONY maintained her single-minded focus on woman suffrage for nearly fifty years, and by the end of the century was the most widely recognized proponent of women's rights in the country. She was, in suffragist Helen Gougar's words, "our grand old standard-bearer." In 1891 Anthony announced she was "retiring" to the Rochester, New York, home she shared with her sister Mary and no longer would be in Washington D.C. half of every year lobbying while Congress was in session.

Friends celebrated her coming domesticity by presenting her with dishes, towels, and household items but the gift that she particularly treasured was a desk with cubbyholes, the first she had ever owned. Naturally her "retirement" lasted less than six months; she was elected NAWSA president in 1892.

Eight years later, however, as she approached 80, Anthony announced that she would step down as NAWSA president in 1900.

Above: Susan B. Anthony at her desk. Right: Taking after former president Grover Cleveland in 1905 after he declared, "Sensible and responsible women do not want to vote."

The four-starred flag represented the four "free states" where women enjoyed equal voting rights with men. The suffrage flag became a popular image, appearing on leaflets, badges, and handmade items like the silk pillow case above. For years the four states stood, one suffragist wrote, "like a democratic oasis in a desert of pretension." Suffragists across the country asked male voters the same question (below): "Why Not Our State, Too?" The U.S. continued to attract men and women from around the world towards the end of the century (upper left), and the population grew dramatically in size and diversity. A turn-of-the-century cartoon (left) stressed that shackles bound not only women but also the entire nation.

Preparing for the Twentieth Century

BY THE end of the 19th century four states offered tangible proof that equal suffrage was possible and that the staunch labors of suffrage supporters could eventually bear fruit. But, as women were finding out, the road to enfranchisement was long and filled with obstacles.

For over three decades suffragists had tried to win the support of legislatures, political parties, and constitutional conventions. They had waged fourteen referendum campaigns in ten states between 1867 and 1899 and had won only two. Despite advances in education, the professions, and other areas, women's political condition remained "helpless and degraded" despite everything suffragists could do. Still, work continued throughout the country, carried on by dedicated women in small local clubs and impoverished state associations.

Carrie Catt continued her organizing work with NAWSA, traveling over 13,000 miles in 1899 to attend suffrage meetings and deliver speeches in twenty states. Anna Howard Shaw, NAWSA's Lecturer at Large, was also on the circuit continually, speaking as both a paid lecturer and a campaign worker. As the early pioneers passed away, the mantle fell to a new generation. ◆

AMERICAN WOMANHOOD –
"You release my shackles and I'll release yours."

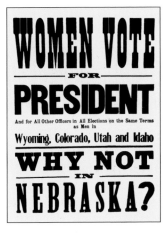

Chapter 4: 1900-1909

New Leadership for a New Century

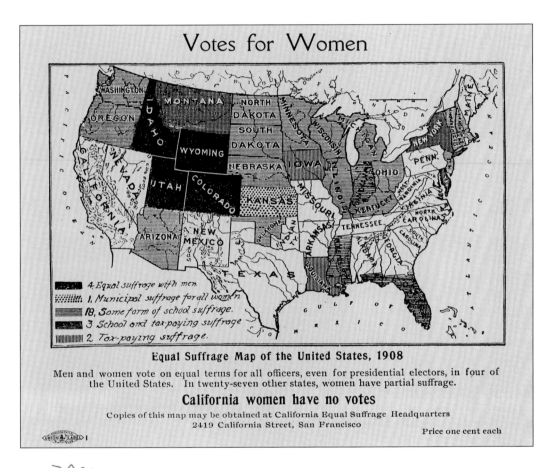

Votes for Women

Equal Suffrage Map of the United States, 1908

Men and women vote on equal terms for all officers, even for presidential electors, in four of the United States. In twenty-seven other states, women have partial suffrage.

California women have no votes

Copies of this map may be obtained at California Equal Suffrage Headquarters
2419 California Street, San Francisco

Price one cent each

Suffragists began to use stars, state symbols, and other imagery more broadly to represent their cause in visual terms in the early 1900s. One of the most effective portrayals was the Suffrage Map (left). Graphically highlighting the four adjoining states, the map emphasized their combined size as evidence of growing acceptance in a substantial part of the country. The map cleverly downplayed the states' small populations and relatively weak political influence. Maps would become a favorite means of illustrating suffrage gains.

THE WOMAN suffrage movement went through a period of unparalleled growth and development between 1900 and 1909, taking on a more political identity, attracting broader support, and experimenting with innovative methods. Suffragists promoted the existing four equal suffrage states as proof of the "rightness" of women voting. They faced continual setbacks, though, in their ef-forts to win another state. Despite the momentum of the previous decade, progress proved to be disappointingly slow.

At best, it usually took sup-porters several years – when they were successful – to get a state legislature to approve a suffrage bill which would send the question on to the voters. Many legislatures only met every other year, consti-tutional amendments gener-ally had to be approved by two successive legislatures, and many politicians were unsympathetic to women voting. With little hope for progress in Washington D.C., suffragists were forced to deal with different conditions in each individual state.

Facing page: Justice displayed the emblems of the equal suffrage states on this patriotic 1908 march.

A New President for NAWSA

IN 1899 Susan B. Anthony announced that in 1900, at the age of 80, she would retire from the National American Woman Suffrage Association presidency she had held for seven years. The times "demand stronger hands, younger heads, fresher hearts," she declared.

Anna Howard Shaw, the orator and ordained minister who had traveled with her for twelve years, was anxious to follow her as president. Carrie Chapman Catt, chair of NAWSA's Organization Committee, shared the same ambition and had shown her skill in organizing work nationally. Also, Catt was married, economically secure, and able to devote more time than Shaw who was constantly traveling and lecturing to make a living.

Faced with a difficult choice, Anthony endorsed Catt as best suited for the job. She was elected and Anthony persuaded Shaw to continue to serve as vice-president. Lillie Devereux Blake from New York withdrew as a third candidate.

Catt brought new drive and ability to the presidency. She immediately launched efforts to attract more young women to the cause and to organize supporters both nationally and internationally.

Following the election, NAWSA officers met at the Anthony home in Rochester (above) in late August 1900 to clear the air after "personal ambitions, prejudices and misunderstandings reared their heads," in historian Alma Lutz's words. A sense of unity was restored.

Above: NAWSA officers in 1900. From the left: Harriet Taylor Upton, Rachel Avery, co-hostess Mary Anthony, Anna Howard Shaw, Alice Stone Blackwell, Laura Clay, Susan B. Anthony, Carrie Catt, and Catharine Waugh McCulloch (behind Catt).

Parlor Meetings Bring Suffrage to "Respectable" Women

PARLOR MEETINGS offered private opportunities for turn-of-the-century women to hear about woman suffrage and other controversial matters. Suffragists used these informal settings to reach women who would never attend a lecture or public meeting. "You had these little afternoon gatherings of women," remembered Minnesota suffragist Sylvie Thygeson. "While we were drinking tea, I gave a little talk and they asked questions about what was going on."

Carrie Chapman Catt was 41 when she was elected head of NAWSA. A detail-oriented administrator, known for her careful planning, she had participated in several state campaigns as chair of NAWSA's Organization Committee during the 1890s. "Catt had a magnetic personality in these early years," historian Eleanor Flexner observed, "combined with a certain youthful brashness and lack of tact." International work seasoned her and she became a "commanding platform presence." In 1902 Catt presided over both NAWSA's convention and the first international woman suffrage conference (below) which she organized in Washington D.C.

Visiting speakers would occasionally be entertained before their public lectures, which was probably the case at the tea party above with Carrie Catt on the far left. She recommended recruiting new members through such social gatherings and involvement with civic and charitable organizations.

Seeking a new respectability for the suffrage cause, she encouraged supporters in the states to adopt her "Society Plan" which entailed enlisting wealthy women, club women, and social leaders. With their influence and financial backing, suffragists hoped to appeal to a much larger constituency.

The elite plan brought only limited success but, as historian Sara Graham observed, "Name recognition, handsome contributions and social prestige were welcome boons to an organization that had borne the stigma of fanaticism for decades." In due course the stylish gatherings even led one observer to refer to the suffrage cause as a "gilt-chair movement."

As women's clubs proliferated among affluent white women, the parallel club movement among Black women also grew, but their energies were rarely integrated. Black suffragists and dedicated proponents from other races and ethnic backgrounds nonetheless did important work in their own neighborhoods and communities across the country.

Above: A 1905 parlor meeting in Chicago.

Maud Wood Park, a senior at Radcliffe, resolved to recruit more young women to the suffrage cause after finding herself the youngest delegate at a NAWSA meeting in 1900. She immediately organized the College Equal Suffrage League with Inez Haynes Gillmore (later Irwin) and spent several years setting up chapters throughout the country. In 1901 Park became executive secretary of philanthropist Pauline Agassiz Shaw's Boston Equal Suffrage Association for Good Government and in 1909 took an eighteen month world tour, financed by Shaw, to study the condition of women in other countries. Park, Gillmore, and Ruth Delano (below, from right) posed together at Radcliffe.

WOMAN'S LEAGUE MEETING AT STANFORD CHAPTER OF THE COLLEGIATE WOMAN EQUAL SUFFRAGE LEAGUE ROBLE HALL SATURDAY 2 PM SHARP

Signing Up College Women

B Y 1900 thousands of wo-men were graduating from colleges each year and many agreed wholeheartedly with the goal of equal rights. Recognizing their potential, the College Equal Suffrage League was formed to enlist young women and men "both before and after graduation" in the suffrage movement. In 1908, with chapters in fifteen states, NAWSA sanctioned a National College Equal Suffrage League with Bryn Mawr dean M. Carey Thomas as president. Over the next nine years, with Maud Wood Park serving as vice-president, the league mobilized thousands of young women and proved to be a vital force in many state campaigns.

Above left: Denver Judge Ben Lindsey, with supporters in 1907, defended equal suffrage in Colorado. Left: One of the new "college women" demonstrated her strength to a group of astounded men in a turn-of-the-century cartoon. Facing page: A handmade poster featuring an image of Joan of Arc announced a College League meeting at Stanford University in California around 1910.

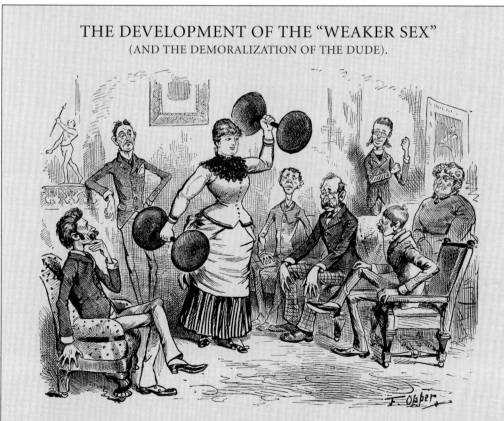

THE DEVELOPMENT OF THE "WEAKER SEX"
(AND THE DEMORALIZATION OF THE DUDE).

VASSAR GRADUATE – "These are the dumb-bells I used last term in our gymnasium; won't one of you gentlemen just put them up? It's awfully easy."

Charting a New Course for NAWSA

WHEN Carrie Chapman Catt took the helm of the National American Woman Suffrage Association in 1900 she brought her unique strategic vision and administrative drive. To formulate national policy she began to gather information through the existing state associations to determine the opportunities for woman suffrage in each state.

More State Efforts

Catt and other NAWSA officers traveled to numerous states in 1901 speaking with suffragists and assessing conditions. A national suffrage bazaar in Madison Square Garden took in an extraordinary $10,000. In 1902 Catt joined organizers Gail Laughlin and Laura Gregg in Montana trying to get a suffrage referendum approved by the legislature. While this effort, like many others, was unsuccessful, the women left behind some thirty new clubs in Montana, a network that would prove useful later.

When the New Hampshire legislature surprised suffragists in December 1902 by agreeing to place the measure before the voters, Catt personally took charge of the campaign, the second held on the east coast. She set up headquarters in Concord, brought in fifteen speakers, and canvassed the state through the cold weeks of January and February. After a short, difficult campaign,

New Hampshire voters defeated the measure on March 10, 1903 by a vote of 21,788 to 14,162.

To help relieve Catt of many of the routine business details, NAWSA's headquarters was moved in 1903 from New York City to the home of

done by mail and at annual conventions.

A New President

In January 1904 Catt announced that she would not stand for re-election. She was both suffering from poor health and concerned about

Susan B. Anthony posed with NAWSA officers in 1904. Outgoing president Carrie Chapman Catt is in the foreground and newly elected president Anna Howard Shaw is standing in the center behind Anthony.

treasurer Harriet Taylor Upton in Warren, Ohio, and later to the first floor of the county courthouse. For the next six years, Upton covered many administrative duties while most association business was

caring for her ill husband. She had served for four years as the unpaid head of the struggling, factional National Association, trying to reinvigorate and inspire suffragists across the country, but always

moving in the shadow of Susan B. Anthony.

Organizationally, Catt left NAWSA in better shape than ever. There was $12,000 in the treasury. The number and size of state suffrage clubs had increased. New members were being enlisted. Personally, however, Catt faced a difficult time. Biographer Jacqueline Van Voris wrote that after Catt's husband died in October 1905, "her grief so eroded her own health that for a long time she expected to die at any moment." She took rooms in a New York hotel and asked her friend Mary Garrett Hay to stay with her.

In February 1904, Anna Howard Shaw was elected without opposition to lead NAWSA, although she later admitted, "I had lost my ambition to be president." Bowing to pressure from Anthony, who "actually commanded me to take the place," Shaw accepted the post with a heavy heart. The 57-year-old veteran made a personal promise to her mentor to lead the organization, a pledge which she was to keep, despite challenges, for the next eleven years.

In 1906 she was relieved to learn that Baltimore philanthropist Mary Garrett and M. Carey Thomas of Bryn Mawr had raised a fund of $60,000, enough for five years salary and expenses, to free her to work full time as NAWSA president. ◆

Nannie Helen Burroughs worked through the Baptist church to empower Black women academically and politically. Beginning in 1900, when she was 21, Burroughs energetically promoted equal suffrage through the church's new Woman's Convention. The vote, she argued, would help Black women defeat segregationists and "reckon with men who place no value on her virtue." By 1912 the Convention represented over 50,000 Black women and was the largest such organization in the country. Burroughs (below, left) opened the National Training School in Washington D.C. in 1909 to help Black women become self-supporting wage earners. While promoting self-determination, she remained unsparing in her denunciation of racial segregation, lynching, and disfranchisement.

In 1903 national suffrage headquarters was moved from New York City to Harriet Taylor Upton's stately family home (left) in Warren, Ohio. However, the out of the way location was not conducive to regular meetings. Throughout the decade suffragists worked in their own states with only limited contact with the national association. Black women were active simultaneously with white suffragists, promoting equal rights in overlapping regions. Black organizers like Marichita Lyons of the Woman's Loyal Union in New York, whom co-workers praised as "one of the most brilliant women in the North," lectured throughout the early 1900s. Increasingly, suffragists set their sights on young women like those above at the new National Training School in Washington D.C.

WARREN, O.   NATIONAL HEADQUARTERS OF THE NATIONAL AMERICAN
WOMAN SUFFRAGE ASSOCIATION.

Years of public life and constant traveling helped make Susan B. Anthony one of the best known women in America by 1900. Her once-controversial image had been softened by time and familiarity, and she had become a living symbol of women's demand for equality. On her eightieth birthday in 1900 Colorado suffragists presented her with the silver cup below, and for many years her image graced commemorative stamps (above), buttons, and medals issued by the movement. Activist Lucy Burns later praised Anthony's "genius for action" and observed, "she lived her life in the spirit of a warrior, battling for the mental liberty of women." Fondly referred to as Aunt Susan, Anthony posed on the porch (right) of her Rochester, New York home. Anthony's sister Mary was also widely respected for both her loyalty to her sister and her own long service to the cause.

Susan B. Anthony: A Time of Celebrity and Honors

IN HER later years Susan B. Anthony attracted public attention and honors wherever she went. "The stones once flung at her had become roses," Carrie Catt later observed. Traveling to Europe in 1904 for the founding congress of the International Woman Suffrage Alliance, the tall, gray-haired Anthony received an effusive outpouring of praise. In the U.S. she was treated with increasing adoration at NAWSA's annual conventions. She came to be recognized by the press and the public as the leading figure in the struggle for votes for women.

After years of hard work and travel, Anthony retired to the home at 17 Madison Street in Rochester, New York, which she shared with her sister Mary. In 1900 the two sisters were the determining force in opening the University of Rochester to women. Even in her eighties, however, the inveterate campaigner barely slowed down. Between 1900 and 1906, Anthony visited eighteen states and toured several European countries.

Suffragists Look to the West

Hopeful that neighboring states could be won after the gains of the 1890s, suffrage leaders paid particular attention to developments in the west. To support an initiative in Oregon, NAWSA held its 1905 convention in Portland, coinciding with the great Lewis and Clark Exposition. Special railroad cars carried nearly 100 delegates to the city, where the mayor welcomed them and heartily endorsed woman suffrage. At the Exposition, Susan B. Anthony spoke at the unveiling of a beautiful bronze statue honoring Sacajawea, the Shoshone woman who was an advisor, emissary, and interpreter for Lewis and Clark. Her fortitude as the only woman, roughly 19 years old, carrying a newborn child through the wilderness still inspires awe, and suffragists adopted her as a symbol. State leader Abigail Scott Duniway declared that in honoring Sacajawea, "we pay homage to thousands of uncrowned heroines whose quiet endurance and patient efforts have made possible the achievements of the world's great men." Anthony praised Alice Cooper Hubbard's lyrical sculpture as "the first statue erected in this country to a woman because of deeds of daring," and called on the women of Oregon to similarly lead the way during the 1906 suffrage campaign.

Left: Sacajawea's statue in Portland, Oregon.

Henry B Blackwell   Antoinette Brown Blac[k]
Laura Clay;   Susan B.
Alice Stone Blackwell   Abigail Scott Duniway
Florence Kelley,

Oregon Hosts the 1905 NAWSA Convention

In June 1905, suffrage supporters from around the country journeyed to Portland, Oregon, for NAWSA's annual convention. Susan B. Anthony, a legendary figure at 85, posed with other delegates and guests (above) on the steps of the Oregon Building at the Lewis and Clark Exposition. In the center of the front row (left to right) are Dr. Mary Thompson (in white), Antoinette Brown Blackwell, Dr. Annice Jeffreys, Susan B. Anthony, Abigail Scott Duniway, Anna Howard Shaw, Kate Gordon, Mary Anthony, and Hon. Jefferson Meyers.

Meyers, president of the Exposition Committee, was married to Jeffreys, who was vice-president under Duni-

(handwritten signatures on photograph)
Kate M. Gordon
Gail Laughlin
Smith Eaton
Carrie Chapman Catt

Abigail Scott Duniway
came to personify woman suffrage in the Pacific northwest from her earliest days as a journalist in Portland, Oregon. Her extensive work in Oregon, Washington, and Idaho, beginning in the 1870s, helped lay the groundwork for later suffrage victories. A frequent lecturer and prolific author, she wrote the first novel to come out of the northwest as well as innumerable articles and editorials. Forceful and opinionated, Duniway clashed on occasion with other suffragists over such issues as campaign strategies, regional rivalries, and prohibition. "Her salty language, freewheeling humor and sarcasm, religious skepticism and iconoclasm," wrote biographer Ruth Moynihan, "echoed her milieu and well represented the many other 'strongminded women' of the American frontier." Duniway led the Oregon Equal Suffrage Association during four unsuccessful campaigns. At age 78 she was confined to a wheelchair during the final victorious drive in 1912. Widely honored for her years of service, she became the first woman in Oregon to register to vote.

way of the state suffrage association. Both groups had invited NAWSA to hold its convention during the Oregon Exposition. Laura Clay is in the second row between Blackwell and Jeffreys, and author Charlotte Perkins Gilman is behind Shaw. The national gathering gave new life to the cause in Oregon and helped persuade the legislature to place suffrage on the 1906 ballot. Before returning home, Anthony and other suffragists toured neighboring Washington and California, encouraging supporters and generating publicity for the cause.

Above: Suffragists met in Oregon during the Lewis and Clark Exposition in 1905.

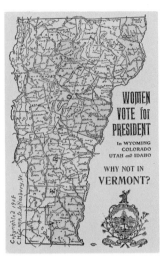

For years supporters across the country tried to persuade their legislatures to put suffrage on the ballot. Failing that, women in some states used the new initiative and referendum process, collecting signatures on petitions to force a statewide vote. Between 1900 and 1909 the measure went to voters only four times, once in New Hampshire and three times in Oregon. Abigail Scott Duniway led the 1900 campaign in Oregon which tried to avoid the problems of 1894. She nearly succeeded as the measure lost by just over 2,100 votes, 28,402 to 26,265. Duniway favored the "still hunt" method of campaigning which involved quietly and unobtrusively enlisting the support of influential citizens and avoiding publicity-generating events which would arouse the opposition. NAWSA leaders blamed Duniway's approach for the two defeats and in 1905 decided to take control.

Challenges from Within and Without in Oregon

IN OCTOBER 1905 NAWSA assumed management of the suffrage campaign in Oregon and sent organizers Mary Chase and Gail Laughlin to prepare a more systematic statewide drive. State leader Abigail Scott Duniway was appalled by the "eastern invasion" but avoided an open break.

Recognizing that the campaign had been so important to Susan B. Anthony, many former colleagues returned to Oregon after Anthony's death in March 1906. Local women under state association president Viola Coe were joined by a remarkable group of suffragists, including Laura Clay, Mary Bradford, Emma DeVoe, and Laura Gregg, who traveled and helped women throughout the state. Alice Stone Blackwell, together with Susan B. Anthony's sister Mary and niece Lucy, sent out literature and press information, and Kate Gordon organized parlor meetings. NAWSA president Anna Howard Shaw spoke and managed the campaign.

Suffragists eventually spent over $18,000. They found, however, that many voters opposed woman suffrage because they believed it would lead to prohibition. As Duniway had feared, the meetings and the presence of outsiders helped arouse the opposition.

On election day, June 4, 1906, suffragists endured drenching rain outside the polls to plead their case to the voters one last time. Groups of anti-suffrage men in Portland argued with the women while passing out blue cards that read "Don't Handicap Greater Oregon with Woman Suffrage." The measure was defeated for the third time by a vote of 47,075 to 36,902. Duniway led another drive two years later but it proved even less popular and lost 58,670 to 36,858.

Above: An Oregon supporter shielded Susan B. Anthony and Anna Howard Shaw from the sun during their 1905 visit. Left: A 1906 leaflet.

Susan B. Anthony: *"Failure is Impossible"*

SUSAN B. ANTHONY worked for equal suffrage most of her life and eventually won international praise for her "single minded, earnest and unselfish" work, as one journalist wrote. At a Washington D.C. tribute on her 86th birthday, one of her last public appearances, she thanked all those "true and devoted to the cause" and declared, "with such women consecrating their lives failure is impossible." Her words became a rallying cry for the final generation of suffragists.

Widely Mourned

The revered leader died in her Rochester home on March 13, 1906 with her sister Mary and her close friend Anna Howard Shaw by her side. "All who knew her will mourn her," Carrie Catt observed, "and long will they miss her wise counsel, her hearty cheerfulness and her splendid optimism." Shaw declared, "The ages to come will revere her name." More than a thousand glowing editorials appeared in the nation's newspapers.

At her memorial Anthony's coffin was draped with a large American flag, crowned with a wreath of laurel and palms, and surrounded by an honor guard of young women from the University of Rochester. Flags fluttered at half-mast as over ten thousand people paid their final respects. "The object of her life," Shaw reminded mourners, "was to awaken in women the consciousness of the need of freedom and the courage to demand it not as an end but as a means of creating higher ideals for humanity."

Susan B. Anthony was 77 when she posed for this portrait in 1897. Her friend Frances Willard called her a "heroic figure, sure to stand out in history as plainly as any of our presidents."

Anthony's memory would be kept alive by a reinvigorated national movement, members of which would come to refer to the Federal suffrage bill as the Susan B. Anthony Amendment.

Anthony also left a notable international legacy. Following her earlier efforts to organize the International Congress of Women, which steered away from endorsing suffrage, Anthony was persuaded by Catt to help found a new association and to chair its founding congress in Berlin in 1904.

After an initial meeting in 1902, the International Woman Suffrage Alliance was officially launched with eight national auxiliaries at a congress in June 1904 where Anthony was the guest of honor. The Berlin meeting garnered tremendous publicity because, in suffragist Mary Peck's words, "Votes for Women was a radical movement in 1904 and Susan B. Anthony's name had gone 'round the world." Anthony described the exuberant welcoming reception she received in Berlin as a high point in her life.

International Influence

The congress elected Catt as its president and she presided over congresses in Copenhagen in 1906, Amsterdam in 1908, and London in 1909, by which time the Alliance counted member associations in twenty countries. After the first meeting in 1904, Annie Furuhjelm had returned to Russian-controlled Finland to organize Finnish women. A short time later, after unforeseen political changes, they became the first European women to win the right to vote.

Anthony recognized that participation in international work challenged the prejudices and provincialism of American suffragists and encouraged them to see the struggle for equal rights in a worldwide context. In that broader realm it was the American leader herself who became a recognized symbol of women's rights, an indomitable figure the German press referred to as "Susan B. Anthony of the World." ◆

Anna Howard Shaw's Unsettled NAWSA Presidency

D RAFTED IN 1904 to lead the organization of which she had been vice-president for twelve years, Anna Howard Shaw took over a fragile National Association that had but a toehold in many states. Shaw was widely respected as a captivating orator and a rugged campaigner. But she was neither a strategist nor an administrator.

Moreover, despite the warmth of her personality, she was sometimes difficult to work with, showing poor judgment and harboring suspicions and jealousies about those who disagreed with her. As historian Eleanor Flexner noted, the movement "needed strong yet flexible guidance which she was unable to provide."

As a result, NAWSA lagged behind rather than led developments which were largely driven in the states by local activists and initiatives. Although state associations particularly in the west showed new life, the National Associ-ation was plagued by disagreements and turnover of staff and board members. Work for the Federal amendment nearly ceased and most national business was conducted by mail from headquarters in Ohio. With no clear strategy guiding work nationally, members of state associations grew increasingly dispirited at the lack of tangible progress.

Above: Anna Howard Shaw (center) in Stockholm in 1911.

News from Abroad

WHILE SUFFRAGISTS in the U.S. tried to win another state, women in Great Britain were raising the call for equal rights to a new level. The Women's Social and Political Union, founded in October 1903 by Emmeline Pankhurst, rejected the role of quiet and patient petitioner and instead launched a series of controversial political actions. Demanding enfranchisement from Parliament, the women took to the streets to rouse public support. They staged parades with great pageantry and color and organized well-publicized protests of every sort. Beginning in 1905, British suffragists were repeatedly arrested and jailed for aggressively demanding equal rights. Their fearless stance led to a dramatic change in the public perception of suffragists.

Suffragists in America were impressed by the bold new tactics of the women in Britain. There, activists held open-air meetings (left) to reach men in the street while others (below) were jailed for trying to enter Parliament. In January 1908 two suffragists in London demanding a hearing with the Prime Minister chained themselves to his gates (bottom left). They spoke to the gathered crowd as police cut their chains and then arrested them. The more traditional suffrage societies were appalled, but the press and the public took notice. The Women's Social and Political Union's weekly newspaper, *Votes for Women* (above), reached a circulation of 40,000 by 1910. American papers also widely reported developments in England.

A New Militant Suffrage Movement

The woman suffrage movement in Great Britain went through dramatic changes during the first years of the 20th century. Although suffragists had been actively seeking enfranchisement since the 1860s, the rise of the Women's Social and Political Union and its campaign for "immediate enfranchisement" forced the matter onto the public agenda. The militant stance of the WSPU had a tremendous influence on women in the U.S. and around the world.

Since 1897, the National Union of Women's Suffrage Societies, led by veteran suffragist Millicent Garrett Fawcett, had focused its energy on educating, lobbying, and petitioning to win the government's support. By contrast, the WSPU, founded in 1903, adopted a more assertive style in keeping with the image of a "suffrage army in the field" envisioned by founder Emmeline Pankhurst. Some women supported both organizations despite their different styles.

"Suffragettes"

Late in 1905 two WSPU members were arrested after disrupting a political meeting. They attracted enormous publicity when they accepted jail rather than pay the fine.

The following year, the WSPU organized deputations of women who tried to "rush"

"The Bugler Girl" advertised the moderate National Union of Women's Suffrage Societies' 1908 procession in London. The striking poster was published by the Artists' Suffrage League.

past police into the House of Commons, leading to dozens of arrests and two to four weeks in jail. Fear of prison did not deter these new "suffragettes," as *The Daily Mail* derisively labeled them. The WSPU proudly adopted the term which clearly set it apart

from the more law-abiding suffragists.

On June 30, 1908 two suffragettes were arrested for throwing stones through the Prime Minister's windows after others had chained themselves to his gate when he refused to see their deputa-

tions. The WSPU later officially endorsed window smashing. The tactic was defended as far less violent than others chosen by men to win their political independence.

Grand Pageantry

Seeing the publicity generated by public spectacles, the National Union organized a great march on June 13, 1908, independent of the WSPU. Suffragists from throughout England and from other countries paraded through London to a mass meeting in Albert Hall, while spectators threw flowers from their balconies. Catharine McCulloch of Illinois witnessed this "monster parade" and wrote back to *The Woman's Journal*, "I never saw such crowds! Twenty thousand women were parading, carrying over a hundred beautiful banners, among them banners for Susan B. Anthony, Elizabeth Cady Stanton and Lucy Stone." Anna Howard Shaw gave a rousing speech which "brought the English to their feet roaring with applause."

A week later, the WSPU sponsored a brilliant "Women's Sunday" parade on June 21 which saw 30,000 suffragists converge on London's Hyde Park. There speakers addressed an unprecedented audience of over 250,000 from twenty platforms.

At the rally the WSPU first popularized its signature colors of purple, white, and

Gains Strength in Great Britain

green, symbolizing dignity, purity, and hope. Vibrant colors became a hallmark of the British suffrage campaign. The National Union's colors were red, white, and green, and the Women's Freedom League, a militant nonviolent group led by Charlotte Despard, chose green, white, and gold.

Force-Feeding

Suffragettes continued to be arrested and jailed throughout this period, many for minor infractions. In July 1909, after being denied her request to be treated as a political prisoner, Marjorie Wallace Dunlop began a hunger strike to protest women's treatment in prison. New prisoners also refused to eat.

At first they were released when they became dangerously weak. But in September prison authorities began to force-feed the women to keep them from starving. This punishing ordeal entailed forcing a tube down the nose or throat of the restrained prisoner and pouring liquid directly into her body. An ugly and painful experience, it left the women sore, nauseous, and barely nourished. By the end of 1909 nearly 500 women had been imprisoned, including several American supporters.

News of their torments filled the papers and won the suffragettes wider support. When the government pro-

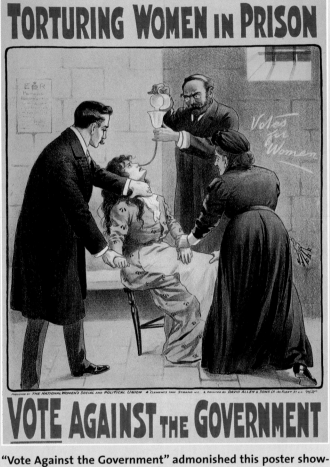

"Vote Against the Government" admonished this poster showing British prison officials force-feeding a suffragette. The WSPU campaigned against the ruling Liberal Party at elections because it blocked votes for women.

posed a Conciliation Bill, the WSPU agreed to a truce. But on November 18, 1910, frustrated over the lack of progress, Emmeline Pankhurst and 500 supporters tried to enter the House of Commons. A violent battle ensued. The women were beaten back and roughly thrown between police and men in the crowd. Many were

injured during the fierce struggle. After six hours of clashing, police arrested 119 suffragettes on what became known as "Black Friday."

To encourage the government to act, the WSPU resumed its truce and on June 17, 1911 all the British suffrage groups participated in a spectacular parade in London a week before King George

V's coronation. An estimated 60,000 women marched in the Women's Coronation Procession, the largest and most impressive of the British demonstrations. Festive spectacles like this, which included 70 bands, floats, and over 1,000 colorful banners, had a powerful effect on Americans who would soon emulate the pageantry of their English sisters.

When the government abandoned the Conciliation Bill, there was another uprising on November 21, 1911 during which hundreds of WSPU members smashed the windows of commercial and government buildings in London. Over 200 were arrested and sentenced to two months in Holloway Gaol.

Fed up with government delay and betrayal, the WSPU adopted more violent, but not life-threatening, methods including vandalism and arson. In March 1912, after further window breaking, police raided WSPU headquarters and arrested its leadership for conspiracy. Moderate suffragists further distanced themselves from the militants. Many recognized, though, that the WSPU had made the issue of woman suffrage a hotly debated political topic which was gaining broad popular support. Whether that support was strong enough to win over the government, however, remained to be seen. ◆

Drawing Inspiration from Events in England

MANY AMERICAN suffragists visited England during this period and brought back news to supporters in the U.S. Alice Paul (above), a social worker from New Jersey, joined the Women's Social and Political Union while studying in England and was imprisoned six times in 1909. American women including Lucy Burns, Anne Martin, and Alice Morgan Wright, also served time in jail. Many others, including Inez Milholland, Florence Luscomb, and Margaret Foley, participated in demonstrations and observed the workings of the British movement.

American supporters were fascinated by the imaginative and aggressive methods British suffragettes had adopted, and shocked at the government's harsh reprisals.

Under their "From Prison to Citizenship" banner, 700 British suffragists who had been imprisoned (above) led the Women's Coronation Procession, one of several major demonstrations in London. Bringing news of the suffrage situation in England, Alice Paul (above left) addressed a New York audience on February 18, 1910 with Harriot Stanton Blatch and Inez Milholland seated on the stage behind her. Paul also spoke at the 1910 NAWSA convention. Like their British counterparts, suffragists in New York (left) used "human billboards" to publicize a 1911 meeting.

SUFFRAGETTE PROCESSION JUNE 17, 1911.

Emmeline Pankhurst, the inspirational and militant British suffrage leader, helped make women's rights a vital issue in England and exerted a powerful influence on American suffragists. Charismatic and autocratic, the 45-year-old widow founded the Women's Social and Political Union in 1903 with the motto "Deeds Not Words." Through it she brought new levels of activism and self-sacrifice to women's forty-year struggle in England. Although she could be a passionate and eloquent speaker, "her calm, quiet, cultured manner appealed to us all," remembered activist Annie Kenney. Speaking in the U.S. in November 1913, Pankhurst voiced her pride in American activists Alice Paul and Lucy Burns. "In a way, they are my children," she told her audience, since they had trained and worked together in the WSPU. An American button (below) showed Pankhurst's influence.

British Suffragists Impress American Audiences

Excited by the struggle in England, groups in the U.S. sponsored numerous speaking tours for British suffrage leaders. Emmeline Pankhurst visited on four occasions between 1909 and 1915, and her daughters, Sylvia and Cristabel, also toured several times. Other British activists who gave lectures to American audiences included Ethel Snowden, Emmeline and Frederick Pethick-Lawrence, Annie Cobden-Sanderson, and Ethel Arnold. Audiences were swept up by their accounts of the courageous actions of women in England.

In addition to lecturing on the east coast, British representatives inspired local supporters to establish new

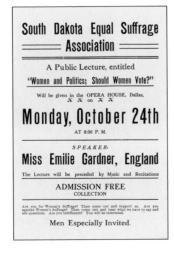

South Dakota Equal Suffrage Association

A Public Lecture, entitled "Women and Politics; Should Women Vote?"

Will be given in the OPERA HOUSE, Dallas, ㅈ ㅈ on ㅈ ㅈ

Monday, October 24th

AT 8:30 P. M.

SPEAKER:

Miss Emilie Gardner, England

The Lecture will be preceded by Music and Recitations

ADMISSION FREE COLLECTION

Are you for Women's Suffrage? Then come out and support us. Are you against Women's Suffrage? Then come out and hear what we have to say and ask questions. Are you indifferent? You will be interested.

Men Especially Invited.

groups in Connecticut, Missouri, North Dakota, and elsewhere. Several visiting speakers joined the efforts to convert voters during the campaigns in California, Wisconsin, Nevada, Massachusetts, and other states.

While they were winning sympathy and funds for their own struggle, British suffragists were also forging close relationships with American activists and helping revitalize the American movement with new methods and a new determination.

Left: Bringing news to South Dakota in 1910.

A Pioneer's Daughter Returns

CHARISMATIC AND full of confidence, Harriot Stanton Blatch was a persuasive speaker when she took the podium urging working women to mobilize for the vote. Taking a different approach from Carrie Catt's Society Plan, Blatch, the daughter of Elizabeth Cady Stanton, founded the Equality League of Self-Supporting Women in New York City in the autumn of 1906 "to bring to suffrage the strength of women engaged in wage-earning occupations."

Blatch returned to the U.S. in 1902 at the age of 46 after living in England for twenty years. Fresh from her experience in the Fabian Society and other British reform groups, she brought a genuine appreciation of the importance of militant trade unions and of working women (and men) in the struggle for equal rights.

Blatch was critical of America's woman suffrage activity, particularly the "unin-spired" regime of tea parties and parlor meetings. Confronting the New York suffrage movement, Blatch later declared it "completely in a rut." She accused suffragists of simplicity and naivete, and observed that "there did not seem to be a grain of political knowledge in the movement."

Through work with the recently formed Women's Trade Union League she met other politically active women including Leonora O'Reilly and Rose Schneiderman. With their help she set about involving rank and file women in the suffrage cause and drawing on some of the energy and vitality of the labor movement. "Blatch's special contribution," noted biographer Ellen DuBois, "was her understanding of the bonds and common interests uniting industrial and professional women workers."

Above: Harriot Stanton Blatch on the platform. At right is Rose Schneiderman.

The Equality League of Self-Supporting Women Confronts the New York Legislature

SHORTLY AFTER forming the Equality League of Self-Supporting Women, Harriot Stanton Blatch arranged for trade union women to testify before the New York legislature in Albany in 1907. "To be left out by the State just sets up a prejudice against us," trade unionist Clara Silver told the attentive lawmakers. "Bosses think and women come to think themselves that they don't count for so much as men." The hearing began Blatch's campaign to pressure the legislature to pass the suffrage measure on to voters.

Sponsored by the Equality League, over 300 "self-supporting" and professional

A Band of "American Suffragettes" Boldly Takes to the Streets of New York

DESPITE THE winter chill, the American Suffragettes, including Lydia Commander and librarian Maud Malone, began holding weekly open-air meetings in New York City's Madison Square on December 31, 1907. This was seen as a daring breach of propriety as a woman speaking publicly on the streets to crowds of men was considered scandalous behavior.

Several weeks later, under the name the Progressive Woman Suffrage Union, the women called for the first New York parade for equal suffrage (below). Although denied a permit by police, at least 23 "marching suffragists" still made their way up Broadway from Union Square on February 16, 1908 with hundreds of men and women following them. The event drew positive press coverage and paved the way for more public actions.

Above left: The first unofficial suffrage parade in New York ended with a meeting in a school gymnasium. Top: Police escorted Sophia Loebinger (center) and friends from City Hall on October 28, 1908, after they called on the mayor to discuss women's rights.

women boarded a special train to Albany on February 19, 1908 to attend another hearing on the suffrage amendment. Hundreds of women would subsequently attend legislative hearings as the Equality League grew into a visible force in state politics. Members also began to chart the positions of representatives and to interview and secure pledges from new candidates. Blatch helped direct lobbying work in Albany along with executive secretary Caroline Lexow and lobbyist Hattie Graham.

Visiting English activist Anne Cobden-Sanderson spoke in New York for the Equality League in late 1907 and vividly described the growing militance in the British suffrage movement. Within weeks a band of "American Suffragettes," organized by British activist Bettina Borrman Wells, sprang up to promote the cause with new energy and to try out in New York some of the imaginative actions of their English comrades.

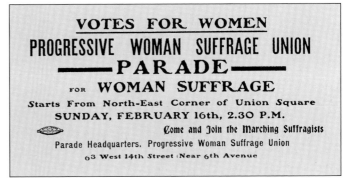

The spectacle of "American Suffragettes" speaking in the street (left) drew a huge crowd of curious men outside New York's City Hall on October 28, 1908. Sophia Loebinger (above) was one of the speakers who addressed the throng. Fearless of ridicule and willing to challenge conventional ideas of femininity, the Suffragettes saw themselves as insurgents organizing bold public events to shake up the social order. "We glory in the reproach that we are theatrical," the monthly *American Suffragette* declared. "The suffragists believe in milder and more conciliatory methods sitting in comfortable parlors and halls. We on the other hand believe in standing on street corners and fighting our way to recognition." The American Suffragettes disbanded in 1911 confident that they had helped the movement outgrow a more timid and restrained time. Few other Americans used the term "suffragette," which sounded diminutive and, ultimately, too British. The preferred term in the U.S. was "suffragist."

Remembering Elizabeth Cady Stanton and the 60th Anniversary of Seneca Falls

To PUBLICIZE the renewed effort for suffrage in New York, and to honor the memory of their mother and other pioneers, Harriot Blatch and her sister Margaret organized a celebration of the sixtieth anniversary of the 1848 Woman's Rights Convention at Seneca Falls.

The May 25, 1908 memorial included the dedication of a bronze tablet on the wall of the old Wesleyan Chapel where the 1848 convention had been held. Designed by Mrs. St. John Matthews, the plaque (above center) pictured a woman in a long dress holding a laurel wreath and a call for justice, standing next to a shield which read: "On this spot . . . Elizabeth Cady Stanton moved this resolution, which was seconded by Frederick Douglass: 'That it is the duty of the women of this country to secure to themselves their sacred right to the elective franchise.'"

The observance provided the daughters of Stanton, dead nearly six years, with an opportunity to uphold the memory of their mother's achievements. The growing popularity of Susan B. Anthony had threatened to eclipse her brilliant and less single-minded colleague.

The Seneca Falls gathering also served as a send-off for the Equality League's first open-air speaking tour. Blatch and Maud Malone followed the celebration with a strenuous two week "trolley car campaign" eastward through upstate New York. Using mainly public transportation, the two women held open-air meetings in town after town, addressing men in the street and outside factories before ending with a meeting at Vassar College in Poughkeepsie.

Above: Dedicating the plaque in Seneca Falls.

Inez Milholland was drawn to the Equality League after graduating from Vassar in 1909. Talented and idealistic, she testified at legislative hearings, organized meetings, and often shared the platform with Harriot Blatch. Daughter of a wealthy progressive, Milholland traveled to England, studied law, and picketed with the shirtwaist strikers. Attractive, passionate, and well educated, Milholland epitomized the New Woman of popular culture. Her adventures in academia and on the picket line were featured in an unusual illustrated "strip" (below) from 1910. Once charged with "inciting a riot" in a police station, she was a suffragist the media could love.

College junior Inez Milholland agreed to arrange the final meeting of the Equality League's speaking tour at Vassar, Harriot Blatch's alma mater, in June 1908. However, the college president refused to permit any suffrage gathering on the campus. Not to be outdone, Milholland moved the meeting to the lawn of a neighboring cemetery. There forty students gathered to hear Blatch, Charlotte Perkins Gilman, and industrial worker Rose Schneiderman speak about the cause.

The Equality League was also helping women establish a presence in the rough wards of New York City. After the league won the right for women to act as poll watchers to help guard against ballot fraud, league vice-president Elizabeth Ellsworth Cook (above) proudly took her place among election officials in November 1909. Blatch and Alberta Hill also served as watchers and when they encountered two drunken officials they had them removed. Through their involvement and persistence suffragists began to participate in, and reform, the all-male political world.

WEDNESDAY THE NEW YORK EVENING JOURNAL, JANUARY 19, 1910. WEDNESDAY

Scenes in the Life of Miss Milholland, Arrested as a Strike Picket, Illustrated

Miss Inez Milholland, daughter of wealthy John E. Milholland, with every luxury that money could buy, goes to Vassar winning class honors.

Upon graduating she went to England to help the Suffragettes, is shown in the top picture; underneath she is shown studying law at New York University.

While acting as a picket for the girl shirtwaist strikers in Waverley place she is warned away and roughly handled by a policeman, who forces her to cross the street, where she waits until she sees other girls arrested and taken to the police station.

Upon following the girls who have been arrested, she is arrested herself in the police station and charged with disorderly conduct, the charge being afterward changed to that of inciting a riot.

When arraigned in the police court she accuses Police Captain Henry of striking one of the girl shirtwaist strikers, and also complains of being roughly treated by the police herself while in the station house.

Revitalizing the Suffrage Movement in New York City

Harriot Blatch not only recruited "self-supporting" professional and working women to the suffrage cause, she also involved a number of wealthier benefactors. One of Blatch's early converts was New York society leader Katherine Duer Mackay, the wife of the founder of International Telephone and Telegraph. With Blatch's encouragement Mackay started her own Equal Franchise Society in December 1908 which drew other "women of fashion" to the cause and gave it a respectability in the city which it had not enjoyed be-

fore. Mackay also supported Blatch's lobbying efforts in Albany for several years, although she considered more publicity-oriented methods too unladylike.

Alva Belmont, flamboyant wife of a railway magnate, was another important recruit. Inspired by the militant English suffragettes and influenced by Anna Howard Shaw and Ida Husted Harper, Belmont formed her own Political Equality Association in 1909 and offered to help financially strapped NAWSA.

Blatch built up her political base in New York City. With support from wealthy and

middle-class women, and the involvement of working-class women, she worked to orchestrate public opinion to show politicians in Albany the growing demand for suffrage. The Equality League increased its political involvement, sending deputations to the state capital, testifying before the legislature, canvassing election districts, and organizing in workplaces. Within a few years Blatch shaped a program to convince legislators that, regardless of their own beliefs, it would be both wise and expedient of them to place woman suffrage before the voters.

Biographer Ellen DuBois noted: "Blatch was particularly drawn to the 'virile' world of politics, which she characterized as a male 'sport' she was sure she could master." Blatch was delighted that executive secretary Caroline Lexow, who came from Barnard and the College Equal Suffrage League, "loved the game of politics as much as I did."

Above: Harriot Blatch, in the rear, her daughter Nora Blatch at the wheel, and other Equality League members demonstrated outside the polls in 1908.

"The New Woman – Wash Day"

"I tell you woman's suffrage would strengthen the solar plexus of the world."

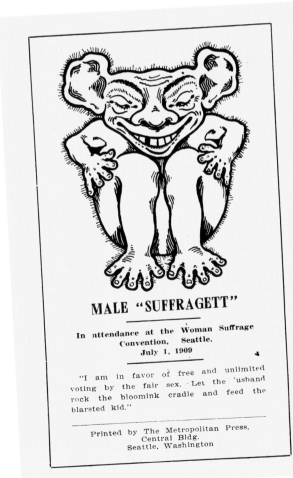

MALE "SUFFRAGETT"

In attendance at the Woman Suffrage Convention, Seattle, July 1, 1909

"I am in favor of free and unlimited voting by the fair sex. Let the 'usband rock the bloomink cradle and feed the blarsted kid."

Printed by The Metropolitan Press, Central Bldg. Seattle, Washington

Entering Popular Culture in New Ways

IN THE early 20th century, as suffrage activity grew in the U.S. and Great Britain, the cause began to enter popular culture in new ways. Widely circulated media like magazines, post cards, photo-view cards, and moving pictures usually treated the idea of women voting in a humorous or derogatory way. But occasionally they were quite serious and captured the true ·spirit of the movement.

Hundreds of popular songs and post card parodies, along with scores of silent comedies and melodramas, were produced between 1900 and 1915. But portraying suffragists in print and on the giant screen lent them new importance, and cute or even insult- ·ing depictions similarly kept the idea before the public.

Before long, American suf- fragists began producing their own propaganda, including post cards, posters, songs, car- toons, novelties, and even a few motion pictures which cultivated an attitude of re- spect instead of ridicule. Dozens of pin-back buttons also popularized the cause.

Some businesses began to incorporate woman suffrage into their marketing – a clear indication that things were changing. Advertisements for products such as stove polish, toothpaste, breakfast cereal, and tea carried a Votes for Women appeal, and particu- lar accessories like hats, capes, and umbrellas were adopted by supporters and used to further advertise the cause.

Above: Humorous panels from two stereo-view cards. Left: A post card ridiculed male supporters at NAWSA's 1909 convention in Seattle.

SUFFRAGETTE MADONNA

Women Writers' Suffrage League.

Advertisers and commercial publishers of sheet music (facing page) and inexpensive picture post cards (above) exploited the theme of woman suffrage in a variety of ways. While many depictions were satirical or even vicious, others showed ironic humor and honest conviction. Some popular cards were printed and collected in sets.

Suffragists produced a number of post cards themselves, including some which reprinted artwork from the British movement (above, bottom center) where symbolic imagery was more developed. Favorable color illustrations such as these carried a strong visual power in the early 20th century and gave suffragists greater control over how their cause was perceived by the general public.

Harriot Blatch's Equality League Becomes a Force in New York

Harriot Stanton Blatch and the Equality League of Self-Supporting Women created a stir on October 25, 1909 by inviting the controversial leader of the militant British suffragettes, Emmeline Pankhurst, to speak in the U.S. Her sold-out meeting of over 3,000 in Carnegie Hall was the largest suffrage meeting held in New York up to that time. Blatch shared the platform with Anna Howard Shaw, who welcomed the magnetic British figure to the U.S. Pankhurst won over her listeners with her eloquence, poise, and clarity of purpose. "It is by going to prison, rather than by any arguments we have employed . . . that we will eventually win over all England," the fiery orator declared at one point in her two hour speech. Her month-long American tour was a tremendous success and influenced numerous supporters in other states.

Above: Harriot Stanton Blatch in New York.

Carrie Catt Creates a New Suffrage Party

Four days after Emmeline Pankhurst spoke, Carrie Catt used the same hall to launch the Woman Suffrage Party of Greater New York. The meeting was called by an Interurban Council of 20 suffrage societies which Catt had organized earlier in the year. Eight hundred delegates and 200 alternates agreed with Catt that suffrage work in the city should be organized along political lines. Offering a moderate alternative to British-style militancy, Catt told the new coalition that the WSP would convert New York by dividing it into election precincts, the way voters were organized. This would allow suffragists to wage a more systematic and effective political battle. In the growing rivalry between Catt and Harriot Blatch, the WSP would serve as the political "machine" which would come to dominate the New York movement.

Above: Carrie Chapman Catt. Left: Catt (center) addressed the 1909 founding meeting.

Defining the Moment for a New Revolution

THE CREATION of the Woman Suffrage Party in October 1909 signaled women's readiness to take united action to win their political freedom. Borrowing from John Trumbull's famous painting, *The Declaration of Independence* (left rear), artist Paul Stahr placed the gathering in a flattering historical context for the May 14, 1910 issue of *Harper's Weekly*. The picture featured leading suffragists in patriotic poses. Party founder Carrie Catt sits at the desk with Harriot Blatch, Katherine Mackay, and other suffrage leaders standing before her. Alva Belmont is seated second from the left. One reporter observed that when women of wealth went into the equal rights movement, "the papers were compelled to follow. . . . Suffrage became popular, practically overnight." But as middle- and upper-class women became more active in suffrage organizations, they tended to displace working and trade union women whose influence gradually declined. When the WSP grew more centralized and bureaucratic, both Blatch and Belmont withdrew. Over the following years the party thrived on many of the innovations pioneered by the Equality League and encouraged the drive to win over the New York legislature.

Left: "Another Declaration of Independence."

The program cover for the 1909 International Congress (above) bore the image of a woman in darkness waiting for the coming dawn. Ancient symbols on the post card below emphasized the "sacred law" of equality. When challenged to comment on the "militant" tactics of British suffragettes, alliance members resolved that "since riot, revolution and disorder have never been construed into an argument against man suffrage, we protest against the practice of the opponents of woman suffrage to interpret 'militancy' employed by the minority in one country as an excuse for withholding the vote from the women of the world."

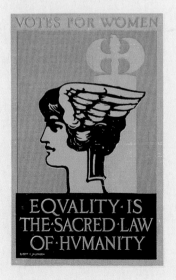

Building the International Woman Suffrage Alliance

THE INTERNATIONAL Woman Suffrage Alliance had been officially organized in Berlin in 1904. It grew steadily over the following ten years under Carrie Catt's leadership. Congresses were generally held every other year in countries showing favorable prospects for benefit from such an impressive international gathering.

After a popular 1909 congress in London, delegates from 24 countries with suffrage associations met in Stockholm in 1911 and in Budapest in June 1913. Decorating each congress were colorful flags and suffrage banners including the Alliance's own (displayed above and right), with "Justice" embroidered in gold on white satin, which was a gift of Swedish suffragist Lotten von Kroemer.

The Budapest congress welcomed the admission of the Chinese Woman Suffrage Association, although members were unable to attend. Dr. Aletta Jacobs, widely-traveled president of the Netherlands Association, told the conference that she had heard Chinese women speak in crowded meetings "with an eloquence none of us can surpass." She added, "You cannot imagine how hard is the struggle for liberty which

they have to make."

Organized by Rosika Schwimmer, the Budapest congress was the last before the outbreak of World War I. It was fondly remembered by its participants for strengthening connections between women of countries soon to be at war and building ties that outlasted the terrible conflict. The International Woman Suffrage Alliance, headquartered in London and financed largely by Americans, stayed open throughout World War I and kept publishing its official monthly paper, *Jus Suffragii*, but there were no congresses for seven years. ◆

Above: Carrie Catt presides at the Budapest congress in 1913. **Inset:** A promotional stamp portrayed women around the world joining hands before the rising sun.

Dr. Aletta Jacobs and Carrie Catt (seated above, third and fifth from left) joined the Chinese Women's Rights Convention in Shanghai in 1912. The two feminist leaders traveled around the world between April 1911 and November 1912, holding public meetings in towns and cities in Europe, Africa, and Asia. "We spoke with many women all over the East who had never heard of a 'woman's movement,'" Catt reported, "yet isolated and alone they had thought out the entire program of woman's emancipation, not excluding the vote." Uniformed pages (left) greeted delegates to the International Woman Suffrage Alliance's 1911 Congress in Sweden.

Chapter 5: 1910

Forging New Tools

THE YEAR 1910 WAS full of unprecedented activity for woman suffrage. "Politicians took notice," reported journalist Ida Husted Harper, "but they remained cold. This political question had not yet entered politics."

That, however, would soon change.

The rise of a progressive reform movement in several states and the campaigns of suffragists in Great Britain inspired American suffragists to experiment with more innovative methods, including open-air meetings, parades, and automobile tours. Buoyed by the energy of a new generation of activists, suffragists across the country rebuilt their state organizations, often after years of decreasing activity. They launched new campaigns to persuade their legislatures to place a suffrage amendment before the voters.

In four western states, Washington, Oregon, Oklahoma, and South Dakota, the measure was placed on the November 8 ballot and suffragists conducted vigorous campaigns. Harriot Stanton Blatch and the Equality League continued working to gain support in the New York legislature, organizing the first large woman suffrage parade, interviewing and pledg-

Nora Blatch, granddaughter of Elizabeth Cady Stanton, graduated from Cornell University in 1905 and became the first female civil engineer. Predictably, she was also an active suffragist.

ing new candidates, and waging their first campaign to defeat a political opponent.

Suffrage leaders continued to make annual presentations to congressional committees but there was no legislative progress. Politicians felt no

Youthful and stylish suffragists wearing yellow sashes and carrying signs graced the cover of the July 4, 1909 magazine section of the pro-suffrage *San Francisco Sunday Call* (facing page). The newspaper editorialized that equal suffrage would abolish "the anomalous and indefensible distinction between the human rights of the being born male and the being born female." Four stars still represented the four "free states" in 1910, but members of a new generation of women were joining older suffragists to forge new tools to advance their cause.

pressure and NAWSA's tiny Congressional Committee reflected its parent body's ambivalence about political lobbying, as well as doubts about the prospects of a woman suffrage amendment to the U.S. Constitution.

Across the country suffragists tried to put their demand before the public in a growing number of ways. In addition to hosting lectures, distributing literature, issuing press material, and writing letters, local societies often sponsored floats in 4th of July and Labor Day parades. The one above, from Chicago's July 4, 1910 parade, carried a tableau of women and a popular quote from Abraham Lincoln. Suffragists also attended state and county fairs where they could reach visitors from all parts of the state. Young volunteers (right) displayed their banners to fairgoers in front of their Votes for Women booth in Hartford, Connecticut.

Petitioning Congress for a Constitutional Amendment

IN 1909 suffragists launched a year-long drive to collect one million signatures asking Congress to pass the Federal suffrage amendment. Carrie Chapmen Catt proposed the ambitious effort as a way for NAWSA to take a more active role in directing the energies of its state associations. National petition drives were a method abolitionists and temperance advocates had used earlier.

While the drive for signatures gave direction to local supporters, it also stretched the resources of many groups, like the Pennsylvania association which only had a small core of workers, no headquarters, and virtually no money. Suffragists in the states still did their best to meet NAWSA's request. Wisconsin collected about 18,000 signatures, Utah obtained 40,000, Nebraska secured 10,386, Minnesota furnished 20,300, and New York gathered over 72,000.

Florence Luscomb in Massachusetts described the method behind such efforts. "Sometimes we hired booth space at the county fairs, sometimes only had a crew of workers among the crowds passing out leaflets, soliciting signatures to the petitions, and arguing with all comers. Suffrage campaigning was always one petition after another, which gave one a reason for approaching strangers and an opening for discussion."

A parade of fifty decorated automobiles filled with suffragists (above) finally delivered the "monster petition" containing over 404,000 signatures to Congress in mid-April 1910. Congressmen, however, barely took notice. Without the vote, the women were told, they were politically powerless. The familiar refrain, even from supportive politicians, was "Go win more states." The Federal suffrage amendment had not been called out of committee for fourteen years.

Above: A parade of fifty automobiles delivered suffragists' 1910 petition to Congress.

VOTES FOR WOMEN

WOMAN SUFFRAGE HEADQUARTERS

W.S.H.

WOMAN SUFFRAGE HEADQUARTERS 505 FIFTH AVE. NEW YORK.

Alva Belmont Helps NAWSA Move into New Headquarters in New York City

ONE RESULT of the International Woman Suffrage Alliance meeting in London in 1909 was the involvement of wealthy New York society figure Alva Belmont. Recently widowed, and inspired by the vigor of the English suffragettes, Belmont began to devote her time and fortune to the suffrage cause in the U.S. She generously paid the costs of moving NAWSA headquarters from Warren, Ohio, to New York City.

Belmont rented the entire seventeenth floor of a new office building on Fifth Avenue and for two years covered the rent for NAWSA and the New York State Woman Suffrage Association as well as the expenses of a new national press bureau. NAWSA later moved to quarters at 171 Madison Avenue. Belmont's Political Equality Association organized new clubs of wage-earning women and was the first white New York suffrage society to involve Black women.

Relocating to cosmopolitan New York offered NAWSA greater public visibility, more access to the press, and an opportunity to grow at a critical time.

Above: A new home.

United Under a Common Cause, Divided on Tactics and Style

SUFFRAGISTS (ABOVE) from around the country met in Washington D.C. on April 14, 1910 for NAWSA's annual convention. President Anna Howard Shaw praised the "unprecedented rising suffrage sentiment," but NAWSA itself was wracked with division. Members in some states resented taking directions

from national leaders who were almost all from the east. In addition, many southern women opposed a constitutional amendment because they feared Federal intervention would erode states' rights.

Regional concerns, differences in style and experience, and personal rivalries all played out in the national association, making progress difficult. Without strong leadership or clear direction, NAWSA drifted for many years. As a consequence, women in the individual states were left to carry out their own campaigns with limited national support.

President William Howard Taft welcomed the suffragists at their 1910 convention, but when he suggested that the "least desirable" citizens voted initially when a new class was enfranchised, "a slight hissing" reportedly arose from the audience, some of whom were voters from the west. NAWSA formally apologized for the audience's behavior, but it was becoming clear that the patience and quiet tolerance of some women were coming to an end.

Above: Anna Howard Shaw (front row, center) with 1910 convention delegates, NAWSA officers, and state leaders in Washington D.C.

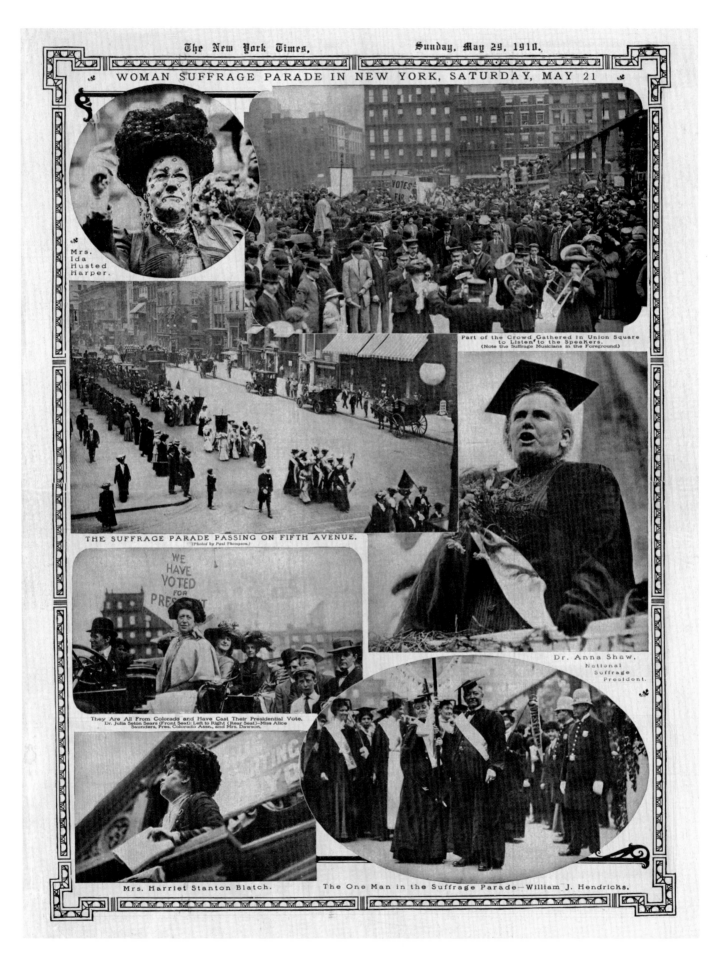

WOMAN SUFFRAGE PARADE IN NEW YORK, SATURDAY, MAY 21

Mrs. Ida Husted Harper.

Part of the Crowd Gathered in Union Square to Listen to the Speakers. (Note the Suffrage Musicians in the Foreground.)

THE SUFFRAGE PARADE PASSING ON FIFTH AVENUE. (Photo by Paul Thompson.)

WE HAVE VOTED FOR PRESIDENT

Dr. Anna Shaw, National Suffrage President.

They Are All From Colorado and Have Cast Their Presidential Vote. Dr. Julia Seton Sears (Front Seat); Left to Right (Rear Seat)—Miss Alice Saunders, Pres. Colorado Assn., and Mrs. Dawson.

Mrs. Harriet Stanton Blatch.

The One Man in the Suffrage Parade—William J. Hendricks.

The First Large Suffrage Parade in New York Sounds a New Tone of Urgency

As a "PROTEST against the legislature for its indifference to our demands for woman suffrage," Harriot Stanton Blatch and the Equality League of Self-Supporting Women organized the first major woman suffrage parade in New York City on May 21, 1910. Over four hundred determined women, most dressed in dark outfits, marched four abreast in a tight column down Fifth Avenue past several thousand curious onlookers to a mass meeting in Union Square.

The women carried banners protesting the inaction of the state legislature and demanding "Not Favor but Justice." Suffragists had been working for several years to advance the measure but kept encountering stubborn opposition in Albany. Speeches by suffragists and local politicians climaxed the demonstration, which energized supporters and increased pressure on representatives in the state capital.

Blatch's call for a suffrage parade had met with opposition from some of the more conservative women, who thought that such a public display was undignified. Society women like Alva Belmont refused to take part, and Blatch remembered being told that "a parade would set suffrage back fifty years." Despite the early dissension, however, the suffrage parade was such a success that it became a popular annual event and a key barometer for growing public support.

Facing Page: News of the May 21, 1910 suffrage parade. Above: Supporters rally in Union Square.

The Equality League Tries to Unseat a Political Opponent

Faced with the refusal of the New York legislature even to consider the woman suffrage measure, Harriot Blatch and the Equality League implemented a new strategy in September 1910. They chose a prominent New York City anti-suffragist, Republican Assemblyman Artemus Ward, and launched a campaign to defeat him in the upcoming election.

Their diligent activity led *The New York World* to report with some amazement, "The ladies are campaigning. Early and late, afoot and in the horseless, from the curbstone and the top of tables, on street corners and door steps . . . they are demanding the vote and the scalps of the enemy." Ward was re-elected by the narrowest of margins, but suffragists were delighted to test their strength in the political world and to gain experience for the future.

In November 1910 Blatch announced that the Equality League of Self-Supporting Women would change its name to the Women's Political Union to reflect the broader interests of the organization and its more political focus. Acknowledging the influence of Emmeline Pankhurst's Women's Social and Political Union in England, Blatch even adopted the British group's colors – purple, white, and green.

The Woman Suffrage Party was also growing in numbers and influence. During much of 1911 and 1912, while Carrie Catt was out of the country, the WSP recruited new members and continued its political district organizing work under Mrs. W.W. Penfield, Harriet Burton Laidlaw, and others. Mary Beard edited *The Woman Voter*, the party's monthly journal.

Above: Campaigning in New York. Below: Targeting a political opponent.

Political Rally of Woman Suffragists

TWENTY-FIFTH ASSEMBLY DISTRICT

IN

UNION SQUARE

Thursday Evening, November 3d, at 8 o'clock

ORGANIZED TO HELP

DEFEAT ARTEMAS WARD, Jr.

TORCHLIGHT HERALDS line up at 43 East 22d Street, 7.30 p.m.

Come and Bring Your Chinese Lantern to Help the Women of the Twenty-fifth

Charlotte Perkins Gilman: "Woman must stand free with man."

Charlotte Perkins Gilman
was the foremost feminist
intellectual of her time and
a strong advocate of woman
suffrage. For years on the
edge of poverty, Gilman, 25,
left an unhappy marriage
following a nervous break-
down in 1885 and moved to
California where she began
writing and lecturing to support herself and her young
daughter. Although shaken
by the "scandal" of her
divorce in 1894, she concentrated on her writing. Her
books, short stories, poetry,
and prose won her international fame. She also produced *The Forerunner,* a
monthly magazine (below),
for seventeen years. Her life
ended with characteristic
controversy when she com-
mitted suicide in 1935 rather
than become incapacitated
by incurable breast cancer.

CHARLOTTE PERKINS
Gilman had been active
with Harriot Blatch and the
Equality League since 1908. A
passionate and persuasive advocate for equal rights,
Gilman championed political
and economic independence
for women. "Set the woman
on her own feet, as a free, intelligent, able human being,"
Gilman wrote. "Woman must
stand free with man."

The popular writer was
widely sought as a speaker at
meetings and conventions.
She broke through conven-
tional notions of gender roles
with keen insight and ironic
humor. Gilman promoted the
ideal of a free, financially
independent, and socially involved woman – the very
image suffragists advanced.

Gilman's reputation grew
following the publication of
her "feminist manifesto,"
Women and Economics, in
1898 and its translation into
seven languages. In this
provocative call to rethink the
way society is organized,
Gilman raised such new "social organization" ideas as co-
operative kitchens and
centralized nurseries to help
free women for greater social
involvement.

Gilman was a favorite of
college women and suffragists
although her progressive
views sometimes clashed with
those of more conservative
women. She was enormously
influential and, as historian
Eleanor Flexner noted, "None
of her contemporaries who
labored for women's rights
was untouched by her thinking." Carrie Catt and other
suffragists credited Gilman
for revolutionizing popular
attitudes towards women.

**Above: Charlotte Perkins
Gilman spoke from an automobile at the Union Square
rally following the 1911 suffrage parade. Alice Park of
California is on the right.**

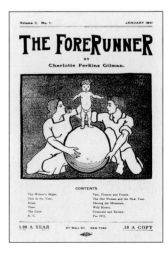

Out Into the Open Air: Early Street Meetings in Boston

FOLLOWING the brief "trolley-car campaign" in New York in 1908, open-air street meetings grew in popularity, and supporters began new efforts in several eastern states. Suffragists realized that outdoor meetings were an effective way to reach large numbers of voters. The women also learned, from their audiences' immediate feedback, to make their cause as exciting, important, and easy to grasp as possible. Boston's first street meeting was held during the summer of 1909 at Bedford Common by Mary Ware Dennett, Teresa Crowley, Lenora Little, Susan Walker Fitzgerald, and Katharine Dexter McCormick.

In August, Fitzgerald, secretary of the Boston Equal Suffrage Association for Good Government, proposed a wider trip. During their

first "trolley tour" the women usually spoke in three separate towns, finding audiences in parks and on street corners in the afternoons and evenings and at factory gates at noon.

During the summer of 1910, Massachusetts suffragists organized a series of outdoor meetings throughout the industrial part of the state. The speakers, including three British suffragists, addressed immigrant men and women with the help of interpreters who translated their speeches into Italian, Yiddish,

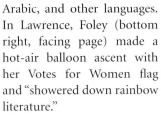

Arabic, and other languages. In Lawrence, Foley (bottom right, facing page) made a hot-air balloon ascent with her Votes for Women flag and "showered down rainbow literature."

Open-air meetings were held throughout Boston and the beach resorts for years and women in other states were encouraged to try similar methods. Philadelphia suffragists started open-air meetings in July 1911.

Above: Suffragists spoke on Bedford Common in 1909. Left: Florence Luscomb (center) waited by the tracks with Katharine McCormick and Margaret Foley on the left, and Susan Fitzgerald and Teresa Crowley on the right, before their first open-air trolley tour.

Florence Luscomb was one of the young college women drawn to the suffrage movement in the early 1900s. Luscomb, who was five years old when she first heard Susan B. Anthony speak, observed the English movement in 1911 and later participated in several state campaigns. An MIT graduate in architecture, she volunteered as a newsgirl (left) when *The Woman's Journal* began to reach out to a larger public through street sales. She recalled averaging eight sales an hour every Saturday afternoon on the "coldest and windiest" corner in Boston. She could often be found distributing literature (above), and she remained a activist until her death at 98 in 1985.

Automobile Tours Reach Rural Voters

Using the relatively new automobile to carry the suffrage message to areas throughout a state was another method that was quick to catch on. Grace Wilbur Trout, president of the Chicago Political Equality League, organized the first automobile tour in central Illinois on July 11, 1910. It included Ella Stewart, Grace Nicholes, and Catharine McCulloch and reached out to voters in sixteen towns who were alerted by posters and press announcements. As a rule, McCulloch addressed the legal aspects, Nicholes offered the working woman's view, and Stewart gave an international perspective. A man usually drove.

One of the traveling suffrage speakers (above) made a point before a rural Illinois audience on August 19 from a platform covered with patriotic bunting. Additional tours were organized in Illinois and other states.

Left and above: Reaching voters in rural Illinois.

With bonnets securely fastened, a carload of Massachusetts suffragists (left) set out on an open-air automobile tour from Boston's Copley Square in 1910. Women quickly incorporated the new "horseless carriages" into their parades and campaigns. A post card and poster (above) publicized tours in Connecticut and Illinois.

Suffragists Win a Stunning Victory in Washington State

By the end of 1910 the late Susan B. Anthony had become, in historian Sara Hunter Graham's words, a "suffrage saint" personifying the cause and uniting women nationwide. NAWSA leaders promoted a somewhat sanitized image of the pioneer reformer, giving her long career a new respectability attractive to middle-class women who generally avoided political controversy but whose support was critical to the movement.

THE 1910 campaign in Washington state resulted from the persistent efforts of suffrage organizer Emma Smith DeVoe. A protegee of Susan B. Anthony, DeVoe had worked on NAWSA's Organization Committee with Carrie Catt in the 1890s. When DeVoe settled in Washington she called together local supporters.

The suffragists quietly and skillfully lobbied representatives in the state capital and in February 1909 won their overwhelming approval for the referendum. DeVoe was elected president of the Washington Equal Suffrage Association and ran the twenty-month campaign with little fanfare. She decided on a "campaign of partly speech making and

partly 'still hunting.'" Resisting eastern efforts to run the drive, she maintained harmonious relationships with visitors but insisted that most volunteers be state residents. The emphasis was on intensive work among women – the wives, sisters, and mothers of the men voting.

Avoiding large or spectac-

Woman Suffrage!
MASS MEETING
TO CELEBRATE
THE VICTORY
FOR WOMAN SUFFRAGE
IN THE
State of Washington
AT
COOPER UNION
Thursday, November 10th
8 P. M.
Fine Speakers   Music   All Welcome

ular events, organizers addressed meetings of church groups, Granges, farmers, and labor unions, asking voters to "Give the Women a Square Deal." DeVoe's low-profile approach did not reveal the movement's strength until it was too late for the opposition to respond.

On November 8, Washington voters approved equal suffrage nearly two to one, 52,299 to 29,676, and supporters across the country rejoiced. The fourteen-year drought of state victories had finally ended.

Above: Washington suffragists posed with signs and sashes. Facing page: College women posted signs before the election. Left: Celebrating in New York.

Emma Smith DeVoe, as president of the Washington Equal Suffrage Association, led the campaign that won woman suffrage in that state. DeVoe became one of the most effective suffrage leaders in the west after working for years in various states. A former NAWSA organizer, she had set up suffrage clubs in South Dakota, Illinois, and Idaho before settling in Washington with her supportive husband. Her work in Oregon in 1906 showed her the strengths and weaknesses of different campaign strategies and led to her success in Washington. Described as "talented, brilliant and logical" by the press, DeVoe was a pragmatic, sensible leader who was also an accomplished vocalist. The victory in Washington added a fifth star to the suffrage stamp below.

Voters Defeat Woman Suffrage in Three States

ALTHOUGH DELIGHTED by the victory in Washington, suffragists faced a familiar series of defeats in Oregon, South Dakota, and Oklahoma on November 8, 1910. The legislature had approved the measure in South Dakota but suffragists had to use the new initiative and referendum process to place the amendment on the ballot in the other states.

The Oregon state association under Abigail Scott Duniway ran its fifth campaign, the stillest of "still hunts," with little organizing and a controversial measure

limiting suffrage to taxpaying women. It lost 58,800 to 36,200.

In South Dakota, a third attempt was led by Lydia B. Johnson, head of the state Political Equality League, but it also was defeated 57,709 to 35,290. Suffragists in both states began to plan new campaigns.

In Oklahoma, women collected over 38,500 signatures of voters to put suffrage on the ballot and under Kate H. Biggers' leadership waged a heroic but woefully underfunded drive. State officer Adelia Stephens remembered

going into "the most hostile part of the state" and speaking "from boxes and wagons; in little dark school houses with only one smoky kerosene lamp . . . [and] before large, unsympathetic crowds at open-air meetings. It was an experience that tested endurance and loyalty almost to the breaking point."

The measure was opposed by the powerful Democratic machine and voters defeated it by over 40,000 votes, 128,928 to 88,808. Still, the victory in Washington restored hope that progress was actually possible. ◆

"The Unknown" (right), a cartoon from the July 10, 1912 issue of *Puck* magazine, suggested that the concept of equal rights was as mysterious, and as frightening, to the average politician as fire was to chimpanzees. Suffragists encountered similar reactions. In 1910, as they had for years, NAWSA leaders appeared before congressional committees to plead their case even though the bill had not been called out of committee since the 1890s. Harriet Taylor Upton challenged the House Judiciary Committee "to report against us if you will not report for us. . . . but break your long years of silence." Laura Clay was even more direct. "Must we crawl on our knees to ask you for that which we feel we have a right to demand?"

Meanwhile women who had won equal rights in the west were beginning to organize themselves. In January 1911 a National Council of Women Voters was established in Tacoma, Washington, and Emma Smith DeVoe was elected president. The non-partisan, non-sectarian organization aimed to educate new voters, extend suffrage, and secure legislation "in the interest of men and women, of children and the home." As new states passed equal suffrage they joined the Council which DeVoe led until it was merged in 1919 with the League of Women Voters.

THE PUCK PRESS

Expressing the Attitu

THE UNKNOWN.

erage Politician Toward the Woman Suffrage Movement.

Chapter 6: 1911

Tasting Victory in California

THE VICTORY in Washington and the rise of a progressive political movement in the west renewed suffragists' hopes for success in additional states. In 1911 all eyes turned to California, the site of the year's only electoral contest.

Women had been working since 1896 to have the measure put before the voters again. On August 27, 1908, three hundred suffragists marched to the state Republican Party Convention meeting in Oakland to demand a plank endorsing votes for women. The suffrage parade, the only one held in California, was led by Lillian Harris Coffin of the state association and Mrs. Theodore Pinther who carried a hand-embroidered yellow silk suffrage banner. "Vehicles were halted, and the inhabitants gazed open-mouthed at so unusual a sight," reported suffragist Selina Solomons. The ruling Republicans, predictably, declined to act. Regardless, women gradually built up support throughout the state, including most of the rural and foreign-language newspapers.

There was virtually no action being taken on the national level. The long-dormant suffrage amendment was introduced in each ses-

California suffragists marched to the Republican Convention in Oakland in August 1908 seeking its support.

sion of Congress, but the ensuing hearings had become formalities which the politicians involved quickly forgot.

In New York, the Women's Political Union stepped up its drive to win approval from the state legislature. In addition to organizing another

parade, the WPU again selected opponents in the state Assembly and campaigned openly to defeat them.

Even where suffrage was not on the popular ballot, elections were becoming showdowns over the question of equal rights.

Five stars proudly symbolized the equal suffrage states in 1911 on this flag from the Votes for Women Club in San Francisco and on buttons produced during the year. Suffragists in California held fervent hopes that their efforts would add a sixth star. California artist Bertha Boye promoted the cause with her beautiful, warmly colored image (facing page) of a draped woman posed against the Golden Gate with the setting sun behind her. The College Equal Suffrage League printed the award-winning poster. For an entire week in late August 1911 merchants throughout San Francisco displayed it in their shop windows, accompanied by festive decorations in suffrage yellow which supporters called "the color of success." Across the country the cause was drawing more serious attention.

Florence Kelley was one of the college-educated social reformers who came through Jane Addams' Hull House in Chicago and connected woman suffrage with wider social issues. Kelley traveled and spoke widely as an active Socialist and NAWSA board member, encouraging workers and labor activists to support the struggle for equal rights. After the mass meeting in New York advertised below, she and Leonora O'Reilly founded the Wage Earners Suffrage League. Working women like this young Chicago activist (right) learned to speak out in labor disputes by putting their case directly to the public. Many suffragists followed their example.

Building pressure on the New York legislature, suffragists held a second major parade in New York City on May 6, 1911. Distinguished suffrage pioneers, including Rev. Antoinette Blackwell and Anna Garlin Spencer (above), rode in carriages decorated with the Women's Political Union's purple, white, and green flags past tens of thousands of spectators. Also marching, and enduring jeers and insults, were 89 intrepid members of the Men's League for Woman Suffrage (left) led by banker James Lees Laidlaw and professors John Dewey and Vladmir Simkhovitch.

The 1911 Parade Links Labor and Woman Suffrage

Showcasing the growing strength of the New York movement, an extended column of 3,000 women marched down the center of Fifth Avenue during the May 6, 1911 suffrage parade. Organized by the Women's Political Union, the demonstration demanded legislative action and emphasized how working women in particular needed the ballot. Participants marched by trades and professions to show that woman's place was no longer limited to the home. Colorful standards, floats, and marching bands gave the controversial spectacle a contagious excitement. The demonstration included hundreds of trade union women, many society women, and a delegation of college educated women dressed in caps and gowns to emphasize that women were well prepared to vote responsibly. Thousands followed the parade to a rally in Union Square.

Right and above: The March 6 suffrage parade in New York. Below: Rallying afterwards in Union Square.

Targeting Political Opponents
in the New York State Legislature

THREE DAYS after the May 6, 1911 suffrage parade in New York City, fifty members of the Women's Political Union traveled to the state capital in Albany to demand action once again on the suffrage bill. Led by Harriot Stanton Blatch, the women attempted to carry their banners all the way into the Assembly chamber itself. They were politely intercepted by capital guards. Less than a week later, the suffrage bill was finally reported out of committee and scheduled for the first full Senate vote. Opponents, however, were able to forestall action until July. Then the measure was narrowly defeated.

In response, the WPU selected two prominent Democratic opponents in the Assembly and actively campaigned to defeat them in the November election. The suffragists succeeded in overcoming Ron Carew while Louis Cuvillier barely survived. Cuvillier later fumed against "the cunning and shrewdness" of the suffragists. "Woman is dangerous when she wants to gain a point. She will stop at nothing."

"We knew now we could influence an electorate," Blatch remembered with delight. "We could lower majorities. We could drive a man down to defeat."

Above: Harriot Stanton Blatch addressed a Wall Street crowd. Right: Going after an anti-suffragist.

The Campaign for California

SUFFRAGISTS IN California organized a vibrant, open campaign in 1911. With little central direction they harnessed the energy of women and men across the state, helped create countless local suffrage clubs, and built up solid support for equal rights.

The legislature approved the measure early in the year after progressive Republicans were swept into office. Suffragists waged an eight-month "whirlwind campaign" before the special election set for October 10.

Dividing the State

Early in the campaign, state suffragists divided their territory. The California Equal Suffrage Association, led by Elizabeth Lowe Watson, took the northern half. The less populated south was covered by two organizations, the Political Equality League of Los Angeles, founded in April 1910 by Pasadena businessman John Hyde Braly, and the Votes for Women Club, led by pioneer attorney Clara Shortridge Foltz. Involving both men and women, the Political Equality League lined up prominent citizens and helped mobilize support in the legislature.

The public attitude was more amused and indifferent than hostile, noted Louise Herrick Wall of the College League, so "it seemed best for us to put forth positive arguments of a hopeful, constructive sort rather than

Hoping that an intensive campaign in rural areas would offset opposition in the cities, women like the two mounted suffragists above reached voters in the small towns and country districts of California during the 1911 drive.

arguments that ended in criticism or irony."

Experienced organizers from other states lent their talents including Gail Laughlin from Colorado, Jeannette Rankin from Montana, Helen Hoy Greeley from New York, and Helen Todd, Mar-garet Haley and Catharine McCulloch from Illinois. They spoke to members of the Grange, labor unions, women's clubs, and other organizations in each county.

Other volunteers sent out personal letters and generated press material.

Marketing Suffrage

Hardly a "still hunt" which avoided publicity, the California campaign featured early signs of mass marketing and brand advertising. The suffragists refined their message, choosing a "positive, constructive" strategy. They used the most modern means of advertising then available:

giant posters, billboards, leaflets, buttons, pennants, banners, electric signs, and lantern slides at night. Voters were made aware of the issue constantly throughout the year. The Blue Liner, a seven passenger "campaigning car," played an important role, ferrying speakers, organizers, and supplies around the San Francisco Bay Area.

During the campaign, supporters distributed over three million pieces of literature plus over 90,000 Votes for Women buttons and 13,000 pennants in southern California alone. State suffragists sold 50,000 of the popular gold and white "dinner plate" pin (below) during the campaign while Oakland activists appealed to homemakers by furnishing grocers with 10,000 printed paper bags recommending woman suffrage "FOR HOME AND FAMILY."

The contest drew national attention because, in the words of one journalist, votes for women had become "the three small words which constitute the biggest question in the political world today." ◆

To draw a crowd before an open-air speech, a bugler usually sounded a call, which was followed by a song. A chairwoman introduced each speaker and tied all their points together before taking leave of the crowd "instead of allowing it to leave us!" One speaker recalled that the most .popular opening lines were, "I appeal to you as a mother, a grandmother, as a garment worker, a school teacher, a trained nurse . . . as the case might be." Margaret Haley (top, right), a prominent Chicago teacher, was one of several organizers who helped in the California campaign.

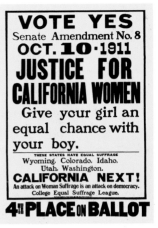

Suffrage workers (left) gathered for a committee meeting in San Francisco during the 1911 campaign. They found that their most effective paid advertisements were the eight-foot-high posters (above), visible for half a block, which appeared on 250 city billboards a month before the election. Huge signs were also erected at the Oakland and San Francisco baseball grounds. Just before the election anti-suffragists posted counter billboards and took out full-page advertisements in the city papers. "Trademark" Amendment 8 buttons (below) were produced by the Clubwoman's Franchise League early in the campaign. Suffragists also produced fliers in Spanish (left), as well as French, Italian, and German, and a post card (facing page) which argued that the ballot was the tool women needed to clean up politics, corruption, and moral decay.

A Massive Effort in California

THREE MONTHS before the election suffragists organized a Central Campaign Committee in northern California to coordinate work among the five most active organizations: the California Equal Suffrage Association, Woman Suffrage Party, Wage Earners League, Clubwoman's Franchise League, and the College Equal Suffrage League. In southern California, the Political Equality League under Mrs. Seward A. Simons printed leaflets in many languages and distributed them door to door to immigrant voters. Supporters at first publicized the number of the amendment (8) before deciding instead to emphasize its place on the ballot (fourth) to lessen voter confusion. The measure was one of 23 on the October 10 ballot.

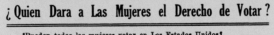

HOMBRES Y MUJERES

¿Quien Dio Al Hombre El Derecho De Votar Y Cuando?

¿Pueden votar todos los hombres en Los Estados Unidos?

Si, si son mayores de 21 años y son nacidos en el país ó naturalizados. (En algunos Estados deben tambien saber leer).

¿Han pedido todos estos hombres el derecho de votar?

No, Ninguno lo ha pedido. El derecho les ha sido concedido por las leyes del país.

¿Cuando las leyes fueron hechas pidieron todos estos hombres el derecho de votar?

No, los representantes que hicieron las leyes, fueron suficientemente previsores para saber que no podrían formar una república con los pocos ciudadanos, á quienes era permitido votar en los tiempos Coloniales— aquellos hombres que llenaban los requisitos de religión, nacimiento y que tenian propiedades—y en consecuencia todos éstos requisitos fueron suprimidos y á la mayoria de los hombres les fué concedido el derecho de votar.

NOTA, ésto fué hecho por razones políticas y no porque los hombres pidieron el derecho de votar.

LOS DESCENDIENTES de estos hombres han votado desde entonces.

¿ Quien Dara a Las Mujeres el Derecho de Votar ?

¿Pueden todas las mujeres votar en Los Estados Unidos?

No, solamente aquellas que viven in Los Estados de Colorado, Idaho, Utah, Wyoming y Washington.

¿Han pedido todas las mujeres en Los Estados Unidos el derecho de votar?

No, pero el NUMERO DE MUJERES QUE HAN PEDIDO el derecho de votar es mayor que el NUMERO DE HOMBRES QUE HAN PEDIDO ALGUNA cosa en toda la historia de nuestro pais.

Las mujeres son ciudadanas de este país, "aunque sean ó no sean oficialmente reconocidas."

La mujer debe obtener el derecho de votar por las mismas razones políticas por las que el hombre lo ha obtenido y no PORQUE lo pide.

La mujer forma parte del pueblo y nadie se atrevería á negar ésto. Abraham Lincoln definió una república ideal "como un gobierno, formado del pueblo, elegido por el pueblo y para el pueblo," pero el nuestro esta formado del pueblo por la mitad del pueblo.

El país necesita la cooperación de todos sus ciudadanos.

Los hombres y las mujeres necesitan la oportunidad, de trabajar juntos para el mismo fin y en igualdad de condiciones.

Votese por Dar la Mujer de California el Derecho de Votar
EN LA ELECCION DEL 10 DE OCTUBRE, 1911

Political Equality League, Choral Hall, Auditorium Building, Los Angeles, California. Precio, cien por 20 centavos

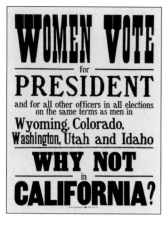

WOMEN VOTE for PRESIDENT and for all other officers in all elections on the same terms as men in **Wyoming, Colorado, Washington, Utah and Idaho** **WHY NOT in CALIFORNIA?**

Signs comparing one state with others (above) were aimed at fostering indignation and a friendly competitiveness among male voters in non-suffrage states. Although politicians in California refused to mention the suffrage amendment, believing it would lose, labor unions endorsed it and Socialist women were particularly active in the south. Members of Local 197 of the Women's Union Label League in San Diego (right) created a float for the 1910 Labor Day parade that displayed a straightforward call for economic equality. The following year, suffragists in San Francisco created a beautiful horse-drawn float which Maud Younger, founder of the Wage Earners' Equal Suffrage League, drove in the Labor Day parade. The float carried several working women with "plain, tired faces" busy with their trades. The sincerity of the appeal, one suffragist observed, "reached men who know what it is . . . to ask for a withheld right."

VOTES FOR WOMEN

John Hyde Braly founded the Political Equality League in Los Angeles and was instrumental in convincing members of the California legislature to put woman suffrage on the ballot. A former educator and retired banker, Braly believed that women's enfranchisement was "a man's job" since it was the men who had to vote on the matter. Braly, who turned 76 in 1911, had come west with his parents by wagon train in 1847. He and his wife helped establish public schools in California and he founded a series of savings banks in Fresno and San Diego. In the early months of 1910 he took the lead recruiting "men of prominence" in Los Angeles and Pasadena who supported equal rights for women. The ensuing Political Equality League, which soon included women, quickly grew into a major organization which ensured approval in the legislature and worked in the multi-ethnic region to win voter approval. Braly, a prosperous, civic-minded business man, exemplified the enthusiastic and principled support for woman suffrage by far-sighted men nationwide.

Reaching Voters Throughout California

THE CALIFORNIA campaign involved an estimated 10,000 suffragists and set a new standard of activity and innovation for state campaigns.

Anticipating strong opposition by saloon and business interests in the cities, suffragists concentrated particularly on the rural districts. To reach distant voters the state suffrage association, College League, and other groups sent speakers, organizers, automobile tours, and press material to the remote corners of the state. Organizers tried to set up small groups in each locality to work up public interest and reach individual voters.

As election day drew near, a College League member in San Francisco described the excitement: "Each day brought a worker in from the field, from far Del Norte, or wooded Humboldt, from logging-camps and mining-ledges, where we had sent our best – wan, brown, laughing

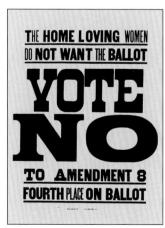

THE **HOME LOVING** WOMEN DO **NOT WANT** THE **BALLOT**

VOTE NO

TO **AMENDMENT 8** FOURTH PLACE **ON BALLOT**

women, worked down to the nerve, but the nerve gay and steady, full of stories of camp and field, of joyous prophecy, full of delight and confidence in the men of the open."

Suffragists encountered more organized opposition than ever before. Groups of business men and socially prominent women were formed to oppose the measure but one supporter dismissed their claims that most women did not want to vote as "largely historical superstitions."

Above: Campaign workers in San Francisco compared notes outside a polling place. Left and facing page: Anti-suffragists' claims.

TO THE VOTERS OF NORTHERN CALIFORNIA

We, the women of the Northern California Association Opposed to Woman Suffrage, urge you not to thrust the womanhood of this State into the political arena, at the request of the small minority of women who are asking for the ballot.

Mrs. Harriet Stanton Blatch, one of the leaders of the world suffrage movement, in Pearson's Magazine, February, 1910, said:

"I've given up the American woman. She's hopeless. If it depends upon her, women will never have the ballot!"

The National Woman Suffrage Organization circulated an appeal in this State during this campaign in which, under the signature of Jessie Ashley, national treasurer, it is admitted that there are only 75,000 organized Suffragists in the United States, working among 93,000,000 people, and that the 75,000 organized Suffragettes are not sufficiently interested in the agitation to give a dollar each to the movement.

In 1895 the question of woman suffrage was put to a referendum vote of the women of Massachusetts. Out of nearly half a million women who might have voted on the question only 22,000 were sufficiently interested to cast a vote either way.

Since that time, the Suffragists have fought every attempt to put the question to a vote of the women, even as they fought it here in California.

When in the polling booth, we ask you to remember that the vast majority of California women do not want to vote.

We ask you not to put upon our shoulders the responsibility of man's work.

The advance of woman—moral, intellectual and economic—has been made without the vote.

Woman now stands outside of politics and may appeal to any party on matters of education and reform.

The ballot does not govern the law of supply and demand, and so cannot affect the wages of woman. It has never raised the wages of man—why should it be expected to do so for woman?

The woman suffrage movement is a backward step in the progress of civilization. Do not permit California to take a step backward.

Women Are Not Free in Suffrage States.

In his story, "The Beast," on page 307, Judge Ben Lindsey has this to say of the Hon. Alma Lafferty: "I went at the beginning of the campaign to practically all the woman's suffrage leaders, who, at national meetings, had been telling how much the women had done for the Juvenile Court in Denver;

and none of them dared help me. Women like Mrs. Mary C. Bradford and Mrs. Lafferty (who was a member of the last Legislature) took the platform against me and supported the System in its attempt to 'get' the Juvenile Court."

On page 306 of the same volume, Judge Lindsey says: "I talked to a number of school teachers . . . they told me they dared not make themselves conspicuous . . . the teachers were afraid of losing their positions."

On page 307 of "The Beast," Judge Lindsey says again: "If anyone believes that woman suffrage is a panacea for all the evils of political life, he does not know what those evils are . . . . The women are as helpless as the rest of us . . . . They are bound by the same bread-and-butter consideration as the rest of us. Their leaders in politics are politicians; when they get their nominations, from the corporate machines, they do the work of the corporations, and there is almost no way . . . .to get a party nomination except from a corporation machine. Women in politics are human beings; they are not 'ministering angels' of an ethereal ideality; and they are unable to free us, because they are not free themselves."

Suffrage Leaders Abuse Their Freedom.

Rev. Anna Shaw, President of the National Woman's Suffrage Association, says:

"I would make motherhood a Governmental institution. I would pension all mothers and have them provided for, first to last, by the State. I believe that motherhood should be independent of man.

"One crying need of our civilization is the presence of women on the police force. I would place a woman policeman at the door of every saloon and dance hall, every nickel theater and every factory."

Mrs. Carrie Chapman Catt, President of the International Woman Suffrage Alliance, says:

"I believe that the time will come, and that comparatively soon, when every American woman who does not earn her own living will be considered a prostitute."

These are the lengths to which the leaders of this movement are willing to go, and any one who favors it, favors them, and must be ready to take the consequence.

Is This a Direct Blow at the American Home?

Mrs. Harriet Stanton Blatch, one of the leaders of the world suffrage movement, said in her discussion of the economic emancipation of woman that she rejoiced in every co-operative working woman's dwelling, because it aimed a blow at the isolated house, and she repeated her proposition regarding the institutional care of children.

Another leading Suffragist, in an article on woman's work in America, says: "Suffrage aims to benefit woman by recognizing her as a perfect equal of man, politically and socially, and by fixing woman's means of support by the State so as to render her independent of man."

Nothing Sacred to Suffragists.

The Suffragists have travestied the Bible, the Declaration of Independence and the American flag.

They have travestied the Bible with their "Woman's Bible," in which they take exception to the Creator as a Heavenly Father, instead of a Divine Pair.

They have travestied the Declaration of Independence—have mocked the most hallowed document of the Nation, and assert that man "has made her (woman), if married, in the eye of the law, civilly dead. He has endeavored, in every way that he could, to destroy her confidence in her own powers, to lessen her self-respect and to make her willing to lead a dependent and abject life."

The tenth count in the Suffrage Declaration of Independence is: "He has usurped the prerogative of Jehovah himself, claiming it is his right to assign for her a sphere of action, when that belongs to her consciousness and her God."

The editors add: "Quite as many false ideas prevail as to woman's true position in the home as elsewhere. Womanhood is the great fact of her life, motherhood and wifehood are but incidental relations."

The American Flag is not good enough for the Suffragists. They have made a mockery of the National emblem, by flaunting the flag with but five stars in the field, signifying that only those five States in which women vote are worthy a representation on the National emblem.

WOMEN DON'T WANT BALLOT.

The great majority of California women do not follow the suffrage flag; they do not want to vote; they depend upon the manhood of California to protect them from the responsibility of the ballot. They rely on manhood suffrage and a safe and sane government.

Vote Against the Woman Suffrage Amendment!

ISSUED BY

The Women of Northern California Association Opposed to Woman Suffrage

Native-born Asian women in California, like the young Chinese-American woman in San Francisco at left, were able to cast their first votes for president in the November 1912 election. After California added a sixth star to the suffrage constellation, suffragists used the figure of the Statue of Liberty in New York on the post card above to help the rest of the country relate to events in the far west. Adopting a similar theme, Triggs' editorial cartoon below pictured Betsy Ross putting "A New Star in the Flag." On the facing page, a stylish and confident western lady easily balanced her public and private lives, symbolized by the ballot box and the nursery cradle, in this illustration from the July 4, 1909 issue of the *San Francisco Sunday Call.*

A Dramatic Victory in the Golden State

THE DRIVE in California gained its full momentum in the final two months, aided by workers and funds contributed by other state associations. In southern California fifty to sixty meetings a week were held, climaxing on September 30 with a gathering of 4,000 people in Los Angeles. In northern California a "monster rally" on October 6, followed by fireworks and a band concert, drew over 10,000 people to San Francisco's Dreamland Rink.

On October 10 the fervent hopes of many were dashed when surprisingly strong adverse votes were reported in San Francisco and Oakland, and Los Angeles barely passed the measure. Stunned and heartbroken, supporters slowly began to plan a new campaign, but not before posting a guard over

the vaults where the city ballots were stored to avoid any tampering.

As the days passed, however, favorable returns began to come in from distant villages and country districts.

Julia Bracken Wendt created the plaque above for the California campaign, complete with a yin/yang symbol over the inscription, "Intelligence Has No Gender."

When the long count was finally completed, suffragists had won by a mere 3,587 votes out of a total of 246,487. This represented an average majority of one for each voting precinct in the state. The final tally was 125,037 to 121,450. As they had hoped, supporters' efforts in the rural districts had successfully overcome the more organized opposition in the cities.

At one stroke the number of women with full suffrage doubled and San Francisco became the most populous city in the world in which women could vote. Equal suffrage now reigned in six western states with a total of 37 electoral votes for the presidency. Women in other states were exultant and gained new hope in their efforts to place the measure on their own state's ballot. ◆

Suffragetts at Long Beach

1912.

Chapter 7: 1912

New Life in the States

I N 1912 suffragists through-out the country dedicated themselves to putting their cause before the voters. The October victory in California had surprised and aroused the opposition, and suffragists realized that subsequent efforts would become much more difficult.

In Virginia, for the first time, a resolution seeking a suffrage amendment to the state constitution was introduced only to be soundly defeated by the legislature. In New Jersey, suffragists tried to impress lawmakers by staging a parade of 1,000 in Newark on October 25 while in Maryland, supporters presented a petition of 30,000 voters to both Houses requesting submission of the suffrage bill. Both measures were voted down. In other states like Connecticut supporters resubmitted bills for full and

partial suffrage as they had done for years.

However, four states – Ohio, Wisconsin, Michigan, and Kansas – were persuaded to schedule a vote. And in two other states, Arizona and Oregon, supporters successfully circulated initiative petitions and raised the number to an unprecedented six state contests. From Maine to Alabama, supporters continued to circulate petitions, lobby political leaders, and demand a public vote.

Facing page: Reaching out to vacationers in Long Beach, a group of white-clad suffragists prepared to sell pennants and enroll new members during the summer of 1912. Left and above: A sixth star celebrated the victory in California.

Rose Schneiderman, an immigrant from Russian Poland, started working in New York's Lower East Side at 13 and began organizing at 16 when she worked in a New York cap factory. A passionate and eloquent speaker with flaming red hair, she rose to become one of the leading figures in the trade union movement. Vice-president of the Women's Trade Union League in New York and active in the International Ladies' Garment Workers' Union's organizing drives, she was an early ally of Harriot Blatch and a leader of the Equality League for Self-Supporting Women. A life-long labor organizer and union official, Schneiderman later influenced the views of both Eleanor and Franklin Roosevelt on labor relations. In the 1930s, Schneiderman helped win the eight-hour day and minimum wage legislation in New York.

SENATORS *vs.* WORKING-WOMEN

Sentimentality of New York Senators
in Equal Suffrage Debate Answered
by Common Sense of Working Women

JOINT MASS-MEETING

Wage-Earners' League and Collegiate Equal Suffrage League

Cooper Union, April 22d, 8 p.m.

" Now there is nobody to whom I yield in respect and admiration and devotion to the sex."   Answered by MOLLIE SCHEPPS, Shirt Waist Maker.

" Cornelia's Jewels.   Where are they to-day ? "
            Answered by MELINDA SCOTT, Hat Trimmer.

" The anti-suffragists tell me: 'Be careful, be careful, how you destroy the incentive to motherhood.   We speak for motherhood.   Save that.' "
            Answered by LEONORA O'REILLY, Shirt Maker.

" Women—they are peaceful ; they are sympathetic ; they minister to man in the home."   Answered by MRS. HEFFERLY, Neckwear Maker.

" Now there is no question in the world to my mind but what the family and family relation are a more important thing than any law or any law-making or holding of office."   Answered by MAGGIE HINCHEY, Laundry Worker.

" We want to relieve women of the burdens and responsibilities of life."
            Answered by CLARA LEMLICH, Shirt Waist Maker.

" Get women into the arena of politics with its alliances and distressing contests—the delicacy is gone, the charm is gone, and you emasculize women."
            Answered by ROSE SCHNEIDERMANN, Cap Maker.

Instructions for the Suffrage Parade, May 4th
Elizabeth Freeman of England

Free tickets can be obtained at the Women's Trade Union League, 43 East 22nd Street. Admission without ticket after 8 P. M.

Working Women! Don't fail to come and hear what Senators McClellan, Thomas, Sage and some of the Assemblymen have said about women

They forgot all about the four-hundred thousand working women in New York City. They forgot the eight hundred thousand working women in New York State. **Come just to show the gentlemen we have arrived.**

Building Political Pressure in New York

Working women in New York increasingly spoke out for equal rights with the encouragement of both suffragists and trade union leaders. For several years Harriot Stanton Blatch worked through existing labor organizations to get the suffrage message out to their members. But after her Equality League for Self-Supporting Women became the Women's Political Union with a broader membership, other groups including the Wage Earners Suffrage League and the Woman Suffrage Party made efforts to recruit working women.

Above: Answering the "sentimentality" of New York state senators.

Fed up with legislative delays, Harriot Stanton Blatch (above, second from right) led three hundred women up the steps of the New York state capitol in Albany on March 12, 1912 to demand that Senator Robert Wagner schedule a vote on the suffrage bill. He did. Members of the Women's Political Union (left) posed as "Parasol Girls" to announce that the May 4 suffrage parade would take place "rain or shine." From the left are Eleanor Brannan, Jane Schneiderman (Rose's sister), Mary Woods Smith, Elizabeth Selden Rogers, and Elizabeth Mayer.

Harriot Stanton Blatch had become one of the most influential suffragists in the country by 1912, re-energizing the movement in New York and leading the effort to convert the state legislature. Earlier in the year Blatch had won widespread publicity when she stationed "Silent Sentinels" in the Albany State House. "Whenever the Judiciary Committees were in session," she reported, "two of us stood at the door of the committee room, typifying the patient waiting that women had done since Elizabeth Cady Stanton made the first demand for our enfranchisement in 1848." When opponents in the New York legislature narrowly defeated the measure in March, the Women's Political Union organized its annual parade as a protest before turning its attention to winning favorable planks in the state Democratic and Republican platforms. Party endorsements, Blatch believed, would force opponents to fall in line. Blatch had actually lost her citizenship twenty years earlier when she married English businessman William Henry Blatch and did not regain it until after his death in 1915.

The Women's Political Union Organizes a Spectacular Parade Up Fifth Avenue

Carrying purple, white, and green flags, the Executive Board of the Women's Political Union, including president and parade organizer Harriot Stanton Blatch, led the annual woman suffrage parade on May 4, 1912.

The impressive parade, which protested the failure of the legislature to pass the suffrage measure, drew between 15,000 and 20,000 women from all walks of life including trade union members, so-ciety women, domestic workers, professionals, and other "self-supporting" women. Carefully planned to show the breadth of women's demand for the vote, the parade included divisions of marchers organized by occupations, political districts, organizations, and states. There was also a brigade of several dozen street speakers with portable rostrums, a contingent of Black members of the Political Equality Association,

Woman Suffrage Parade

Organized by the Women's Political Union
46 East 29th Street, New York City

Saturday Afternoon, May 4th
RAIN OR SHINE

Mass Meeting, Carnegie Hall, 6 p.m.

Upon YOU rests the responsibility of securing political freedom for this generation.

The plain duty of every suffragist is to demonstrate that she is one of the great body of women who demand votes. Your co-operation is needed NOW to make the parade of May 4th so overwhelming that no political tactics next session will be used to prevent the advancement of our bill.

Politicians yield to public opinion. WITHOUT DELAY help express the overwhelming public opinion already existing in favor of woman suffrage by signing and mailing the attached pledge to march shoulder to shoulder with other women on May 4th.

TIME OF PROCESSION. The head of the parade will start up Fifth Avenue from Washington Square at 5 P. M.

FORMATION:—

Washington Square. Women Riders on horseback, Flag bearer, Executive Board of the Women's Political Union, Ushers for Carnegie Hall, Street Speakers.

Washington Square North. East of Fifth Avenue:—Senatorial Groups of the Women's Political Union, General Sympathizers.
West:—Public School Teachers, Private School Teachers, Students, etc.

9th Street, East. Women's Political Union;—Professional Women—Doctors, Lawyers, Investigators, Nurses, Writers, Musicians, Artists, Actresses, Craftsmen, Librarians, Lecturers, Social Workers, etc.

9th Street, West. Women's Political Union—Industrial Workers—Millinery, Dress, Shirtwaist, Laundry, etc., Domesti Workers.

10th Street, East. Women's Political Union;—Business Women—Managers, Tearooms, Buyers, Shopkeepers, etc. Secretries, Bookkeepers, Stenographers, Telephone Operators, Department tore Clerks, etc.

10th Street, West. Women's Political Union;—Suffrage Pioneers, Civil ants, Voters from Suffrage States, Scar etc.

11th Street, East. Non-suffrage State—ational Board, Connecticut, Maryland, Massachusetts, Nebraska, New Hampshire, New Jerse Pennsylva , Tennessee, Vern Virginia, Washingto Gre tive League.

11th Street, West. New York State Association, Equal Franc ty Legislative League.

15th Street, East. Men's League for Woman ffrage, Men Sympathizers.

17th Street, East, from Union Square. Woman ffage Party College League, Wage Earners' League, Women's Trade Union League, etc.

27th Street, East. Political Equality A tio Women's Political Union div from uptown stores.

See to it that your name is enrolled with this great army of women he will march for their principles on May 4th.

One week before the Parade all marchers whose names are filed office will receive a post card giving full directions.

SUGGESTIONS: Be punctual. Reach point of formation by 4 p. m. Wear white if po. Low heeled boots.

Appearance of parade depends on each marcher. Head erect. Shoulders back. Keep step. No talking. Eyes to the front. Remember you are marching for a principle. OBEY YOUR MARSHAL.

PLEDGE TO MARCH
IN

Woman Suffrage Parade
NEW YORK CITY
SATURDAY AFTERNOON, MAY 4, 1912
Starting 5 P. M., Rain or Shine

Name..

Occupation (if any) or Group....................................

Address...

Send to **WOMEN'S POLITICAL UNION**, 46 East 29th Street, New York
Telephone, Madison Square 9880

---

several suffragists from China, a large number of Socialist women, and a division of over 600 men. The vibrant procession, witnessed by over half a million people, took two and a half hours to pass.

Leaflets advised marchers to gather on streets that fed into the main parade. "Remember you are marching for a principle," one flier read, adding that participants should wear white if possible and low-heeled boots. The WPU publicized the demonstration extensively and recruited women for months to ensure a large turnout. The march also started later than in the past so that more working women could take part.

Above: Harriot Blatch (center foreground), in her dark academic gown, led the 1912 parade with WPU officers. Right: Blatch (center) discussed plans with fellow suffragists at headquarters.

The May 4, 1912 suffrage parade in New York drew an enormous crowd of spectators along the route, particularly in front of the Public Library (left) where observers surged into the street. Suffragists continued marching up Fifth Avenue but later charged police with neglect of duty for allowing the crowd to nearly block the parade's path.

The colorful demonstration was led by a "suffrage cavalry" of over fifty horsewomen in riding gear (above) and included marching bands and several floats portraying the changing status of women. The largest parade to date, it eliminated any lingering doubts as to the propriety of women marching for their rights.

Reversing direction from previous years, the parade headed uptown to a mass meeting in Carnegie Hall instead of downtown to labor-associated Union Square. The shift reflected a larger change within the movement. Society and middle class women (below) increasingly drew attention and exerted more influence in suffrage organizations, although working women still marched and organized.

The parade won extensive coverage and triggered intensified attacks. *The New York Times* warned its readers that women would "play havoc" with the vote if men were not "masculine enough to prevent them."

Alice Stone Blackwell
continued to publish *The Woman's Journal* after the death of her parents, Lucy Stone and Henry Blackwell. She proved to be a hardworking editor and forceful writer whose well-informed arguments and pointed wit won her a level of respect afforded few suffragists. One admirer remarked that Blackwell "thought like lightening" and another praised her skill at "ridiculing, analyzing, checkmating" the absurd claims of opponents. A longtime leader in both the Massachusetts and New England Woman Suffrage Associations, she reminded younger workers of the values and sacrifices of women before them. The rousing stamp below encouraged *Journal* subscriptions.

Each State 1000
August 13

WOMAN'S JOURNAL
AND
SUFFRAGE NEWS
BOSTON

IF YOU BELIEVE IN SUFFRAGE
USE YOUR SUFFRAGE PAPER

WOMAN'S JOURNAL

OFFICIAL ORGAN OF THE NATIONAL AMERICAN WOMAN SUFFRAGE ASSOCIATION

VOL. XLIII NO. 36   SATURDAY, SEPTEMBER 14, 1912   FIVE CENTS

WHEN DR. SHAW SPEAKS

There is perhaps no other woman in this country who can stir and inspire an audience as can Dr. Anna Howard Shaw, the National President. It has been said that the most fascinating of intellectual treats is to watch the faces of her listeners.
Dr. Shaw is at present touring the campaign States. In Ohio she wound up the campaign with a two-hour address and held the crowded thousands spell-bound from the first to the last. Dr. Shaw reports her Ohio trip on the last page of this week's Woman's Journal.

NEW YORK HAS BIG SUFFRAGE WEEK

Broadway Placarded with "Votes for Women"—Suffragists Hold Picturesque Performances at Hammerstein's Vaudeville House

MRS. JAMES DUANE LIVINGSTON

(Continued on Page 293)

The Woman's Journal: Shining a Steady Beacon of Light

THE WOMAN'S JOURNAL was of tremendous importance during its 47 years of continuous weekly publication as a source of news, opinion, and support to activists across the country. Founded by Lucy Stone and Boston-area supporters in 1870 and later edited by Alice Stone Blackwell, the *Journal* became the official organ of NAWSA between 1910 and 1912. However it proved to be too expensive and NAWSA returned it to Blackwell. She continued publishing it until June 1917 when it was merged into *The Woman Citizen*. Carrie Chapman Catt compared the *Journal* to "a pillar of light" that guided women through the darkest times.

Uniformed suffrage "newsies" (left) carried bundles of *The Woman's Journal* to sell at a Long Island pageant in May 1913. British activist Elisabeth Freeman is in the center. Freeman, in the driver's seat above, and Ida Craft used a yellow buggy modeled on Lucy Stone's to sell the *Journal* on the streets of New York in July 1913. The button below commemorated *Journal* founder Lucy Stone.

Motion Pictures Advocate the Cause

MOTION PICTURES, a new medium at the turn of the century, drew the attention of suffragists, and suffragists themselves attracted silent movie producers. Scores of commercial anti-suffrage comedies and melodramas were produced that featured rebellious "suffragette" caricatures including Thomas Edison's *How They Got the Vote* (1913) and Charlie Chaplin's *A Busy Day* (1914).

In response, supporters made their own movies and screened them nationally. In 1912 NAWSA produced the melodrama *Votes for Women* which included speeches by Anna Howard Shaw and Jane Addams, and footage of the New York parade. That same year the Women's Political Union produced a romantic comedy, *Suffrage and the Man,* followed in 1913 by a melodrama, *80 Million Women Want What?* NAWSA officer Ruth Hanna McCormick produced an ambitious feature film, *Your Girl and Mine,* in 1914. Despite favorable reviews it was never commercially distributed.

Above: The "ghost" of Abraham Lincoln looked on approvingly during a suffrage speech in *Your Girl and Mine*. Right: Film announcement.

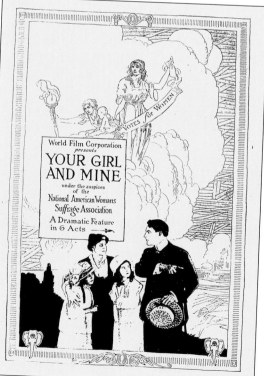

Recognized as an inspirational orator, NAWSA president Anna Howard Shaw (above and left) enjoyed traveling and speaking much more than working in an office. Like her mentor Susan B. Anthony, Shaw spent much of each year giving paid lectures as well as suffrage speeches throughout the country, particularly in campaign states. Administrative assistant Mary Ware Dennett managed NAWSA affairs in the New York office.

LET OHIO WOMEN VOTE

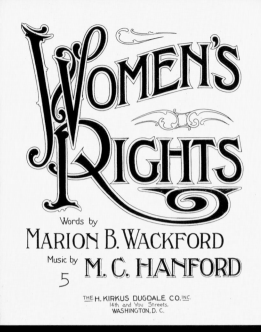

WOMEN'S RIGHTS

Words by
MARION B. WACKFORD
Music by M. C. HANFORD
5

THE H. KIRKUS DUGDALE CO. INC.
14th and You Streets.
WASHINGTON, D. C.

KANSAS

EQUAL SUFFRAGE

VOTE
BALLOT BOX

FOR A BETTER GOVERNMENT
OF THE PEOPLE BY THE PEOPLE
AND FOR THE PEOPLE

VICTORY VICTORY

VOTES FOR WOMEN

★ CAMPAIGN ★
IN

OHIO - NEW HAMPSHIRE
KANSAS - MICHIGAN
WISCONSIN - OREGON

OHIO NEXT

LET MOTHER VOTE

EQUAL SUFFRAGE

Cadillaqua Auto Parade. 1912 — Detroit

Suffragists in Michigan (left) drew attention to the 1912 referendum with a parade of artfully decorated automobiles. Supporters in the state Woman's Christian Temperance Union estimated the property taxes women paid and issued a flier (above) challenging male voters, "Do you really believe that taxation without representation is tyranny?" Supporters publicized their cause in new, eye-catching ways in 1912 (facing page). They produced colorful postcards, pin-backed buttons, sheet music, and publicity stamps – including one (bottom left) which mistakenly listed New Hampshire instead of Arizona as a campaign state. One pamphlet cover (left) showed Liberty holding her torch high while crushing a serpent before the rising sun. Six stars represented the equal suffrage states.

Campaigns Put Suffrage to Voters in Six States

CONTESTS WERE waged in six states in 1912 as suffragists convinced the constitutional convention in Ohio and the legislatures in Wisconsin, Michigan, and Kansas to put votes for women on the ballot. Supporters also collected enough signatures under the initiative process to qualify the measure in Oregon and Arizona.

Suffragists in Ohio and Wisconsin were relatively well-organized under longtime leaders, but Arizona was a brand new, sparsely populated state. Quieter, less spectacular drives were carried out there and in Kansas while more energetic, open campaigns in the other states included district organizing, mass meetings, automobile tours, and parades to establish woman suffrage as a popular election issue.

For decades Ohio suffra-

gists had lobbied their legislature, submitting bills which year after year would be lost in committee or otherwise ignored. Finally, in late May 1912 a constitutional convention voted to submit a suffrage amendment to the voters, giving supporters just three months before the special election scheduled for September 3.

Harriet Taylor Upton, longtime NAWSA treasurer, led the Ohio state association assisted by Elizabeth J. Hauser. Over fifty volunteer field workers, many from the east, assisted local women in the populated industrial state. In August, a festive suffrage parade of 5,000 supporters filled the streets of Columbus.

There was strong opposition to suffrage in Ohio and in other midwestern states where the liquor and brewery industries were strongest. Fears of prohibition were fanned by the opposition even though not all women favored the reform. Suffragists tried to keep the issues separate, realizing that most men would never approve of votes for women if they believed it would lead to liquor being outlawed.

Harriet Taylor Upton led the campaigns of the Ohio Woman Suffrage Association and was a beloved figure in the national movement for thirty years. The daughter of an Ohio congressman, she served as his hostess in Washington D.C. while a young woman and acquired an ease in political circles that later aided the suffrage drive. Originally converted to the cause while gathering material for an anti-suffrage article, Upton joined NAWSA in 1890 and was elected treasurer in 1894. Good-humored, fair-minded, and politically astute, she traveled and spoke extensively for equal suffrage, testified before congressional committees, lobbied congressmen, and was active in NAWSA's annual conventions. She also edited NAWSA's official organ, *Progress*, from 1902 to 1910 and authored numerous articles, children's stories, and several books on Ohio history.

The 1912 campaign in Ohio drew countless volunteers to suffrage headquarters (above) on Euclid Avenue in Cleveland. Florence Allen, later a Federal judge, is in the center holding the flag. Suffragists grew tired of mysterious "hit pieces" which circulated anonymously before the election and unsuccessfully offered a $100 reward (right) to find out who the "vicious interests" were behind the attacks. In Cincinnati Susan Fitzgerald and Louise Hall (facing page) tried to avoid the mud while they glued up suffrage posters at Main and Canal Streets on May 17. The posters, produced by the College Equal Suffrage League, carried a popular quote from Abraham Lincoln.

WHO PAYS THE BILLS ?
$100 Reward !

Cash on delivery for a straight tip as to the authorship of spurious hand bills being circulated to defeat Amendment 23, Woman Suffrage, at the special election Sept. 3. THESE HANDBILLS ARE ANONYMOUS and are worded to deceive the reader into thinking they were put out by the Anti-Saloon League but the Anti-Saloon League denies any knowledge of their authorship.

THEY ARE WITHOUT THE UNION LABEL which prevents their being traced to a reputable printer.

Anonymous Authorship
Fake Copy   **Scab Printing**

are hall marks not only of these hand bills but also of the street car ads. which are appearing "Skidoo 23" everywhere.

THE OHIO WOMAN SUFFRAGE ASSOCIATION WANTS TO KNOW WHO PAYS THE BILLS INCURRED TO DEFEAT AMENDMENT 23.

Money is poured out like water to defeat Woman Suffrage by people who are AFRAID TO TELL THE PUBLIC WHO THEY ARE. The Ohio Woman Suffrage Association is poor but it has $100 cash down to pay for information that will DRAG THESE VICIOUS INTERESTS INTO THE OPEN before September 1st.

EVERY HONEST MAN will recognize this kind of attack and resent it by GIVING THE WOMEN OF OHIO POWER TO PROTECT THEMSELVES by electing lawmakers.

Men of Ohio make your women political equals of the gamblers, white slavers and all other interests that are spending thousands to keep them disfranchised.

Vote for Amendment 23, Woman Suffrage
OHIO WOMAN SUFFRAGE ASSOCIATION. ━━ Headquarters, Warren, Ohio

Adella Hunt Logan, an influential educator and writer, organized suffrage activity among Black women at Tuskegee Institute in Alabama. In addition, her incisive articles countered anti-suffragists' claims and reached a national audience through the Black press. Logan joined the faculty of Tuskegee in 1883 at the age of 20, married the school's treasurer in 1888, and gave birth to nine children. A member for two decades of the Tuskegee Woman's Club, founded by Margaret Murray Washington in 1895, Logan organized debates and other events promoting equal suffrage on campus. A life member of NAWSA, she used her light complexion to gain entrance to segregated meetings of white suffragists and brought back news to her own community. In 1913 Logan encouraged Black women to march in the suffrage parade in Washington D.C. after reading it was to be segregated. She agreed with fellow educator Mary Talbert of Buffalo that one reason Black women should try to organize other Black women was that white women were never going to do it.

Votes for Women!

The Suffragist's Alphabet

A is for Antis who sneer at us all.
B is for Ballot we'll win in the Fall.
C is for "Con-Con" which passed The Great Clause
D is for Duty we owe to our Cause.
E is for Effort we women must make.
F is for Faith which we know it will take.
G is for Good we believe we can do.
H is for Home to which we'll be true.
I is for Ideals we need in our land.
J is Justice which we NOW demand.
K is for Knowledge our Leaflets will spread.
L is for the Light on our problems they shed.
M is for Men we hope to persuade.
N is for Numbers that swell the parade.
O is for Obstructions men place in our way.
P is for Precinct we're polling today.
Q is for Queries we answer with ease.
R is for Reason---as much as you please.
S is for SUFFRAGE for ALL of THE NATION.
T is for Taxes WITH Representation.
U is the Union we take for our text.
V VOTES FOR WOMEN! **OHIO THE NEXT!**
W is for Women---for Wages---for Work.
X the Xample we set to the shirk.
Y is for Youth who our Banner will bear.
Z is the Zest in which we all share.

OHIO WOMAN SUFFRAGE HEADQUARTERS
HARRIET TAYLOR UPTON, President
WARREN, OHIO

Enthusiastic in her appeal, Margaret Foley of Boston (above) addressed an Ohio crowd in 1912, emphasizing women's need for the ballot. Foley was a dynamic speaker and member of the Hat Trimmers' Union who studied the British movement in 1911. She brought new tactics home to the states including, for a while, heckling politicians. Adella Hunt Logan of Alabama was another of over fifty volunteers who came from out of state to help Ohio women win the vote. A rhyming leaflet (left) spelled out their case. Making a classic suffrage point, Orson Lowell's illustration for *Life* magazine, "Four Voters" (facing page), contrasted an upper class but unenfranchised woman with four "socially inferior" men who could vote.

PRO-SUFFRAGE
NUMBER

Life

PRICE 10 CENTS
Vol. 62, No. 1616. October 16, 1913
Copyright, 1913, Life Publishing Company

BLACK
HAND

ORSON
LOWELL

FOUR VOTERS

Courting Voters in Kansas and Arizona

Led by Lucy B. Johnston, president of the Kansas Equal Suffrage Association, over 2,000 women were involved in the 1912 campaign in Kansas plus a large number of influential men. Suffragists covered the state with a dignified, well-organized campaign and reached out personally to voters on farms and at conventions, circuses, and public events.

Arizona women put suffrage on the ballot immediately after statehood using the new initiative process of collecting voters' signatures. NAWSA organizer Laura Gregg, who had helped set up suffrage clubs throughout the territory in 1910, returned in September for a final, strenuous ten-week campaign during which she helped win the support of every labor organization.

Mrs. Frances W. Munds, who was later elected state senator, led the small but effective Arizona suffrage organization. NAWSA President Anna Howard Shaw spoke for a week in the principal cities, and Alice Park came from California to oversee distribution of literature. There were no parades or demonstrations, and opponents did not realize the cause's strength until the closing days.

Above: Welcoming voters at a fair in Winfield, Kansas. Below: A leaflet from Arizona highlighted labor and organizational support.

A Last-Minute Michigan Contest Challenges Supporters

A LAST MINUTE act by the Michigan legislature put woman suffrage on the 1912 ballot but allowed for only a five month campaign. With less than $250 in their treasury, Michigan suffragists felt unprepared and virtually alone since national organiz-

Oregon, Again

A CAMPAIGN POST CARD (above) encouraged Oregon voters to "fill the gap" to make the entire Pacific coast pro-suffrage. The well-respected Portland Woman's Club helped initiate the sixth campaign in Oregon and directed a carefully organized statewide drive with NAWSA's support. Abigail Scott Duniway's state association remained independent. Numerous local societies were also active, including leagues of college women (below), society women, men, and even an Every Body's League for otherwise unattached supporters. They organized groups in towns and villages throughout the state.

ers and financial resources had already been committed to other states.

Clara B. Arthur, president of the Michigan Equal Suffrage Association, led the "short and unexpected" campaign with assistance from the college and men's leagues, the WCTU, state Grange, farmers' clubs, and various labor organizations. Headquarters were opened in Detroit, Grand Rapids, and Kalamazoo. Feeling confident, liquor dealers did not mount as active an opposition as in most other states.

A well-appointed team of suffragists (above) set out on a 1912 speaking tour from Lawrence, Kansas, in a campaign automobile decorated with flags, banners, and bright yellow sunflowers.

Defending American Womanhood –

WHILE SUFFRAGISTS fought state by state for the right to vote, a combination of forces grew up to block their progress. In addition to people who simply did not agree that women should vote, there were powerful economic interests and political concerns that helped determine electoral results.

Opposition to woman suffrage generally came from three basic sources: business interests concerned that women would vote for prohibition and other reforms, politicians and party bosses afraid of a vast and unknown addition to the electorate, and individuals who felt that enfranchised women would threaten the social pillars of the home and family. Opponents of all sorts paid more attention to suffrage campaigns after the 1911 victory in California.

Business Opposition

The principal financial opposition came from the brewery and liquor industries and from related business interests which were often hard to identify. The powerful U.S. Brewers Association exerted tremendous influence in many states, particularly where beer and whiskey were manufactured. Under publicity head Percy Andreae, the Brewers Association raised millions of dollars which it spent through its political committee and assorted

SHALL THE TAIL WAG THE DOG?

LESS THAN 10 PER CENT DEMAND THE BALLOT

AT LEAST 90 PER CENT OF MASSACHUSETTS WOMEN DO NOT WANT TO VOTE

WOMEN'S ANTI-SUFFRAGE ASSOCIATION OF MASSACHUSETTS
Mrs. JOHN BALCH, President   Mrs. CHARLES P. STRONG, Secretary

Anti-suffragists claimed that the vast body of Massachusetts women did not want to vote and used "man's best friend" on the flier above to graphically make their point.

"front" groups in a skillfully coordinated campaign against both woman suffrage and prohibition. Afraid that women would vote for prohibition, members of the association, including distillers and retail liquor dealers, formed what was by far the best funded source of opposition, largely responsible for the anti-suffrage campaigns

in most states.

The Brewers Association was joined by allies in agriculture, railroad, banking, and other industries who were able to influence large blocks of voters and key politicians. A national Man-Suffrage Association representing business interests was organized in 1912 and led by Everett P. Wheeler, a corporate attorney

in New York. Historian Eleanor Flexner noted that Wheeler was "considered by suffragists to be the evil genius of the opposition." Wheeler filed appeals to strike down suffrage gains and sued to have suffrage bills invalidated.

Male politicians were similarly hostile to women becoming voters, fearing they

Against Equal Suffrage for Women

would disrupt the entrenched political machines and demand civic reforms. Party leaders realized that the behavior of such a large block of new voters would be hard to control or predict. When suffragists campaigned against opponents in their state legislatures, as they did in New York, it only confirmed their worst fears. Elected officials often tried to sidestep the issue by sending the bill to committee, delaying a vote, or using other legislative maneuvers. They were rarely held accountable.

Regional Politics

Resistance to woman suffrage also reflected regional concerns. Opponents in the south feared that laws enforcing racial segregation and white supremacy would be overturned if Black women had political power which was backed by the Federal government. In the midwest, opponents warned voters that woman suffrage would lead inevitably to prohibition which would cause economic collapse. In the east, the drive was led by machine politicians anxious to maintain the status quo, along with liquor trade representatives. With such strong and varied opposition, suffragists faced contests that were increasingly complex, difficult, and expensive.

Some anti-suffragists were women who established their

own organizations in several states. Female opponents also testified against suffrage legislation at the state and national levels, campaigned to defeat measures in state elections, and lent a certain legitimacy to all those who opposed equal rights.

Defenders of the Home

Both male and female anti-suffragists put themselves forward as defenders of the home, champions of the family, and responsible guardians of women's sphere. They argued that most women did not want to vote and that political decisions should be left to men. Several prominent anti-suffrage women were active in social welfare work and

Anti-suffrage leaders such as Mrs. James Wadsworth, Jr. (left) claimed that women voting was both unnecessary and wrong since political decisions were the responsibility of men.

philanthropy; others were successful authors and university professors.

The Massachusetts Association Opposed to the Further Extension of Suffrage to Women, founded in 1882 and revived in 1895, became the most active of the anti-suffrage groups, providing literature and speakers to other states. The MAOFESW later changed its name to the Women's Anti-Suffrage Association of Massachusetts. Anti-suffrage women in Illinois had similarly organized in the late 1880s.

A National Association Opposed to Woman Suffrage was founded in New York just after the California victory to draw together groups in seven

states and the District of Columbia. Josephine Jewell Dodge led the association until 1917 when Mrs. James Wadsworth, Jr., wife of the influential senator from New York, became president and focused on opposing the Federal amendment.

"The women who led the movement were usually members of the social aristocracy," noted historian Jane Camhi. "They were, for the most part, urban, wealthy, native born, Republican, and Protestant – members of established families either by birth or marriage, or both." By entering public life these women "went to lengths inconsistent with their goals in order to prevent the extension of suffrage to women."

Going beyond their traditional "sphere," anti-suffrage women organized clubs, gave speeches, held meetings, hosted dances, and organized public events particularly in campaign states. But despite their activity, these women were consistently dismissed by suffragists who treated them as merely fronts for male interests and failed to acknowledge their ability, strength, and influence as women, albeit ideological opposites. Because they became active in the public sphere, women who opposed equal rights actually reflected women's overall progress and their growing involvement in social and political affairs. ◆

Dual Campaigns Take On Wisconsin

Two organizations led the Wisconsin campaign in 1912, the Wisconsin Woman Suffrage Association, run for over 25 years by Olympia Brown, and the Political Equality League, formed in 1911 by younger suffragists seeking more dynamic leadership. After the legislature was persuaded to submit the question to the voters, these two groups campaigned separately for seventeen months, their actions loosely coordinated by Brown's daughter, Gwendolen Brown Willis.

While the state association pursued the traditional methods of parlor meetings and touring speakers, the Political Equality League, led by Ada James, organized street meetings and several automobile tours which generated publicity and reached residents throughout the state. The league also helped form a society of Black women led by Carrie Horton and energetically recruited men and women of more diverse backgrounds.

Above: Plotting strategy in Wisconsin beneath an election district map. Ada James, who was deaf and read lips, is in the center in a plaid dress. Below: A suffrage speaker addressed men on a street in Cooperstown. Inset: Olympia Brown.

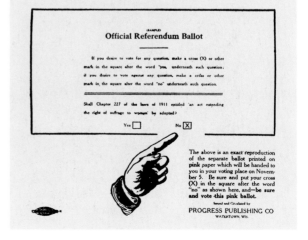

DANGER!

Woman's Suffrage Would Double the Irresponsible Vote

It is a MENACE to the Home, Men's Employment and to All Business

(SAMPLE)
Official Referendum Ballot

If you desire to vote for any question, make a cross (X) or other mark in the square after the word "yes" underneath such question; if you desire to vote against any question, make a cross or other mark in the square after the word "no" underneath such question.

Shall Chapter 227 of the laws of 1911 entitled "an act extending the right of suffrage to women" be adopted?

Yes ☐   No ☒

The above is an exact reproduction of the separate ballot printed on pink paper which will be handed to you in your voting place on November 5. Be sure and put your cross (X) in the square after the word "no" as shown here, and—be sure and vote this pink ballot.

Issued and Circulated by
PROGRESS PUBLISHING CO
WATERTOWN, WIS.

Crystal Eastman, a dynamic organizer and eloquent speaker, served as campaign manager for the Political Equality League during the 1912 suffrage contest in Wisconsin. A graduate of Vassar, Eastman was a labor attorney and investigator who helped win passage of the first worker's compensation laws. After marrying in 1911 she moved from New York to Milwaukee and immediately became involved in the suffrage drive. Nearly six feet tall, Eastman (below) was a natural leader with a keen political sense. One friend described her as "a symbol of what the free woman might be." After the Wisconsin campaign, Eastman worked with Alice Paul to redirect suffrage efforts towards winning a constitutional amendment.

"A typical village meeting" in Sister Bay, Wisconsin (above) saw Catharine Waugh McCulloch speaking to townspeople and answering questions in front of the Post Office and General Store. Wisconsin suffragists took to the Wolf River (left) to promote votes for women at "riverboat rallies" in towns along the shore. An opposition leaflet (far left), which claimed that women voting "would double the irresponsible vote," exemplified the vague threats and mysterious authorship of many anti-suffrage pieces.

Stumping Rural Wisconsin for Votes for Women

SUFFRAGE SPEAKERS traveled by horse, train, and automobile throughout rural Wisconsin during the 1912 campaign to reach voters in small villages and distant settlements.

Talking directly with male voters of many nationalities allowed the women to dispel common objections, fears, and misconceptions. Experienced speakers like Catharine McCulloch, a Chicago attorney and veteran campaigner, were skilled at persuasive dialogue, helping to win male voters one by one. Many other speakers came from outside the state including Jane Addams, Inez Milholland, Anna Garlin Spencer, and both Emmeline and Sylvia Pankhurst.

Wisconsin suffragists also wooed voters at some 75 county fairs, and even persuaded a pilot to scatter fliers from his plane over the state fair in Milwaukee. As in Michigan, suffragists were particularly concerned be-cause the question was printed on a separate ballot with which opponents could easily tamper. The measure was strongly opposed by the state's powerful brewing industry which feared women would vote for prohibition. ◆

Suffragist Catharine McCulloch (above), a Justice of the Peace in Illinois, spoke with workers at a construction site during an automobile tour of Wisconsin before the 1912 election.

Close Victories, Discouraging Defeats

As THEY APPROACHED the 1912 elections, suffragists were cautiously hopeful that their new momentum might double the number of equal suffrage states.

During the year NAWSA was able to offer some limited financial aid thanks largely to philanthropist Pauline Agassiz Shaw of Boston who over time secretly donated $30,000 to Anna Howard Shaw (no relation) to be used to win more states. The NAWSA president rejoiced, "It enabled us for the first time to establish headquarters, secure an office force, and engage campaign speakers." Finances, however, were tight. Women in each state worked hard to raise the money needed to reach the voters.

Mixed Results

The first contest was in Ohio at a special election on September 3. In the most populous state to consider suffrage to date, the measure was defeated by 87,455 votes, 336,875 to 249,420. Suffragists who had raised about $40,000 blamed saloon interests and public indifference and immediately began an initiative drive to put the measure before the voters again.

The general election on November 5 brought much better news. In Kansas, forty-five years after the first equal rights referendum, voters approved the measure 175,246 to 159,197, a majority of over

"Tearing Off the Bonds," by Annie Lucosta "Lou" Rogers, appeared in the October 19, 1912 issue of *Judge*. Pen and ink cartoons, particularly by women artists, became an important means of illustrating suffragists' cause.

16,000. Because the results were reported first, Kansas claimed the position as the seventh equal suffrage state.

In Arizona every county carried as men approved woman suffrage two to one, 13,442 to 6,202. Votes for women finally passed in Oregon as well, but with a margin of only 4,161 votes out of 118,000. By a count of 61,265

to 57,104, the west coast became solidly for suffrage.

The two other contests were less encouraging. Wisconsin voters, many believing that woman suffrage would lead to prohibition, defeated the measure by 91,479 votes, 227,024 to 135,545. The state's two suffrage societies merged after the election and a friendlier legislature ap-

proved another vote in 1913. The governor, however, vetoed it.

Voters seemed much more receptive in Michigan where, out of nearly 500,000, the measure officially lost by only 760 ballots, 248,135 to 247,375. However no one could be sure of the accuracy of the count. Widespread fraud was clearly apparent in unexplained delays, lost ballot boxes, and other forms of tampering. The situation infuriated suffragists, who felt they had been robbed of victory.

Fighting Fraud

With charges flying, the Michigan legislature approved a second vote at a special election on April 7, 1913, the only electoral drive held that year. This time anti-suffragists and liquor interests made an open fight against the measure and it was defeated by 96,144 votes, 264,882 to 168,738.

Women continued to make slow progress in other states. In Iowa, for example, suffragists worked throughout the year and in early 1913 succeeded in persuading the state legislature to pass the question on to the voters. However the measure had to be approved again in 1915 before it could be put on the ballot in 1916, over three years from the first approval. Each state had its own rules, making coordinated strategies nearly impossible. ◆

The growth of the Progressive Party in the west contributed to suffrage gains in several states during this time, and when the party went national in 1912, Jane Addams (above, right) played a leading role. The convention in Chicago included enthusiastic women delegates (top) who got an early taste of active party politics. Presidential candidate Theodore Roosevelt had to be converted, however. Only "tepidly in favor" of suffrage, his earlier rhetoric (right) had left unenfranchised women wondering if "The People Rule" then "We're What?"

"LET THE PEOPLE RULE"

WE'RE WHAT?

WE'RE THE PEOPLE

WE'RE THE ANIMALS

DEMOCRACY---a government for all the people by all the people

Celebrating the Western Victories

A SPECTACULAR torchlight parade of 20,000 suffragists took place in New York City the evening of November 9, 1912 as a "Celebration of Suffrage Victories" in the west. Resembling "a long river of fire" according to one account, the parade began at 54th Street and ended in a blazing display in Union Square.

"If we do not celebrate our victories we will be considered indifferent," Men's League head James Lees Laidlaw had declared. "If we do not show life, and protest loudly against defeats, we will be considered discouraged and out of the contest." The night-time procession organized by a Cooperative Parade Committee left no doubt that suffragists were very much "in the contest."

A Torchlight Parade

"It was a line, miles long, of well-dressed, intelligent women, deeply concerned in the cause they are fighting for; of girls in their teens, overflowing with enthusiastic exuberance, and of men," reported *The New York Times*. Fifth Avenue was packed with an estimated half a million spectators.

"It was not necessary to flash the word down the line that the suffragists were coming," observed *The Times*. "The glare of those big pumpkin-shaped lanterns was all that was needed. First . . . it appeared like a single big

line of fire that was yards wide and only inches deep. But the width of the picture was short lived, and as the minutes passed the red river

A cartoon by Rollin Kirby after the 1912 election pictured Father Knickerbocker, a symbol of New York, peering out at the evening suffrage parade and declaring, "Goodness! Women At This Time o' Night! *There must be something in it!*"

grew longer and longer until, when the head of the column reached a point abreast of St. Patrick's Cathedral, the spectacle as seen by those south of Forty-Second Street was that of a rolling stream of fiery lava."

The New York Tribune reported that the crowd was "almost solemn. Almost unbroken silence reigned among the thousands who gazed,

from start to finish. It was as if they were saying to themselves: 'What is this force that is marching upon us?'"

New York suffragists had additional reason to celebrate after the election. Not only had several opponents in the

legislature been defeated, but enough pledged candidates had been elected to guarantee passage of the suffrage bill.

Regional Efforts

Women throughout the country celebrated the western victories. Abigail Scott Duniway, of newly enfranchised Oregon, was elected Honorary President of the National Council of Women Voters led by Emma DeVoe of Washington state. Both women had long recognized the irony of eastern suffragists offering advice to western women about winning the vote when all the suffrage victories had occurred in the west.

Without strong leadership, financial resources, or a clear strategy, New York-based NAWSA was of limited help and remained largely unable to capitalize on the new energy in the states. To help balance NAWSA's predominantly eastern orientation, Catharine McCulloch and others organized an annual Mississippi Valley Conference in 1912 and Kate Gordon of Louisiana established a southern states conference.

Despite difficulties, however, the movement posted significant gains in the 1912 elections which in turn led to more favorable representatives in Congress. Woman suffrage was finally positioned to emerge as a serious, and realistic, national political issue. ◆

Night-time rallies and parades added a special allure to women's cause. The torch-light parade on November 9, 1912 was particularly memorable. 5,000 Chinese lanterns had been imported from Paris, and New York suffragist Gertrude Brown reported that "the great yellow globes of lights, like harvest moons in the darkness, made an enchanting sight." Young women (below), bundled up against the cold, waited for the start of the parade. Excited suffragists (right) displayed their lanterns, paper sunflowers, yellow sashes, and fashionable tricorn suffrage hats.

These and other images from this intense period of suffrage activism were taken by Jessie Tarbox Beals (above), one of the first successful American women photojournalists.

Official Program WOMAN SUFFRAGE Procession

VOTES for WOMEN

Washington
D.C.
March 3, 1913

Chapter 8: 1913

Rebirth of the Federal Amendment

Despite their victories in the 1912 elections, suffragists were reminded of the difficulties and limits of the state-by-state approach.

At the November 1912 convention of the National American Woman Suffrage Association two young activists, Alice Paul and Lucy Burns, secured Anna Howard Shaw's approval to take over NAWSA's barely active Congressional Committee in Washington D.C. Paul and Burns, both of whom had worked with Emmeline Pankhurst in England, planned to organize a parade in support of the long-dormant Federal suffrage amendment. At the time Elizabeth Kent, wife of a California congressman, headed the committee as a volunteer with an annual budget of $10. Woman suffrage was last debated by the Senate in 1887 and had never reached the floor of the House. There had been no House or Senate committee report at all since 1896, although perfunctory hearings were held annually.

Paul and Burns, together with Mary Ritter Beard who had edited *The Woman Voter*, attorney Crystal Eastman who knew Burns from Vassar, and Dora Lewis, an aristocratic widow from Philadelphia, revitalized the committee within a matter of weeks and recruited a host of new workers. The novel idea of a political parade in the capital for the Federal amendment appealed to many suffragists who felt that congressional action was long overdue and that organized pressure should be applied on a national scale, not just in individual states.

The parade was both a ringing cry against injustice and a vibrant celebration of women's progress. "We march in a spirit of protest," the organizers declared in the official program, "against the present political organization of society from which women are excluded."

Left: An elegant mounted herald set the tone for the ambitious parade.

Elisabeth Freeman brought her experience with the militant suffrage movement in England to the U.S. where she helped organize public demonstrations to bring the cause to a wider audience. After setting up a successful outdoor rally which opened NAWSA's annual convention in Philadelphia in 1912, she helped plan the ambitious New York to Washington D.C. Pilgrimage. She followed the pilgrims along the route, driving a yellow horse-drawn suffrage cart which carried supplies and extra literature. Freeman, a Socialist and trade unionist, had spent two months in a notorious English prison and was a particularly effective speaker with factory workers. A "Pilgrim March," inspired by an earlier hike to Albany, was featured at a benefit dance (below) in New York for the Woman Suffrage Party.

HELP!! **WE NEED IT**

You Give It by Attending the

Unique Entertainment and Dance

given by the

WOMAN SUFFRAGE PARTY
of the 27th ASSEMBLY DISTRICT

January 31st 1913
8.30 P. M.

180 Madison Avenue

Special Features:
Pilgrims March with the Albany Hikers
Ballot Box Quadrille   The Anti Glide-by
The Suffrage Trot   Voters' Dip
            Anti Back-step

Tickets 25 Cents Each   On Sale at 30 E. 34th St.

Hardy Women Make a Winter Pilgrimage from New York to Washington D.C.

AFTER BEING appointed chair of NAWSA's Congressional Committee, Alice Paul began recruiting suffragists in surrounding states to participate in the Washington D.C. parade. In New York City activist Rosalie Gardiner Jones proposed a Votes for Women Pilgrimage from New York to Washington D.C. to publicize the parade and appeal to newly-elected President Woodrow Wilson to support the Federal amendment. The formidable march would cover 295 wintry miles in 16 days.

On February 12, 1913, Jones and over a dozen other pilgrims began their long trek to the nation's capital. Jour-

Triggering patriotic comparisons by journalists and editorial cartoonists, "General" Rosalie Jones and her band of pilgrims drew national attention as they hiked from New York to the nation's capital during the winter of 1913. James Donahey's drawing (above) from the *Cleveland Plain Dealer* compared the women's action to Washington crossing the Delaware, delighting suffragists who welcomed such parallels with America's revolutionary tradition. *The Woman Voter* boasted that "no propaganda work by the State had ever achieved such publicity."

Dressed in long brown woolen capes for the freezing weather, the pilgrims passed out leaflets and buttons and made countless speeches along the way. Arriving triumphantly in Washington D.C. (below), the women and their supporters were met by a mounted honor guard sent by NAWSA's Congressional Committee, which escorted them past a welcoming crowd on February 28. The pilgrims again drew cheers when they marched in the great parade for the Federal amendment three days later.

nalists immediately dubbed her "General" Rosalie Jones, assisted by "Lieutenant Colonel" Ida Craft, a New York state suffrage officer, and "Surgeon General" Lavinia Dock, a pioneer settlement house nurse. A total of sixteen women came from seven states to form the core of what the press humorously referred to as "The Army of the Hudson." Their ranks were substantially increased by supporters in each town.

Above: Rosalie Jones (left), Ida Craft (third from left), and other pilgrims with their walking sticks and bags of literature before starting their 1913 hike.

NAWSA's New Congressional Committee Attracts a Wealth of Talent

ALICE PAUL was 27 when she became chair of the NAWSA Congressional Committee in Washington D.C. Her plan for the first suffrage parade in the nation's capital attracted women of all ages who offered a wealth of talent and experience.

A few of these women posed (above) in front of the committee's first headquarters in the basement of 1420 F Street which opened on January 2, 1913. In the front row from the left are Glenna S. Tinnin, a theatrical producer who organized the pageant feature of the procession, Helen H. Gardener, a novelist and capital resident who served as press representative, and Alice Paul. Next to her is former committee chair Eliz-

abeth Kent, a congressional wife who arranged for the bands and the Continental Hall meeting, and Genevieve Stone, another congressional wife and former assistant superintendent of schools who

organized marchers from the non-suffrage states.

In the back row are Gertrude Leonard, a Washington D.C. attorney who oversaw suffrage headquarters and the section of lawyers in the pa-

rade, Nina Evans Allender, an artist with the Treasury Department who secured all the permits for the outdoor meetings, Lulu Hemingway of Alabama who supervised literature sales at headquarters, Hazel MacKaye, a professional actress from Cambridge, Massachusetts, who directed the Allegory on the Treasury steps, and Elsie Hill, a Vassar graduate who organized the college women's section of the procession. The heads of thirty-seven committees were assisted by dozens of other volunteers over the two hectic months.

Above: Procession organizers. Left: Alice Paul and Helen Gardener discussed publicity.

Leafleting men in the streets of the capital, members of NAWSA's Congressional Committee (left) advertised the March 3, 1913 suffrage parade while others organized marchers, costumes, bands, and logistics. Mrs. J. Otto Stevenson and Elizabeth Kent are on the left and Jane Burleson and Mrs. George Grove are on the right. The committee encouraged state associations to send delegations to show widespread support for the Federal amendment. Before their hike, pilgrims and activists in New York City (above) promoted a rally which featured NAWSA vice-president Jane Addams as speaker.

Alice Paul joined Emmeline Pankhurst's Women's Social and Political Union while studying in England in 1909. A Quaker from Moorestown, New Jersey, Paul had graduated from Swarthmore College and studied social work at the University of Pennsylvania. In England, she sold newspapers and attended meetings before joining a demonstration and getting arrested. Paul was jailed several times and endured forced feeding while on hunger strikes in prison. Returning to the U.S. (below) she helped launch open-air meetings in Philadelphia.

A Dynamic Partnership Brings New Life to the Federal Amendment

WITH ONLY eight weeks to plan, NAWSA's newly-staffed Congressional Committee worked to make the March 3 parade in Washington D.C. an unforgettable experience. Depending solely on volunteers and raising their own funds, Alice Paul and Lucy Burns crafted a spectacular event that built on, and in some ways surpassed, the pageantry of earlier parades in New York and London. Scheduled for the day before Woodrow Wilson's inauguration, when the city was full of people, the parade announced unequivocally that there was important new energy in the suffrage ranks.

The procession featured

Lucy Burns, a native of Brooklyn, New York, developed into an effective street speaker and seasoned activist while working for two years as a salaried organizer with the Women's Social and Political Union in England and Scotland. Tall and athletic with blue eyes and red hair, Burns was an outstanding scholar at Vassar before traveling to Europe to study languages. She met Alice Paul when they were both arrested during a suffrage protest in London in 1909. A natural leader, Burns was repeatedly jailed and force-fed during hunger strikes in British prisons. Paul called her "a thousand times more valiant than I." In recognition of their sacrifice, prisoners including Burns and Paul were awarded the Holloway jail brooch (below) by British leader Emmeline Pankhurst. The Americans would later create a pin of their own.

colorful banners, marching bands, symbolic floats, and regiments of women marching by countries, states, and professions in matching costumes. At the head, just behind the color guard and mounted marshals, the Amendment Float broadcast the demand for a constitutional amendment.

Paul and Burns made a powerful and complementary team. Paul was a focused executive who thought strategically and was able to raise money and attract publicity with unusual skill. Women from widely different backgrounds were drawn by her charismatic personality and single-minded focus on the Federal amendment. Burns was a passionate leader who helped formulate and carry out these innovative campaigns. Their partnership would have a powerful impact on the movement and on the entire country.

Above: The Amendment Float and lead units.

Beauty and Power Combine in Washington D.C. Suffrage Parade

The Woman Suffrage Procession got off to a festive start on the afternoon of March 3, 1913 passing before covered reviewing stands and excited crowds. The Amendment Float was followed by fifty ushers dressed in blue and gold and the officers of NAWSA headed by Anna Howard Shaw and Jane Addams.

A band led the way for Carrie Catt and the first section of the parade, "The World-Wide Movement for Woman Suffrage," which included delegations of women in their native costumes representing countries with full or partial suffrage. Other sections represented "The Appeal of the States," "The 75 Year Struggle for Freedom," and "Women in Business and the Professions."

The legions of gaily-dressed marchers widely proclaimed that women throughout the country, and around the world, wanted the vote and had a rightful claim to it. An estimated 6,000 to 8,000 women took part in the parade along with ten bands, twenty-six floats, and six golden chariots representing the first six suffrage states. Significantly, a number of congressmen and politicians also marched.

Hundreds of thousands of spectators from every part of the country, most in town for the inauguration and the change in political parties, witnessed the event. Observers were amazed at the beauty and dignity of the unique procession; even most suffragists had not known what to expect. As *The New York Times* reported the following day, "It was an astonishing demonstration."

Above: Passing the reviewing stands near the Capitol.

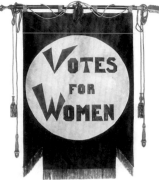

"The Free Woman of the Future"

AT ALICE Paul's invitation, Inez Milholland (left) of New York led the Washington D.C. suffrage parade dressed as a mounted herald. Insisting on symbolizing the future rather than the past, Milholland updated the idea. She told Paul that she would ride not as a medieval herald "but as something suggesting the 'free woman of the future' – crowned with the star of hope – armed with the cross of mercy, circled with the blue mantle of freedom, breasted with the torch of knowledge, and carrying the trumpet which is to herald the dawn of a new day of heroic endeavor for womanhood." *The New York Times* reported that she was "by far the most picturesque figure in the parade, an imposing figure in a white broadcloth Cossack suit and long white-kid boots. From her shoulders hung a pale-blue cloak, adorned with a golden Maltese cross." Mounted on Gray Dawn, a friend's horse, Milholland made a lasting impression on suffragists and observers alike, embodying the energy, beauty, and youth of the renewed movement for women's rights.

Left: Inez Milholland

Theater and Art Bring New Life to the Cause

In addition to marshaling supporters and focusing attention on the Federal amendment, the suffrage parade in Washington D.C. also gave participants an opportunity to represent the goal of women's equality in new ways. One beautiful float (left), from the section of "Countries Where Women are Working for Suffrage," featured elaborately costumed Women of the Bible Lands. The cast included, from the Old Testament, the judge Deborah, the priestess Miriam, and the scholar Huldah, and from the New Testament, the four daughters of the evangelist Philip who were public speakers and teachers. The remarkable display was arranged by Lydia Von Finkelstein Mountford of Jerusalem.

Despite objections from some southerners, the parade was integrated to a degree. Black women were not actively recruited but a strong contingent of Black students from Howard University marched in the college women's section. Eminent suffragist Ida B. Wells-Barnett, refusing to tolerate segregation, boldly joined her state delegation flanked by white supporters. When President-elect Wilson arrived in the capital and found the streets empty, he was told that all the people were over on Pennsylvania Avenue watching the woman suffrage parade.

Left: Biblical women.

In a beautifully coordinated display of color and pageantry, costumed divisions of nurses (top right), homemakers, teachers, lawyers, and women in other occupations marched through the streets of Washington D.C. while hundreds of yellow flags and brilliant banners fluttered in the wind. The parade illustrated the worldwide progress of woman suffrage over the past 65 years. One series of floats showed women working alongside men in the field (right), in the factory, and in all other areas of life except the halls of government. A final float displayed the nine enfranchised states on an oversized Suffrage Map. Following the gaily-decorated route of the next day's inaugural parade, the procession included delegations from nearly every state, including Massachusetts (bottom) whose members carried a banner honoring early suffragist Julia Ward Howe. NAWSA's own colorful pennant (above) featured the figure of Justice and the rising sun surrounded by a wreath wrapped with a ribbon inscribed with the words Freedom, Service, Cooperation, Patriotism, and Equality.

Stalled and Threatened by a Near-Riot

THE STREETS were clear and the crowds were orderly in front of the Capitol at the start of the March 3 suffrage procession. But farther away, rowdy and intoxicated spectators surged into the street until they had surrounded and completely blocked the parade.

As the unrestrained crowd pressed in on the marchers some men grabbed at the women, tearing at their clothing and ripping banners from their hands. "Some marchers were struck in the face by onlookers, spat upon, and overwhelmed with ribald remarks," recalled Harriot Blatch, "and the police officers as a whole did nothing."

The Baltimore American re-ported the women "practically fought their way foot by foot up Pennsylvania Avenue, through a surging throng that completely defied Washington police, swamped the marchers, and broke their procession into little companies. The women, trudging stoutly along under great difficulties, were able to complete their march only when troops of cavalry from Fort Myer were rushed into Washington . . . No inauguration has ever produced such scenes, which in many instances amounted to nothing less than riots."

Above and left: Crowds close in, then completely block the parade, forcing it to a halt.

Women Confront a Hostile Mob and Indifferent Police

Anxious yet resolute, suffragists in their colorful felt parade costumes had their courage tested as they marched or rode slowly down a narrowing path through an increasingly hostile crowd during the March 3 parade. As one participant remembered, "We struggled along, with lumps in our throats, fighting back tears. We thought all was lost."

Stalled for over an hour, the marchers were shaken by the abusive behavior of men and furious at the indifference of the police. "The treatment accorded us was simply unspeakable," Glenna Tinnan told *The New York Times*. "It was more than a question of an undermanned police line. Those who were assigned to the task not only did little or nothing, but even seemed to encourage the hoodlums in . . . breaking up the parade." Dr. Nellie V. Mark testified, "I have never heard such vulgar, obscene, scurrilous, abusive language as was hurled at us that day by men – the voters of the country – and it amused the police."

Harriot Blatch blamed the government which "held in light esteem the affairs of women. When women were sponsors of a project, that project immediately became a matter of small account in the eyes of the official class." Blatch charged that the parade was broken up "because the State taught lack of respect for the opinion of women," and that the mob "reflected the State's opinion of its women citizens."

Above: A float of costumed suffragists continued down a narrowing route.

WE DEMAND
AMENDMENT TO
CONSTITUTION O
UNITED STA
ENFRANCHISIN
WOMEN OF THIS C

Suffragists, Boy Scouts, and sympathetic spectators at first tried to force the crowd back so that the marchers could pass. But the unruly mob "surged forward and . . . soon the entire procession was engulfed by rowdy, half drunken men and boys," recalled Gertrude Brown of New York. A mounted squad of the 15th Cavalry (left), called in by the Secretary of War, eventually opened a way for the women to proceed (above). Suffragists were finally able to march past the Treasury building where a dramatic Allegory of Women had been waiting to welcome them. It took the parade three hours to cover one mile.

From the steps of the U.S. Treasury building, Liberty (above) and her attendants greeted the procession of women during the March 3 suffrage pageant. Heralds announced the long-delayed marchers with a bugle fanfare and a grand, multi-phase performance began. Beautifully-robed figures representing Liberty, Justice, Charity, Hope, and Peace slowly appeared and swept down the steps with their attendants to gather around Columbia (below) to witness and bless this new "Crusade of Women." The performance artistically portrayed the ideals toward which both women and men continued to strive.

A Spectacular Tableau Encourages the New Crusade of Women

SPECTATORS LINED the roof of the Treasury building on March 3 to view the beautiful allegory that welcomed the suffrage procession. Dancer Florence Flemming Noyes portrayed the commanding figure of Columbia who, with striped cape and eagle scepter, took her place as leader in the dramatic spectacle to the strains of "The Star Spangled Banner."

Each allegorical figure had her own colors and music. Liberty, "unfettered and free," swept down to the plaza to the *Triumphal March* from Aida followed by dancers waving scarves of crimson and rose. Justice, in purple and violet, and Charity in blue, preceded Liberty to the tunes of *Pilgrims Chorus* and

Demanding an Official Investigation

FRONT PAGE reports of the frightening mob scene and inadequate police protection brought national attention to the new campaign for the Federal suffrage amendment. Alice Paul and others demanded a congressional investigation and a lengthy but ultimately inconclusive hearing kept the matter in the news for several weeks.

NAWSA's Congressional Committee was quick to take advantage of its new visibility and immediately began to organize a new lobbying effort in the capital. The committee sent delegations to the new president, speakers to congressional hearings, and lobbyists to individual congressmen to push for the suf-

frage bill. The women also launched a series of dramatic new initiatives to show widespread support for the Federal amendment.

Paul and Lucy Burns provided the passion and energy needed to lead this new assault on the capital. As historian Inez Irwin reported, "They displayed astonishing executive ability, gathered about them a small army of women and during the next twelve months raised $27,378." NAWSA, with a $42,000 annual budget, kept its focus on state campaigns.

Above: Columbia leads the tableau. Below: Young dancers followed Hope during the Allegory.

Handel's *Largo.* White-clad girls carrying golden balls danced down the steps of the Treasury after the hesitant figure of Hope, clothed in rainbow colors. After the silvery figure of Peace, dancers bore golden cornucopias symbolizing Plenty that follows Peace.

The procession climaxed with a rally at Continental

Hall. A relieved yet shaken Anna Shaw and Carrie Catt spoke but Helen Keller had to cancel because of the near riot. The dramatic and shocking events of the day were reported in detail by visiting journalists sent to cover the inauguration.

Above: The Allegory on the Treasury steps.

Forcing Congress to Respond

NAWSA's CONGRESSIONAL Committee organized a second parade on April 7, 1913, focused on the opening of the 63rd Congress. Suffragists representing each of the 435 congressional districts marched under their state banners to present their petitions and resolutions in support of the Federal amendment to Congress. Reaching the Capitol steps, the women were welcomed by congressmen who formally reintroduced the amendment. The bill became known as the Bristow-Mondell Amendment after its sponsors, but it was the same suffrage bill first presented in 1878 at the behest of Elizabeth Cady Stanton and Susan B. Anthony.

Above: The figure of Peace released a white dove symbolizing a new beginning during a high moment in the March 3, 1913 tableau. Right: The April 7 suffrage parade reaches the Capitol steps.

The Congressional Union Focuses Exclusively on the Federal Amendment

To MAKE the Federal amendment a national priority, Alice Paul formed a new but not very distinct national organization in April 1913 called the Congressional Union for Woman Suffrage (CU) to work beyond the confines of a NAWSA lobbying committee. Adopting purple, white, and gold as its colors, symbolizing loyalty, purity, and light, the CU began to reach out to women throughout the country. During the summer it sent salaried organizers to half a dozen eastern states to raise money and build support. On June 13 the Senate Woman Suffrage Committee is-

sued its first favorable report in twenty years.

The summer also saw a dozen automobile pilgrimages of suffragists to Washington D.C. from congressional districts across the country. The coordinated action climaxed with a great procession to Congress on July 31 which delivered petitions with 200,000 signatures asking for passage of the Federal amendment.

Above: Suffragists marched state-by-state in the April 7 parade. Below: A delegation of suffragists brought the issue to the attention of the new president.

"We knew by experience that waiting to get money for action was short-sighted policy," Harriot Stanton Blatch remembered. "Do something and the money will come to foot the bill." With that hope, the Women's Political Union launched its own biweekly newspaper, *The Women's Political World*, on January 6, 1913 edited by Blatch's daughter Nora and Beatrice Brown. The March 1 issue (facing page) featured a warrior on the ramparts sounding "The Call" to action. The image was borrowed from the British and modified by adding nine stars to the flag to represent the equal suffrage states.

Ringing a bell to attract attention, Mrs. Calvin Tomkins and Mrs. Sidney Borg (above right) sold tickets to a suffrage ball in front of the library on January 29. Dancers (right) prepared for a suffrage pageant in January 1914 while a sophisticated couple graced the program cover above.

Building Support in New York

WHILE THERE were hopeful new developments in Washington D.C., women in the states continued their work. In New York, suffragists raised money for their campaign by organizing lectures, art exhibitions, performances, and benefits of all sorts. Supporters also held several great balls which attracted both society women in glittering ball gowns and working girls in simple shirt waists. "We learned," Harriot Stanton Blatch recalled, "that sermons and logic never convince, that human beings move because they feel, not because they think. For that reason we began to dance about our cause at great balls, instead of sitting in corners and arguing." Ticket prices were deliberately kept low and the 1913 ball attracted over 8,000 people.

THE
WOMEN'S POLITICAL WORLD

IMMEDIATE·OBJECT: SECURING·WOMAN·SUFFRAGE·IN·NEW·YORK·STATE·IN·1915

VOL. I. No. 5.   NEW YORK, MARCH 1, 1913.   PRICE 2 CENTS.

THE CALL

The Women's Marseillaise

Arise, ye daughters of a land
That vaunts its liberty!
Make legislators understand
   That women must be free,
   That women WILL be free.
Hark! Hark! The trumpet's calling!
Who'd be a laggard in the fight?
With victory even now in sight,
And stubborn foemen backward falling.

   Chorus:

To Freedom's cause till death
We swear our fealty.
Repeat—March on! March on!
   Face to the dawn,
    The dawn of liberty.

Marching On

It is mete that the next great procession of women should awake the national capital, for we march for unity, for a common citizenship among women from coast to coast, from lake to gulf. The woman of the South will stand with the woman of the North, the woman of the East will meet in fellowship the woman of the West, the enfranchised woman will join with the disenfranchised—we will march as American women demanding equality between ourselves, demanding that there shall be uniformity in the laws governing our political status throughout the nation.

No statutes in the separate States stand in greater contrast than those dealing with the political rights of women. While some women exercise electoral rights which belong to citizens in a republic, others have no part in the political life of the community in which they live. Between these extremes our States illustrate every stage in political evolution from a complete sex aristocracy to a free self-governing people. These contrasts stir a deep discontent. We will march in protest against such inequality.

Our procession will enter new territory, and therefore our soldiers must meet the test of courage. Every believer in the enfranchisement of women must find her place in our ranks. Our numbers must not be deprived of one marcher through lack of enthusiasm, through lack of courage in any. Those who stand not with us will be counted against us. Our march will be a test of devotion to our common cause.

A great procession draws marcher to marcher. As we stand marking time, as we move forward keeping step, comradeship is born, and waxes strong. Our march will fill our hearts with fellowship.

A great procession carries conviction of earnestness, of devotion to onlookers who doubt or disbelieve. It stirs their emotions, it convinces as logic and sermons cannot. Our march will draw converts to our cause.

Let us march, then, for our own soul's good, let us march for the conversion of men, let us march shoulder to shoulder for the joy of the comrade beside us.

The procession of women will know no sectionalism. Forward we will press as a unit for liberty. The woman of the enfranchised State understands full well that so long as her sister-women in other Commonwealths are enslaved politically, she herself suffers degradation. The disfranchised woman, feeling her equal worth, regards her enfranchised sisters as but pointing the way which she must quickly tread. Our procession of women on March 3 will be inspired by a common ideal—special privileges for none, liberty for all. We will march for equality—equality between women.

Our march will be a parade of protest against the injustice of keeping some women in political tutelage, while others enjoy political freedom. We will march demanding for women a common ground of citizenship.

HARRIOT STANTON BLATCH.

The New York Legislature Yields to Suffragists' Pressure

IN LATE January 1913 both Houses of the New York legislature for the first time approved the bill which passed the suffrage question on to the voters. Supporters used the May parade to mark the start of the long-awaited referendum campaign. The women were confident that they could get the measure passed again by the next state legislature, as required, so New York men could vote on suffrage in 1915.

Due to the efforts initiated by Harriot Blatch and carried out by suffragists throughout the state, delegates to both the Democratic and Republican state conventions in 1912 were persuaded to include planks in their parties' platforms which supported putting the suffrage question to the voters. With party endorsement suffragists were delighted and relieved to see that even old enemies in the legislature felt duty bound to place the measure before the voters out of party loyalty.

Blatch explained that although most representatives opposed women voting, "they considered the according of the referendum sound democracy. This idea had been put into their minds by the Women's Political Union, and their acceptance of it proved the value of the propaganda we had pushed. . . . At last everyone knew the difference between believing in woman suffrage and believing in a referendum on woman suffrage."

The victory would not have been possible without the electoral pressure the WPU had put on selected opponents the previous years, working to defeat several politicians and putting others on notice. Suffragists in Massachusetts facing a similarly hostile legislature adopted the same strategy. Meanwhile, supporters in several states were successful in having the question placed on the 1914 ballot.

Above: Leading the New York State Woman Suffrage Association's division in the 1913 parade were (from left) Harriet Burton Laidlaw, Mrs. Albert Plimpton, Augusta Hughston, Mrs. Frank Stratton, and Helen Rick.

Verina Morton-Jones was a pioneering physician and leading club woman in Brooklyn, New York, who, in the words of historian Thea Arnold, "fought to win the vote for all women and fought to protect the right to vote of all Black Americans." Born in Cleveland, Ohio, Morton-Jones was 23 when she graduated from the Woman's Medical College in Philadelphia in 1888. She became the first woman to practice medicine in the state of Mississippi. After moving to Brooklyn, she became an important figure in community affairs. She served as president of the Brooklyn Equal Suffrage League, monitored cases of racial discrimination, testified before government committees, and encouraged voter education efforts. A board member of the National Association for the Advancement of Colored People, she also headed the Lincoln Settlement House, originally an extension of the Henry Street Settlement, which sponsored classes and services for the growing Black community in Brooklyn.

Carrie Catt Returns to Organize the New York Campaign

IN LATE 1912, after nearly two years traveling abroad, Carrie Catt returned to New York to find a suffrage movement bursting with new life. After the legislature passed the suffrage bill in January 1913, officers of the state association asked Catt to take charge of the upcoming referendum campaign.

She proposed merging all the various suffrage societies, mostly in New York City, into one statewide campaign committee. While most groups went along with the plan, Alva Belmont's Political Equality Association and Harriot Blatch's Women's Political Union chose not to be swallowed up and lose their independence and resources. Instead, Blatch advocated that they work together in a "friendly rivalry."

Catt divided the state into twelve campaign districts, each with its own chair overseeing leaders in a total of 150 assembly districts. Mary Garrett Hay took charge of the First Campaign District, New York City, which included 63 assembly districts. Through its precinct organizing, the Woman Suffrage Party tried in particular to reach women in the home – the wives, mothers, and family members of voters – leaving women in the workplace to the WPU. But as the WPU came to depend more on wealthier supporters to fund its campaigns, the WSP began to attract more working women as well.

Above: Carrie Catt led the first suffrage school in New York in 1911. Below: Gertrude Foster Brown, Harriet Burton Laidlaw, and Helen Rogers Reid installed a Votes for Women hood ornament (facing page).

TO THE WOMAN IN THE HOME

How can a mother rest content with this—

When such conditions exist as this?

There are thousands of children working in sweat-shops like the one in the picture. There are thousands of children working in mines and mills and factories. Thousands more are being wronged and cheated by Society in countless ways.

IS NOT THIS **YOUR** BUSINESS?

Intelligent citizens WHO CARED could change all this—providing always, of course, that they had the power of the ballot.

DO **YOU** CARE?

Mothers are responsible for the welfare of children—all children. Do your duty as a mother and demand

VOTES FOR WOMEN!

NATIONAL AMERICAN WOMAN SUFFRAGE ASSOCIATION
505 FIFTH AVENUE   NEW YORK CITY

Mary Ellen Sigsbee, a painter and Socialist who contributed her work to the suffrage movement, illustrated these two fliers (above and top right) issued by NAWSA around 1912. The handouts promoted an enlarged concept of the home and homemakers, and emphasized women's responsibilities in larger society. Like several other women artists, including Lou Rogers, Nina Allender, and Fredrikke Palmer, Sigsbee chose the cartoon form as the most effective propaganda medium to reach the widely diverse, and not always literate, male voters. Allender, a versatile and prolific artist, later became the Official Cartoonist for the Congressional Union.

A Climactic Parade in New York Celebrates a Key Victory

AN ESTIMATED 30,000 suffragists filled New York's Fifth Avenue during the Women's Political Union's suffrage parade on May 3, 1913. The marchers celebrated passage of their bill by the legislature and demonstrated again to New York voters the strength and breadth of their cause.

Dressed in riding gear and on horseback, Inez Milholland drew cheers as she led the parade up Fifth Avenue carrying an American flag. Behind her, eight women in blue carried silk banners bearing the names of the parade's co-sponsors. Great divisions of white-clad suffra-

TO THE MALE CITIZEN

If this is womanly—   Why not this?

Housekeeping is woman's work—no man denies that.

Government is public house-keeping—practically everybody agrees to that.

Isn't it foolish, then, to keep out of government the very people who have had most training for a large part of its functions?

Men have never regarded it as unwomanly for women to do the scrubbing and cleaning indoors—even in public places, like office buildings.

Why, then, should they think it unwomanly for women to keep the streets clean?

Be logical and insist that women should no longer shirk their duty as house-keepers. You need their help.

DEMAND VOTES FOR WOMEN!

NATIONAL AMERICAN WOMAN SUFFRAGE ASSOCIATION
505 FIFTH AVENUE   NEW YORK CITY

gists followed carrying brilliantly colored pennants, flags, and ribbons and marching with well-drilled precision from Washington Square to Central Park. Although everyone wanted to participate, Harriot Blatch noted, it was left to the Women's Political Union to organize and pay the bills for the march. She had recommended that women wear a plain white tailored suit with a Votes for Women sash.

Thirty-five bands played while members of the WPU and the Woman Suffrage Party, representing every borough of greater New York, marched eight abreast by the

thousands in unbroken lines by ward, district, trade, and profession. The two-hour parade included over a thousand students from the eastern women's colleges, regiments of Black women, and several Native American women performers from Buffalo Bill Cody's Wild West Show. Other delegations represented local Greek, Jewish, Italian, and Syrian suffrage societies, showing both the diversity and the unity of modern women.

Above: Inez Milholland rode at the head of the May 3, 1913 suffrage parade in New York City.

Legions of women in white wearing suffrage yellow sashes marched sharply up Fifth Avenue during the May 3, 1913 suffrage parade (below). As an accessory, some marchers wore the patriotic tricorn suffrage hat which could be decorated to each woman's taste. Carrying their walking sticks and

newsbags, the New York to Washington D.C. pilgrims (bottom left), led by "General" Rosalie Jones, won applause from many spectators along the route. Jones organized other hikes in New York state. The city parade took place just two months after the spectacular procession in Washington D.C.

"Heels clicked on the asphalt like hammer taps," wrote one reporter as suffragists took over New York City's Fifth Avenue on Saturday afternoon, May 3, 1913. Marchers dressed uniformly in white carried a forest of yellow banners along the three-mile route, passing before of over a quarter of a million spectators (right). Fifty beautiful and expensive new Women's Political Union banners unified the march. *The New York Times* called it suffragists' "showiest" parade yet.

One added feature of the parade was a Reviewing Stand (below and far right) in front of the Public Library for legislators, state and city officials, and business and professional men. Although not every observer was an advocate, Harriot Blatch noted, "by his presence he registered his approval of women marching for their principles." The parade ended with mass meetings at Carnegie Hall and in the four corners of Central Park Plaza. Having won over the legislature, suffragists now focused on reaching individual voters.

The Men's League for Woman Suffrage in New York City was started in 1910 by Columbia professor Max Eastman, brother of suffragist Crystal Eastman, Oswald Garrison Villard, grandson of William Lloyd Garrison, and Rabbi Stephen S. Wise. Eastman observed that "the main function of the league would be to exist" and the visible support of prominent community leaders did help reassure male voters and bestow greater legitimacy on the suffrage drive. The New York league sponsored meetings in New York (below) often featuring speakers from the equal suffrage states. New York banker James Lees Laidlaw (above, with his wife Harriet) led the National Men's League.

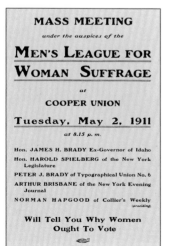

Men Show Their Support for Equal Rights

MEN CAME to New York from several states to participate in the annual parades and to show their support for equal suffrage. Members of the Connecticut chapter of the Men's League for Woman Suffrage marched by the hundreds behind their state banner in the 1913 parade while men from the New York league brought their own cavalry brigade.

The previous year over 600 New York men had marched four abreast in a line that extended five blocks long. There was a lot of teasing or "guying" of the male marchers, one newspaper reported, but "they took it in good part and generally responded with about as good as they got." Most, however, followed pa-

Organizing Men's Leagues for Suffrage

To lead the Men's Leagues for Woman Suffrage in different states suffragists recruited distinguished citizens including former governors, public officials, judges, military and religious leaders, and influential business and professional men.

In Illinois the Chicago Men's Equal Suffrage League was organized in 1909 with former Senator Thomas J. McMillan as its head, and in New York George Foster Peabody, a prominent banker and financier, agreed to serve as first president. Attorney Leonard J. Grossman organized a Men's League in Georgia in 1913 and also advised the state suffrage association. Other loyal supporters included Wilmer Atkinson of Philadelphia, editor of the *Farm Journal,* and Wellington Rankin, brother of Jeannette Rankin and later Attorney General of Montana, whose stature helped attract other forward-looking men.

James Less Laidlaw, a wealthy banker whose wife was very active in the movement, succeeded Peabody in New York and also served as president of the National Men's League which counted 20,000 members in 1912. He was aided by Omar E. Garwood, a former Assistant District Attorney from Colorado who defended equal suffrage in that state. Garwood became secretary of the National Men's League and with Laidlaw organized branches in other states and participated in a number of state campaigns.

Although often subjected to criticism and ridicule for endorsing women's rights, male supporters recognized that as voters they could best influence other voters, and that men should stand up for women's equality. Because of their effectiveness, men's leagues became active parts of nearly all of the state campaigns. Members helped remind voters that it was not a "women against men" issue, but a question of equality and justice.

rade discipline and kept silent.

Dozens of Men's Leagues were organized after 1910, usually connected to pending state campaigns, to help win voters and coordinate the efforts of male supporters. Members gave speeches, held meetings and rallies, organized dinners, balls, and theatrical performances, and carried out campaign activities of all kinds. They also contributed important advice on legislative problems, assisted with state campaigns, and helped raise money.

Above and upper right: Male supporters marched in the 1913 New York parade. Left: A league button advertised support for equality.

MARCH ON! MARCH ON! FACE TO THE DAWN!
THE DAWN OF LIBERTY

JOIN THE MARCH TO VICTORY
WOMAN SUFFRAGE PARADE
Baltimore, Saturday, May 31, 5 P. M.
STARTING FROM WASHINGTON'S MONUMENT, 5 P. M. RAIN OR SHINE
THE LYRIC, MAY 31st, 8 P. M.
MORALITY PLAY: WOMAN. By Mrs. Christian Hemmick
100 in Cast
SPEAKERS : State Senator Helen Ring Robinson of Colorado
U. S. Senator William E. Borah, of Idaho
Rev. James Grattan Mythen, of Baltimore
Tickets on sale at Albaugh's Ticket Office, 817 N. Charles St., and at the Lyric on the
night of the performance. Boxes $15 and $10, Orchestra seats $1.00 and 75c.; balcony 50c.
and 25c.

The growing success of suffrage parades encouraged supporters in other states to schedule their own. Suffragists organized parades in both New Jersey and Maryland in 1913 and used a Joan of Arc figure (above) to call on supporters to join "The March to Victory" in Baltimore. During the summer, members of the Women's Political Union in New York hit on a novel idea to reach voters. They offered visitors to the Suffolk County Fair free child care at their Suffrage Tent (right) which was decorated with the Union's colorful purple, white, and green banners and equipped with toys, games, clean cots, and cradles. The large shady tent was staffed by kindergarten teachers and a trained nurse, leaving parents free to enjoy the fair. They were naturally impressed. The sign on the far left claimed ten equal rights states, still counting Michigan where the election was contested.

Illinois Passes Presidential Suffrage

AFTER TWENTY years of effort, Illinois suffragists scored a key victory in 1913. They persuaded sympathetic state legislators to pass a suffrage bill in keeping with the legislature's power under the state constitution. The bill, which was signed by the governor on June 26, allowed Illinois women to vote for president of the U.S. as well as for many local candidates. Referred to as "presidential suffrage," the measure marked a strategic milestone in the struggle for equal suffrage. Chicago at the time was the second largest city in the country.

While only an amendment to the state constitution approved by the voters could grant full suffrage for state and national offices, the presidential suffrage bill specifically gave women the right to vote for presidential electors and for candidates and measures in municipal elections.

A Unique Campaign

The unique Illinois campaign was carried forward on many fronts simultaneously. Successive state suffrage leaders Ella S. Stewart and Grace Wilbur Trout promoted the strategy (long advocated by Henry Blackwell) and attorney Catharine McCulloch drew up the bill. Ruth Hanna McCormick, later a member of Congress, directed publicity, and Antoinette Funk and Elizabeth K. Booth supervised the work.

John T. McCutcheon's cartoon (above) from the *Chicago Tribune*, "The First One East of the 'Mother of Waters,'" showed suffragists triumphantly crossing the Mississippi at last. Supporters in Chicago (top) were ecstatic.

Booth waged a remarkable and inconspicuous personal campaign with individual legislators during the session, getting to know them and winning their trust while riding on the trains that brought them to and from the state capital. The strength of Progressives elected in 1912 provided the opportunity to win the legislature's approval.

Elizabeth Upham Yates of NAWSA called it an "extraordinary victory," noting that women voted in nine states with 54 electoral votes only after campaigns "that involved vast outlay of time and treasure." Simply by legislative act, Illinois added 29 more, With women having a voice in 83 electoral votes in the next presidential election, excited suffrage leaders noted that women voters might actually hold the balance of power in a close election.

After their victory, Illinois suffragists had to fight to protect the ground they had gained. Anti-suffragists filed lawsuits which challenged the constitutionality of the law and also tried to repeal the bill in the legislature. It took nearly four years before the U.S. Supreme Court ruled that the measure was constitutional, allowing other states to follow.

Alaska

Meanwhile, one of the last U.S. territories, Alaska, was "won by correspondence" in March 1913. Since Alaska had no suffrage organization, NAWSA officials pledged its 22 territorial legislators by mail and telegraph to back suffrage for women and they approved it unanimously. ◆

Defeating Opponents in Massachusetts

The Women's Political Union continued its statewide efforts in New York and during the summer of 1913 helped suffragists in New Jersey organize a WPU chapter of their own which worked alongside the New Jersey state association.

Supporters in Massachusetts also followed the WPU's lead in mounting political campaigns against selected opponents in the state legislature. Their first campaign in 1912 caused a sensation when they helped defeat Senator Roger Wolcott, uncooperative chair of the Constitutional Amendments Committee.

The following year the women mounted a larger attack. The Boston Equal Suffrage Association defeated one man and the state suffrage association, working with the Progressive Party, defeated two candidates, including Charles Underhill (left) in the primaries. They ousted another two men in the election including the powerful Republican president of the Senate. As in New York, Massachusetts politicians were being forced to see the wisdom of passing the suffrage question on to the voters. Chapters of the Woman Suffrage Party were also established in several eastern states, and local suffrage leagues evolved into political district organizations.

Above: New York suffragists wore signboards along a Coney Island beach, much to the astonishment of male bathers.

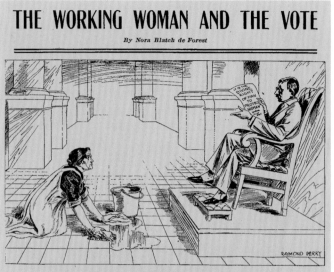

THE WORKING WOMAN AND THE VOTE

By Nora Blatch de Forest

Senator Root says: "In the divine distribution of powers the duty and the right of protection rests with the male."

But working women are underpaid and exploited. In many industries in New York State over half the women workers get less than **$6.00** a week.

In 50 per cent. of the suffrage States the woman voter has secured for herself a minimum wage, while only 10 per cent. of the other States have granted this.

60 per cent. of the suffrage States and 58 per cent. of the other States regulate the hours of women's work.

In the suffrage States the woman voter has decided that she will work no more than eight hours and forty-two minutes, while in the other States the law decrees that she must work ten hours if her employer requires it.

The woman voter sees to it that the laws are enforced and do not lie as dead letters on the statute books.

THE CHIVALROUS MAN REALIZES THAT WOMAN NEEDS THE VOTE TO PROTECT HERSELF.

VOTE FOR THE WOMAN SUFFRAGE AMENDMENT IN NOVEMBER, 1915.
JOIN THE WOMEN'S POLITICAL UNION, 25 WEST 45th STREET, NEW YORK.
25 cents initiation fee, no dues.
SUBSCRIBE TO THE WOMEN'S POLITICAL WORLD, 25 WEST 45th STREET, NEW YORK.
Published semi-monthly, subscription price 50 cents per year.
This leaflet for sale at Women's Political Union headquarters. Price 10 cents per 100, postpaid 15 cents, or $1.00 per 1,000, express extra.

Personifying the third generation of suffragists, Nora Blatch produced literature (top) for the Women's Political Union, and even mounted a "Horseback Campaign" in 1913 to reach New York voters. She is shown speaking (above) with Harriet Porritt on October 10. Nora was briefly married to radio pioneer Lee de Forest.

Resentments and Political Differences Grow Within NAWSA

As STATE suffragists prepared for referendum campaigns, Alice Paul and NAWSA's Congressional Committee continued to promote the Federal amendment as a critical political issue. During 1913 the committee repeatedly sought President Wilson's support through delegations of distinguished women. He responded first

A Painful Separation

COLOR STAMPS like the one above publicized several of NAWSA's annual conventions, including the 1913 meeting hosted by Alice Paul's energetic Congressional Committee. Here simmering differences finally boiled over. Despite praise for the committee's remarkable accomplishments, NAWSA leaders called on Paul to explain its finances and its relationship to the Congressional Union which she also led. Since the CU and the committee were nearly indistinguishable, had raised their own funds, and had successfully championed the Federal amendment despite NAWSA's indifference, a conflict was probably inevitable. The clash over authority, strategy, and funds led to Paul's dismissal and the resignations of other committee members. "The real difficulty," historian Eleanor Flexner noted, "arose from the rift growing between dynamic and static methods of work and aims." Anna Howard Shaw appointed new members to the decimated committee and the CU soon separated from NAWSA.

that he had have never considered the matter, later that the tariff laws took precedence, and still later that it was a matter for each state to decide.

Meanwhile, the Congressional Union grew to include over 1,000 members, and in November began publishing a weekly news magazine called *The Suffragist.* The venerable but impoverished National Association had no publication of its own and some members resented the success of newer and smaller suffrage groups. Soon there were calls for a change in policy.

Late in the year Carrie Catt began a successful drive to require all member societies to pay a percentage of their revenue to NAWSA. She also raised questions within NAWSA about the Congressional Committee's independent finances.

Above: Alice Paul (second from right in front) and Congressional Union members wore purple, white, and gold sashes for a hearing before the House Rules Committee in 1914.

Militant Confrontations Shake Britain

FRUSTRATION, DISSENSION, and violence marked the final years of the British suffrage movement, almost overshadowing the courage and tenacity of dedicated suffragists.

Faced with an intransigent Parliament in 1912, Emmeline Pankhurst, released from jail, intensified the Women's Social and Political Union's militant campaigns while moderates simultaneously stepped up their efforts. Pankhurst took aim at "the security of property" since it was "something governments care for more than human life."

Destroying Property

Over the following years, government and shop windows were smashed. Golf courses and postal boxes were vandalized. Several unoccupied government buildings, politicians' residences, churches, and railway stations were set on fire as part of the suffragettes' "guerrilla warfare."

British suffragists, as well as many American supporters, grew deeply concerned over the extreme and increasingly unpopular tactics of the militants. "The whole spirit engendered by attempting to gain by violence or threats of violence what was not conceded to justice and reason was intensely inimical to the spirit of our movement," declared Millicent Garret Fawcett, head of the National Union of Women's Suffrage Societies. Membership in the moderate federation grew from 130 groups in 1910 to over 600 in 1914. The National Union

Police arrested Emmeline Pankhurst outside Buckingham Palace on May 21, 1914. After suffrage was won, a statue of the controversial but widely respected leader was erected by supporters a short distance from Parliament.

and other groups continued to organize and lobby despite the WSPU's warfare.

In October 1912, Emmeline Pankhurst and her daughter Christabel purged the WSPU of those who questioned their policies and began a new weekly paper, *The Suffragette*, which Christabel edited.

Arson and further violence led police to raid WSPU offices, and indignant members of the public took to attacking suffragettes themselves. One woman distributing leaflets was stripped and tarred; others were pelted with food and heavy objects.

Through all this the government remained unmoved. On June 4, 1913, suffragette Emily Wilding Davison, after being jailed nine times and repeatedly force-fed, ran onto the race course in protest during the Epsom Derby and was killed by the king's race horse. Proclaiming "She Died For Women," the WSPU honored her with a martyr's funeral which drew tens of thousands of mourners.

The following year, protesting the harsh treatment of Emmeline Pankhurst, one supporter slashed a painting in the National Gallery causing museums and art galleries to close to the public and resentment to increase. A final confrontation with police on May 21, 1914, witnessed by a crowd of over 20,000, saw sixty women including Pankhurst arrested outside Buckingham Palace when they tried to send a deputation to plead with the king.

An Abrupt End

Militant and mainstream actions ended abruptly just after the start of World War I on August 4, 1914. Immediately nearly all suffragists pledged themselves to the war effort and imprisoned suffragettes were released. The WSPU was even enlisted by the government to recruit women for war work. In January 1918, Parliament finally approved a bill which, with certain conditions, enfranchised women over 30, thereby preserving a male majority. In 1928 all women in Great Britain over 21 were enfranchised. ◆

Militants

AS THEY ARE

AS THEY THINK THEY ARE

Rodney Thomson
with apologies to
Orson Lowell

AS THEY APPEAR TO THE POLICE AND SHOPKEEPERS

Looking Backward

Issue of Militancy Challenges the U.S. Movement

FEARS THAT Americans might embrace the alienating tactics of the British suffragettes lay at least partly behind NAWSA's break with Alice Paul and Lucy Burns in late 1913. Once the more politically confrontational approach of these two young, British-trained activists became clear, NAWSA leaders moved to regain control over their Congressional Committee and to challenge the need for the Congressional Union which, they argued, duplicated their own work. Neither Anna Howard Shaw nor Carrie Catt approved of the militants' approach and were distrustful of those women who did.

Although Paul and Burns had returned from England "irrevocably radicalized and firmly militant," in historian

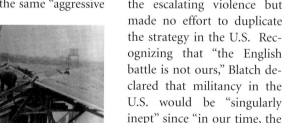

Linda Ford's words, they did not endorse violence or property destruction. But, as Ford notes, they did bring to America the same "aggressive and determined stance."

Harriot Stanton Blatch and others also maintained their support for the WSPU despite the escalating violence but made no effort to duplicate the strategy in the U.S. Recognizing that "the English battle is not ours," Blatch declared that militancy in the U.S. would be "singularly inept" since "in our time, the vote has not been won through violence."

Left: Saunderton Railway Station in England, burnt down by suffragettes in 1913. Top left: Different perceptions of "Militants." Above: "Looking Backward."

TULLIA

Suddenly concerned that women might hurt their own cause, male commentators in 1913 earnestly cautioned against aggressive tactics and the "shackles" of "militancy." Editorial cartoonists had a field day combining time-tested caricatures of dour old suffragists with images of bomb-wielding, torch-waving "militants." Fears of pillaging feminists were played out in cartoons of women on the war path, abandoning their children, sweeping men off the face of the Earth, and even of legendary "Tullia" (left, by Rodney Thomson), who rode over her father's corpse to seize power. Above: "To the Glory of the Militant." Below: "Handicapped."

Fears Remain After British Militance Ends

ALTHOUGH NO American suffrage leader ever advocated violence, arson, or vandalism, fear of British-style militance did not immediately disappear. For some time, critics and conservative suffragists remained extremely wary that any new activity might trigger similar unlawful behavior in the U.S. But despite labels and accusations hurled at Harriot

Blatch, Alice Paul, and other innovators, the actions of American suffragists were almost entirely legal and firmly within the tradition of democratic politics.

Nonetheless, inflammatory images of frightening militants continued to be used until the sudden end to nearly all suffrage activity in England in August 1914. Afterwards, the image of the

violent suffragette had little to reinforce it in the U.S., and it gradually died out, allowing artists to return to more creative and patriotic comparisons. ◆

Facing page: Josef Keppler, Jr.'s cartoon warning of "militant lawlessness," entitled "The Feminine of Jekyll and Hyde," appeared in the June 4, 1913 issue of *Puck*.

Judge

Fourth of July Number

JUNE 27, 1914
PRICE, **10** CENTS

VOTE

JAMES MONTGOMERY FLAGG

INDEPENDENCE DAY

Chapter 9: 1914

Campaigns in Seven States

In 1914 women in seven states waged electoral campaigns for equal rights, making it a pivotal year for the suffrage movement. In addition, the Congressional Union in Washington D.C. continued to press vigorously for passage of the Federal amendment.

Capitalizing on the publicity of the 1913 parade and the numerous delegations and demonstrations that followed it, the CU made a systematic effort to win the support of members of Congress. Under the charisma and single-mindedness of Alice Paul, the CU kept 40 lobbyists busy, far outnumbering the three associated with NAWSA's recently re-staffed Congressional Committee.

As a result of this renewed activity, the U.S. Senate scheduled a vote on the amendment on March 19, 1914, the first vote since 1887. The measure won a majority of the votes cast, but 35-34 was still 11 votes short of the necessary two-thirds. There was no action in the House of Representatives until late in the year.

The CU also continued to pressure the president and the ruling Democratic Party. Turning to women in the nine equal suffrage states in the fall, the CU began to mobilize

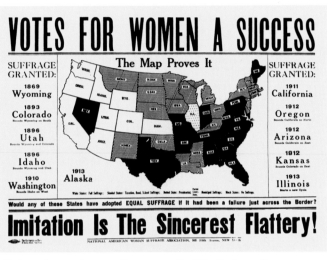

A "triumphant, threatening army of white States..."

enfranchised women to demand that Congress pass the suffrage amendment. Rather than trying to persuade male legislators and voters to approve state measures, the CU aimed at convincing women who had the vote to help other women get it nationally by supporting the drive for the Federal amendment.

Increasingly the CU emphasized women's power as voters in nine states. "Our argument is not one of justice or democracy or fair play," Crystal Eastman informed the House Judiciary Committee in March. "It is one of political expediency.... Our plea is simply that you look at the little suffrage map. That triumphant, threatening army of white States

growing rapidly eastward toward the center of population is the sum and substance of our argument. It represents 4,000,000 women voters."

"When we go to the voters of a campaign state to ask them to vote 'yes' on a woman suffrage amendment," she told the congressmen, "we go as petitioners with smiles and arguments and unwearied patience. . . . We reason and plead with them, try to touch their sense of honor, their sense of justice, their reason, whatever noble human quality they possess." However, she explained, this way of getting suffrage was "a long, laborious and very costly way" which offered no guarantee of success. What was needed was an amendment to the constitution.

A woman voting was still a noteworthy sight in 1914, meriting a portrayal by James Montgomery Flagg (facing page) on the cover of the Fourth of July issue of *Judge*. Some buttons, like the one above, displayed ten stars, counting presidential suffrage in Illinois. In 1914 suffragists tried to win seven more states, including Nevada, the last "dark spot" in the west on the Suffrage Map (left). Women had won the right to vote equally with men in the nine white states plus presidential suffrage in Illinois; women in the gray states exercised some sort of partial suffrage. Liberty held two torches on a stamp (below) publicizing the drive in Missouri.

Coordinated Suffrage Events Increase Pressure for the Federal Amendment

IN ONE of the greatest coordinated actions in the drive for woman suffrage, May 2, 1914 was declared national Suffrage Day. Women throughout the country organized over one thousand demonstrations, parades, and rallies. The nationwide actions were organized by the Congressional Union and endorsed by NAWSA to send a clear, simultaneous demand to Congress from all the states for immediate passage of the Federal amendment.

Thousands of supporters took to the streets in large cities and small towns across the nation, winning front page coverage for the cause.

There were sixty open-air meetings and celebrations in cities and towns throughout New York state plus "flying banners and eloquent oratory" in New York City, according to *The Suffragist*. An evening meeting at Carnegie Hall featured speeches by the mayor of New York and leading suffragists including organizers Alice Paul and Lucy Burns of the CU.

Above: Patriotic suffragists in a Baltimore, Maryland, parade carried Revolutionary War slogans to emphasize their democratic demand. Right: Celebrating Suffrage Day in New York City.

SUFFRAGE DAY CELEBRATION

Saturday, May 2d
8:15 P. M.
UNDER THE AUSPICES OF THE
WOMEN'S POLITICAL UNION
Mass Meeting
AT
CARNEGIE HALL

Among the Speakers will be
HIS HONOR THE MAYOR OF THE CITY OF NEW YORK
Dr. Katherine B. Davis
COMMISSIONER OF CORRECTIONS
Miss Josephine Casey
GENERAL ORGANIZER FOR THE LADIES' INTERNATIONAL
GARMENT WORKERS
Miss Alice Paul
Mrs. Norman deR. Whitehouse
Chairman
HARRIOT STANTON BLATCH

ALL SEATS FREE

Suffragists in Hartford, Connecticut, celebrated Suffrage Day with one of the finest parades in the country and an immense crowd turned out to see it. One memorable float (above) featured the figure of Liberty surrounded by girls representing each of the 48 states. Students (left) stressed that equal education was the key to equal citizenship. Connecticut had a state suffrage association since 1869 but the legislature had what one suffragist called "only a melancholy record of defeats." Suffrage Day offered supporters throughout the country a reason to initiate their own actions in support of the Federal amendment.

Lila Meade Valentine led the Equal Suffrage League of Virginia for eleven years from its founding in 1909. Valentine was widely known for her work advocating educational and public health reforms including kindergartens, visiting nurses, vocational training in public schools, and a campaign against tuberculosis. In 1913 alone she made over one hundred public speeches for suffrage across the state, addressing supporters, opponents, and the undecided (below). Two years later, trying to win the governor over, she led a march of 200 suffragists to his office along with the great, great granddaughters of Thomas Jefferson and George Mason, author of the Virginia Bill of Rights. Unlike those southern women wedded to states' rights, Valentine supported the Federal amendment and later served on NAWSA's Congressional Committee lobbying in Washington D.C.

Massachusetts Woman Suffrage Association

SUFFRAGE PARADE HEADQUARTERS

587 BOYLSTON ST., BOSTON

Speaking Daily at 3 and 8 P. M.   Afternoon Tea

All Suffragists are asked to Come in and Pledge to March in the

Massachusetts Suffrage Parade

SATURDAY, MAY 2nd, at 5 P. M.

Mass Meeting at Tremont Temple at 7 P. M.

Line forms on Beacon St. at 4.00.   Line starts at 5 sharp rain or shine.

The route will be Beacon St. past the State House where the Governor and the
Mayor will review us, School, Washington and Eliot Sts. to Park Square,
Boylston and Tremont Sts. to Tremont Temple.

There will be in line of march:
Mounted Police
Boy Scouts on Duty
Ushers in Costume
Bands of Music
Marching Chorus
Decorated Floats
Horsemen and Women
City Women
Country Women
Home Women
Business Women
Artists
Actresses
Nurses
Teachers
Doctors
Lawyers
Farmers
Wage Earning Women
Men's Section
Labor Unions
College Students
Junior Section, etc., etc.

Automobiles for those who cannot
walk.

National Suffrage Day, May 2nd.
There will be Suffrage Parades all
over the Union to call public attention to the campaigns in Nevada,
Montana, North and South Dakota,
and Nebraska.

The vote on Women Suffrage will be
taken in these states next November.

The Massachusetts Senate passed the
Suffrage Bill 35–3 on March 10th.

This is the first great Victory in Massachusetts for Votes for Women.

The Suffrage Parade on May 2 will
celebrate this Victory.

The Floats and Costumes will make
it beautiful, the Bands will make it
gay, but NUMBERS alone will make
it impressive.

We need YOU to make it a success.

WILL YOU MARCH?

JOIN ANY SECTION YOU PLEASE.

No Special Costume Necessary.   White Preferred.

EVERYTHING FREE.

Every person pledged will receive full instructions where to form, etc., before
the day of the Parade.

BRING OR SEND YOUR NAME TO PARADE HEADQUARTERS

587 Boylston Street, Boston, Mass

The Libbie Printing Co.   242 Dover St., Boston

Proud members of the Equal Suffrage League of Richmond, Virginia (above), posed with their banners and suffrage sashes. The women celebrated Suffrage Day with a grand rally on the steps of the State Capitol in Richmond (left), which featured speeches by politicians, community leaders, and equal rights advocates. Lila Valentine is seated just behind the speaker, Rabbi Edward N. Calish. Festivities in other southern cities included a rally in Atlanta, Georgia, and parades in both St. Louis, Missouri, and Chattanooga, Tennessee.

Boston's Suffrage Day Parade was "a record breaking performance" according to *The Suffragist*. The parade, which featured an estimated 12,000 marchers plus several bands and beautifully decorated floats, passed in review before both the governor and the mayor. Divisions of women marched by professions (left) along with groups of Self-Supporting Women (below) and representatives from all the women's colleges in the state. Popular suffrage speaker Margaret Foley rode in an open motorcar (above) carrying an oversized red paper rose bearing a challenge to anti-suffragists. The red rose was the chosen symbol of the opposition. Her "deft and amusing stunt" was greeted with shouts of laughter from the crowds. Other marchers included the direct descendants of suffrage pioneers Angelina Grimke, Abby Kelley Foster, and William Lloyd Garrison. Between 200,000 and 300,000 enthusiastic onlookers witnessed the impressive spectacle. The Massachusetts Senate had just passed the suffrage bill, opening the way for a public vote in 1915.

Suffrage Day Celebrations Reflect New Life in Minnesota

Parades and rallies organized by the Minneapolis and St. Paul suffrage clubs marked Suffrage Day in Minnesota. Clara Hampson Ueland, a civic reformer and mother of eight, revitalized the state association in 1914. She led local suffragists in organizing supporters, raising funds, and working with the legislature and NAWSA. Besides the state association, Minnesota was home to a Women's Welfare League, Women Workers' Suffrage Club, and the Everywoman Suffrage Club of Black women in St. Paul.

Minnesota suffragists tried repeatedly but unsuccessfully to win legislative action. The bill, championed by Senator Ole Sageng who earned the title "The Father of Woman Suffrage in Minnesota," suffered defeat four times in a row between 1909 and 1915 although never by more than four votes in either House. Supporters in other states had similar experiences with their legislatures. Throughout the

Appealing to the large number of immigrant voters in Minnesota, women in the Scandinavian contingent of the Suffrage Day parade (above) carried the Norwegian and Swedish flags through Minneapolis on May 2, 1914. The parade, which followed mass meetings in Minneapolis and St. Paul, stretched more than a mile in length and included over 2,000 supporters. Minnesota voters (below) crowded around automobiles to hear suffrage speakers in St. Paul's Rice Park during the celebration.

The Congressional Union was overjoyed by the success of the nationwide demonstrations. *The Suffragist* reported with delight, "Women have proved that they can organize on a huge scale, that they can capitalize an enormous project, and that they can carry out a big plan and do it nobly."

country, however, Suffrage Day revealed a growing movement with energetic new members, able leadership, and diversified support in clubs, schools, civic groups, and political organizations.

Above: The Votes for Women Club at Hamline College in St. Paul, Minnesota.

WAGE EARNER CONVENTIONALITY DEGRADATION

The Suffragist Arousing her Sisters

Supporters in Wilmington, Delaware, enthusiastically observed Suffrage Day by decorating the main streets with suffrage yellow for the first big demonstration in that state. New Jersey suffragists held rallies in nearly every county seat while supporters in New Hampshire

and Maine organized automobile parades followed by mass meetings. Women in Ohio completed the daunting task of collecting the signatures of over 131,000 male voters to put the question on the ballot a second time. Supporters staged a pageant and parade in Cleveland

(below) on Suffrage Day to kick off the campaign. One popular allegory, portrayed in tableau and on parade floats, was "The Suffragist Arousing Her Sisters" (above) showing the Suffrage Herald trying to stir the Wage Earner, Conventionality (dozing), Vanity, and Degradation.

Parades, Festivities, and Pageantry Focus on Congress

Louise deKoven Bowen was such a powerful and respected presence in Chicago that there was talk of running her for mayor in the 1920s. The unprecedented notion greatly amused her. A community-minded philanthropist, Bowen was widely admired for her administrative skill and no-nonsense leadership in efforts for social welfare, juvenile justice, education, and municipal reform. She was president of the influential Woman's City Club and was an active supporter and board member of Hull House for over forty years, helping it survive following Jane Addams' death. Both a benefactor of NAWSA and an officer in 1912, Bowen spoke nationally for woman suffrage and marched in the 1916 Chicago parade at age 57. When Anna Howard Shaw was once asked which women she thought would have made a good president of the U.S., she listed Susan B. Anthony, Jane Addams, and Louise Bowen.

THE SUFFRAGE Day parade in Chicago involved an estimated 15,000 women from all political parties and backgrounds. Onlookers packed the sidewalks along windy Michigan Avenue to view the bands and horse-drawn floats. Prominent Illinois suffragist Grace Wilbur Trout served as grand marshal and led the parade carrying a large American flag.

With women organized into divisions, wards and associations, "the parade was literally an army with banners" according to *The Suffragist.* Governor Edward F. Dunne called it "a grand procession." The parade included a large delegation from the Women's Trade Union League, a group of waitresses on strike, an impressive battalion of Black women, and a division from the Wage Earners' Suffrage League wearing distinctive white "liberty caps" with blue stars. Hundreds of thousands of spectators lined the two mile route. As one journalist reported, "The sense of gaiety, of joy and inspiration, of the new-born comradeship of women was in the air."

In a dramatic climax to the national action, the Congressional Union organized a parade of several thousand women in Washington D.C. on May 9 to deliver the Suffrage Day resolutions to Congress. With the kind of colorful pageantry the CU had already become known for, women representing each of the 531 congressional districts marched to the Capitol and presented the petitions for the Federal amendment while a throng of supporters outside sang *The March of the Women.* Members of the House of Representatives, however, still refused to act.

Above: Chicago's Suffrage Day parade.

Ida B. Wells-Barnett organized the first suffrage club for Black women in Illinois and became a prominent community leader in Chicago. Wells married newspaper owner Ferdinand Barnett in 1895 and had four children while building an international movement against lynching. Through lectures and articles based on careful research, she catalyzed organizing among Black Americans and helped shift white public opinion against lynching and racial violence. Wells-Barnett integrated the 1913 suffrage parade in Washington D.C. when she refused to march at the end of the procession. She also led her club members in the 1916 suffrage parade in Chicago. The anti-lynching flag below hung from the office of the National Association for the Advancement of Colored People in New York City.

The Alpha Suffrage Record

Vol 1   Chicago, Ill. March 18 1914   No. 1

THE ALPHA SUFFRAGE CLUB.

The Alpha Suffrage Club is the first suffrage club organized among Afro-American women, having been organized January 30, 1913, and is now in the third year of its existence. It has a membership of two hundred women. It has fifteen women judges and clerks of election, who have been serving the city in every election for the past year. It did the work of getting out the Afro-American women's registration a year ago. Though its members, other political clubs have been formed in Hyde Park, the South and West sides of the city.

The Alpha Suffrage Club meets every Wednesday evening at the Reading Room, 3005 State street, at 8 o'clock. All women interested in knowing how to become good citizens are cordially invited to become members. Its officers are: Mrs. Ida B. Wells-Barnett, President; Mrs. Mary Jackson, First Vice-President; Miss Viola Hill, Second Vice-President; Mrs. Vera Wesley Green, Recording Secretary; Mrs. Sadie L. Adams, Corresponding Secretary; Miss Laura Beasley, Treasurer: Mrs. K. J. Bills, Editor.

RESOLUTIONS.

Whereas, For the first time in our country's history, a champion for American womanhood has raised his voice in the halls of Congress, demanding safeguards and protection for that womanhood, and,

Whereas, This same champion has also led the successful battle against the African Exclusion Amendment, and the Jim Crow Car bills in the same Congress, therefore be it,

Resolved, That this public meeting composed of thousands of his constituents do now join with the Afro-American womanhood of Chicago, in voicing its heartfelt thanks to Congressman Martin B. Madden for the faithful discharge of his duty in defending and protecting our rights, and those of the Afro-American throughout the United States.

Resolved, That as a further proof of our gratitude for his able championship of our rights and liberties in the nation and at home, we endorse our young giant Oscar De Priest for Alderman of the Second Ward and Wm. Hale Thompson for Mayor, and pledge ourselves to leave no stone unturned to secure their election April 6th; we realize that in no other way can we safeguard our own rights than by holding up the hands of those who fight our battles.

The Alpha Suffrage Club is enthusiastically working to elect Hon. Oscar De Priest as the first negro alderman to the City Council. It is therefore very proud to know that the Afro-American race throughout the country is endorsing its stand. The following editorial is taken from the New York News of last Saturday.

Fellow citizens, the womanhood of the race urges you to read this editorial over and over again. Especially the last line which says, "We as a race everywhere expect you to do your duty."

ALL HAIL CHICAGO.

Chicago, as we have said many a time before, points the way to the political salvation of the race. Her colored men are colored men first—Republicans, Progressives and Democrats afterwards. In the last twenty years, but on one spot in the entire broad United States has the black man received anything like adequate political recognition and that one spot is Chicago. The corollary of this proposition is that on only one spot in this broad United States have colored citizens demanded anything like adequate political recognition, and that one spot is Chicago.

Oscar De Priest, a popular and capable colored man, formerly County Commissioner, has been designated over four candidates, two white and two colored, in the Republican primaries for Alderman from the Second Ward. He is and was the regular organization candidate. The white Democratic candidate nominated the same day is "Al" Russell, a saloonkeeper and himself popular with many colored people. It is said that the Democrats are trying to induce one of the defeated colored primary candidates to enter the field. We do not believe that so base a traitor to his race lives in Chicago. We do not believe that any colored man or woman of Chicago, and especially of the Second Ward, fails to grasp this grand opportunity. A colored man has never been elected an Alderman in your city. You now have it in your power to do so. The eyes of the country, white and black, are upon you. We as a race everywhere expect you to do your duty!

EXTRACTS FROM SPEECH

Mr. Speaker, I am opposed to the intermarriage of the races. The Negroes themselves are opposed to such marriages. But I am also opposed to legislation making such marriages a crime. If a white man and a black woman want to marry it should be a matter for them to decide. I think they would both be foolish to thus ostracise themselves from association with their own people and that is what they do when they marry but if they want to ostracise themselves, that is a personal matter between them and it should be.

To make such marriages criminal and void would leave the children of such marriages without the protection which they need and should have. Instead of bettering moral conditions such a law would make them worse. It would leave many young girls at the mercy of brutes willing to take advantage of their virtue and then desert them to a life of shame. I cannot conceive of a condition under which white men should be allowed to cohabit with a black woman not his wife with out being compelled by law to marry her or to provide for the care of her children. Why should innocent women of the Negro race not have the same protection of the law which is accorded to women of any other race? It will not do to say there is no such condition as that to which I have alluded Everyone knows better else how does it happen that we have so many people of mixed blood in the United States,

The Negroes are willing to confine their marriages to their race, indeed the would prefer that, but they have a right to demand that the women of their race shall not be considered the legitimate prey of men of other races. (Applause) * *

CHICAGO HONORS MARTIN B. MADDEN

The Alpha Suffrage Club tenders a public reception to Hon. Martin B. Madden, representative of the 1st Congressional District for his splendid work in the last Congress in defense of Negro Womanhood and successful fight against race discrimination, at Quinn Chapel Church, Thursday evening, March, 18-at 8 o'clock.

Grand old Quinn Chapel

The Women of the club desire to acknowledge their debt of gratitude to the pastor and officers of Quinn Chapel for the use of this beautiful and historic edifice in which to hold a reception to our Congressman.

It is both a recognition and encouragement to our womanhood and a fine tribute to the man who stood before the nation and defended the cause of the race three times already since the beginning of the New Year i.e. on the African Exclusion Amendment to the Immigration Bill; on the Inter-marriage Bill and again on the Jim Crow Street Car Bill for the District All of these measures were defeated and largely through the efforts of our Congressman. The whole race everywhere through out the nation has benefitted and because of that fact Quinn Chapel rose to the occasion and donated the use of the beautiful auditorium as its contribution to the race's effort to honor its champion.

Black Suffrage Groups Make Their Presence Felt

IDA B. WELLS-BARNETT founded the Alpha Suffrage Club, one of the first for African-American women, in Chicago in 1913. In print (above) and at weekly meetings she encouraged members to register local women so that they could use their new power to help elect Black candidates. They eventually did exactly that.

Other leading Black suffragists in the northern states included Mary Eleanora McCoy in Detroit, Gertrude Bustill Mossell in Philadelphia, and Bertha Higgins in Rhode Island. Women active in the south included Adella Hunt Logan and Margaret Murray Washington in Alabama, Lugenia Burns Hope in Atlanta, and Christia Adair in Texas. Logan began the Department of Suffrage for the National Association of Colored Women and joined the campaign in Ohio in 1912.

There were also a number of Black suffrage groups across the country including the Colored Women's Suffrage Club in Los Angeles, the St. Louis Suffrage Club in Missouri, and the Colored Women's Progressive Franchise Association in Washington D.C. A few white clubs accepted a small number of Black members and some Black societies were accepted as NAWSA auxiliaries but these were the exceptions, not the rule. As in other efforts, Black women were left to work independently to advance their interests.

Above: Organizing Black voters in Chicago.

Internal Dissension in NAWSA Splits Focus

NAWSA took what many considered to be a wrong turn in March 1914 when its newly re-staffed Congressional Committee, including Antoinette Funk and Ruth Hannah McCormick of Illinois, endorsed a woman suffrage amendment substantially different from the original one already under consideration.

Partially to satisfy southern Democrats, the Shafroth-Palmer Resolution aimed at getting around states' rights objections and restrictions in certain states regarding constitutional questions. The proposed amendment would require a state to hold a referendum on woman suffrage if 8% of the legal voters petitioned for it. However many suffragists sensed an attempt to evade the issue. They realized that, after a tremendous amount of work getting this new constitutional amendment passed and ratified, they would be right back in the same place facing repeated state campaigns.

Doris Stevens of the Con-gressional Union called it a "red herring" and an "evil compromise" which diverted NAWSA's focus and divided congressional support. She lamented that it "had been accepted by the conservative suffragists evidently in a moment of hopelessness."

NAWSA president Anna Howard Shaw also opposed the idea but she yielded to some members of her board. Her Congressional Committee members had endorsed the measure without the approval of the national board. This led Jane Addams to step down as vice-president. After much heated debate, it was abandoned late in 1915.

CU members strongly opposed the diversion and kept their focus on the original Bristow-Mondell Amendment which they called the Susan B. Anthony Amendment and which NAWSA called simply the Federal amendment.

Above: Congressional Union marchers carried a banner endorsing the original amendment. Below: Learning to vote in Chicago.

Alva Belmont, rich, flamboyant, and imperious, still possessed a true militant spirit according to her comrades in the Congressional Union. Born Alva Erskine Smith in Alabama and educated in France, she bore three children before scandalously divorcing her husband, William K. Vanderbilt, for adultery in 1895. She married O.H.P. Belmont a year later and devoted herself to equal rights after his death in 1908. In 1883 she appeared as a Venetian princess (below) at her extravagant society costume ball.

Wealthy Alva Belmont Backs Federal Action

Popularizing the cause of woman suffrage among the wealthy was a role for which Alva Belmont was well positioned. After generously supporting NAWSA and founding her own Political Equality Association, Belmont joined Alice Paul and the Congressional Union and began to contribute substantially to the drive for the Federal amendment.

A recognized if controversial figure in New York society, Belmont also owned Marble House, a mansion in fashionable Newport, Rhode Island, which she opened for suffrage meetings. In late August 1914 leaders of the CU met there to plan their election strategy.

An admirer of the British suffragettes, Belmont favored bold actions to make suffrage a political issue, especially in the upcoming election. She was attracted by Paul's approach of organizing enfranchised women to support the Federal amendment, feeling that, in historian Inez Irwin's words, "it was more dignified of women to ask the vote of other women than to beg it of men."

Top and above (left): Alva Belmont at Marble House in Newport on July 8, 1914.

Congressional Union for Woman's Suffrage
National Summer Headquarters

Old Strategic Differences Surface Again

WITH THE renewed activity nationally for the suffrage amendment, Alice Paul and her colleagues were optimistic that Federal action would be forthcoming. The new Democratic administration, however, neither embraced nor advanced the measure. Paul had also hoped that NAWSA would put its weight behind the drive, but differing political outlooks as well as personal rivalries made such a commitment impossible at this time.

NAWSA leaders felt that they needed to win more states for the Federal amendment to have any chance of success in Congress. Paul and the Congressional Union, on the other hand, believed that direct pressure on Congress, supported by activity in all the states, would force politicians – particularly the ruling Democratic Party – to act.

Members of the Congressional Union (above) prepared to court wealthy vacationers in Newport, Rhode Island, on July 13, 1914. Alva Belmont is in the second row, second from left, and Doris Stevens is next to her in white. Beach towns, like state fairs, offered suffragists a chance to reach residents from all over the state.

THE ELUSIVE WHITE HOUSE MAN

He wriggles out of every hold I get.

WILSON

VOTES FOR WOMEN

SUPPORT OF WOMAN SUFFRAGE

F. Fox

Opposing the Party in Power

PRESIDENT WOODROW Wilson's position on woman suffrage was hard to pin down, and the 1914 cartoon above captured some of the Congressional Union's frustration. To persuade Wilson to support a constitutional amendment during 1913 and 1914, Alice Paul sent seven separate deputations to him, including groups of working women, women voters, and 500 club women. To this last delegation he restated his position that suffrage was a state, not a Federal, issue and, after the briefest of exchanges, he expressed his annoyance at being "cross-examined" further. Lucy Burns wrote of the rebuff, "Only fitfully do women realize the astounding arrogance of their rulers."

When the Democrat-controlled Congress continued to block the suffrage bill, the CU announced that it would hold Democrats responsible as the "party in power" and would campaign against them in the coming election.

The strategy of holding a political party accountable for inaction on legislation was a new and bitterly controversial one, praised for its directness by supporters but condemned by the non-partisan NAWSA and by Democratic allies. There was no such thing as party responsibility in the U.S., claimed Carrie Catt; the idea was just another misguided militant tactic imported from England. Paul countered that "ours is a government by parties," and the CU Advisory Committee approved the plan in late August. The Union sent over a dozen "envoys" west to ask women voters to use their political power against the Democratic Party to help win the vote for all the women in the country. The tactic virtually guaranteed the CU extensive publicity.

Above: A 1914 cartoon

Envoys Campaign Against Democratic Candidates in the West

ON SEPTEMBER 14, 1914, the Congressional Union sent teams of organizers into the nine equal suffrage states to make woman suffrage an issue in the November election. Alice Paul recognized that nearly four million voting women offered a "great lever" in the suffrage struggle and resolved to use it to move Congress and the president.

Lucy Burns and Rose Winslow traveled to San Francisco, Jessie Hardy Stubbs and Virginia Arnold went to Portland, and Margaret Whittemore and Anne McCue worked in Seattle.

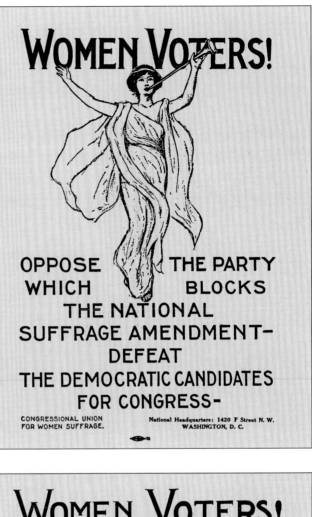

WOMEN VOTERS!

OPPOSE THE PARTY WHICH BLOCKS THE NATIONAL SUFFRAGE AMENDMENT— DEFEAT THE DEMOCRATIC CANDIDATES FOR CONGRESS—

CONGRESSIONAL UNION FOR WOMEN SUFFRAGE.

National Headquarters: 1420 F Street N. W. WASHINGTON, D. C.

WOMEN VOTERS!

THE DEMOCRATIC ADMINISTRATION REFUSES VOTES TO WOMEN THOUGH IT ADVOCATES VOTES FOR FILIPINOS— DEFEAT THE DEMOCRATIC CANDIDATES FOR CONGRESS

CONGRESSIONAL UNION FOR WOMEN SUFFRAGE

NATIONAL HEADQUARTERS 1420 F STREET. WASHINGTON, D. C.

Other organizers set up in Denver, Phoenix, Kansas City, Salt Lake, Cheyenne, and Boise. In addition, Mabel Vernon helped Anne Martin campaign for suffrage in the state of Nevada.

The envoys publicized the record of the Democratic Party in blocking woman suffrage. They traveled to small towns, homesteads, and camps, speaking in schoolhouses and on court house greens, and often received a warm welcome from audiences who appreciated their insight into current Washington politics.

"The first entry of women into a national election on the suffrage amendment was little more than a quick, brilliant dash," remembered Stevens, but it quickly angered the Democratic Party and made the campaign "a very hot one." Suffragists visiting each state were "invited" to leave immediately and Democrats were forced to redirect resources to fight this new initiative.

Above: Rose Winslow, Lucy Burns, and Doris Stevens (from left) and other envoys leave for the west. Right: Congressional Union fliers appealed to women voters during the 1914 campaign.

Suffragists Launch Drives in 7 States

SUFFRAGISTS WAGED campaigns in seven states in 1914, putting the question to voters through legislative approval in Montana, Nevada, North and South Dakota, and through initiative petitions in Ohio, Missouri and Nebraska. There were many all too familiar parallels with the drives of 1912.

Determined Efforts

Organizers worked in each state during the campaign months soliciting support, forming local leagues, and preparing the way for speakers. At the same time officers and volunteers at headquarters planned the drives, raised money, scheduled speakers and automobile tours, and circulated leaflets and press material to inform the public about the ballot measure. With varying success suffragists tried to win the endorsement of the state political parties and both urban and rural newspapers.

In nearly every county, and often in every voting precinct, local women reached out to voters repeatedly through personal contact, house-to-house canvassing, informative leaflets, and public meetings which often featured well known national speakers. These women, and a few men, were usually sent by NAWSA or recruited by the state officers and many came at their own expense from some distance. Katharine Devereux Blake jour-

Special Suffrage Editions were prepared by supporters for newspapers across the country, including the one above which showed a dirty politician getting a good scrubbing after spoiling the suffrage "pudding" with graft and "crooked methods."

neyed to Montana from New York, Annie Kenney came from England to support the Nevada drive, and Rosalie Jones and Ida Craft worked in several states.

Anna Howard Shaw traveled and spoke for over a week in each of the campaign states and New Yorker James Lees Laidlaw helped form new chapters of the Men's League. NAWSA created a speakers bureau, headquartered in Chicago, to which many Illinois women gave their active support.

Distinguished and articulate speakers were always helpful. Shaw in particular was praised for her strenuous work and "untiring beautiful

spirit." NAWSA field secretary Jane Thompson, who herself had journeyed over 8,000 miles through the campaign states, later conveyed the states' appreciation to the 67-year-old leader, "Always ready to meet whatever situation arose, regardless of fatigue, you encouraged the believers, braced up the uncertain and converted the unbelieving."

Powerful Opposition

Anti-suffragists were also active in each state, speaking and circulating literature which claimed that women did not want to vote. Josephine Jewel Dodge, president of the National Association Opposed to Woman Suffrage, and Minnie Bronson, its secretary and circuit rider, came from New York and they or an associate spoke in each campaign state. Mainly, however, these "antis" served to mask the behind-the-scenes efforts by businessmen, saloon interests, and conservative politicians who feared the results of women voting. Liquor and intertwined business interests, along with generally conservative voters, formed the backbone of the opposition, particularly in the midwest. As they did in numerous state elections, the powerful U.S. Brewer's Association and the brewery-related German-American Alliance forcefully and stealthily opposed the measure. ◆

Supporters in Missouri Come to Life

AROUND the turn of the century the state suffrage association in Missouri, like many others, had essentially stopped functioning. A decade later, however, supporters had been re-energized by organizers and speakers from the east and from Great Britain.

The electoral campaign in 1914 was led by successive presidents of the Missouri Woman Suffrage Association, Mrs. George Gellhorn and Mrs. Walter McNab Miller, who later served as NAWSA vice-president. With the help of the Woman's Christian

Temperance Union, Missouri suffragists sidestepped the unsupportive state legislature and gathered enough signatures to put the measure on the ballot themselves.

For six months they waged a modest, intensive campaign

which included active press work, a speakers bureau, participation at state and county fairs, and the creation of dozens of local suffrage clubs as well as leagues of business women and men in St. Louis. Meetings featured notable

speakers including Jane Addams and Ruth McCormick of Illinois, Desha Breckinridge of Kentucky, and Helen Todd of California. Male voters were encouraged to follow the example of the western states and make Missouri women fully equal in political affairs.

Above: Local supporters led a back yard meeting in Marthasville, Missouri after the 1914 election from a platform precariously perched in a tree. Left: Volunteers worked at headquarters where the latest Suffrage Map reminded them of recent gains.

A Second Try to Win Ohio

Ohio suffragists undertook the initiative process in 1914. Two thousand women gathered the signatures of over 131,000 voters to put equal suffrage on the ballot just two years after it had been defeated. During the hectic campaign, supporters canvassed the towns in every county. They held hundreds of meetings and rallies and distributed huge quantities of literature. Opposition was particularly strong as Ohio was the fifth largest brewing state.

In the midst of the drive, suffragists paid homage to the past with a March to the Oak in Newbury, a center of early suffrage activity. Over forty years earlier, pioneer suffragists had planted an acorn as a sign of their faith and it had grown into a sturdy oak. Under its spreading branches modern suffragists held a service to honor those earlier women of vision and to rededicate themselves to the same ideals.

¶ Great is that nation whose men and women work together, for its strength is thereby doubled.

REPRODUCED BY COURTESY OF

Top: Cleveland physician Dr. Julie Green, state suffrage leader Harriet Taylor Upton, and supporters followed a wreath bearer from Freedom Chapel on a March to the Oak to honor the early equal rights pioneers.

NAWSA organizer and state association chair Jeannette Rankin (above) spoke to voters and interested women from an automobile during the campaign in Montana. Inspired by the victory in Washington state in 1910, Rankin spent a year traveling to the spread-out towns and settlements in Montana, recruiting workers and building up a favorable public climate. Automobiles became crucial for canvassing the small towns and vast rural areas of the western states. A post card from Ohio (left) showed the ideal of a woman and a man together at the ballot box.

Jeannette Rankin discovered her love of democratic politics when she was drawn into the 1910 suffrage drive in Washington state. Born on a Montana ranch in 1880, the oldest of seven children, Rankin was an energetic and independent girl who broke her nose playing basketball in high school in Missoula. She embraced the drive for equal rights after growing dissatisfied with teaching and social work. Returning to Montana in 1911, she became the first woman to address the state legislature, then considering a suffrage bill, and helped make women's rights a live issue in the state. Rankin refined her skills working in the California, Ohio, and Wisconsin campaigns, and in 1912 joined NAWSA as a field secretary, lobbying the legislatures and organizing suffragists in over a dozen states. She was the driving force in the 1914 Montana campaign and became one of the best known figures in the state.

Suffragists Wage a Strong Campaign in Montana

After Montana suffragists convinced the major political parties to support a state amendment in 1912, they launched a campaign against an anti-suffrage representative just before the election. This put politicians on notice that they would be wise not to antagonize the women. In January 1913 the various suffrage leagues formed the Montana Equal Franchise Society, electing Jeannette Rankin as chair, and the legislature agreed to put the amendment before the voters at the 1914 election.

The Woman's Christian Temperance Union helped suffragists canvass every county. They visited small settlements and mining camps where rallies were often followed by a dance. Harriet and James Laidlaw, wealthy supporters visiting from New York, organized a men's league chapter and advanced $600 when the state bank collapsed in the midst of the campaign, taking the suffrage treasury with it. The measure was opposed by the politically powerful copper mining companies which feared women voters would back a workmen's compensa-

tion law.

The climax of the drive came in late September with a festive parade through Helena during the state fair. The parade featured thousands of marchers, as many men as women, from across the state. Led by Rankin, state leader Dr. Maria M. Dean, and Anna Howard Shaw, the mile-long demonstration included a band, numerous floats, and supporters on horseback and in automobiles. But despite widespread interest, NAWSA organizer Antoinette Funk sensed "an undertow of fierce opposition."

Business Men Oppose
Woman Suffrage

Supplementary Report of Investigating Committee, Business Men's Association of Washoe County, Nevada.

On investigation, we find that Constitutional Amendment, relating to the Adoption of Equal Suffrage for the State of Nevada, which will appear on the Ballot, at the General Election to be held Tuesday, November 3rd, 1914, is antagonistic and not in harmony with the issues which your Association have adopted in their platform.

The issues we are supporting are intended to develop and foster business conditions throughout the State generally, and particularly in Washoe County, and we earnestly feel that the time is not ripe for the adoption of a constitutional amendment, which will radically affect these issues, hence we urgently recommend that it be the sense of this Association and the duty of every member to work diligently and faithfully against its support, and vote "NO" on this Amendment.

**Business Men's Association of
Washoe County**

Authorized and Published by Business Men's Association of Washoe County, Nevada.   Printed by the Reno Printing Company, 41 East Second Street, Reno, Nevada.

Good Business Men
Support Woman Suffrage

The so-called "Business Men" and the "Business Men's Association of Washoe County" who announce themselves opposed to woman suffrage, are working for a WIDE OPEN TOWN and a WIDE OPEN STATE.

Their alleged object to "develop and foster business conditions generally" is to be accomplished by restoring Nevada as the wide-open gambling resort of the United States.

Certain vested and certain evil interests have always opposed woman suffrage in every suffrage campaign ever carried on. These same vested and evil interests are opposing woman suffrage in Nevada.

A Vote for Woman Suffrage is a Vote for Good Government in Nevada

Good Government Means Prosperity Good Business Men are Supporting Woman Suffrage

Vote "YES" on the Suffrage Amendment

Published by the Nevada Equal Franchise Society, 153 N. Virginia St., Reno, Nev.

3

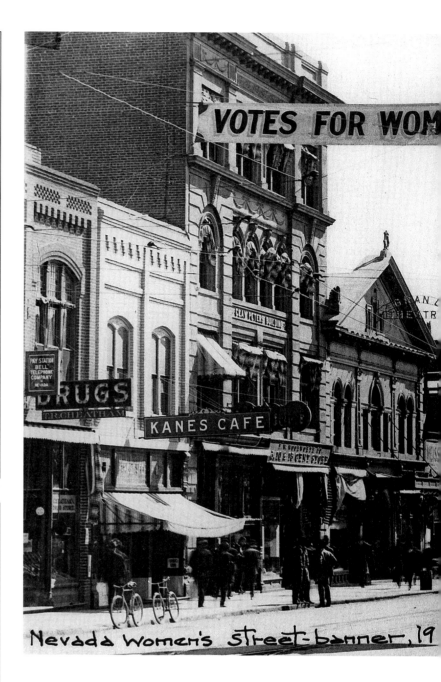

Nevada Women's Street-banner, 19

A Systematic Drive Envelopes Nevada

"NEVADA NEXT" was the goal in the last non-suffrage state in the far west in 1914. Large banners (above) showing Nevada as "the black spot" on the Suffrage Map were strung across the streets of the larger cities to urge voters to catch up with their equal suffrage neighbors.

After enlisting the support of the state's political parties, suffragists had persuaded two successive legislatures to approve placing the amendment

NEVADA NEXT.

...owing "the black spot"

Anne Martin was 36 when she returned from England in 1911 determined to win equal suffrage in her native Nevada. The state's first woman tennis champion, she had studied at Stanford University before founding the history department at the University of Nevada. While traveling abroad she encountered the British suffrage movement and was inspired by Emmeline Pankhurst. When Martin was arrested in London in 1910 her college friend Lou Henry Hoover sent her husband Herbert, later president of the United States, to bail her out. In Nevada Martin led a skillfully organized campaign emphasizing personal contact and "fair play" designed to appeal to the state's independent male voters. NAWSA organizer Antoinette Funk reported admiringly of Martin, "I believe she could address every voter by his first name." Shortly after the drive Martin parted ways with NAWSA, joined the Congressional Union, and rose to national leadership. Forceful, dedicated, and temperamental, she became one of the strongest voices for woman voters. "Equality for women," she wrote, "is a passion with me."

on the ballot. Anne Martin, president of the Nevada Equal Franchise Society, secured financial pledges from eastern supporters at NAWSA's 1913 convention and helped the campaign raise "an adequate fund" of $7,000 which Martin and others supplemented by paying their own expenses.

Since Reno, the largest city, was full of saloons and gambling halls, suffragists concentrated on the mining camps, remote ranches, and rural districts of the sparsely populated state. Under the slogan "Every Vote Counts," organizers traveled to distant settlements and even descended into mines "prospecting" for votes. Local supporters in Reno formed a Men's Suffrage League to counter a so-called Business Men's Association which opponents organized.

The Nevada campaign was unusually well planned and carefully executed. Every county was organized and there were women leaders in over 180 of 240 precincts. Margaret Foley, Maud Younger, Sara Bard Field, and Charlotte Perkins Gilman spoke throughout the state and Jane Addams gave speeches over four days, leading up to an overflow meeting in Reno two weeks before the election.

Above: A street banner caught attention in Nevada. Far left: Soliciting business men.

Persuading Voters in Nebraska, North Dakota and South Dakota

SUFFRAGISTS IN North Dakota, South Dakota, and Nebraska had to contend with organized anti-suffragists, intimidating brewery interests, and recently-arrived voters from many countries during their strenuous 1914 campaigns.

Nebraska

With no support in their legislature, members of the Nebraska Woman Suffrage Association under Henrietta I. Smith circulated initiative petitions throughout 1913 to put the measure on the ballot. Required to bring in 37,000 names from 38 counties, they collected over 50,000 signatures from 63 counties after working days and evenings for months.

Building on earlier work by Laura Gregg and Gail Laughlin, suffragists organized over 500 clubs in the state and arranged automobile tours which covered over 20,000 miles. They were able to reach half of the state's voters in over 500 towns and villages. NAWSA sent two organizers and contributed $4,000.

Opponents fought the effort with a vengeance. Businessmen married to suffragists were blatantly pressured to oppose the measure and to force their wives to withdraw from public activity. Grace Wheeler and Mary Williams wrote in The History of Woman Suffrage that "a committee of business men was formed by the brewing interests, which visited the husbands of various women engaged in the effort for the amendment. They said 'suffrage means prohibition,' and threatened the husbands in a business way unless their wives retired from the work. This committee watched the papers and when names of women were given as interested in suffrage, even to the extent of attending a luncheon for some celebrity, the husbands promptly were visited. Through this intimidation many women were forced to withdraw and many men who would have subscribed generously did not dare give more than $25, as the State law required the publication of names of all contributing over this sum."

North and South Dakota

In both North and South Dakota, where work for suffrage had long been intertwined with the Woman's Christian Temperance Union's efforts, women won the approval of the state legislatures to place the measure on the ballot. Mary Shields Pyle, who was elected president of the Universal Franchise League in 1911, directed the state campaign in South Dakota. Organizers divided the state into four districts. They set up branch leagues and circulated an influential weekly suffrage newspaper, The South Dakota Messenger. Local and national speakers toured both states. NAWSA's Antoinette Funk gave away 20,000 yellow badges in one day at the state fair in Huron where, she reported, Native American women danced with suffrage banners.

In North Dakota, supporters formed 100 clubs involving around 2,000 members. Clara L. Darrow, wife of a pioneer physician and mother of five, led the newly-formed North Dakota Votes for Women League. To reach rural voters, suffragists organized automobile tours, generated press material, and spoke at meetings and fairs.

Both states' drives faced severe difficulties. Some supporters referred to the North Dakota effort as "hard and hopeless." The measure needed a majority of all votes cast at the election, not just on the measure itself, and ballots not marked were counted against it. In South Dakota recent male immigrants could become qualified voters after having merely declared their intention to become citizens, and although many had failed to complete their naturalization, they were still able to vote. Suffragists feared that newly-arrived men from the "old world" would oppose equal rights for women. ◆

Nebraska volunteers solicited support from headquarters.

WHY WE DO NOT APPROVE
─┤OF├─
WOMAN SUFFRAGE

BECAUSE: We feel that the ballot makes absolutely no difference in the economic status of woman. Whether she votes or not, her charities, great and small, will continue, professions will extend diplomas to her intelligence, and trade will grant recompense to her ability. As for the protection of the ballot to working women, it will protect them no farther than it protects men who, in spite of their voting power, find themselves unable to cope with labor conditions by legislation and form themselves into unions outside of law and law making.

BECAUSE: Our hospital Boards, our social and civic service work, our child welfare committees and countless other clubs and industries for the general welfare and uplift need women who can give non-partisan and unselfish service, the worth of which service would be greatly lessened by political affiliations.

BECAUSE: Behind **law** there must always be **force** to make it effective. If legislation was shaped by a majority of women over men we should soon have, not government, but chaos.

BECAUSE: It is an attested fact that politics degrade women more than women purify politics.

BECAUSE: We believe that American men would speedily remedy all conditions needing reform if urged with half the force now brought to bear in favor of suffrage.

BECAUSE: We believe that the interests of all women are as safe in the hands of men as in those of other women.

BECAUSE: Thorough investigation of the laws of suffrage states shows that non-suffrage states have by far the better and more humane laws, and that all laws are more strictly enforced than in suffrage states.

BECAUSE: We believe that if franchise for women would better general conditions, there would be some evidence of that betterment in states where it has been exercised for twenty and up to forty-four years.

BECAUSE: Women make little use of suffrage when it is given them. School suffrage has been a lamentable failure, the women vote averaging scarcely two per cent in any state.

BECAUSE: The energies of women are engrossed by their present duties and interests, from which men cannot relieve them, and there is great need of better performance of their present work rather than diversion to new fields of activity.

BECAUSE: The suffrage movement develops sex hatred which is a menace to society.

BECAUSE: Of the alliance of suffrage with socialism which advocates free love and institutional life for children.

BECAUSE: The greatest menace to the morals of today lies in the efforts of suffragists to convince the world that vice is predominant. In the mad rush for the ballot and the consequent advertisement of immorality, reverence has been dethroned and reticence annihilated. It is high time for the right thinking, purity-loving women to arise and undo the terrific impress made on the public mind by the preachments of these pursuers of vice.

BECAUSE: The great majority of intelligent, refined and educated women do not want enfranchisement. They realize no sense of injustice such as expressed by the small minority of suffragists. They have all the rights and freedom they desire, and consider their present trusts most sacred and important. They feel that the duties which naturally must ever revert to their sex are such that none but themselves can perform and that political responsibilities could not be borne by them without the sacrifice of the highest interests of their families and of society.

Nebraska Association Opposed to Woman Suffrage.

The Case Against Woman Suffrage

Anti-suffrage sentiment was particularly strong in Nebraska and in those states where much of the economy was tied to the liquor or brewery industries. Women's presumed support for prohibition, however, was not raised as one of the reasons to oppose equal suffrage on the "anti" leaflet above.

There were much more serious and sinister ramifications to consider.

According to the authors, if suffrage won it would mean chaos, the degradation of women, less humane and enforceable laws, sex hatred (yet free love), and the institutionalization of children. In their "mad rush" for the ballot, the writers claimed, women had advanced immorality, rejected the social graces, and become "pursuers of vice." The simple solution was for women to avoid diversions – like their own political enfranchisement.

Above: A disapproving leaflet from 1914.

During the Nebraska campaign in July 1914, thirty lawyers, bank presidents, and businessmen in Omaha issued an infamous Manifesto, similar in tone to the leaflet at left, which summarized their opposition to woman suffrage. Calling it "inconsistent with the fundamental principles upon which our representative government was founded," they declared, "We do not believe that women are adapted to the political work of the world.... There are spheres in which feeling should be paramount. There are kingdoms in which the heart should reign supreme. That kingdom belongs to woman – the realm of sentiment, the realm of love, the realm of gentler and holier and kindlier attributes that make the name of wife, mother and sister next to the name of God himself, but it is not in harmony with suffrage and has no place in government." In every state women encountered a similar mix of complex fears, prejudice masquerading as reason, and flowery yet condescending rhetoric. And behind the words lay substantial political and economic power.

Mixed Results from the 1914 Election

THE NOVEMBER 1914 elections showed mixed results for woman suffrage. After all their effort and expense. suffragists won two new equal suffrage states, Montana and Nevada, but lost the five other contests.

The exhausting campaign in Nevada was a clear victory, capturing 60% of the vote and passing 10,936 to 7,257. Strong support in the small towns and mining camps successfully outweighed opposition in the city.

In Montana the amendment passed by less than 4,000 votes, 41,302 to 37,588. NAWSA and other state associations had contributed over half of the campaign's $9,000 budget. Montana suffrage groups promptly reorganized as Good Government Clubs to support reform legislation and women candidates.

Anne Martin (fourth from left) and co-workers campaigning for suffrage in rural Nevada in 1914.

A Familiar Story

Results from the five other contests reflected the disinterest of voters and the power of brewery and other business interests which tied woman suffrage to popular fears of prohibition and reform. In Nebraska, support was strong but the measure was defeated 100,842 to 90,738. In Missouri it lost by 140,206 votes, 322,463 to 182,257.

In Ohio the measure registered gains in every county since the loss two years earlier, but voters again defeated it 518,295 to 335,390. After the loss, state suffragists abandoned efforts for a referendum and worked for municipal and presidential suffrage through their legislature.

In South Dakota the amendment was defeated for the fourth time, losing 51,519 to 39,605. Suffragists returned to the state legislature undeterred the following year with a new campaign.

The measure lost in North Dakota 49,348 to 40,209 although supporters felt that if the unmarked ballots had not been counted against the measure it would have passed. Suffragists in North Dakota were not able to get two successive legislatures to approve the measure again for a public vote until November 1920.

Sending a Message

The psychological effect of the Congressional Union's campaign to organize women voters against Democratic candidates in the west "was soon evident in Congress," claimed Doris Stevens, where even "the most backward member realized for the first time that women had voted." A year-end CU report noted, "All candidates, indeed, seemed to develop a marked increase in the fervor of their allegiance to the Suffrage Amendment."

Alice Paul told a congressional committee shortly after the election, "We campaigned against forty-three men running for Congress on the Democratic ticket in the suffrage states and only nineteen we campaigned against came back to Washington D.C." While not claiming full credit, suffragists had shown their willingness to organize politically to defeat their enemies. The CU continued to lobby for congressional action, and also began planning for the next important national election. ◆

Forcing Action on the Federal Amendment

E VEN WITH the defeats, the 1914 elections showed the growing strength and ability of women across the country. Running seven complicated statewide campaigns, plus a brief but well-publicized drive against Democratic candidates in nine western states, helped convince politicians that women were becoming a force to be reckoned with.

The House Rules Committee, for example, had refused to act on the suffrage bill throughout the entire year. It reversed itself immediately after the election and scheduled a vote for early January. The measure had never been debated on the House floor.

While there were signs of progress nationally, there was growing discontent within NAWSA. In mid-November, younger members including Anne Martin contested Anna Howard Shaw for leadership of the embattled association at its annual convention in Nashville. Shaw won re-election, but a third of the ballots were left blank by delegates unhappy over the association's direction yet unwilling to vote against her. Six of eight board positions turned over and some dissatisfied members gravitated towards the more vigorous and focused Congressional Union.

NAWSA set its sights, and hopes, on the four state contests scheduled for 1915, but pressure was clearly building for it to work harder for the original Federal amendment or else continue to lose members, funds, and political influence to its upstart rival.

In March 1915 the CU formally became a national organization and reached out to suffragists in every state, arguing that a constitutional amendment was the only way to guarantee the enfranchisement of women nationally.

Above: Signs and banners decorated a suffrage booth in New Jersey.

Fannie Garrison Villard, the only daughter of abolitionist William Lloyd Garrison, was an influential philanthropist and uncompromising pacifist who helped found the Woman's Peace Party in 1915. A distinguished social reformer, Villard was over sixty when she began speaking for woman suffrage, addressing rallies, testifying before legislative hearings in three states, and even speaking to crowds on the street. Believing that women would redeem politics, she worked with the New York state suffrage association and chaired its legislative committee during the height of activity in Albany. Her leadership also helped revitalize work for international peace.

Leading the Drive for Peace

ONE OF the first responses in the U.S. to the outbreak of war in Europe was a solemn Women's Peace Parade which suffragists and peace advocates organized in New York on August 29, 1914. Over fifteen hundred women, most wearing black armbands, followed parade chair Fannie Garrison Villard who carried a single banner for peace at the head of the procession. The marchers, including seasoned suffragists, social workers, and working women, walked with quiet dignity down Fifth Avenue to the beat of muffled drums.

The women mourned the early victims of the war and called for diplomacy and mediation to end the hostilities. Suffragist Mary Peck reported that "the sight was deeply

moving. Men took off their hats and many of the observers burst into tears. . . . The peace parade was a symbolic funeral for all the lives, hopes, and possibilities the world war would destroy." Nearly all suffrage activity abroad stopped completely when war was declared.

Top: The 1914 peace parade passes St. Patrick's Cathedral. Above: Fannie Garrison Villard (center) led the memorial.

The Woman's Peace Party Calls for Mediation in the Face of War

WITH THE encouragement of Carrie Catt, British suffragist Emmeline Pethick-Lawrence, and Rosika Schwimmer of Hungary, Jane Addams called a convention of American women's groups on January 10, 1915 to respond to the war in Europe. The convention formed the Woman's Peace Party which included numerous suffragists as officers and members.

In April the new party sent a large and enthusiastic delegation to an International Congress of Women at The Hague. The meeting brought together suffragists from all over Europe and symbolized the solidarity of women against war. The congress sent European and American emissaries including Addams, Dr. Alice Hamilton, and Emily Greene Balch to the leaders of the warring countries to urge them to consider mediation by a conference of neutral nations. The women called for a "Concert of Nations" to replace the "Balance of Power."

Although ridiculed in the press, the unenfranchised women found evidence that neutral mediation and leadership by the U.S. might help

resolve the conflict before it intensified. President Wilson's administration, however, was unresponsive.

The Woman's Peace Party grew to include 25,000 members and the reinvigorated peace movement clearly reflected the influence of experienced suffragists. As the war continued, however, it was not advantageous to be linked with peace and less dedicated members, including Catt, withdrew. Others, like Crystal Eastman, intensified work opposing preparedness in New York. The war was a constant concern for Americans during these years, and peace became an additional cause for many suffragists. After the war the Woman's Peace Party merged into the Women's International League for Peace and Freedom which Jane Addams also led. ◆

**Above: Emmeline Pethick-Lawrence (far left) of Great Britain stood beside Jane Addams and other delegates on their way to The Hague.
Left: A global peace float sounded the theme in the Suffrage Day parade in Cleveland, Ohio.**

Chapter 10: 1915

The Eastern Campaigns

THE YEAR 1915 SAW a showdown in four of the largest eastern states as woman suffrage measures finally came to a public vote in New Jersey, New York, Massachusetts, and Pennsylvania. The four states included more than one-fifth of the population of the United States, over 20 million people, which was nearly double the population of all the existing equal suffrage states combined.

Following the 1914 elections suffragists continued to pressure the Democratic-controlled 63rd Congress to act on the Federal amendment, leading to the first vote on the measure ever recorded in the U.S. House of Representatives. On January 12, 1915, the entirely male body defeated the bill 204 to 174, well short of the two-thirds needed, but the historic vote helped suffrage lobbyists

identify key opponents. Congress ended with little progress to show on woman suffrage and the new Congress did not convene until after the November elections, leaving a long summer break which saw widespread suffrage activity.

Since progress in Washington D.C. was dependent on pressure from the states, NAWSA's state associations stepped up their efforts to win legislative support for full or partial suffrage. Simultaneously, the Congressional Union pressed each state legislature to endorse the Federal amendment.

Since NAWSA still refused to put its full energy behind the suffrage amendment, Alice Paul built up CU chapters across the country. "We want to organize in every state in the Union," she told her Advisory Council on March 31. "We want to make woman suffrage the dominant political issue from the moment Congress reconvenes." The year marked a move from the CU's original F Street headquarters to Cameron House, a stately old mansion members called the "Little White House," strategically located on Lafayette Square directly opposite the White House.

During the previous year's

campaign, when the CU encouraged western women to vote against Democratic candidates, suffragists had succeeded in alarming many politicians who now openly wondered what the women would plan next. Longtime supporters, however, were encouraged that there was finally an active campaign focusing on the Federal amendment, which they recognized as the only realistic way of winning suffrage nationally.

With drives proceeding in four heavily populated states throughout 1915, the cause

engaged an unprecedented number of citizens. Well aware of the scope of their effort and the challenges they faced, suffragists still broadcast their hope for a complete "Eastern Victory."

Campaign workers distributed several million colorful pin-back buttons and badges (above) during the 1915 drives in the four eastern states. Publishers also produced a wide variety of sheet music sympathetic to the cause, some featuring "new women" on the covers (left). The musical composition *Woman Forever* (facing page), dedicated to the "Womanhood of the Universe," featured a triumphant central figure on its cover, adorned with garlands and backed by a radiant sun. Justice, Liberty, Equality, and Victory effortlessly carried her in regal procession.

VOTE FOR THE
WOMAN SUFFRAGE AMENDMENT
NOV. 2

Suffragists Gear Up for an All Out Eastern Victory

VOTE YES ☒
for
WOMAN SUFFRAGE
1915
NEW JERSEY NEW YORK,
Oct.19th MASS.,PENN,
Nov.2nd
© APP. FOR E.C.L.SUMMIT, N.J.

Suffragists in the campaign states made votes for women a prominent part of the 1915 elections. Each of the four populated industrial states had woman suffrage associations dating back to the 1870s and each state had a large delegation in Congress. A complete "Eastern Victory" would be an enormous step for the cause nationally.

All of the state campaigns had strong leadership and involved legions of women and their male supporters. Independent groups supplemented the efforts of each state suffrage association and NAWSA provided what organizers, funds, and literature it could.

NAWSA president Anna Howard Shaw had led the organization for eleven years and the inspiring orator remained a unifying presence in the movement throughout this period of increased state activity. She was an embattled figure, however, who oversaw a nearly bankrupt association wrought with conflicts over organizational direction. Although it seemed to be losing ground to the Congressional Union's Federal amendment campaign, NAWSA remained focused on winning more states to propel the measure forward nationally.

During the year, several of Shaw's supporters paid tribute to the veteran leader by presenting her with a new Saxon automobile (above) painted a vivid, attention-getting suffrage yellow. Shaw, then 68, took two weeks off to learn to drive and on August 13, 1915, with flags waving, led a procession up Fifth Avenue in New York.

Facing page: Norman Jacobsen's 1915 campaign poster captured some of the determination and crusading spirit of the eastern campaigns. Above: Anna Howard Shaw in her yellow coup. Left: A 1915 publicity stamp.

An Intensive Drive to Win Pennsylvania

Pennsylvania suffragists waged a strenuous effort to win their state after the legislature narrowly approved passing the measure on to the voters in 1913 and again in March 1915. The Keystone State had long been a center of suffrage activity and home to several woman's rights pioneers. They had learned early on that the phrase "all men are created equal" in the Declaration of Independence, signed in Philadelphia, did not necessarily include women and that new legislation was needed. The suffrage measure enjoyed the support of labor and of all the main political parties except the Republican.

Facing page: Paul Stahr's cover for *Life* magazine imaginatively captured suffragists' cause. Pennsylvania supporters produced a Key to Justice (below) and the angelic campaign stamp above.

During extensive automobile and trolley tours throughout Pennsylvania, women spoke at open-air meetings and outside factory gates (above) where the Suffrage Map helped illustrate women's gains. Suffragists were confident that years of work in their progressive state would finally pay off in 1915. Seventeen organizers covered the eight largest counties and eighteen other women, including Jeannette Rankin and Laura Gregg Cannon, worked the rest of the state. They held meetings, formed new organizations, and reached out to voters at Chautauquas, churches, and county fairs. At one rally, future voters, dressed in white (below), lined up with American flags while a speaker addressed their parents and neighbors. The state association scheduled over sixty speakers through its speaker's bureau and every week its publicity department sent news bulletins to more than 300 newspapers.

1776—RETOUCHING AN OLD MASTERPIECE—1915

A Patriotic Symbol Adds Weight to the Drive in Pennsylvania

THE MOST effective publicity feature of the Pennsylvania campaign was a life-size replica of the Liberty Bell in Philadelphia which suffragists called the Women's Liberty Bell or the Justice Bell. Commissioned by Mrs. Charles W. Ruschenberger, the weighty symbol of freedom toured every county during 1915, traveling nearly 4,000 miles on a specially reinforced truck.

Suffragists used the truck's raised platform to address rural audiences who often approached the bell with as much reverence and ceremony as they would the original. The powerful symbol was credited with securing thousands of votes. Sales of novelty bells and collections taken during the tours helped cover expenses but the great weakness of the campaign remained its lack of money.

The state drive was led by Jennie Bradley Roessing of Pittsburgh, president of the Pennsylvania Woman Suffrage Association, and Hannah J. Patterson, chair of the state Woman Suffrage Party which organized supporters into political districts rather than suffrage clubs. Other groups included the Equal Rights Association in Philadelphia and the Equal Franchise Federation of Pittsburgh which was led by Julian Kennedy, one of the few men to serve as president of a woman suffrage organization. There was also an active Men's League headed by Wilmer Atkinson which helped recruit Black voters.

A bustling press bureau published an official newspaper, *The Pennsylvania Suffrage News,* and distributed a popular weekly collection of the best cartoons with suffrage content. Supporters also produced buttons, blotters, hairpins, and even washcloths with the inscription "Taxation Without Representation is Tyranny."

Right: Speaking next to the Women's Liberty Bell. Above: Seeds for "suffrage yellow" flower gardens.

Working to Win Back the Vote in New Jersey

NEW JERSEY suffragists finally saw their measure scheduled for a public vote at a special election on October 19, 1915, after being approved by two successive state legislatures.

Lillian F. Feickert, president of the New Jersey Woman Suffrage Association, traveled extensively to organize support for the initiative. Reflecting the changing image of suffragists, she won praise from *The Patterson Morning Call* when it reported on a 1913 visit, "She came here last night and those of us who heard her went away with the impression that Mrs. Feickert was

aggressive, a campaigner, a politician, a fighter, and an extremely practical woman, all rolled into one."

NAWSA president Anna Howard Shaw also traveled the eastern states extensively before the elections and rarely missed an opportunity to remind her audiences that women in New Jersey were entitled to vote after the Rev-

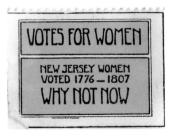

olution until that right was taken away by the legislature in 1807. She enjoined supporters that it was time to win the ballot back.

Shaw believed that enough state victories would make Federal action unavoidable. Countering the premise of Alice Paul and the Congressional Union, she claimed that "there is not a single reason given upon which to base a hope for congressional action that does not rest upon the power and influence to be derived from the equal suffrage states, which power was secured by the slow but effective method of winning state by state."

New Jersey suffragists (facing page) posted signs by the Asbury Park Boardwalk announcing a 1915 lecture by Anna Howard Shaw. The veteran leader (above) delivered hundreds of speeches in the campaign states during the year. As historian Ida Husted Harper noted, "Only a fine constitution and supreme will power enabled her to endure the strain, and with it all her fund of humor was never exhausted and her courage never faltered."

Saturating the Garden State

SUFFRAGISTS VISITED every city and town in New Jersey in 1915 to educate voters, recruit workers, and win the support of influential citizens. The state suffrage association held over 4,000 outdoor and 500 indoor meetings while four paid and thirty volunteer organizers worked in the field. They were assisted by the well-organized Women's Political Union of New Jersey, led by Mina Van Winkle, and active chapters of the Equal Franchise Society and Men's League. The four groups formed a Cooperative Committee to coordinate the ambitious state campaign.

Teams of suffragists journeyed to small towns throughout the state speaking, distributing literature, and canvassing house to house. Supporters used illuminated signs, street banners, concerts, and special events to draw attention to the October 19 election.

Members of the Women's Political Union in New Jersey canvassed towns (left) throughout the state, leafleted at railway crossings (above), and struck up the band (below) to promote local suffrage events.

A shady yard in Newark was the perfect spot for members of the New Jersey chapter of the Women's Political Union to pitch their Votes for Women tent (above) and reach out to passing citizens during the summer of 1915. The WPU maintained a large and active headquarters in Newark and their suffrage booth (right), flying purple, white, and green flags, was the hub of activity on the Asbury Park Boardwalk. Anti-suffragists also maintained a presence at the summer resort. By the end of the campaign, supporters had distributed over three million pieces of literature and 400,000 buttons throughout the state.

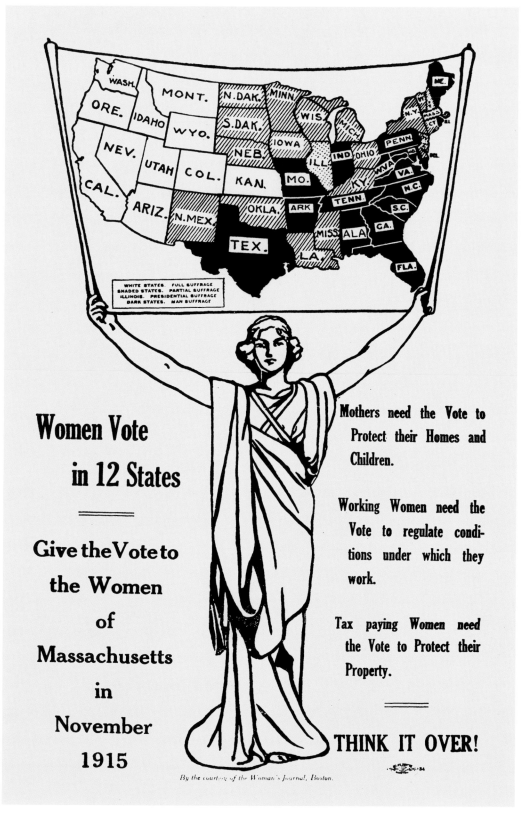

Women Vote in 12 States

Give the Vote to the Women of Massachusetts in November 1915

Mothers need the Vote to Protect their Homes and Children.

Working Women need the Vote to regulate conditions under which they work.

Tax paying Women need the Vote to Protect their Property.

THINK IT OVER!

By the courtesy of the Woman's Journal, Boston.

Forcing a Vote in Massachusetts

AFTER YEARS of disappointment, suffrage was finally put on the ballot in Massachusetts in 1915 and supporters launched a coordinated drive to win passage. The bill had won a two-thirds vote by two successive legislatures only after suffragists had targeted prominent political opponents, including a state senator in 1912 and four other candidates in 1913, and mounted vigorous campaigns to defeat them. Other politicians could no longer ignore the determination of these unenfranchised women.

Gertrude Leonard led the venerable Massachusetts Woman Suffrage Association and Teresa Crowley headed its Legislative Committee that chose which men to oppose. Also active were Pauline Agassiz Shaw's well-funded Boston Equal Suffrage Association for Good Government, the College Equal Suffrage League, a Political Equality Union of working women and men, and a state-wide Woman Suffrage Party.

During the Massachusetts campaign suffragists distributed dozens of different fliers including the one above which reminded male voters that women needed the ballot because they were mothers, workers, and taxpayers. The Suffrage Map showed that women exercised full or partial suffrage in a growing number of states.

Throughout the year Massachusetts workers organized systematic trolley tours, large indoor rallies, street speaking, and mass meetings every Sunday in Boston.

Reaching Voters in the Bay State

Tens of thousands of brightly painted tin Votes for Women bluebirds (above) were posted in conspicuous places throughout Massachusetts in 1915 to publicize the upcoming election. Having won eleven western states, suffrage leaders hoped that a major victory in the east would provide an important psychological breakthrough as well as a substantial increase in political support in Congress. Future Supreme Court Justice Louis D. Brandeis later praised the "intelligence, devotion and intensity" of the women's campaign and noted that "it should silence any doubt as to their fitness for enfranchisement." Leaders of the ruling state Republican party, however, remained staunch opponents.

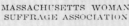

Noble Men of Massachusetts

You want to protect the Home. So do we. Give us the ballot and we will help you defend its sanctity, the welfare of the children and all good things.

This amendment will come before you November 2nd. Vote "Yes."

Shall the following proposed Amendment to the Constitution enabling Women to vote be approved and ratified?

YES	X
NO	

Gertrude Halladay Leonard   MASSACHUSETTS WOMAN
Teresa A. Crowley   SUFFRAGE ASSOCIATION

THOUSANDS OF volunteers worked in Massachusetts during the 1915 drive along side nine organizers and five salaried speakers. Together they built up over 200 local clubs which reached out to voters throughout the state. Agnes Morey and Florence Luscomb directed automobile trips to the country districts throughout the summer and fall, and open-air meetings were held every day. During an extensive house-to-house canvass, suffragists reached over half of the registered voters and obtained pledge cards from 100,000. Leaflets and signs emphasized faith in women and concern for the welfare of children as reasons to support the amendment.

Above: Mt. Holyoke students prepared to march in Springfield. Left: A two-sided card used simple arguments to sway male voters.

HOME   SCHOOL

CHILDREN

PLAYGROUND

ALL THESE ARE PRECIOUS TO YOU AND TO US. LET US VOTE THAT WE MAY HELP YOU TO PROTECT THEM

Suffragists Face Strong Opposition in All Four States

DURING THE 1915 drives, opponents in Massachusetts worked not only in their own state but in all the campaign states to defeat the suffrage measures.

The Massachusetts Association Opposed to the Further Extension of Suffrage to Women was the oldest and best organized of the state anti-suffrage groups. Socially prominent women made up its leadership as well as that of most of the other state associations opposed to suffrage. Men organized groups of their own including the Massachusetts Anti-Suffrage League and the Men's Anti-Suffrage League in New Jersey.

Anti-suffragists published booklets, publicity stamps, and several periodicals in-cluding *The Woman's Protest* and *The Remonstrance,* which was produced in Boston from 1890 to 1920. *The Remonstrance* summarized the shared belief that "the great majority of their sex do not want the ballot, and that to force it upon them would not only be an injustice to women, but would lessen their influence for good."

To raise money for their campaign, suffragists in Boston held annual bazaars, sold novelties, and on August 14, 1914, collected jewelry for their Suffrage Melting Pot (above). Susan Fitzgerald is in the center foreground. An editorial cartoon by Sykes (left) showed dour old Miss Anti-Suffrage blocking Massachusetts from joining the "free states." Below: An opposition stamp.

WHY CAN'T I PLAY TOO?

Reprinted from
The Springfield Republican
Suffrage Number, April 15, 1915

Men of Massachusetts, Make Our State Free

VOTE NO ON WOMAN SUFFRAGE

Anti-suffragists in the east increasingly adopted the tactics of their adversaries, although on a lesser scale, as they tried to defeat votes for women. Not only did opponents testify before legislative bodies, lobby, and publish fliers (above), they also organized public meetings, gave interviews, and held automobile tours. In some cities, like New York, they even opened up storefront offices. Like suffragists, opponents issued leaflets targeting specific groups of voters. The anonymous one below, addressed to the "working man," claimed simply that woman suffrage, "the opening wedge to feminism," meant that men would lose their jobs to women.

Working Against Equal Suffrage

DURING THE 1915 contests anti-suffragists campaigned more publicly than ever before to counter growing public support for equal suffrage. Their 1914 leaflet (right), written before the victories in Montana and Nevada, made the case for restricting woman suffrage "to its present limits" and predicted "the heaviest defeats" in the 1915 elections. The National Association Opposed to Woman Suffrage (above) tried to draw different state groups together to present a united front of opposition. Their dominant theme was that most women did not want to vote.

Above: New Yorkers read window notices outside the opposition's storefront headquarters.

The Empire State Campaign Takes On New York

NEW YORK had long been home to many active suffrage societies and before the state campaign most joined together to coordinate work. The Empire State Campaign Committee, organized in 1913 with Carrie Catt as chair, included the state suffrage association headed by Gertrude Brown, the Woman Suffrage Party in New York City, the College Equal Suffrage League, Men's League, and other groups. Alva Belmont's Political Equality Association remained independent as did Harriot Blatch's comparatively well-funded Women's Political Union which organized its own parallel campaign.

By 1915 there were over 700 clubs and committees in the state filled with workers for whom the prospect of winning equal rights in the most populated and economically important state in the Union was unbelievably exhilarating. Supporters emphasized themes of enlightenment, justice, and cooperation throughout the campaign. However, no major political party actually endorsed the amendment.

Left: The evocative cover of a New York campaign booklet.

Mary Garrett Hay, a veteran of over twenty years of suffrage work, ran the Woman Suffrage Party in New York City with a firm and confident hand. Rooted in politics from her youth in Indiana, Hay helped shape the political form of the later suffrage movement. Displaying a shrewd, street-wise manner which some suffragists found unsettling, Hay helped convert the General Federation of Women's Clubs and neutralize the opposition of Tammany Hall. While her friends called her "Mollie," reporters referred to her as "The Big Boss," echoing the world of machine politics she emulated. Hay first met Carrie Catt on NAWSA's Organization Committee in 1895 and they worked and traveled together from then on. After Catt's husband died in 1905, the two close friends shared a home together for 23 years. Maud Wood Park praised Hay for possessing "a remarkable degree of the executive ability and the knowledge of practical politics" needed by the movement. "Mrs. Catt was essentially a statesman; Miss Hay, a politician, and together they were, in most cases, invincible."

Organizing: The Key to New York State Vote

THE EMPIRE State Campaign Committee divided New York into twelve districts each with a woman chair. Under them were 150 assembly district leaders and 5,524 election district captains. In Gertrude Brown's words, "organization was the keynote to success." Suffragists held meetings in every county during 1914 and 1915. They organized suffrage schools along with automobile tours, booths at fairs, and countless other forms of voter contact. Forty paid organizers and an estimated 200,000 volunteers worked in some capacity during the drive. Organization was most devel-

oped in New York City but between May and November over 10,000 meetings were held all over the state.

Carrie Catt was the driving force on the committee, making plans, raising money, writing, speaking, and coordinating the enormous undertaking. She is pictured in the lower right hand corner (above) while chairing a meeting with suffrage leaders from throughout the state. As in the other states, the demanding campaign prepared women to take on greater responsibilities in the future.

Above: A meeting of Empire State campaign leaders.

A steady stream of campaign literature issued forth from the tidy shipping room (left) of the New York Woman Suffrage Association during the 1915 drive. Suffragists distributed twenty tons of leaflets (above) in 24 languages throughout the diversely-populated state.

Finding new ways to raise money, Vera Boarman Whitehouse, chair of publicity for the Empire State Campaign Committee, tested out the new Votes for Women "Hopperie" game (above) before it opened at New York's Luna Park. Whitehouse, a wealthy socialite originally recruited by Nora Blatch, became a widely respected state leader and outstanding fundraiser. Her suffrage game of hopscotch was one of many innovations used to popularize the cause. Parading "Kewpies" (below) drawn by Rose O'Neill, an ardent suffragist, appealed to men to "give mother the vote." Right: A paper cup from the 1915 campaign.

Imaginative Campaign Targets New York Voters

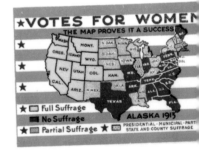

As New York City's Woman Suffrage Party grew in size and influence it adopted all the techniques developed in previous campaigns to awaken voter interest, excite supporters, and counter the claims of anti-suffragists.

Historian Inez Irwin later wrote that the WSP "was on the job day in and day out. In every 'exclusive district' of upper Fifth Avenue, in every great apartment house, in every block of tenements on the East Side, the leader and her assistants were cajoling, persuading and arousing tenants of both sexes. Wherever women gathered, the suffragists tried to present their cause – in clubs, at teas, at special parlor meetings. Wherever men gathered – at firemen's parades, Tammany picnics, Wall Street dinners – they spoke, distributed literature and staged picturesque 'stunts.'"

Special "Suffrage Days" focused on particular groups of voters including firemen, barbers, bankers, street cleaners, clergymen, factory and rail-

Twelve Reasons
Why Women Should Vote

1. **BECAUSE** those who obey the laws should help to choose those who make the laws.
2. **BECAUSE** laws affect women as much as men.
3. **BECAUSE** laws which affect WOMEN are now passed without consulting them.
4. **BECAUSE** laws affecting CHILDREN should include the woman's point of view as well as the man's.
5. **BECAUSE** laws affecting the HOME are voted on in every session of the Legislature.
6. **BECAUSE** women have experience which would be helpful to legislation.
7. **BECAUSE** to deprive women of the vote is to lower their position in common estimation.
8. **BECAUSE** having the vote would increase the sense of responsibility among women toward questions of public importance.
9. **BECAUSE** public spirited mothers make public spirited sons.
10. **BECAUSE** about 8,000,000 women in the United States are wage workers, and the conditions under which they work are controlled by law.
11. **BECAUSE** the objections against their having the vote are based on prejudice, not on reason.
12. **BECAUSE** to sum up all reasons in one—IT IS FOR THE COMMON GOOD OF ALL.

VOTES FOR WOMEN

NATIONAL WOMAN SUFFRAGE PUBLISHING CO., INC.
171 Madison Avenue,   New York City

road workers, lawyers, ditch diggers, and longshoremen. Suffragists visited businessmen on Wall Street as well as Irish laborers in the subway excavations.

Twelve thousand New York City public school teachers formed a branch of the Empire State Campaign under Katharine Devereux Blake and many gave up their summer vacation to work for the amendment. Suffragists printed over seven million leaflets and distributed over one million pin-back buttons during the drive. They also produced playing cards, publicity stamps, posters, "Vote Yes" matches, paper cups, and 35,000 fans featuring the Suffrage Map.

Costumed women (above) representing the different states staged a suffrage tableau outside Central Park before the 1915 election. Liberty, in the center, raised the torch of freedom while enfranchised women in white held identifying shields. The totally unenfranchised women on the right, shackled and clothed in black, cried out for freedom.

Prominent east coast writers (above) participated in "An Author's Evening" for woman suffrage in New York City in 1915. Standing (left to right) are Flora Gaitliss, Ellis Jones, Elisabeth Freeman, William Hard, Paula Jakoti, Frederick C. Howe, and Marie Jenney Howe. Seated are Will Irwin, Edwin Markham, Lincoln Steffens, Arturo Giovannitti, Percy MacKaye, and Dr. W.E.B. Du Bois. The flier (top) summarized the basic suffrage arguments, repeated over the years, ending with "It is for the common good of all."

The Women's Political Union Wages Its Own Statewide Drive

THE 1915 campaign stood at the pinnacle of Harriot Stanton Blatch's years of work in New York. After winning the legislature's approval, the Women's Political Union worked to persuade voters in the city and upstate industrial regions.

One approach the WPU tried during the summer of 1914 was a tent campaign in the western part of the state. Erecting their portable headquarters in a central spot in each town, suffragists branched out to leaflet and hold meetings outside local factories and in public parks. One tour in Jamestown (above) included several young Syracuse University students and was led by Jane Pincus who Blatch called "the most fearless, the most determined, and the most relentless of our young workers."

While the WPU gave its full

energy to the campaign, Blatch faced several difficulties of a more personal nature, particularly the death of her husband of 34 years. After William Blatch was killed by a fallen electrical wire in August, she sailed to England to settle his estate and returned just four weeks before the election.

Blatch also faced the erosion of her once-prominent place in the movement. To preserve her political autonomy and keep her financial backers, she had always kept the WPU independent of the state suffrage association. But in 1914 a new NAWSA consti-

tution backed by Carrie Catt required such affiliation plus a percentage of revenue from every member. In response, the WPU withdrew from NAWSA. As her biographer Ellen DuBois observed, this subsequently weakened Blatch's national influence.

Upon her return to the U.S. she hosted a well-publicized luncheon at the Hotel Astor to commemorate the centennial of the birth of her mother, Elizabeth Cady Stanton, and to climax the New York campaign. Although rival state leaders Catt and Gertrude Brown shunned the event, the reception drew over 800 celebrants and won substantial press coverage just days before the election.

Above: Jane Pincus (second from left) and crew in Jamestown. Left: Commemorative button.

The Women's Political Union's 1915 campaign in New York, led by Caroline Lexow, showed the same creativity and drive that marked the WPU's earlier efforts. Acquiring an old lunch wagon (above), Union members in New York City painted it purple, white, and green and then used it both as a roving shop for selling literature and as a platform for making speeches. Harriot Blatch (center) practiced speaking from the wagon accompanied by (from the

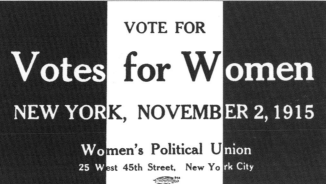

VOTE FOR
Votes for Women
NEW YORK, NOVEMBER 2, 1915

Women's Political Union
25 West 45th Street, New York City

left) WPU executive secretary Alberta Hill (leafleting), finance chair Eunice Dana Brannan, Ethel R. Peyser

(behind Blatch), Lucy Eastman, Mildred Taylor, and Kathleen Taylor on the right. To reach upstate residents

and working class audiences, the WPU enlisted well-known suffragists Helen Todd from California, Helen Ring Robinson from Colorado, Fola LaFollette from Wisconsin, and Rose Winslow of New York. They spoke to thousands of voters. In the city, the WPU worked relatively harmoniously with the Empire State Campaign Committee but there were jurisdictional clashes in some upstate areas. Buttons and a 1915 card (left) displayed the WPU's signature colors.

Maud Younger was 45 when she joined the Congressional Union following the Panama-Pacific Exposition in 1915 and moved from San Francisco to Washington D.C. There she soon led the CU's lobbying drive for the Federal amendment. Younger, who had inherited a fortune as a child after her mother died, worked at the College Settlement House in New York City for five years where she learned about poverty, trade unionism, and women's rights. She earned the nickname "the millionaire waitress" after taking jobs in New York restaurants to expose their exploitation of women, and then writing about the experience in *McClures* magazine. In San Francisco she organized and led a waitresses' union and helped secure the eight-hour-day law for women. A compelling speaker, she also enlisted labor support in the California and Nevada suffrage campaigns. Younger became an influential force in Washington D.C. by emphasizing political pressure rather than the friendly alliances favored by her NAWSA counterpart Maud Wood Park. Younger and her dog Sandy (above right) prepared to drive to Washington D.C. in 1920.

AT WORK IN THE CONSTITUENCIES OF MEMBERS OF CONGRESS

Scene in the New York Headquarters of the Congressional Union

Mrs. William Colt, Member of the Advisory Council of the Union, Explaining the Vote of N. Y. Congressmen on the Suffrage Amendment

Building Pressure on Congress

WHILE CAMPAIGNS continued in the eastern states, members of the Congressional Union kept their focus on Congress. Following the January 12 defeat in the U.S. House of Representatives, Mrs. William Colt (left) appeared on the cover of the CU's weekly magazine reviewing a chart showing the votes of New York's congressmen. Lobbyists kept track of each representative's stand along with his political statements and various personal details on a confidential Congressional Index Card File which made some men very nervous. Meanwhile, suffragists in the congressional districts kept local constituents informed and built up broad political support.

Left: Tabulating support.

A Transcontinental Automobile Trip Dramatizes the Federal Amendment

WHILE NAWSA and the state suffrage organizations were busy in the east, the Congressional Union turned again to the voting women in the west to strengthen the demand for Federal action. Taking advantage of the long Congressional recess, Alice Paul organized a Convention of Women Voters in San Francisco, scheduled to coincide with the Panama-Pacific Exposition.

The climax of the convention came on September 16 with the dramatic torch-lit send-off of two envoys and two drivers carrying a petition to Washington D.C. signed by half a million people calling for passage of the Federal amendment.

When one envoy, Frances Joliffe, fell ill, Sara Bard Field was left to face the speaking and public demands of the cross-country journey on her own until New York City. Field traveled with two Swedish women from Rhode Island, Maria Kindberg and Ingeborg Kindstedt, who had volunteered to drive the envoys across the country in their new Overland touring car. The three intrepid travelers braved a "transcontinental

highway" that was in some places little more than an unmarked muddy track or old wagon trail.

In between large rallies and warm welcomes the trip was an exercise in endurance. The travelers got lost in the Utah desert, sank into a mud hole on a rainy night in rural Kansas (where a patient farmer could only remark, "Well, you girls got guts"), and broke an axle near Syracuse. Mabel Vernon went ahead by train to arrange welcoming receptions and interviews in each city. The women also established CU chapters along the way.

The remarkable 5,000 mile journey took nearly three months. When the women and their weather-beaten automobile finally arrived in Washington D.C. on December 6 they received a hero's welcome. A festive procession of thousands of women organized by novelist Mary Austin welcomed the envoys to the capital.

Above: Gathering signatures at the San Francisco Exposition. Left: Sara Bard Field (left foreground) and companions before crossing the continent.

Sara Bard Field, poet and journalist, was 33 when she agreed to cross the country by automobile for woman suffrage. Married at 18 to a minister twice her age, she served with him in India for two years. Before their divorce they moved with their two children to Portland, Oregon. There Field became involved with the 1910 suffrage campaign and met her future husband, attorney and poet Charles Erskine Scott Wood. She worked as a paid organizer during the successful 1912 drive. Slender and attractive, "a woman of rare spirituality and humor" in Maud Younger's words, Field became an eloquent speaker and a skilled field worker. During her 1915 trip she supported herself writing articles but worried constantly about debts, her children, and her safety. Disregarding a serious heart condition, she continued the journey despite growing exhaustion. Field withdrew from public activity after her son died in 1918 and made her home in Los Gatos, California, a center for west coast artists and writers.

Right: Under her "Great Demand" banner, Sara Bard Field spoke to a "sea of people" from the steps of Chicago's Art Institute.

Like Susan B. Anthony, pictured in her favorite red cape on the stamp above, the Congressional Union was becoming a familiar presence in the capital. When Sara Bard Field and her companions reached Washington D.C. on December 6, 1915, congressmen welcomed them with speeches and President Wilson received them, eyeing the petition of over half a million signatures with interest. Mindful of the president's opposition to Federal action, the diplomatic Field observed, "Like all great men you have changed your mind on other questions." He replied that he would consider the matter "very carefully" and then helped roll up the great petition. A meeting (below) rallied supporters.

CONGRESSIONAL UNION
FOR WOMAN SUFFRAGE

Mass Meeting

BELASCO THEATRE
Sunday, December 12
3:30 P. M.

SPEAKERS

Mrs. Sara Bard Field, Oregon ⎫ ENVOYS OF
Miss Frances Jolliffe, California ⎭ WOMEN VOTERS

Senator George Sutherland, Utah
Representative Frank W. Mondel, Wyoming
Miss Maud Younger, California
Mrs. O. H. P. Belmont, New York
Chairman, Mrs. Margaret Zane Cherdron, Utah

TICKETS 25c, 50c, 75c, $1, $1.25, $1.50
1420 F Street N. W.

Look forward, women, always; utterly cast away
 The memory of hate and struggle and bitterness;
Bonds may endure for a night, but freedom comes with the day,
 And the free must remember nothing less.

Forget the strife; remember those who strove—
 The first defeated women, gallant and few,
Who gave us hope, as a mother gives us love,
 Forget them not, and this remember, too:

How at the later call to come forth and unite,
 Women untaught, uncounselled, alone and
Rank upon rank came forth in unguessed migh
 Each one answering the call of her own wil

By HY MAYER

They came from toil and want, from leisure and ease,
   Those who knew only life, and learned women of fame,
Girls and the mothers of girls, and the mothers of these,
   No one knew whence or how, but they came, they came.

The faces of some were stern, and some were gay,
   And some were pale with the terror of unreal dangers;
But their hearts knew this: that hereafter come what may,
   Women to women would never again be strangers.

Alice Duer Miller.

Suffragists Look Forward to "The Awakening"

AFTER THE gains of 1914, the west was solidly for woman suffrage and over four million women in eleven states could vote equally with men. But while more states could probably be won, it was clear that in some even prolonged efforts might prove unsuccessful. When President Wilson congratulated Anne Martin after the 1914 victory in Nevada saying, "This is the way I believe it should come, by the states," she immediately responded that "referendum campaigns are killing work" and that she personally supported the Federal amendment which would "end the long struggle."

A fully enfranchised west was the theme of Hy Mayer's 1915 illustration for *Life* magazine, "The Awakening" (left). It pictured Liberty bringing the torch of freedom to the darkened east where women reached out for the light of enfranchisement. "I am impressed anew with the change in the tide of progress," wrote Sara Bard Field during her cross-country trip. "Of old, it went from the east westward. Now it moves from the west eastward." Suffragists hoped "progress" would reach the four eastern states in time for the 1915 elections.

Left: Bringing the light of freedom to the east.

Louisine Havemeyer was one of Harriot Blatch's most remarkable recruits to woman suffrage. A wealthy patron of the arts and prominent member of New York society, Havemeyer was 53 when her husband died in 1907. With Blatch's encouragement she became increasingly involved with the suffrage drive, supporting it financially and speaking publicly on its behalf. Educated abroad, Havemeyer was a vibrant and strong-willed matriarch who possessed a directness and enthusiasm that audiences loved. Her speeches became known for their colorful, old-fashioned earthiness and she became one of the Women's Political Union's most successful speakers. Blatch described her as "a great personality . . . vital to her finger tips. She was loyalty itself to friends, to her family, to her class, to the cause she espoused. She was an artist in the very fiber of her being." An astute art collector with her husband, Havemeyer followed her friend Mary Cassatt's guidance and built up an exquisite collection of Impressionist paintings which she later bequeathed to the Metropolitan Museum of Art.

The Torch of Liberty Inspires New York Voters

The Women's Political Union's principal propaganda event during the 1915 drive was a classic, carved Torch of Liberty which attracted crowds throughout the state. Harriot Blatch conceived the campaign and reported that the torch, a visual symbol of women's enfranchisement, "met enthusiasm, even awe," wherever it was used. The painted wooden prop impressed audiences "from Montauk Point to Lake Erie" who gathered around and reverently reached out to touch it.

Louisine Havemeyer of New York City made numerous speeches with the torch, often from the WPU's roving shop. She recalled one noontime speech: "I lifted the torch as high as I could and for once I did not have to think –

After the suffrage torch had served its publicity purposes in New York, the Women's Political Union passed it to New Jersey suffragists during a dramatic rendezvous in the middle of the Hudson River. Members of the WPU of New Jersey (above) sailed out on a tugboat decorated with Union colors to receive the torch on August 7. Louisine Havemeyer (below, right), representing the WPU in Harriot Blatch's absence, handed the carved symbol to Mina Van Winkle, head of the New Jersey WPU, while their boats were moored together. The torch was immediately pressed into service in the Garden State.

Seeing the effect the torch had on audiences, Havemeyer commissioned another symbolic prop, a beautiful, full-rigged model Ship of State, and used it at night meetings held specifically for working men. She told them that woman "is told that she cannot go on board . . . just because she is a woman." The miniature carved frigate resembled the Mayflower. It featured a rigging of 33 tiny light bulbs which lit up through a battery at a critical moment when the speaker flipped a switch. Havemeyer recognized the model ship's attraction when she observed that to many it "seemed a very attractive toy."

the words came to me as if by inspiration; I could not utter them fast enough; I feared the moments would pass before I had told those men all I wanted them to hear.

"The torch, I told them, was like the one that lighted up our harbor, like the one held aloft by the Statue of Liberty – it stood for liberty and for freedom – the freedom we were seeking – and it greeted the strangers who came to our shores and it did not welcome men only – no, but rather men and women alike, bidding them welcome to the land of the free and the home of the brave." Her audience roared its approval.

Above: Louisine Havemeyer spoke to New Yorkers on June 9, 1915, while holding up the suffrage torch.

With the rising sun behind her, blindfolded Justice called for equal suffrage at the ballot box on the stamp above from the Women's Political Union. Suffragists in each state produced publicity stamps and campaign buttons as well as publications and novelties. Opponents were also extremely active in all the eastern contests. Suffragist Fredrikke Palmer's cartoon (below right) graphically captured the power of the brewery industry, picturing it literally burying the suffrage cause with barrels of money being funnelled through an anti-suffrage "front". She asked, "Will the Government Get Them?" Three years later, during the war, Federal investigators uncovered the industry's secret and widespread involvement in defeating both woman suffrage and prohibition initiatives in the states.

Will The Government Get Them?

Suffrage Torch Ignites Media's Interest

Mina Van Winkle (above), head of the Women's Political Union in New Jersey, proudly held aloft the suffrage torch she had just received from Louisine Havemeyer and the New York WPU. In New Jersey, too, "the welcome was hearty wherever the torch was carried," Havemeyer reported.

When the torch's publicity value wore thin, New Jersey suffragists came up with a final way to extend interest. "The newspapers one morning gave out the startling news that the torch had been stolen," remembered Harriot Blatch. "Strange stories of how it had been spirited away" circulated and suffragists and the general public earnestly followed the news day by day until it died out. Only later did Van Winkle privately confide that the torch had never actually been stolen at all, but had been retired to elicit a final burst of publicity.

Van Winkle was a welfare worker on New York's East Side when Blatch sparked her interest in suffrage. Blatch described her as "a young woman bursting with vitality, fully equipped for service." Van Winkle later became head of the Women's Department of the police force in Washington D.C.

Above: Mina Van Winkle with the suffrage torch. Below: Rousing New Jersey voters.

Wilson Endorses Suffrage in New Jersey

Suffragists in New Jersey covered the state with automobile tours and public rallies during the final weeks of their campaign. The state suffrage association, under the able leadership of Lillian Feickert, grew to include 200 branches in 24 cities. On August 13 state suffragists gathered in East Orange with the leaders from the other three campaign states for a strategic planning meeting. Afterwards they made a pilgrimage to Lucy Stone's old house where her daughter Alice Stone Blackwell unveiled a memorial tablet to the pioneer leader.

As the October 19 election approached, state suffragists pulled off their crowning achievement. They persuaded President Wilson to announce that he would personally visit his home state to vote in favor of the suffrage measure. Although his widely publicized endorsement reinvigorated suffragists, he made it clear that he still firmly opposed Federal action. His position as a Democrat dependent on southern support was that voting was an issue for each state to decide.

Above: Suffragists with New Jersey voters.

Antis Campaign to Block Suffrage

THE WOMEN'S Anti-Suf-
frage Association in New
Jersey met the suffrage campaign with an energetic drive
of its own. It sent around two
organizers and several outside
speakers and claimed 11,000
members in 34 local clubs.

One opposition leader re-
portedly claimed that "we
knew we had the amendment
beaten when the election was
put on Registration Day."
Men could vote on the measure without having previously registered. This allowed
unscrupulous opponents to
import voters or recruit men
in the saloons. But opposition seemed widespread, led
by the state's ruling Democratic political machine.

Suffragists, however, re-
mained undaunted. When a

horse-drawn wagon fes-
tooned with anti-suffrage
messages (above) paraded
through a New Jersey town,
the Women's Political Union
sent an automobile flying the
Union's tricolor flags (foreground) to accompany it.

**Above: Monitoring the
opposition. Right: A flier
from Massachusetts warned
farmers that suffrage would
impose "an unjust political
handicap" on them because
urban women voters would
be indifferent to their
interests.**

Why the Farmer Should Oppose Woman Suffrage

The farmer should oppose woman suffrage for the same reasons
that all others should oppose it, and for this special reason in addition:

**Woman suffrage would place a tremendous handicap upon
the farmer by increasing the proportion of the vote which is
indifferent to his interests.**

With woman suffrage in force, the husband and wife must both
vote and vote the same way in order to make the voting power of the
family as strong as it was under male suffrage alone.

In the city, where the polling place is just around the corner, no
conditions of roads or weather can prevent women who desire to do so,
or who are controlled by the bosses, from going to the polls.

But in the country, with the polling places often miles away, the
women in many cases will be compelled by weather and other conditions to remain at home on Election Day, leaving the men to stand alone
against the men and women of the cities, thus making it easier, for
those who so desire, to secure legislation adverse to the interests of
the farmer.

VOTE " NO " ON WOMAN SUFFRAGE NOV. 2 AND SAVE THE
RURAL COMMUNITIES FROM AN UNJUST POLITICAL HANDI-
CAP.

MASSACHUSETTS ANTI-SUFFRAGE COMMITTEE,
524 Scollay Building, Boston.

JAMES D. COLT, Chairman.
AUGUSTIN H. PARKER, Secretary.   97

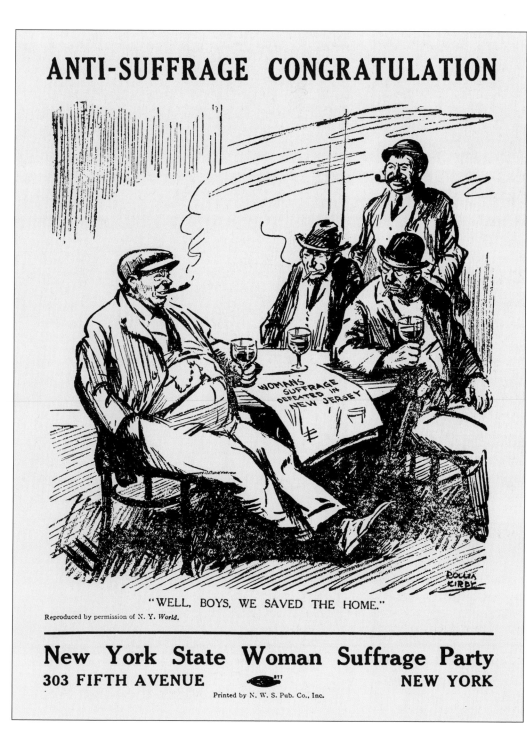

ANTI-SUFFRAGE CONGRATULATION

"WELL, BOYS, WE SAVED THE HOME."

Reproduced by permission of N. Y. *World*.

New York State Woman Suffrage Party
303 FIFTH AVENUE   **NEW YORK**

Printed by N. W. S. Pub. Co., Inc.

Organized anti-suffragists on the east coast gained confidence from their victory in New Jersey and unleashed a final publicity drive just before the election in the three remaining states boasting, "Where we work, we win." As always, the liquor and brewery interests also fought the measure, some saloons even passing out pink slips on election day reading "Good for two drinks if woman suffrage is defeated." A poster in a New York saloon window (above) asked its customers to cast a "No" vote on the issue. In Massachusetts opponents sent every voter an anti-suffrage campaign manual entitled *The Case Against Woman Suffrage* (below) which suffragists charged was "full of misrepresentations."

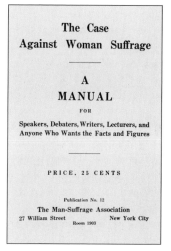

New Jersey Voters Defeat Woman Suffrage

DESPITE THE valiant efforts of supporters, New Jersey voters defeated woman suffrage on October 19, 1915 by a vote of 184,391 to 133,281. The measure lost in every county but one, winning only 42% of the vote.

Immediately after the election supporters in New York circulated the editorial cartoon by Rollin Kirby above to underscore their belief that it was a victory for party bosses in their smoke-filled back rooms. Coming just two weeks before the November 2 national elections, the loss was discouraging to workers in the other three campaign states. Nevertheless, New Jersey suffragists rallied and joined the great New York City suffrage parade a few days later carrying a huge banner proclaiming "Delayed But Not Defeated."

Above: Interpreting the defeat in New Jersey.

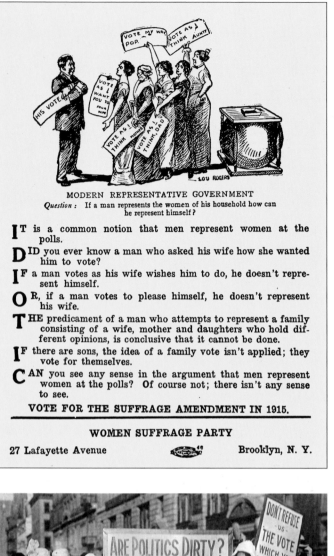

MODERN REPRESENTATIVE GOVERNMENT

Question : If a man represents the women of his household how can he represent himself?

IT is a common notion that men represent women at the polls.

DID you ever know a man who asked his wife how she wanted him to vote?

IF a man votes as his wife wishes him to do, he doesn't represent himself.

OR, if a man votes to please himself, he doesn't represent his wife.

THE predicament of a man who attempts to represent a family consisting of a wife, mother and daughters who hold different opinions, is conclusive that it cannot be done.

IF there are sons, the idea of a family vote isn't applied; they vote for themselves.

CAN you see any sense in the argument that men represent women at the polls? Of course not; there isn't any sense to see.

VOTE FOR THE SUFFRAGE AMENDMENT IN 1915.

WOMEN SUFFRAGE PARTY

127 Lafayette Avenue   Brooklyn, N. Y.

It was "IDIOTIC" to think that men could represent women at the polls according to this flier (top) addressed to New York voters and carrying a cartoon by Lou Rogers. Jane Schneiderman (above, right) and a friend dressed as cleaning ladies to make a classic point during the 1915 New York suffrage parade. Special events, torchlight rallies, and block parties, plus fireworks and huge bonfires, added to the campaign's excitement.

Vibrant Parades Mark the Final Weeks

IN THE FINAL WEEKS before the November 2, 1915 election, suffragists in the three remaining states threw themselves into the campaign. They organized countless meetings and events ending with impressive parades in Boston, Philadelphia, and New York.

With mounted police and the Seventh Regiment Band leading the way (above), between 25,000 and 35,000 marchers filled New York's Fifth Avenue on October 23 for a great "Banner Parade," the largest and most colorful of all the suffrage parades. Spread across the avenue and linked by long garlands, white-clad suffragists carried so many signs informing spectators of the status of woman suffrage nationally and internationally that one observer compared it to a "walking speech."

You ask us to walk with you,
Dance with you, marry you,
Why don't you ask us to Vote with you?

Ethel McClellan Plummer created the stylish poster above for the Empire State Campaign Committee. Eight feet tall, the vibrant image hung in theater lobbies and on billboards throughout New York City. Color played a distinctive role in the campaign, adding excitement and identifying particular groups. During the 1915 parade, *The Woman Voter* reported that color was everywhere, "in flags, banners, sashes, hatbands and pennants. Sometimes the campaign colors, blue, white and yellow flashed forth; sometimes the tricolored City Flag, or the red, white and blue of the National Ensign, or the purple, white and green of the Political Union; but the background was always the yellow of the Woman Suffrage Party, so that all the hues seemed floating in sunlight." Top left and bottom: Suffragists in white, some linked with garlands, filled Fifth Avenue during the October 23 parade.

An Exhilarating Banner Parade Brings the Cause to New York City Voters

The New York suffrage Banner Parade on Saturday, October 23, 1915 was a jubilant affair surging with color and excitement and demonstrating the crusading spirit behind the suffrage drive. The spectacle was carefully planned and executed to impress on voters the importance of suffrage in the upcoming election.

The afternoon was sunny and cold with a biting wind that lifted and tossed the great banners and signs which gave the parade its name. Marchers without signs carried yellow Votes for Women pennants to create what one journalist called "a rippling mass of color."

Leading the parade was an International Division with a huge banner reading "Woman Suffrage is a World Movement" followed by Carrie Catt and "proxy" representatives of the 26 nations in the International Woman Suffrage Alliance. The marchers carried signs but no national flags. Divisions of thousands of suffragists from around the state followed as the music of dozens of bands filled the air.

Right: Creating an international context.

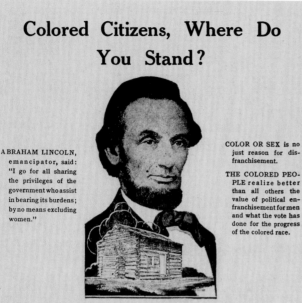

Colored Citizens, Where Do You Stand?

ABRAHAM LINCOLN, emancipator, said: "I go for all sharing the privileges of the government who assist in bearing its burdens; by no means excluding women."

COLOR OR SEX is no just reason for disfranchisement.

THE COLORED PEOPLE realize better than all others the value of political enfranchisement for men and what the vote has done for the progress of the colored race.

DO YOU KNOW that 4,000,000 women, both white and colored, vote in twelve states?

DO YOU KNOW that colored and white women vote in Wyoming, Utah, Colorado, Idaho, Washington, California, Oregon, Arizona, Kansas, Illinois, Montana, Nevada and Alaska?

DO YOU KNOW that the colored women of New York will be eligible to vote for the next President if the men of the Empire State are as fair-minded as the men of the West have been?

DO YOU KNOW that the men of New York State on November 2nd, 1915, will be able to vote on the constitutional amendment enfranchising both the white and colored women of this State?

YOU KNOW that the colored women of New York State are as industrious, intelligent and well educated as the colored women of the West. Why not confer the same political rights upon the women of this State as are enjoyed now by their brothers, sons, husbands and fathers?

THE COLORED RACE believes in freedom—human and political—and it should be the last race to deny freedom to women.

Among the prominent colored leaders who believe in woman suffrage are: Charles W. Anderson, Ex-Collector of Internal Revenue, Port of New York; Dr. W. E. B. Du Bois, Editor of the "Crisis"; Thomas J. Bell, Director of the Colored Men's Branch of the Y. M. C. A.; Rev. William P. Hayes, Pastor of Mt. Olivet Baptist Church, New York City; Rev. G. H. Sims, Pastor of Union Baptist Church, New York City; Frederick H. Moore, Editor "New York Age"; Mr. David Brown, Grand Master of the Odd Fellows of the State of New York and Grand Treasurer of the Odd Fellows of America.

VOTE FOR THE WOMAN SUFFRAGE AMENDMENT ON NOV. 2, 1915
WOMEN'S POLITICAL UNION, 25 WEST 45TH STREET, NEW YORK CITY

Republican President Abraham Lincoln was featured on this Women's Political Union leaflet (top) which appealed to New York's Black voters and listed prominent community supporters. Marchers (above) highlighted the recent endorsement of President Woodrow Wilson, a Democrat. Above right: Informing voters.

A Rousing Climax to a Long Campaign

New York's woman suffrage parade on October 23 made a point of showing convincingly that women in great numbers wanted the vote. Column after column of women from every part of the state marched up Fifth Avenue from Washington Square to 59th Street passing before over one-and-a-half million spectators.

Vera Whitehouse and Mrs. John Blair of the Empire State

"Marching for a Great Cause"

"THERE WAS something in the atmosphere on parade day," state leader Gertrude Brown remembered, that made walking three miles uptown seem easy. "We women who marched in a suffrage parade will never forget the thrill of hearing her own band strike up, the command of her leader, of swinging out into the Avenue in step with the music, passing the multitudes of spectators, head up, eyes straight ahead, in perfect formation, with the conviction that she was marching for a great cause." And it was not just dedicated suffragists any longer. Votes for Women had made its successful appeal to a large cross-section of the population, and to young people in particular. Women's demand for equal rights had clearly entered the mainstream. The 1915 campaigns, full of hope and relatively untouched by war, marked a high point in the idealism and enthusiasm of the revitalized movement.

Above: A campaign stamp featured 1913 flag bearer Cora Anderson Carpenter.

Campaign Committee organized the massive demonstration, taking over what had previously been the realm of the Women's Political Union. Realizing that their innovation was being assumed by others, the WPU board angrily protested that it had not been consulted. But the growing influence of Carrie Catt's coalition was increasingly evident. The WPU did stage its own suffrage parade of several thousand, including a division of municipal employees, through East Side neighborhoods before joining the end of the Banner Parade.

The great procession continued well past dark, New York suffragist Mary Peck remembered. "Six o'clock came and still the marchers poured up the avenue, shopgirls, stenographers, clerks, nurses off duty, everybody who could not get there earlier, walking anyhow, singing popular songs, many a youth locking arms with his sweetheart at the tail of that parade.... The demonstration was to have been concluded with street meetings throughout the city, but the end of it never was seen, for people went home to dinner leaving the boys and girls marching up the avenue in the windy darkness, singing as they went."

Final Efforts Aim for Victory in the Three Eastern States

WITH GROWING excitement, suffragists made a push for victory on November 2, 1915 in the three remaining eastern contests. In each state there were final rallies, parades, and last minute publicity work.

Pennsylvania suffragists placed posters in 5,748 streetcars and organized a stirring parade (above) on the evening of October 22 which filled the streets of Philadelphia. A few days before the election, volunteers sent out 330,000 personal letters to voters each signed by the county chair or a suffragist in his own community. On election day women appeared at polling places to make last minute, often successful, appeals to voters.

Boston was the site of a

hopeful suffrage "Victory Parade" on October 16 which included some 15,000 suffragists from around the state. Over half a million people, including the governor and mayor, reviewed the impressive march through Boston's Back Bay. The festive parade

included women marching by trade union and profession, college women wearing yellow camellias, and a large number of men. Massachusetts suffragists also sent out a last-minute circular to 600,000 voters. 8,000 women stood for hours outside

polling places on election day seeking voter support.

New York state activists climaxed a long series of meetings with rallies in 124 cities. A week before the election, marathon speeches were held in New York, Rochester, Buffalo and other urban centers where supporters spoke continuously for 24 hours to crowds that gathered even in the middle of the night.

Facing page: James Montgomery Flagg's dramatic illustration captured the fighting spirit of suffragists and appealed to eastern voters' Revolutionary roots. Above: College delegations in the Philadelphia parade. Left: Selling newspapers in Pittsburgh.

A Million Men Vote for Equal Suffrage

THE RESULTS of the November 2, 1915 election were a shock to many who had given their all to the campaigns and a sad reminder to veteran suffragists.

In Pennsylvania lack of money and "rockbound conservatism" took their toll as the suffrage measure was defeated 441,034 to 385,348. Of the 55,686 vote difference, 45,272 votes came from the city of Philadelphia. The measure won 47% of the vote and state leaders felt that with another $25,000 they could have won the last 4% needed.

Massachusetts voters soundly defeated the amendment 295,489 to 163,406. A staggering 64% voted against the measure.

In New York, where thousands of women again acted as poll watchers, voters rejected the measure 748,332 to 553,348 with an adverse majority of 82,755 in New York City. Gertrude Brown remembered, "The disappointment was almost crushing. Although the task of persuading the huge cosmopolitan population of New York State to grant equality to women had been recognized as being almost superhuman, the work done had been so colossal that it would have been impossible not to hope for success."

A New Campaign

Rallying once more, New York suffragists took to the streets just after the disappointing results came in to announce that a new campaign would begin immediately. Two nights after the election an overflowing meeting at Cooper Union, chaired by Mary Garrett Hay, announced the drive for another state vote on suffrage in 1917. $100,000 was pledged on the spot "amid boundless enthusiasm." The campaign was reorganized and all groups in the Empire State Campaign Committee were consolidated under the name of the New York State Woman Suffrage Party with Carrie Catt as chair.

The Women's Political Union amalgamated with the Congressional Union after the election. While some WPU members joined the new state campaign, Harriot Blatch regarded a second referendum as a "serious error" and likely disaster. Catt, however, believed that without success in one of the large eastern states the suffrage amendment had no chance of passing in Congress.

Laws in New Jersey and Pennsylvania required a five year hiatus before resubmitting a constitutional amendment. Nonetheless, 2,500 Pennsylvania women with unwavering spirits held a mass meeting on November 30. They declared that their fight would go on and prepared themselves for a new campaign.

New Jersey suffragists tried to win presidential suffrage, but like their Massachusetts counterparts, they believed that another campaign would be futile and turned most of their attention to the Federal amendment.

Despite the string of losses in the eastern states, suffrage leaders could point to a remarkable show of political strength. During the four elections 1,234,593 men had voted for woman suffrage. The four states had given a larger vote for suffrage than they had for the Republican presidential candidate in 1912. Winning that level of support was a critical step towards ultimate victory. ◆

The sheet music for Phil Hanna's 1915 partisan song featured the red rose adopted as a symbol by anti-suffragists to counter the sunflowers and other yellow blooms favored by supporters.

Carrie Chapman Catt Drafted to Lead NAWSA

THREE WEEKS after the eastern defeats, Anna Howard Shaw announced that she would not stand for re-election as NAWSA president at the December 1915 convention. Despite discontent over the years regarding her leadership style, she received a hero's tribute from the 546 delegates at the gathering in Washington D.C. for her many years of service. She was named Honorary President, awarded a life-long annuity, and then was showered with yellow roses.

It was clear to most delegates that NAWSA needed a skilled executive who could give her entire time to vast demands of planning and administrative work, and the overwhelming choice was veteran organizer Carrie Chapman Catt. Catt was then serving as president of the In-

ternational Woman Suffrage Alliance and chair of the new campaign in New York.

At first she steadfastly refused, but after leading suffragists lined up funds for the alliance and convinced the New York delegation to release her, she was persuaded to accept the post. Afterwards she returned to her hotel room and burst into tears. Mina Van Winkle was the convention's second choice. Shaw quietly supported Harriet Burton Laidlaw.

Catt, who carried with her the Leslie bequest of approximately one million dollars to be used for woman suffrage, stipulated that she would choose her own board and set her own agenda. When she addressed her co-workers at the convention she called herself an "unwilling victim." "When I came to this conven-

tion I had no more idea of accepting the presidency of this Association than I had of taking a trip to Kamtchatka. . . . I ask all of you to work harder the coming year than you have ever worked before. I cannot be otherwise than deeply touched by the confidence you have placed in me. I promise you to do my best not to disappoint you."

NAWSA was set to take on its final battle form. Suffragists looked ahead to 1916, an election year when for the first time women in large numbers would be able to vote for president of the U.S.

Above: Harriet Burton Laidlaw addressed New Yorkers in Columbus Circle during a 26-hour street meeting on October 29, 1915. Left: "She Has Just Begun to Fight" by Winsor McCay.

TWO'S COMPANY THREE'S

A Force to Be Reckoned With

BRINGING LIGHT to a shadowy corner, the allegorical figure of woman suffrage caught "Honest Graft" paying off a corrupt Political Boss in this 1912 illustration from *Puck*. Josef Keppler, Jr.'s cartoon, "Two's Company. Three's a Crowd," captured the anxiety and defiance felt by many men in power towards women voting. Corruption, patronage, and payoffs were common in big city politics during the early 20th century, and some men feared that women would demand accountability and reform in the halls of government. In cities like New York and states like New Jersey suffragists encountered entrenched political machines which tightly controlled civic affairs and used their influence to block equal suffrage. Frustrated and stymied, NAWSA followed the Congressional Union's lead and turned with new fervor to the Federal government. However, despite the defeats in the eastern states, many men outside of politics were coming to recognize the simple justice of equal suffrage. ◆

Above: A stylish playing card.
Left: Confronting the Boss.

Evelyn Rumsey Cary's stylish poster from 1917 blended several classical and scriptural references to promote equal rights. The imagery suggested the mythical nymph Daphne, who was transformed into a laurel tree to escape Apollo's pursuit.

Chapter 11: 1916

A New Party and a New Plan

THE ELECTION YEAR of 1916 marked the first time that four million women in the eleven equal suffrage states plus Illinois could help choose the next president of the United States. In addition, the entire House and one-third of the Senate was up for election. New energy and organization marked the state-oriented National American Woman Suffrage Association, and a heightened vitality and spirit characterized the Congressional Union in the capital.

One of Carrie Chapman Catt's first major moves as NAWSA president in early 1916 was to pressure the Democratic and Republican parties to include woman suffrage in their platforms. She and other NAWSA officers also traveled to the non-suffrage states to strengthen or-

ganizations and encourage cooperation with national headquarters. Three more referendum campaigns were underway in Iowa, West Virginia, and South Dakota.

The CU, expanding nationally, laid plans to form an entirely new political party which would have as its sole purpose suffrage for women. Continuing its strategy of opposing Democrats as the "party in power," the CU, much to NAWSA's chagrin, focused public attention on how the Democrats continued to block progress on the Federal amendment. Despite persistent opposition and the growing specter of war, members of both suffrage organizations continued working to make women's enfranchisement a pressing political issue which neither party could afford to ignore.

I MARCH FOR FULL SUFFRAGE JUNE 7TH WILL YOU?

When Carrie Catt became NAWSA president she chose for her board politically experienced and financially independent women who were able to devote most of their time to the cause. Several met with her (left) in Chicago, Illinois, in early June 1916. From the left are treasurer Mrs. Henry Wade Rogers, auditor Mrs. Walter McNab Miller of Missouri, corresponding secretary Hannah J. Patterson of Pennsylvania, recording secretary Mrs. James W. Morrison of Illinois, and Catt. Suffragists converged on Chicago for a great parade to pressure the Republican Party to support the Federal suffrage amendment in their platform. Supporters practiced their marching skills (bottom left) before the June 7 demonstration.

Five thousand supporters cheered the group of Congressional Union "envoys" (above) when they left Washington D.C. aboard The Suffrage Special to organize support for the Federal amendment. As a result of the trip, enfranchised women from the west, including delegates from the Topeka, Kansas, chapter of the CU (right), traveled to Chicago in early June to form a new political party of voting women.

The Suffrage Special Goes West

Believing that suffragists' strength lay with the enfranchised women of the western states, Alice Paul proposed that the Congressional Union help voting women organize an independent political party with the potential of becoming a determining factor in the upcoming election.

To recruit delegates for the new party, the CU sent two dozen envoys west in early April 1916 aboard a gaily-decorated railroad car they named "The Suffrage Special." The envoys included Lucy Burns, Harriot Blatch (now "National Political Chairman"), Alva Belmont, Abby Scott Baker, and other experienced and persuasive speakers. During the well-organized four week tour the women addressed large and enthusiastic crowds in many of the principal cities and created considerable interest in a new political party.

Throughout the year the CU kept drawing politicians' attention to the potential power of the four million women voters in the equal suffrage states. Alice Paul had hoped that the very suggestion of women voting as a block would force action by politicians in the capital, but more was needed.

Above: Lucy Burns (center), western emissaries, and honor guard approach the Capitol on May 16, 1916.

Organizing Women Voters in the West

THE CONGRESSIONAL Union had worked for two years to expand nationally and by April 1916 had branches in 26 states. With greater resources following the merger with Harriot Blatch's Women's Political Union, Alice Paul and the CU made bolder plans.

On May 11, after the four-week tour by The Suffrage Special, western women voters gathered for a convention in Salt Lake City, Utah. There they selected delegates to a June convention in Chicago to form the new political party. They also chose three women to act as "emissaries" to politicians and supporters in the east.

Returning on The Suffrage Special, the emissaries all received a triumphal welcome in Washington D.C. on May 16. A beautiful procession of white-clad suffragists wearing purple, white, and gold sashes and carrying tricolor flags accompanied the representatives to the Capitol. The Senate recessed and nearly 100 congressmen heard the women voters' message and the repeated demand for the Federal amendment.

Above: Lucy Burns prepared to leaflet Seattle from the air. Below: Route of The Suffrage Special across the country.

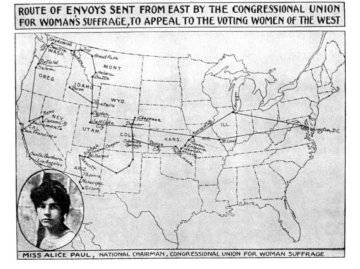

ROUTE OF ENVOYS SENT FROM EAST BY THE CONGRESSIONAL UNION FOR WOMAN'S SUFFRAGE, TO APPEAL TO THE VOTING WOMEN OF THE WEST

MISS ALICE PAUL, NATIONAL CHAIRMAN, CONGRESSIONAL UNION FOR WOMAN SUFFRAGE

Suffrage First

WOMAN'S PARTY
CONVENTION
Chicago ··· June 5,6,7

Mabel Vernon (right) drew
a large audience on a Chicago
street corner in early June
1916. A dynamic and enter-
taining speaker with a clear,
ringing voice, the Congressional Union's first organizer
once described herself and
her comrades as women
"endeavoring to think fearlessly." She was equally direct
with new recruits: "Don't be
afraid to open your mouths
and yell." A warm and outgoing Quaker from Delaware,
Vernon went to Swarthmore
with Alice Paul, then taught
high school before becoming
a key figure in the CU. She
traveled alone in 1915 to Delaware, Ohio, Utah, Colorado,
and Oregon organizing state
conventions to promote the
Federal amendment, and also
recruited women to come
to Washington D.C. to work.
Called a "beloved and gifted
crusader" by Doris Stevens,
Vernon caused a scene on
July 4, 1916 when she twice
interrupted a speech by
Woodrow Wilson asking him
loudly, "Why do you oppose
the national enfranchisement
of women?" before being
ejected.

**Above: A stamp displayed
the Congressional Union's
signature colors.**

Creating a New
Political Party
for Women

"A NEW FORCE marches on-
to the political field,"
announced keynote speaker
Maud Younger at the opening
of the Woman's Party Con-
vention in Chicago on June 5,
1916. "For the first time in a
presidential election women
are a factor to be reckoned
with. . . . With enough women organized in each state
to hold the balance of power,
the women's votes may determine the Presidency of the
United States."

Drawing substantial press
attention, 2,000 women voters and Congressional Union
members met in Chicago two
days before the Republican
National Convention. The
historic gathering voted to
form the National Woman's
Party of Western Women Voters devoted solely to winning
suffrage for women. Dele-
gates chose Anne Martin of
Nevada as chair, Phoebe A.
Hearst and Judge Mary A.
Bartelme as vice-chairs, and
Mabel Vernon (right) as
secretary.

Call to Women Voters

By ANNE MARTIN
Chairman National Woman's Party

WOMEN Voters of the United States:
For over sixty years American women have been battling against heavy odds for political liberty.

As a result of this half-century of struggle, in which the women of all the nation participated, four million women now vote in twelve states.

Women of the East worked side by side with women of the West to secure this portion of our common heritage of freedom. The pioneers of the woman's movement toiled not merely in their own states but in every state in the Union, wherever there was a chance to help. In our states their labors were crowned with success; we are full citizens, with power to control and alter the policies of our country.

ONE POLICY WE ARE DETERMINED TO ESTABLISH: POLITICAL LIBERTY FOR WOMEN THROUGHOUT THE NATION.

It is for this that the ballot was put in our hands—to safeguard and extend the liberties of the American people.

We are called upon at this time as voters, to pass upon the record of the party which has been for four years in power,—to endorse its record or censure it.

WHAT IS ITS RECORD ON THE NATIONAL ENFRANCHISEMENT OF WOMEN?

For four years the Democratic party has bitterly opposed national suffrage; President Wilson has declared against it; his party has voted against it; committees of Congress have used every kind of political trick to defeat it.

A vote for President Wilson and the national candidates of the Democratic party is a vote against the freedom of women throughout America.

We of the West refuse to endorse the record of a party that has fought against justice to women.

Some of us are Progressives, some Democrats, some Socialists, some Prohibitionists. Unite with us in a western movement dedicated to the principle of political liberty for women. VOTE AGAINST MR. WILSON AND THE DEMOCRATIC CANDIDATES FOR OFFICE IN THE UNITED STATES SENATE AND HOUSE.

ANNE MARTIN, Nevada.

NATIONAL WOMAN'S PARTY
National Headquarters, Lafayette Square, Washington, D. C.

Anne Martin's Call (top) summarized the Woman's Party's case: a vote for Wilson, who opposed the Federal amendment, was "a vote against the freedom of women." After being elected head of the new party, Martin (above, left) posed behind the Great Demand banner with Sara Bard Field on the far right. Both the Woman's Party, centered in Chicago, and the Congressional Union immediately sent organizers to the western states.

"Rainy Day" Suffrage Parade, Chicago, 1916

Taking the Republicans by Storm in Chicago

Following the founding convention for the Woman's Party, thousands of members of NAWSA gathered in Chicago to demonstrate at the Republican Convention for a platform plank endorsing woman suffrage. NAWSA organizers planned an elaborate parade to impress delegates and for months had been recruiting women to march.

On Wednesday afternoon, June 7, 1916, in a cold, pelting rain, more than 5,500 suffragists paraded down Michigan Avenue led by two "GOP" elephants, Jennie and her nine-month-old son Chinchin, wearing rubber blankets. Marchers were organized by state, club, ward, and precinct. Many wore yellow raincoats because of the heavy

downpour. The parade also included two dozen marching bands, the Women's Liberty Bell from Pennsylvania, and a large wooden "Suffrage Plank" as a "gentle hint." High and dry in their hotel

rooms, delegates from around the country looked down on the hour-long parade of thousands of women marching in the rain.

Calling it a "show of strength as well as a plea for

justice," Mary Peck noted that there was also something profoundly moving about the spectacle. "Many a man turned away from it with a lump in his throat and shame in his heart."

The successful demonstration culminated when wave after wave of wet but triumphant marchers reached the convention hall. There they dramatically burst into a meeting of the Resolutions Committee just as an anti-suffrage speaker was claiming that women did not want to vote. The speaker looked up aghast, quickly finished, and then fled as exuberant paraders filled the room.

Above: Demonstrating in Chicago. Left: Chinchin shows his support.

ONE MARCHER IN LINE IS WORTH TEN PETITIONS IN THE WASTE BASKET

Thousands of women (above) braved a biting north wind and frigid rain to march in the June 7, 1916 Chicago suffrage parade. As this editorial cartoon (left) from *The Woman's Journal* suggested, NAWSA had moved away from petitions and solidly toward political action. Suffragists did persuade the Republicans to approve a platform plank but it endorsed only the state-by-state method and not the Federal amendment. Disappointed with this significant but partial victory, supporters turned their attention to the Democratic convention in St. Louis.

Theatrical Tactics Bring Suffrage Message to Democrats

Aᴡᴇᴇᴋ ᴀꜰᴛᴇʀ the parade in Chicago, suffragists gathered in St. Louis, Missouri, to pressure the Democratic National Convention to adopt a suffrage plank as well. NAWSA staged a demonstration for the Democrats that *The Woman Voter* called "the most beautiful of any ever made by suffragists."

On June 14, the opening day of the convention, Democratic delegates were greeted by a remarkable protest, a "walk-less parade" called The Golden Lane devised by state publicity chair Emily Newell

Blair. 8,000 suffragists of all ages, dressed in white with gold sashes and carrying yellow Votes for Women parasols, stood side-by-side along the curb on both sides of the main thoroughfare for nearly a mile. For two hours they formed a brilliant but silent lane through which the delegates had to pass to get to the Convention Center.

The Democrats, like the Republicans, refused to back the Federal amendment and instead passed a plank that endorsed suffrage by state means only. Still, these con-

ditional endorsements put both parties on record for the first time as supporting votes for women.

The press regarded the Democratic plank as a great achievement for the suffrage forces, and the *St. Louis Globe-Democrat* even took to verse:

Citizen and Democrat,
Marching down the Golden
  Lane
'Neath the eyes of Mrs. Catt,
Marching down the Golden
  Lane,
Marching out to nominate
Wilson for their candidate —

SILENCE GLOOM SILENCE

THE "GOLDEN LANE."
THE JOYFUL LITTLE ENTERTAINMENT WHICH THE SUFFRAGISTS HAVE PLANNED FOR THE UPLIFT OF THE DEMOCRATS (WHO NEED IT)

10 BEERS QUICK   SAVED

PROBABLE EFFECT OF THE "GOLDEN LANE" ON ABOVE MENTIONED DEMOCRATS

How the Democrats did hate Marching down the Golden Lane!

Concerned about the up-coming election and the publicity-generating activity of the new Woman's Party, Carrie Catt called an Emergency Convention of NAWSA for early September and invited both presidential candidates to address the Atlantic City meeting. Republican Charles Evans Hughes, who announced that he backed the Federal amendment, sent his regrets but President Woodrow Wilson accepted.

Democratic conventioneers (above), including President Wilson in the middle, were shown passing uncomfortably down The Golden Lane, a gauntlet of 8,000 silent suffragists. **At the end of the "joyful little entertainment" delegates sought liquid relief in this June 14, 1916 editorial cartoon by Russell from the** *St. Louis Globe-Democrat.*

A Goddess of Liberty raised her torch high during a striking open-air tableau (above) representing the status of woman suffrage in the U.S. and abroad. The tableau was held under a canopy of golden cloth on the steps of the old St. Louis art museum, midway down The Golden Lane (left of center in photo at left), during the opening of the Democratic Convention. Surrounding the central figure were thirteen women dressed in white to represent the eleven equal suffrage states plus Illinois and Alaska. Women in gray on the right symbolized states with partial suffrage and those in black on the left represented states with no suffrage at all. Their wrists chained, they appealed to the passing delegates to set them free. The costumed women in the foreground represented the equal suffrage countries of Denmark, Iceland, Tasmania, New Zealand, Australia, Finland, Norway, and the Isle of Man.

Wilson Challenged to Commit to the Federal Amendment

On September 8, 1916, President Woodrow Wilson arrived in Atlantic City, New Jersey, with his wife, assistants, and body-guards to address the NAWSA convention. Although he spoke in generalities, suffragists understood that his very presence confirmed their growing power.

Wilson called the suffrage movement "one of the most astonishing tides in modern history . . . which has not only come to stay but has come with conquering power."

"We feel the tide; we rejoice in the strength of it, and we shall not quarrel in the long run as to the method of it," he told the convention, "because when you are working with

masses of men and organized bodies of opinion, you have got to carry the organized body along." He concluded, "I have not come to ask you

"A Tempting Morsel"

to be patient, because you have been; but I have come to congratulate you that there has been a force behind you that will beyond any perad-

venture be triumphant, and for which you can a little while afford to wait."

When he had finished Anna Howard Shaw rose and responded, "We have waited so long, Mr. President, for the vote, and we had hoped it might come in your adminis-tration." The entire audience of women rose in agreement and Wilson bowed and made his exit. But while he did not support the Federal amend-ment for two more years, from then on he kept an open channel with NAWSA leaders.

Above: President and Mrs. Wilson in Atlantic City. Left: Fredrikke Palmer's cartoon showed both parties eyeing the equal suffrage states.

Crafting "The Winning Plan"

THE EMERGENCY Convention of NAWSA, which Carrie Catt called just after the major party conventions, met in Atlantic City on September 4, 1916. There was a "crisis" in the suffrage movement, she declared in her opening address, which called for "new considerations and new decisions."

A Secret Strategy

Undistracted by President Wilson's much publicized visit, NAWSA's Executive Committee composed of national board members and state association presidents met privately to hammer out a plan of action. Going over the situation in great detail, Catt finally suggested an integrated way to make the various state associations work together. In office less than nine months, she was determined to forge a unified battle plan with the highest chance of success or she was prepared to resign.

"The scene in the crowded stuffy room in the basement of the hotel where the Council met is something I shall always remember," recalled Maud Wood Park, "the tired faces of most of the women there; the huge map of the United States, hung on one of the walls; and, most vividly of all, Mrs. Catt herself."

The NAWSA president made a new commitment to the original Federal amendment and endorsed further state work only where a very good chance of success existed. She called for more concentrated effort to have presidential suffrage bills passed in each state, and sought the active involvement

Carrie Chapman Catt was 56 when delegates elected her president of NAWSA for the second time in December 1915.

of women in the equal suffrage states to pressure their representatives to call for the Federal amendment. Looking ahead, Catt wanted every state to be ready when the amendment passed Congress and went to the legislatures for ratification. She also announced an expanded lobby in Washington D.C. and the goal of a one million dollar campaign fund.

This was the basis of what became known as "The Winning Plan," a strategy for simultaneous, complementary state and national work which Catt made her comrades promise to keep secret

until it was successful. She hoped to keep the opposition in the dark while each state association quietly pursued a specific set of tasks to reach the common goal.

Political Decisions

In contrast to Anna Howard Shaw, Catt provided proactive leadership, and formulated a strategic plan based on informed surveys of existing conditions. Catt believed that

unenfranchised women in the north and midwest could win some form of suffrage themselves and so strengthen support for the Federal amendment. Thus she turned away from Alice Paul's strategy of organizing women voters in the west,

One price of NAWSA's plan, however, was the loss of some southern women who, like President Wilson, opposed Federal action on states' rights grounds. Most notably, long-time leaders Laura Clay of Kentucky and Kate Gordon of Louisiana parted with NAWSA and eventually worked against the suffrage amendment because it represented Federal interference in state affairs.

At the end of the meeting Catt presented a compact to be signed by at least 36 state suffrage associations, the minimum number of states necessary for ratification of a constitutional amendment. Park recalled, "When the full number of signatures had been affixed to the compact and we filed out of the room, I felt like Moses on the mountain top after the Promised Land had been shown to him and he knew the long years of wandering in the wilderness were soon to end. For the first time I saw our goal as possible of attainment in the near future. But we had to have swift and concerted action from every part of the country. Could we get i? Could we get it?" ◆

A Second Campaign Targets Democrats in the West

WITH THE 1916 election in sight, the Congressional Union again set out to convince women voters in the west to oppose Democratic candidates, this time with the help of the new National Woman's Party of Western Women Voters. The campaign was carried out on a larger scale than the 1914 effort, but still the idea of uniting women throughout the west was an overwhelming undertaking. More importantly, the issue of war versus peace had voters "excited to an almost unprecedented pitch," remembered Doris Stevens. "We could not have entered a more difficult contest."

Nonetheless, suffrage organizers spoke to as many voters as possible in the weeks before the election. "The appeal was to vote a vote of protest against Mr. Wilson and his Congressional candidates," explained Stevens, "because he and his party had had the power to pass the amendment through Congress and had refused to do so."

Sara Bard Field, Elizabeth Kent, Maud Younger, and other women from the west

were joined by Harriot Blatch, Louisine Havemeyer, Rose Winslow, Gail Laughlin, and others from the east to work in specific states. Katharine Morey went to Kansas, Anne Martin, Mabel Vernon, and Younger worked in Nevada, and Caroline Katzenstein joined Lucy Burns in Montana. Inez Milholland, who had married Dutch businessman Eugen Boissevain in 1913, was appointed special "flying envoy" to make a 12,000 mile swing through all 12 states. Inez Irwin called it a "small army, the members of which were all generals."

Above: Organizing voters in the west. Left: Demonstrating in Chicago.

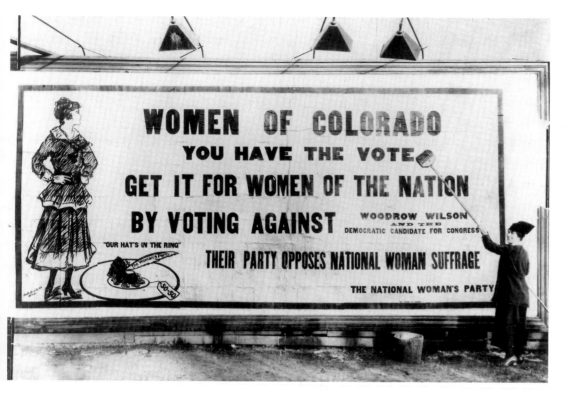

Elsie Hill was one of the intrepid members of the Congressional Union who went west to campaign against Democratic party candidates in 1916. Before the difficult trip she cautioned her fellow organizers, "Don't ask for pity or special consideration. If you can't do the job, don't take it. Don't have them throw it into your face that women can't do these things." Enthusiastic, independent, and highly engaging, Hill grew up surrounded by politics since her father was a congressman from Connecticut for over twenty years. After graduating from Vassar, she taught high school and worked with the College Equal Suffrage League before joining the CU.

Waging an Intense Drive Against Democratic Candidates

A GRUELING schedule drove several suffrage organizers to exhaustion during the Congressional Union's 1916 campaign in the west, but their message was heard by a substantial number of voters. Angry Democrats and hostile audiences, however, made the going rough in some areas. The women also faced accusations of being "fronts" for the Republicans.

Democrats in Arizona hired messenger boys to "counter-picket" and in Denver Elsie Hill was arrested for distributing "anti-Democratic" literature. The suffragists were pressured to withdraw but Alice Paul remained steadfast. "We must make this such an important thing in national elections that the Democrats will not want to meet it again."

Holding the majority party, the "party in power," responsible for legislative progress continued to be one of

the most divisive issues separating NAWSA and the CU. NAWSA members were particularly outraged when long-standing allies were targeted for defeat just because they were Democrats. But the CU pointed out that any man would still have to represent his pro-suffrage constituents.

While the strategy's merits were clear to politically-minded women like Harriot Blatch, Maud Younger, and Alice Paul, it made few

friends among mainstream suffragists. Staunch opponents included Alice Stone Blackwell, Carrie Catt, and Nevada suffragist Bird Wilson who remarked, "It may be politics, but I don't think it's *good* politics."

Top: Posting a billboard in Colorado. Above: Paid counter-demonstrators in Arizona. Right: Elsie Hill answered Wilson's slogan, "He Kept Us Out of War."

Rose Winslow represented the workers, wrote Vivian Pierce in *The Suffragist* in 1916. "Her words had the authenticity of an inspired young evangelist. She herself had come up out of that darkness; and the men of the mines and lumber camps, the women of the remote Arizona towns, listened to her with tears pouring down their faces." Born Ruza Wenzclawska in Poland, Winslow began working in a Philadelphia textile mill at the age of 11 and became disabled by tuberculosis at 19. One of the few industrial women organizers in the Women's Political Union, she joined Lucy Burns in California during the Congressional Union's 1914 drive against the Democrats and worked to near exhaustion during the 1916 campaign (below) with the National Woman's Party.

WOMEN VOTERS
OF THE WEST!

Hear the Appeal of the Voteless WOMEN of the EAST!

Rose Winslow
A Polish Miner's daughter, a Mill Hand in Pennsylvania from the age of 11 until disabled by sickness at 19 THE SPEAKER.

(RUZA WENCLAW)

COME
Learn Why We ask You to VOTE AGAINST National Democratic Party.

MEETING FREE!

NATIONAL WOMAN'S PARTY

Angry Democrats Respond With Violence

SUFFRAGE FIRST

Much to their surprise, many western Democrats who thought that "suffrage wasn't an issue" in the 1916 campaign were forced by Congressional Union and Woman's Party activists to repeatedly explain and defend their party's position. Democratic loyalists, both male and female, deeply resented the "interference" of the suffragists and tried to counter their accusations with literature and speakers who emphasized Wilson's support of suffrage on a state-by-state basis.

Towards the end of the close contest, resentments boiled over into violence. On October 19, one hundred members of the Woman's Party staged a silent protest (above) outside the Chicago auditorium where President Wilson was making a speech. A mob of men gathered and suddenly attacked the women, knocking several down, tearing their banners and clothing, seizing their signs and trampling them in what newspapers the next day called a "near riot."

Alice Paul condemned "the violent attack by Democrats" and claimed that it showed "the seriousness with which they take our campaign." The

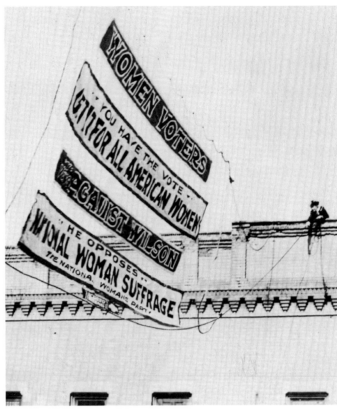

Tragedy Strikes the Western Tour

CAMPAIGNING AGAINST the Democratic Party, the eloquent and beautiful Inez Milholland Boissevain acted as "flying envoy" to tie together the Congressional Union's efforts in the twelve states where women could vote for president. Despite being in poor health, the thirty-year-old attorney kept up a grueling pace speaking in eight states in three weeks during her whirlwind tour. Late in October 1916 she collapsed on a Los Angeles stage after reportedly asking one last time, "President Wilson, how long must women wait for liberty?"

"It was a dramatic scene," the *Los Angeles Times* reported. "A moment before, this remarkable woman, the charms of whose personality have not been exaggerated, held the great audience with the fire and emotion of her oratory. In the middle of an intense sentence she crumpled up like a wilted white rose and lay stark upon the platform, while one of those eloquent silences befell the expectant crowd."

Suffering from exhaustion and undiagnosed anemia, Boissevain lay ill for a month and then died on November 25. Her sacrifice, *The Suffragist* editorialized, "illustrates the waste of life and power that the cruel and bigoted opposition to the political freedom of women is costing the nation. With the nation in sore need of women's help, this long struggle for the power to help it is arousing the deepest resentment . and indignation in every independent woman throughout the country." Inez Milholland Boissevain's death "has fanned that resentment into a burning flame."

violence further publicized the suffragists' efforts and caused many to join the new Woman's Party.

The climax of the drive came at a mass rally on November 5, just before the election, when Harriot Blatch called up a series of twelve mass meetings by long distance telephone from the stage of Chicago's Blackstone Theater and issued a final appeal to western voters.

The full effect of the suffragists' campaign will never be known, but Wilson won only 57 electoral votes from suffrage states as opposed to 69 in 1912. The Woman's Party claimed success since suffrage had been forcefully raised as an issue in the election, politicians had taken note, and women voters had gained new respect as a political force. "Again many women had stood together on this issue," observed Doris Stevens, "and put woman suffrage first."

Above: Picketing the president in Chicago before being attacked. Upper right: Suffragists strung giant banners across city streets to appeal to women voters. Virginia Arnold tied up this sign in Chicago.

Iowa Says No

SUFFRAGISTS WAGED three state campaigns in 1916, the first coming to a vote in Iowa at a special election on June 5, 1916. After the legislature placed the measure on the ballot, Iowa activists waged a vigorous campaign, sending speakers and automobile tours across the state. The Iowa Equal Suffrage Association under president Flora Dunlap organized in every one of the ninety counties and an active Men's League grew to include branches in forty cities. Carrie Catt gave six weeks of her time and workers distributed over five million circulars. Anti-suffragists countered with literature and speakers of their own, particularly in the final weeks. Election results were delayed for several days before it was announced that the measure had been defeated by just over 10,000 votes, 173,024 to 162,683. Supporters more than suspected foul play but realized that it would be futile to contest the vote. Instead they began preparing for another campaign.

Above: An opposition leaflet from Iowa.

Further Defeats in the States

THE IOWA defeat in June was a discouraging reminder of the difficulty, if not the impossibility, of the state-by-state route to suffrage. Still, two more state campaigns were focused on the November 7, 1916 election.

After the West Virginia legislature placed the measure on the ballot, a ten month drive was led by Lenna Lowe Yost, president of the state Equal Suffrage Association. The campaign received considerable aid from NAWSA as well as from other states, and welcomed speakers including Desha Breckinridge from Kentucky, Pattie Ruffner Jacobs from Alabama, and Minnie Fisher Cunningham from Texas. Opponents played up racial anxieties and resentment over prohibition, which had passed the previous year, and the suffrage measure was overwhelmingly defeated by a vote of 161,607 to 63,540.

In South Dakota the ongoing drive for enfranchisement was led again by Mary Shields

PAULINE REVERE

"We do know that it is little short of national scandal that women should be allowed to vote in some States and not in others."

NEW YORK HERALD.

NATIONAL WOMAN SUFFRAGE PUBLISHING COMPANY, INC.
171 Madison Avenue   New York City

Women Revealed as a Political Force

"PAULINE REVERE," a 1916 editorial cartoon by Rollin Kirby which suffragists reproduced on the flier above, used two American legends, Paul Revere and the Pony Express, to dramatize the growing influence of women voters. Kirby recognized the fact that women in the west could actually decide the final election, much to the consternation of eastern men. As it turned out, Wilson's re-election was extremely close in November and the pivotal equal suffrage state of California was credited with ensuring his victory.

The most unexpected result of the 1916 contest, however, was the election of the first woman to Congress in U.S. history. She was suffragist Jeannette Rankin from Montana. Rankin had run a well-organized campaign that capitalized on her visibility and on women's support just two years after they had won suffrage in the state. The former NAWSA organizer was suddenly thrust into the national spotlight.

The war was more a deciding factor in the election than suffrage, but the well-publicized campaign against Democrats in the west succeeded in sending chills through many politicians in Washington D.C. who became increasingly concerned about the potential power of organized women voters. ◆

Above: A late 1916 flier emphasized the growing influence of women voters in the western states.

Pyle, president of the state association. Suffragists covered the state in a familiar but exhausting pattern trying to convince enough men of the justice of their demand. NAWSA provided substantial assistance which helped counter the open campaign waged by opponents. The result was an extremely close contest but the measure was defeated for a fifth time, 58,350 to 53,432, by less than 5,000 votes. Heartened by the close race, South Dakota suffragists prepared for one more campaign. Similarly, women in other unenfranchised states continued their long efforts.

Above: Preparing for the 4th of July parade in Racine, Wisconsin.

INEZ MILHOLLAND BOISSEVAIN

WHO DIED FOR THE FREEDOM OF WOMEN.

Chapter 12: 1917

Picketing the White House

FORWARD
OUT OF DARKNESS
LEAVE BEHIND
THE NIGHT
FORWARD
OUT OF ERROR
FORWARD
INTO LIGHT

Suffragists faced a discouraging situation at the start of 1917. Votes for women had just been defeated in three more states, President Wilson had won re-election without endorsing the Federal amendment, and America's involvement in the long war in Europe was beginning to seem inevitable.

Within their own ranks suffragists mourned the death of a popular and promising young leader, Inez Milholland Boissevain. How long, they asked, would women have to sacrifice their time, their resources, and their very lives to win what was rightfully theirs?

As a tribute to Boissevain, the Congressional Union organized a beautiful memorial service on December 25, 1916 in Statuary Hall under the dome of the national Capitol,

the first time a woman had been so honored. Purple, white, and gold banners draped the great hall and tricolor flags (below) marked each seat. Amid hymns and stately pageantry suffragists, trade unionists, prison reformers, and peace activists paid tribute to Boissevain's short, remarkable life and to women's continuing quest for

recognition.

Following the ceremony a memorial delegation of 300 suffragists called on President Wilson on January 9 but he only restated his opposition to Federal action on states' rights grounds. Until conditions were more favorable, he claimed irritably, his hands were tied. He told the women to go "concert" public opinion; he wanted no more delegations.

Returning to CU headquarters on Lafayette Square, the indignant women discussed their next move. Recalling her experiences in Albany in 1912, Harriot Blatch proposed that silent "sentinels of liberty, sentinels of self-government" take up posts standing outside the president's White House residence. What Alice Paul called a "perpetual delegation" began the next day.

Loved and honored by her comrades, Inez Milholland Boissevain's sudden and untimely death led the Congressional Union and the Woman's Party to treat her as a suffrage martyr whom they immortalized on this golden poster (facing page). "As in life she had been the symbol of the woman's cause, so in death she is the symbol of its sacrifice," Maud Younger observed in her memorial address. The yellow banner above was from the memorial service in Statuary Hall in the Capitol (left). After Boissevain's death a mountain in her native New York was unofficially renamed in her honor. In early January suffragists bearing cloth banners and tricolor flags (above left) took up positions outside the White House gates.

Pickets Escalate the Challenge

"THERE IS a royal blaze of color at the White House gates these nipping winter days," *The Suffragist* reported in mid-January 1917. "For the first time in history the President of the United States is being picketed."

Carrying purple, white, and gold flags and lettered banners, a dozen women set out from Congressional Union headquarters on January 10 to silently stand outside the gates of the White House. Their banners bore the questions they wanted everyone to ask: "Mr. President, What Will You Do For Woman Suffrage?" and "How Long Must Women Wait for Liberty?" Sue White recalled that "the next morning every paper in the United States carried the story and gave the wording of the banners. Something unusual had happened. A news value had been given to suffrage agitation."

Day after day the women picketed, weathering snow, sleet, and hail and winning growing respect and support. Alice Paul argued that women had to keep the issue right in front of the president for him to give it his attention. "If a creditor stands before a man's house all day long, demanding payment of his bill," she reasoned, "the man must either remove the creditor or pay his bill."

Right: Suffrage pickets.

Suffragists picketed the White House in shifts every day except Sunday, week after week, drawing national press coverage and triggering widespread discussion. The women stood silently (above) despite the frigid weather or kept moving by parading in circles (right). "You are brave girls," one old Confederate veteran told them. President Wilson (below) reacted courteously at first but his distaste for the "belligerent" suffragists did not alter. Doris Stevens noted that administration leaders "tried to conceal under an artificial indifference their sensitive- ness to our strategy." But as war drew closer, "the pickets began to be a serious thorn in his flesh." The president's call to defend democracy abroad left him open to criticism for denying democracy at home. Later suffrage banners shrewdly quoted Wilson himself.

Congressional Union Activists Unite as the National Woman's Party

"PATIENCE CEASES to be a virtue," declared 82-year-old Olympia Brown after she picketed the White House during the winter of 1917. "We cannot allow our cause to rest, or to be over-looked, or over-shadowed" even by the increasingly ominous threat of war.

Visitors to the capital found the daily sight of the women standing silently outside the White House through all weather "inspiring, gallant and impressive," according to Doris Stevens. "There was some mirth and joking, but the vast majority were filled with admiration."

Among the pickets were many college graduates, teachers, social workers, trade unionists, factory workers, and even an aeroplane pilot. Others included an admiral's wife, an ambassador's daughter, and the wives and daughters of congressmen, journalists, and professional men.

In early March 1917, two months after the picketing began, members of the Congressional Union and the National Woman's Party of Western Women Voters met in Washington D.C. and voted to merge into the National Woman's Party. They elected Alice Paul chair, Anne Martin vice-chair, and Mabel Vernon secretary. The new party would unite women nationally, including women voters in the west, around the single goal of a woman suffrage amendment to the U.S. Constitution.

Following the founding convention of the National Woman's Party (above), delegates and supporters converged on the White House on March 4, 1917. Forming an extraordinary procession in the pouring rain (right), one thousand banner-carrying suffragists circled the White House for two hours trying to present the convention's resolutions to the newly inaugurated president. At every entrance, however, the gates were locked and the women were turned away. The emotionally powerful procession was witnessed by thousands in town for Wilson's second inauguration. When the president and his wife finally emerged, they sped off past the women without even acknowledging them. Supporters (below) brought hot coffee to women on the picket line.

Stalwart Pickets Maintain a Presence

SUFFRAGISTS PICKETED the White House through the winter of 1917 calling for action on the Federal amendment but the war in Europe commanded most attention. To keep attracting publicity the Congressional Union organized special days featuring women from different states and professions, and when necessary provided rain coats, heated bricks, and wooden boards to stand on to help stave off the cold.

When Congress adjourned on March 3, so did the pickets. But when the new Congress convened on April 2 suffragists resumed picketing the White House and also, for a time, the Capitol. By then, however, the nation was on the very brink of war.

Right: College Day drew women from thirteen colleges. Top right: New York women on the picket line. Bottom right: Answering congressmen's "favorite objections."

MR. PRESIDENT HOW LONG MUST WOMEN WAIT FOR LIBERTY

What Is The Paramount Issue Before Congress?

National Defense? NO!

WOMAN SUFFRAGE

Democracy Must Determine Its Own Defense

The women of the United States should be consulted on defense.

A government responsible to all women, as well as all men, will be less likely to go to war, without real necessity.

THE FEDERAL SUFFRAGE AMENDMENT

"The right of citizens of the United States to vote shall not be denied or abridged by the United States, or by any State, on account of sex."

READ THE ANSWER TO YOUR FAVORITE OBJECTION

OBJECTION 1

Some Congressmen say that they cannot vote for the amendment, because they do not believe in woman suffrage.

ANSWER 1.

This need not deter them.

By voting for the amendment, Congress merely passes the question on for the Legislatures of the States to decide.

ANSWER 2.

Many Congressmen did not believe in the Direct Election of Senators, yet voted for the amendment, because of party pressure. The welfare of political parties now demands the passage of the Suffrage Amendment. The Western Women Voters have decided to penalize the party which has the power and does not use it to secure its passage.

OBJECTION 2

Some Congressmen say that they cannot vote for it because they do not approve of the provision in the Constitution for ratifying amendments, by which a State with a large population counts for only one vote, and carries no more weight than a State with a scanty population.

ANSWER.

Women are not responsible for this law. It was put into the Constitution to please the State Rights men, who did not want large States to discriminate against small States.

It is not a sincere objection, as it was not raised against the Income Tax and Direct Election of Senators amendments.

OBJECTION 3

Some Congressmen say that the amendment violates the principle of local self-government.

ANSWER.

On the contrary, it establishes local self-government for women, nation-wide. It is of the same nature as the clause in the Constitution forbidding any State to deny a citizen the right of trial by jury—a just principle valid in every part of the United States.

OBJECTION 4

Some Congressmen say that there is not a sufficient demand for National woman suffrage, and that it is not wise to go ahead of public opinion.

ANSWER 1.

There is a far greater demand than there was for the Income Tax or Direct Election of Senators amendments. There is practically no demand for the enfranchisement of Philippine men; yet the Democratic Party proposes to grant it.

ANSWER 2.

Even the opponents of woman suffrage admit that it is bound to come; this proves the strength of the demand.

Write your Senators and Congressmen to urge the passage of the amendment.

CONGRESSIONAL UNION FOR WOMAN SUFFRAGE,
National Headquarters, 1420 F Street, Washington, D. C.
New York Headquarters, 13 East 41st Street
Telephone, 5444 Murray Hill

State Activists Win Partial Suffrage and a Critical Victory in the South

BY APRIL 1917 NAWSA members had drawn encouragement from solid gains in presidential suffrage in the midwest. Carrie Catt's still secret "Winning Plan" calling for simultaneous action of all sorts in the states was beginning to show results.

The first state after Illinois to pass presidential suffrage was North Dakota in late January 1917, followed by Indiana and Ohio in February and by Nebraska, Michigan, and Rhode Island in April. These victories, which substantially increased the number of electoral votes women could help decide, came only after years of work by suffragists and in some cases by very close margins. The bill passed the Ohio Senate by only two votes and won ap-

proval in Rhode Island only after it had been brought before the legislature fifteen times. Relentless opponents countered each gain with lawsuits and threats of referendum campaigns of their own. Judges in Indiana ruled the bill invalid and in Ohio antisuffragists managed to have a repeal measure placed on the November ballot.

Suffragists won an important advance in March when Arkansas approved primary suffrage for women, the equivalent of presidential suffrage in that one-party state and the first real breakthrough in the south.

Above: North Dakota Governor Lynn J. Frazier signs the presidential suffrage bill. Right: New inroads.

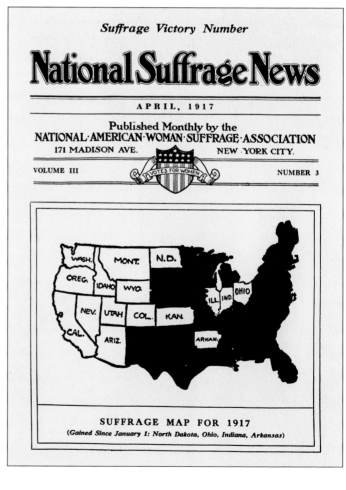

Suffrage Victory Number

National Suffrage News

APRIL, 1917

Published Monthly by the
NATIONAL·AMERICAN·WOMAN·SUFFRAGE·ASSOCIATION
171 MADISON AVE.   NEW·YORK·CITY.

VOLUME III   VOTES FOR WOMEN   NUMBER 3

SUFFRAGE MAP FOR 1917
(Gained Since January 1: North Dakota, Ohio, Indiana, Arkansas)

Jeannette Rankin Steps into History as the Nation's First Congresswoman

BEFORE TAKING her seat in the U.S. House of Representatives on April 2, 1917, first congresswoman Jeannette Rankin (above) made a brief speech to supporters from the balcony of Suffrage House, NAWSA's lobbying headquarters in Washington D.C., where she was staying. Carrie Catt stood behind the former NAWSA organizer who was later escorted to Congress by a motorcade of decorated cars. In the upper right is the yellow national suffrage flag showing a circle of eleven blue stars for the equal suffrage states.

Earlier in the day Rankin attended a breakfast with 200 suffragists held in her honor. Catt was seated on her right with Alice Paul on her left, leading Catt's biographer Jacqueline Van Voris to observe, "By accident or design, the symbolism was apt." It was one of the last times Catt and Paul appeared together.

Having led Montana to adopt woman suffrage in 1914, Rankin was 36 when she campaigned for Congress as a Republican candidate in a Democratic state. With the support of new women voters she ran 25,000 votes ahead of her own party and was one of the few Republicans elected nationally.

After the election Rankin acknowledged her historic position. Besides representing her state, she noted, "it is my special duty to express also the point of view of women," and in particular to encourage passage of the Federal amendment.

For Congress

Jeannette Rankin

REPUBLICAN TICKET

NATIONAL WOMAN SUFFRAGE
PROTECTION OF CHILDHOOD
STATE AND NATIONAL PROHIBITION

Look for the name "Miss Jeannette Rankin" on ballot
If you don't see it ask the Judge of Election

Circulated and Paid for by Montana Good Gov't Organization
(OVER)

Printed by State Pub. Co. Helena.

Above: Jeannette Rankin spoke from NAWSA's lobbying headquarters in the capital after her winning campaign (left) in Montana.

War Threatens to Eclipse Suffrage and Dominate the Congressional Agenda

WHEN JEANNETTE Rankin was formally welcomed to the House of Representatives on April 2, 1917, jubilant women filled the upper galleries for the historic occasion. But later that day President Wilson asked Congress for a Declaration of War. Pacifists Alice Paul and Hazel Hunkins encouraged Rankin to oppose it while Carrie Catt and many political backers pressured her to support it.

When the declaration came to a vote four days later, Rankin voted "no" along with 56 other members of Congress. It was believed to be the first vote ever by a female legislator on the question of war. The conflict in Europe suddenly took center stage.

With the country at war, party leaders in Congress agreed that only legislation included in the president's war program would be considered during the entire session. NAWSA temporarily suspended lobbying work but the National Woman's Party not only continued lobbying and picketing, it also proposed that woman suffrage itself be treated as a war measure.

Above: Jeannette Rankin addressed her colleagues in the House. Right: Cartoonist J. H. Cassel pictured war seizing center stage.

Back in the Limelight

Crystal Eastman was a prime mover in New York's Woman's Peace Party and an outspoken opponent of conscription and "preparedness" for war. A talented journalist and suffrage organizer, Eastman dedicated all her time to peace efforts after 1915 and became an influential member of the American Union Against Militarism, predecessor of the American Civil Liberties Union. Another anti-war organizer, Mary Ware Dennett, had been NAWSA's corresponding secretary and Anna Howard Shaw's able assistant from 1910 to 1914. An early advocate of birth control and sex education, Dennett put her energy into the peace movement with The People's Council (below), a coalition of peace, labor, and farm groups which opposed U.S. entry into the war.

Suffragists Divided Over Entry into World War I

LIKE MEMBERS of Congress, suffragists were split over America's entry into the war. While most approved, there was serious opposition at the outset. Many pacifists and progressives withheld their support and, like Jane Addams and Lillian Wald, concentrated on lessening the painful impact of the conflict and defending civil liberties.

Most Socialist Party members opposed the "capitalist" war, including Rose Cohn, Dorothy Day, and Charlotte Margoles (above), shown selling papers in New York on February 9, 1917. Several Socialists including Day, who would found the Catholic Worker movement in the 1930s, joined the White House pickets in solidarity later in the year when any criticism of the government was attacked as unpatriotic and even treasonous. Doris Stevens reflected the suffragists' resolve, "We must not let our voices be drowned by war trumpets or cannon." But this would be a mighty task. ◆

Above: Anti-war Socialists.

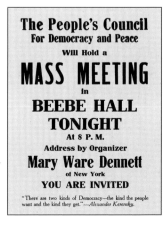

Women Awake!
Your Country
Needs you.
Hazel Roberts. 1916
Learn to be of National Service — Join the Navy League
Help the Navy - Local Headquarters

Chapter 13: 1917-1918

Suffrage, Patriotism, and World War I

THE DECLARATION OF WAR on April 6, 1917 involved the United States in a conflict which had been raging in Europe for nearly three years. Almost overnight the war pushed all domestic issues to the background.

Although it resolved to continue working for suffrage, the National American Woman Suffrage Association offered its organizational resources to the government and initiated an ambitious plan for national service. With Carrie Catt's "Winning Plan" and the second New York campaign underway, suffragists added war-related tasks to work for enfranchisement. The chair of NAWSA's War Service Department, Katharine McCormick, reported that "desks for suffrage work were vacant over all the country" while women gave their energy to the demands of the war.

While Congress considered only war-related legislation, NAWSA lobbyists toured the country strengthening congressional committees in the states so that they could more effectively pressure elected representatives when the opportunity came again.

The National Woman's Party remained focused exclusively on the suffrage amendment, arguing that if

A member of the New York State Woman Suffrage Party (left) registered women for government service in early 1917 while others (below) prepared for a benefit bazaar for the party's War Service Committee. Hazel Robert's "Women Awake!" recruitment poster for the Navy League (facing page) exhorted women to "Learn to be of National Service." By early 1917 many suffragists were already doing national service with groups like the Navy League, YMCA, and American Red Cross, which took over the services pioneered by the U. S. Sanitary Commission during the Civil War. Some 13,000 women served in clerical positions in the Navy during the war.

defending democracy abroad was a critical war measure, then so was establishing democracy for women at home. The NWP's single-minded drive, which included picketing the White House, drew harsher reactions in the wartime environment. Even the patriotism of moderate suffragists who took up the same argument was attacked by opponents during the national mobilization.

Loyalty Parade Racine, Wis. May 30, 1917. Wright Photo No. 11

With children clinging to her, "The Weaker Sex" (above) held up a world of warring men in this evocative cartoon from *Puck* magazine. Following the declaration of war, women joined in patriotic demonstrations such as the Loyalty Parade in Racine, Wisconsin (above right) on May 30. It included pioneer suffragist Olympia Brown on the far left leading the suffrage division. In New York City a huge Wake Up America parade filled Fifth Avenue on April 19, 1917. Madame Kimura Komako (right), a Japanese journalist, was one of 600 marchers in the contingent of suffragists who, according to *The New York Sun,* "were the best marchers in line, barring none, not even the soldiers!" Many more suffragists marched with the nurses, teachers, and other divisions. Kimura's visit prompted a flurry of articles on prospects of woman suffrage in Japan.

War Brings New Difficulties

WHEN President Woodrow Wilson outlined the war's aims in his address to Congress on April 3, 1917, he chose words that suffragists and the rest of the nation could easily relate to. "The world must be made safe for democracy," he declared. "We shall fight for the things we have always carried nearest our hearts, for democracy, for the right of those who submit to authority to have a voice in their own Governments." Despite these lofty aims, Carrie Catt later called this period "the most trying and difficult of my experience." Anti-suffragists not only blocked progress in Congress but also "did their utmost to make the public believe that suffragists were traitors to their country since they did not lay down their work when the U.S.A. went to war." The incessant attacks continued for years.

NAWSA Plans for Wartime Service

BEFORE WAR was declared, the NAWSA Executive Council met in Washington D.C. to hear Carrie Catt propose the adoption of a wartime policy. On February 25, 1917 the council voted 63-13 to offer the services and loyal support of the association and its estimated two million members to the government in the event of national emergency.

This strategic early action helped cement NAWSA's relationship with President Wilson and it received his support from then on. NAWSA emphasized, however, that work for suffrage ("the right protective of all other rights") would continue.

A Controversial Stand

While the association's public pledge to stand by Wilson at a critical time was lauded by politicians, it drew criticism from pacifist, socialist, and other anti-war members who felt betrayed by NAWSA's endorsement. Jane Addams and the Woman's Peace Party appealed to Catt to show patriotism "by refraining from any action tending to increase the war spirit." Crystal Eastman objected that the services of suffragists "had been so lightly pledged to a government which has denied to them for forty years a fundamental democratic right."

Catt, a long-term advocate of peace, responded pragmatically: "Whether we approve or disapprove, war is here. It is not the appeal of war but the call of civilization which is summoning women to new duties and responsibilities."

"Win-the-War Women" were featured on several covers of The Woman Citizen. NAWSA began the weekly magazine in June 1917 with Leslie endowment funds, merging The Woman's Journal, The Woman Voter, and several smaller publications.

NAWSA's war plan set up four new departments: Thrift and Elimination of Waste, which stressed food conservation; Food Production, which included practical gardening and home canning; Industrial Protection of Women partic-ularly within government departments; and Americanization, which offered classes in citizenship, English, and patriotism.

Branches of these four sections were formed by auxiliaries in the states organized under NAWSA's War Service Department. The following year new departments were added for the Women's Oversea Hospital, Child Welfare, Liberty Bonds, and the Woman's Land Army.

The Woman's Committee

To coordinate the work offered by women throughout the country, the Secretary of War established a Woman's Advisory Committee of the Council of National Defense in May 1917 and named Anna Howard Shaw chair. Catt and several NAWSA officers were also appointed. Harriot Blatch worked with the Food Service Administration and other suffragists served in official positions in which for the first time they worked closely with the government.

In addition, Maud Wood Park reported, "hundreds of our state and local officers and members were appointed to leading positions in the state committees that were promptly organized – positions that demanded much, if not all, of their time and thought." By the fall of 1918 *The Woman Citizen* could proudly report that "the leaders in women's work in the Red Cross, YMCA, Liberty Loan, Food [Administration], are almost without exception women who have been trained in their work in our Association."

The war put tremendous pressure and additional demands on suffragists but also provided NAWSA with a powerful new lever with which to pressure the government for the Federal amendment. ◆

Suffragists Drafted for National Service

UNDER THE leadership of Anna Howard Shaw, the Woman's Advisory Committee of the Council of National Defense created chapters in each state and tried to coordinate women's work with government departments. The committee officers (above, left to right) were Maude Wetmore, Mrs. Josiah Evans Cowles, Ida M. Tarbell, Katharine Dexter McCormick (standing), Anna Howard Shaw, Antoinette Funk (standing), Carrie Chapman Catt, Clarinda Pendleton Lamar, and Mrs. Philip North Moore. Agnes Nestor, Emily Newell Blair, and Hannah J. Patterson were appointed later. Wetmore, Lamar and Tarbell were well known anti-suffragists.

Shaw worked nearly full time in Washington D.C. but grew frustrated by the committee's lack of real authority and its poor treatment by male bureaucrats. Nonetheless, when the committee disbanded in March 1919, Shaw and resident director Patterson were awarded the Distinguished Service Medal by the government for their outstanding efforts.

Not all was harmonious, however. Unlike the Woman's Committee, anti-suffragists dominated the National League for Woman's Service, a patriotic group which competed bitterly with NAWSA for prestigious government work like census taking.

New York suffragists, in the midst of their second campaign, circulated this flier (left) which emphasized how war-torn countries depended on the work of women.

Above: The Woman's Committee. Left: Touting "woman's courage, willingness and ability." Facing page: Poster by Charles Dana Gibson.

Gertrude Foster Brown
served as Director General of
NAWSA's Woman's Oversea
Hospitals in France and supervised the establishment of a
gas treatment unit there in
1918. Brown, a trained pianist,
organized a Woman Suffrage
Study Club in New York in
1909 and two years later
spoke on the street for the
first time while campaigning
against an anti-suffrage
politician. In 1913 she left the
Women's Political Union to
head the New York State
Woman Suffrage Association.
Brown later served as vice-
president of NAWSA and
managing director of *The
Woman Citizen*.

NAWSA Organizes Women's Medical Units to Serve Oversea

Early in 1918, NAWSA organized a Women's Oversea Hospital unit made up of female doctors, nurses, and staff. The unit, together with ambulances and supplies, was sent to the European front. The U.S. government had declined the offer of a women's medical unit but the French gratefully accepted. American suffragists served behind the lines offering medical services, organizing relief and assistance to refugees, and running hospitals and schools in the rural French countryside. One hospital was bombed three times during the war.

Dr. Alice Gregory led fifteen women, including a carpenter, plumber, chemist, and chauffeur, who helped establish a 50-bed hospital in the south of France. Suffragists later set up a 300-bed unit for gas cases which treated nearly 20,000 patients. The women

cared for soldiers, refugees, and repatriates until September 1919 when they donated all their remaining equipment to France.

The hospital units included a total of 74 women from across the U.S. and were funded by $178,000 painstakingly raised by NAWSA state affiliates. After the war Dr. Caroline Finley returned to the U.S. as both a Lieutenant in the French Army and a member of the Order of the British Empire, conferred for her work caring for British prisoners of war. Three American surgeons and one nurse were awarded the Croix de Guerre, two doctors were decorated with the Medaille d'Honneur, and France expressed its deepest gratitude for the women's courageous service.

Above: Suffragists bound for France. Inset: The final report on NAWSA's hospitals.

Uncle Sam, Lady Liberty, and other costumed figures shared the 1917 Thrift Stamp Parade float above, sponsored by the Equal Suffrage League in Richmond, Virginia. Representing the "Barge of State," the float highlighted the extensive war service work being done by league members. Suffragists in Ayer, Massachusetts, set up a Suffrage Coffee House (left) to offer hospitality to servicemen and their families outside Camp Devens. Evelyn Peverley Coe of the sponsoring Boston Equal Suffrage Association is standing in the center. Similar houses were opened by suffragists near camps in other states.

The Woman's Land Army Aids Farmers

As the war continued and fewer and fewer men were available to tend the crops, worried farmers began to turn to the organized women for help. In answer, the Woman's Land Army was established in thirty states under the Woman's Advisory Committee and within months had placed roughly 15,000 women on the land for the critical harvest of 1918. Suffrage leaders even consulted with an overalls company to produce a suitable farm uniform for women.

The mostly untrained volunteers cared for animals, learned to operate farm machinery, and helped bring in the harvest from truck farms, orchards, and home gardens. Their hard work and efficiency won the appreciation of both the U.S. government and farmers who depended on their wartime aid.

Above: "Farmerettes" in updated bloomers marched in New York's Liberty Loan parade on October 14, 1918. Right: Answering Uncle Sam's call that "Food Will Win the War." Left: A button celebrated the harvest.

"Boys, the girls are going over the top!"

Bringing in the Wartime Harvest

Recognizing the immediate need for help with the 1918 harvest, women in New Mexico were among the first to organize themselves for war service. Under state chair Isabella Munro Ferguson, women from across the state took men's places on the farms and in the fields. Squads of workers were assigned to districts such as Mimbres Valley where eight women mowed, raked, and stacked sixteen tons of hay. Others helped pick and package the fruit crop.

The war was a great unifying force which underscored men's partnership with women. "We talk of the army in the field as one and the army at home as another," observed Anna Howard Shaw. "We are not two armies; we are one –

absolutely one army – and we must work together." Historian Sara Graham noted, "World War I offered NAWSA suffragists a chance to demonstrate their formidable strength in a show of public-spirited war work. Ironically, they were so successful at pa-

triotic service that commentators would later claim that the war won suffrage for America's women."

In addition to war service at home, over 25,000 women aided soldiers and civilians overseas in hospitals, canteens, and war-torn villages.

Members of New Mexico's Woman's Land Army (top) took a break during the 1918 harvest. Above: Cooling off in a water tank after work. State leader Isabella Munro Ferguson is on the left.

"Teamwork with Uncle Sam" (above) connected women's work at home with the war effort abroad. Produced for the 1917 suffrage campaign in Maine, the drawing showed a woman fashioning an artillery shell for a soldier in the field. Women took on many jobs including operating heavy machinery (below) and assembling holsters (right) during the war, leading the Secretary of War to admit, "If all the women were to stop their work tonight, we should have to withdraw from the war, at least temporarily, until we could entirely readjust ourselves." President Woodrow Wilson later praised the efforts of American women, declaring that "the war could not have been fought without them, or its sacrifices endured."

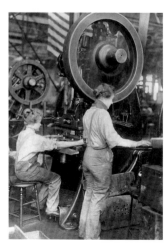

Women's Strengths Revealed in War Work

With men off to war, as many as a million women took on new industrial and manufacturing jobs usually filled by men. These women not only broke down old prejudices but also proved their ability in all sorts of work including critical and hazardous industries.

"Women took jobs in blast furnaces, in the manufacture of steel plate, high explosives, armaments, machine tools, agricultural implements, electrical apparatus, railway, automobile and airplane parts," historian Eleanor Flexner reported, "they worked in brass and copper smelting and refining, in foundries, in oil refining, in the production of chemicals, fertilizers and leather goods. Thousands of women poured into the textile mills producing uniforms for the armed services, the transport services and other occupations."

Since some of the industries women entered were dangerous and barely regulated, the Council of National Defense created a woman's division in January 1918 to oversee safety and working

Like the soldiers in the field, many women on the home front were consumed by the heavy burdens of the war. Taking men's places in countless industries, women could be found in railroad yards moving heavy equipment (above) and in factories weighing wire bed coils (left). "Their skill staggered me," wrote Harriot Blatch. "On all sides women were breaking through the old, accustomed boundaries. America was witnessing the beginning of a great social and industrial change." Although most women had to relinquish their better-paying jobs when the men returned, World War I accelerated women's progress in the workplace and helped secure their recognition as equal members of society.

conditions in munition plants. After the war this grew into the Woman's Bureau of the Department of Labor, directed by suffragist Mary Anderson. She became one of the highest ranking women in the Federal government and a champion of protective legislation for working women.

Regardless of the demands of the war and the benefits of patriotic service, however, many suffragists understood that they still needed to win more states to ensure passage of the Federal amendment. ◆

Chapter 14: 1917

Sentenced to Prison

WHILE THE National American Woman Suffrage Association was focused on the war and the second New York campaign, the National Woman's Party continued picketing the White House and pressuring the president and Congress to pass the Federal suffrage amendment.

The suffrage pickets received a friendly welcome from White House guards and capital police when they resumed their silent, dignified protest on April 2, 1917, as the new 65th Congress convened and suffrage bills were again introduced. Newspapers across the country had publicized the "silent sentinels" outside the White House and tourists in the capital sought out the unusual spectacle.

The messages on the pickets' banners became more defiant as the months passed. These included quotes drawn from President Wilson's own speeches (left) and provocative statements to the public and to White House visitors. The NWP argued that regardless of the war, but very much in keeping with its aims, the president should lead Congress in supporting the national enfranchisement of women.

Suffragists repeatedly emphasized that the war to save democracy abroad was being waged while women were denied democracy at home. The NWP held Wilson, as the president and leader of the majority party, responsible. "Towards women," Alice Paul charged, "President Wilson has adopted the attitude of an autocratic ruler."

Meanwhile, intensive propaganda was rapidly whipping up popular support for the war. Those who did not completely acquiesce were angrily accused of disloyalty, sedition, and cowardice. Many in the country, including most NAWSA leaders, felt that any criticism of the government, and in particular the public protest of "militant" suffragists stationed outside the White House, was inappropriate in war time. Despite objections from NAWSA and the administration, the NWP continued picketing through the spring and summer. The women increasingly faced attacks by mobs hot with patriotic zeal and war fever.

Left: Silently quoting the president.

"America is not a democracy" announced the controversial "Russian Banner" which greeted a delegation to the White House on June 20, 1917. The new Russian Republic had just approved woman suffrage. Moments after the diplomats passed, angry bystanders tore down the sign and ripped it to pieces. The following day Lucy Burns and Katharine Morey returned with an identical banner (above). It, too, was destroyed. Many members of the public agreed with administration officials that the picketing women embarrassed the president and weakened his stature in wartime. "We can only express ourselves by action," countered the National Woman's Party on this 1917 leaflet (right) which put forth the case for picketing and invoked the memory of Susan B. Anthony and her years of "arguing for a cause which was forever inopportune."

WHY WE PICKET

IN the midst of the general national confusion—a confusion of purposes as well as of plans—the clearest testimony to the steadfast faith of our people in democracy is borne by the unfaltering picket lines of the Woman's Party, which, day after day, hold before the doors of Congress and the White House their lovely banners of purple, white and gold, bearing the demand of women for political freedom.

It is beautiful to see the numbers, the devotion, the patience of the women who keep the suffrage banners uplifted.

In the Civil War—the last conflict that really shook the nation—only two women were faithful to the cause of woman suffrage—Susan B. Anthony and Elizabeth Cady Stanton. Now tens of thousands of women hold, or support those who hold, the banners which ask a government demanding women's services to do women common justice.

It is without the shadow of a doubt the finest service a woman can do for the country, to take her place today in the women's picket line.

A strong demand for justice to women at this time can not be disregarded. The claim is too clear. The need of the nation for undivided support is too great. We have only to make now an insistent demand for justice, and we can confer upon our country the imperishable gift of freedom and arouse it to a more passionate defense of its extended liberties.

The difficulty is, in the midst of the alarms of war, to make a clear and steady demand for justice heard at all. The longer our endurance, the more patient our appeal, the less it will be heeded in a time when dissensions, inner and outer, crowd each other off the pages of the press.

We can only express ourselves by action. We can not only hold up the banner of suffrage in our hearts; we can hold it visibly, before the eyes of the world, and before the eyes of those who make our laws. Nothing could be more sorrowful, at a time of national danger, than to see the suffrage banners lowered. It would symbolize the abandonment of the claim of women to liberty, just at the time when their right to liberty is most evident and when the need of the country for their free services is greatest.

One spirit must sometimes haunt the National Capitol—the spirit of Susan B. Anthony, who spent so many patient and courageous hours there, forever arguing for a cause which was forever inopportune. If her spirit watches the women who are, day after day, in snow and rain, through cold and heat, holding up their shining suffrage banners, she must glory to think of the unconquerable army that is now assembled where she, with one other, stood alone and impotent fifty years ago. — *National Woman's Party, Washington, D. C.*

Arrests Keep Women's Cause Alive in Wartime

When violence broke out in response to the Russian Banner, administration officials used it as an excuse to remove the pickets. Police warned Alice Paul on June 22, 1917 that further pickets would be arrested. Paul responded that picketing had been legal for six months and, since the law had not been changed, the protest would continue.

The following day a large crowd gathered in front of the White House. Lines of policemen appeared outside National Woman's Party headquarters. When suffragists attempted to resume picketing, members of the crowd attacked them and ripped their banners away. Instead of protecting the suffragists, the police arrested them. Witnesses, however, could not help but admire the courage and poise of the women in the face of abusive and violent mobs.

Above: Mabel Vernon faced a gauntlet of men on June 23, aware that at any moment she could be arrested or attacked.

After women carrying the Russian Banner were assaulted while the police looked on, unruly crowds gathered repeatedly to harass the White House pickets without fear of arrest. Individual men and packs of boys rushed the women, ripped down their banners, and like the taunting men below, tore them up for souvenirs. Police responded by arresting more suffragists, including organizers Virginia Arnold and Berta Crone (above).

After being attacked on June 22, one determined suffragist (right, center) still held her pole erect with only a tattered scrap of her banner remaining. The silent pickets usually held their positions and clung to their bare poles until new banners were brought from headquarters.

Suffrage Pickets Attacked and Imprisoned on the Fourth of July

VIOLENT ATTACKS continued through the end of June. Angry crowds faced off against the White House pickets and repeatedly assaulted the women. Police arrested twelve more suffragists on June 25, and another nine the next day. Until then, the women had been released after each arrest. Six of this last group were brought to

Alice Paul had led the campaign to force action on the Federal suffrage amendment for nearly five years by 1917. She had won praise as "a master strategist, a great general" from Doris Stevens and "a leader of foresight, genius and courage" from Sue White. Inez Irwin later wrote that Paul had "the quiet of the spinning top." However the months of bitter controversy, violence, and arrests began to take their toll. In mid-July Paul lay ill and exhausted. Friends feared for her life. After an emotional bedside meeting on July 13, Lucy Burns became active "chairman," aided by Mabel Vernon and Hazel Hunkins, while Paul recuperated for several weeks in a Philadelphia hospital. Paul's partnership with Burns, "the cool strategist and passionate rebel" in Steven's words, "provided a complete and unsurpassed leadership." Burns, who admired Paul's "extraordinary mind, extraordinary courage and remarkable executive ability," continued to lead the campaign during Paul's absence.

trial, however, and scolded by the judge for their "unpatriotic, almost treasonable behavior." He sentenced them to three days in the District jail for "obstructing the highways" when they refused to pay the $25 fine.

These six, the first to be thus honored, were national organizers Mabel Vernon, Katharine Morey, and Vir-

ginia Arnold, advisor Lavinia Dock, state officer Maud Jamison from Virginia, and Annie Arneil, a munitions worker from Delaware. The government hoped that imprisoning the women would put an end to the picketing.

But on the Fourth of July eleven women once again attempted to picket. Angry crowds again attacked them

and destroyed their banners including one which quoted the Declaration of Independence, "Governments Derive Their Just Powers From the Consent of the Governed." The judge at their trial, a Wilson appointee, lectured the women not to "bother the president." Then he sentenced them all to three days in the District jail.

Nina Allender's cartoon "News from the Front" (above) was the ironic cover of the National Woman's Party's weekly in late June 1917 as suffragists desperately tried to keep their cause visible in the early months of the war. Over two dozen women were arrested in late June including NWP organizer Katharine Morey of Boston (below) who appeared more defiant than alarmed as she was taken by police to the station house.

A Harsh Sentence Backfires

PICKETING continued despite the threat of jail. On July 14, Julia Hurlbut led a column of sixteen suffragists carrying purple, white, and gold banners to the White House past crowds of jeering men. Commemorating Bastille Day, one woman carried a banner with the French Revolutionary slogan "Liberty, Equality, Fraternity." The pickets, including many National Woman's Party officers, were arrested one by one outside the White House gates.

At their trial each woman spoke in her own defense while the judge kept reminding them to "keep to the charge of obstructing traffic." Matilda Gardner countered that the charge was "political subterfuge" and that the arrests were "purely political." When the women refused to pay a $25 fine for "obstructing traffic" the judge shocked the packed courtroom by sen-

Attacks Keep Suffrage in the News

ONGOING ATTACKS by off-duty sailors, government clerks, and other men together with the arrests of the pickets kept suffrage in the news throughout the summer of 1917. The National Woman's Party continued lobbying and working with sympathetic congressmen, particularly Republicans, on the suffrage bill. Senator Wesley Jones from Washington told the Senate. "I do not see how we can very consistently talk democracy while disfranchising the better half of our citizenship. I may not approve of the action of the women picketing the White House, but neither do I approve of what I consider the lawless action toward these women in connection with the picketing."

A few members of Congress protested the illegal arrests and brutal treatment of the pickets, including Senator William Borah, Representative Jeannette Rankin, and Charles Lindberg, a Minnesota congressman and father of the aviator. Very few members of NAWSA objected because they opposed the picketing strategy.

Above: Disruptive sailors.
Below: Summer pickets.

tencing them to sixty days in the Occoquan Workhouse in nearby Virginia. He warned the predominantly middle-class suffragists, "You will not find jail a pleasant place to be."

The NWP publicized the drastic punishment nationally, which drew a strong public outcry over the severity of the sentence given the type of crime allegedly committed. For three days the prisoners endured miserable and de-grading conditions in the filthy workhouse before public and private pressure forced President Wilson to issue a pardon and release the women. But former prisoner Allison Hopkins responded, "We do not ask pardon for ourselves but justice for all American women." For a time picketing resumed without interference.

Above: Julia Hurlbut led the Bastille Day pickets.

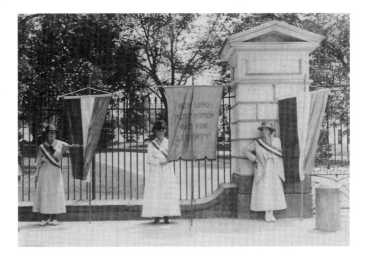

Another Controversial Banner Triggers a Violent Response

AFTER THE sixteen Bastille Day prisoners were released, picketing resumed on July 23, 1917 despite government hopes that jail and the ensuing pardon would put an end to it. New banners protested the president's hypocrisy, Congress' inaction, and the illegal treatment of the pickets by District police and judges.

The appearance of the controversial "Kaiser Banner" on August 14 immediately provoked a new wave of mob violence and national publicity. "We did not expect public sympathy," wrote Doris Stevens of the banner which referred to the president by the title of his German adversary.

Stevens emphasized how strongly the National Woman's Party resented Wilson's constant oratory on freedom and democracy. "We did not regard Mr. Wilson as our president," she wrote. "We felt that he had neither political nor moral claim to our allegiance. . . . Here we were, a band of women fighting with banners, in the midst of a world armed to the teeth."

Above: The Kaiser Banner challenged the president. Upper right: Bastille Day mob. Right: Men repeatedly assaulted the pickets at the White House gates, destroying hundreds of their banners and flags.

Angry Mobs Attack the White House Pickets

O N AUGUST 14, after crowds had twice destroyed their banners, the White House pickets returned to nearby National Woman's Party headquarters. This time the angry mob followed them. Suffragists locked the doors while Lucy Burns and Virginia Arnold climbed out onto the balcony to hold both an NWP tricolor and another "Kaiser Banner." The crowd, which had surrounded the front of the building, pelted the suffragists with fruit and eggs while cheering on several men who climbed up and tore the banners out of the women's hands.

Meanwhile, other suffragists slipped out and resumed picketing before members of the mob noticed them and ripped their banners away. Five times Lucy Burns led women out to resume picketing but each time their banners were destroyed. Later in the day someone fired a shot into the second floor of NWP headquarters, narrowly missing two women. "None of us went to bed that night," recalled Catherine Flanagan. "We were afraid that something – we knew not what – might happen."

Over the following three days the pickets were kicked, dragged, battered, and bruised by members of the crowds and by police. On August 15, Doris Stevens remembered, "yeomen, small boys, and hoodlums attacked the women without hindrance. . . . Alice Paul was knocked down three times. One sailor dragged her thirty feet along the White House sidewalk in his attempts to tear off her suffrage sash, gashing her neck brutally." The following day, more women were injured.

Facing Prison for Equal Rights

O N AUGUST 17, following three days of violence and disorder, police were again directed to arrest the pickets. Catherine Flanagan, a National Woman's Party organizer from Hartford, Connecticut, Madeline Watson of Chicago, and four other suffragists were seized late in the afternoon as government workers passed the White House heading home. Watson's banner read, "Mr. President, How Long Must Women Wait for Liberty?" After a forty minute trial, the judge fined the women $10 for "obstructing traffic." When they refused to pay it, he sentenced them to thirty days in the Occoquan Workhouse. Over the following two weeks ten more pickets were arrested and sent to prison for thirty days. Doris Stevens reported, "The press throughout the entire country at this time protested against mob violence and the severe sentences pronounced upon the women who had attempted to hold their banners steadfast." The women continued picketing despite the violent, unpredictable crowds, well aware that neither the police nor the courts would protect them.

Left: A police matron (center) arrested suffragists Catherine Flanagan and Madeline Watson as a large crowd looked on.

Prison Sentences, Abuse Fail to Discourage Pickets

WOMAN SUFFRAGE remained in the headlines throughout the summer and fall of 1917. Doris Stevens reported that "continuous arrests kept the issue hot and kept people who cared in constant protest."

Off-duty military personnel, government workers, and young "hoodlums" continued to attack the pickets. Many women were injured trying to hang on to their banners and suffrage sashes. "Some members of the crowd made sport of the women," Stevens recalled, while "others hurled cheap and childish epithets at them." A reporter described the men in one crowd as "for the most part disdainful, insolent, or leering."

On September 4, during a Conscription Day parade of drafted soldiers, the National Woman's Party staged a dramatic protest directly in front of the president's reviewing

stand. Edith Ainge and Eleanor Calnan unfolded a golden banner which read, "Mr. President, How Long Must Women Be Denied a Voice in a Government Which is Conscripting Their Sons?" before being arrested. As they were led away, another pair of suffragists approached with a new banner (below) to take their place, followed by others. Police seized each pair as

parade spectators watched intently. Over a dozen women including Lucy Burns, Maud Malone, Lucy Branham, and Mary Winsor were arrested and sentenced to sixty days in the workhouse.

Reflecting growing public discomfort and alarm over accounts of inhumane treatment of the imprisoned pickets, presidential appointee Dudley Field Malone resigned the lucrative post of Collector of the Port of New York in early September in a widely-publicized protest that laid the responsibility squarely on the president. "I think it is high time," he wrote Wilson, "that men in this generation, at some cost to themselves, stood up to battle for the national enfranchisement of American women."

**Above: Attacking the pickets.
Right: Watching police arrest another suffragist in June.**

Imprisoned Suffragists Demand Status of Political Prisoners

Six more women were taken into custody for picketing the White House on September 13 and were sentenced to thirty days in the workhouse along with four others arrested on September 22. This group included several Socialists and trade unionists drawn to the picketing campaign as much for the principle of free speech as for woman suffrage. Together with Lucy Burns they decided to demand recognition as political prisoners since their imprisonment was due to their beliefs and not criminal activity.

These eleven prisoners secretly smuggled out to supporters a letter to the District Commissioners which requested access to legal counsel, contact with the outside, writing materials, and exemption from prison work. When their appeal, believed to be the first sustained demand for political prisoner status in the U.S., went unanswered, the women refused to work. They were all transferred to solitary confinement in the District jail, but suffragists imprisoned after them took up the same demand.

Conditions in both the workhouse and the jail were miserable. Poor quality food weakened and sickened the women, and workhouse authorities pitted Black prisoners against the white suffragists, allowing several beatings. The NWP encouraged congressmen to see their jailed constituents, and a visit by one committee chair shocked him into hastening action in the Senate. Suffragist Ada Kendall later wrote of the Occoquan workhouse, "It was a place of chicanery, sinister horror, brutality and dread."

Lucy Burns "brought a fierceness and resoluteness to the American woman suffrage movement that was rarely equaled," wrote her biographer Sidney Bland. "Burns in her poise and strength of character was a rallying symbol for the more faint-hearted." By 1917 Burns, 38, had served in the Congressional Union and National Woman's Party as co-founder with Alice Paul, organizer, lobbyist, speaker, editor, strategist, and field commander. Her passion for justice and personal integrity had won the respect of congressmen, police, and politicians as well as other suffragists. In the Occoquan Workhouse, however, the superintendent immediately saw her leadership as a serious threat. He had her seized, beaten, stripped, and locked up in solitary confinement. Whenever she could she fought back. Despite an ongoing desire to return to her extended family in New York, Burns stayed in the capital, eventually enduring the longest time in prison of any suffragist.

WHERE THERE IS NO VISION THE PEOPLE PERISH.

White House Pickets Sentenced to Seven Months in Prison for "Obstructing Traffic"

AN ANGRY "White Collar Slave" crushed a suffragist and her plea for democracy in Ryan Walker's 1917 cartoon (above). It criticized the hostile response of "patriots" in Washington D.C. to suffragists demanding their rights in wartime. While many observers considered the pickets misguided and embarrassing, public opinion was split on whether they deserved the severe treatment they received.

With nearly two dozen suffragists in jail, Congress adjourned for two months on October 6 having taken little action on the Federal amendment. In protest, another eleven women, led by Alice Paul, attempted to picket the White House and were arrested. They refused to participate in their trial, agreeing with Paul that "we do not consider ourselves subject to this Court since, as an unenfranchised class, we have nothing to do with the making of the laws which have put us in this position."

After the judge suspended their sentences without explanation, Rose Winslow and three others were arrested again on October 15 and sentenced to six months in jail. On October 20 Alice Paul was arrested picketing the White House and sentenced to seven months.

Above: Blaming women.
Left: More arrests.

Alice Paul in Jail

AFTER BEING sentenced to jail on October 22, 1917 for "obstructing traffic," Alice Paul wrote to reassure her mother: "Dear Mother, I have been sentenced today to seven months imprisonment. Mrs. Lawrence Lewis is going on with the work in my place and will be at headquarters. Please do not worry. It will merely be a delightful rest. With love, Alice."

Paul was taken to the Washington D.C. jail where several other suffragists were being held. They had decided that, in her words, "as long as we were there we would keep up an unremitting fight for the rights of political prisoners."

The Psychopathic Ward

Paul was held in solitary confinement for nearly two weeks in the District jail where the lack of exercise and "the constant cold and hunger of undernourishment" left her severely weakened. On October 30 she and a similarly weakened Rose Winslow were transferred to the prison hospital. "For one brief night we occupied beds in the same ward in the hospital," Paul remembered. "Here we decided upon the hunger strike, as the ultimate form of protest left us – the strongest weapon left with which to continue within the prison our battle against the Administration." She was then removed and kept incommunicado for a week.

Supporters and her attorney tried desperately to find out where she was being held.

"From the moment we undertook the hunger strike, a policy of unremitting intimidation began," she remembered. "One authority after another, high and low, in and out of prison, came to attempt to force me to break the hunger strike."

Isolated from other prisoners, Paul was locked in a boarded-up room with a cell door in the psychopathic ward of the jail hospital. There she was deprived of sleep, harassed, interrogated, and threatened with commitment to the insane asylum if she continued. "It appeared

Alice Paul (above) led a delegation of pickets to the White House gates on October 20, 1917. Her banner quoted one of President Wilson's speeches: "The Time Has Come to Conquer or Submit; For Us There Can Be But One Choice – We Have Made It."

clear that it was their intention either to discredit me, as the leader of the agitation, by casting doubt upon my sanity, or else to intimidate us into retreating from the hunger strike," she later recalled. "All the while everything possible was done to attempt to make me feel that I too was a 'mental patient.'"

Force-Feeding

After refusing to eat for a week she was taken away and force-fed through a tube shoved down her throat while she was being held down by prison guards. When Paul's attorney Dudley Field Malone finally located her, he protested her confinement in the mental ward and had her transferred back to the prison hospital.

Winslow was also brutally force-fed. She was able to smuggle out notes on scraps of paper which contradicted the government's claim that the procedure was "an everyday occurrence" that they submitted to "willingly"!

"Don't let them tell you we take this well," Winslow wrote. "Miss Paul vomits much. I do, too, except when I'm not nervous, as I have been every time against my will.... We think of the coming feeding all day. It is horrible.... One feels so forsaken when one lies prone and people shove a pipe down one's stomach." Dora Lewis protested that forced feeding was an inhumane practice which amounted to an additional punishment.

In late November Winslow wrote to supporters, "The women are all so magnificent, so beautiful. Alice Paul is as thin as ever, pale and large-eyed. We have been in solitary for five weeks. There is nothing to tell but that the days go by somehow. I have felt quite feeble the last few days – faint, so that I could hardly get my hair brushed, my arms ached so." Paul and Winslow endured the torture of force-feeding several times a day for three weeks as they continued their hunger strike. Supporters outside publicized and protested their brutal treatment. ◆

"Women Must Stand by Women"

DESPITE THE imprisonment of their leader, members of the National Woman's Party organized one of the largest and most dramatic demonstrations of the picketing campaign on November 10, 1917.

As an expectant crowd watched almost silently, wave after wave of suffragists marched slowly from Cameron House to the White House holding their tricolor banners high. They protested both the "wanton persecution of their leader," in Doris Stevens' words, and the delay in passing the Federal amendment.

Police arrested forty-one women from sixteen states and, when they were released, most returned to picket and were arrested again. Thirty-one women were sentenced to between six days and seven months in the District jail but

most were taken instead to the dreaded Occoquan Workhouse. Mary Nolan, a 73-year-old picket from Florida whose nephew was fighting for democracy in France, told the judge, "I should be proud of the honor to die in prison for the liberty of American women."

NWP members in New York organized a Meeting of Women Voters to rally support on November 11, and the next day Mary Beard led a protest delegation of fifty women to the White House to demand freedom for the pickets and passage of the Federal amendment.

Above: Suffragists converged on the White House on November 10, 1917. Right: Recently enfranchised women in New York met to support the pickets.

FIRST JOB FOR WOMEN VOTERS
GET THE PICKETS OUT OF JAIL.

SHALL WE LET THESE WOMEN DIE FOR A CAUSE WE HAVE WON?

Women Must Stand by Women

The pickets are risking their lives for a principle.

Won't you invest $20 and a day of your time and make a stand for liberty?

A COMMITTEE OF A THOUSAND WOMEN INVITE YOU TO A
Meeting of Women Voters

Sunday Evening, November 11th, at P. S. 40,
314 EAST 20th STREET, AT 8 O'CLOCK.

———

Come with your bag in hand ready to leave for Washington by the midnight express Sunday night, to
APPEAL TO PRESIDENT WILSON TO ENDORSE THE FEDERAL AMENDMENT AND TO RELEASE THE PICKETS.

· ·

I will join the deputation to Washington.

NAME ·

ADDRESS ·

(Call up Nora C. Smitheman, Spring 7033, for particulars.)

MARY BEARD,
Temporary Chairman.

Supporting her imprisoned leader, Lucy Branham (above) publicized the suffragists' demand for political prisoner status in 1917. From late September through November members of the National Woman's Party traveled throughout the country to inform people about what was happening in the capital and to rally support for the imprisoned pickets. In many places news had been substantially censored, but when the women were able to present their case directly to an audience they often won its sympathy. In some cases, wartime hysteria and government pressure led local officials to cancel meetings and refuse meeting halls. An NWP banner (below) reflected suffragists' solidarity.

Protesting the Treatment of Imprisoned Suffragists

To publicize the treatment of their imprisoned comrades, former suffrage prisoners donned replicas of their coarse prison uniforms to meet the press in Washington D.C. on November 12, 1917.

The National Woman's Party liked to highlight the political lineage of its more prominent members, including those seated in the middle row (above, from left). Eunice Dana Brannan was the daughter of the founder of the *New York Sun* and wife of the head of Bellevue Hospital. Elizabeth Seldin Rogers was a descendant of Roger Sherman, a signer of the Declaration of Independence. Dora Lewis counted among her ancestors the first U.S. Treasurer, and Allison Turnbull Hopkins was married to the leader of the Progressive Party.

Seated on the floor are Julia Hurlbut, NWP vice-chair in New Jersey, Nina Samarodin, a union organizer and teacher from Russia, and Elizabeth Stuyvesant, a dancer active in birth control and settlement work. Virginia Bovee (back, center), was an officer at the workhouse who had been discharged in September. She confirmed suffragists' claims of mistreatment and unsanitary conditions.

Above: Former prisoners.
Below: A 1917 cartoon from the *New York Call*.

"Not the White House, the Work House."

Suffragists Endure Beatings, Brutality,

WHEN THE SUFFRAGISTS arrested for picketing the White House on November 10, 1917 were taken to the Occoquan Workhouse they were subjected to frightening brutality, mistreatment, and outrageous threats far removed from their crime or demeanor.

The Night of Terror

When these 27 women arrived at Occoquan on the evening of November 14 they demanded to be recognized as political prisoners and refused to be processed. After they waited several hours for Workhouse Superintendent Raymond Whittaker, he suddenly burst into the room with a battalion of guards "in a frenzy of rage." At his command they seized the women, dragged them away, and brutally threw them into cells, injuring several and ignoring all protests. Of the attack Eunice Brannan later said, "Its perfectly unexpected ferocity stunned us."

Guards threw Dora Lewis into a tiny cell where she was knocked senseless when her head struck the iron bed. Her comrades feared that she was dead. Alice Cosu became desperately ill from a possible heart attack but she was denied medical attention. The night was filled with the moans and cries of the injured women accompanied by the sounds of large rats scurrying between cells.

"The Modern Inquisition," a drawing issued by the Women's Social and Political Union in England around 1910, illustrated the horrors of force-feeding. Suffragettes in England, including Alice Paul and Lucy Burns, had been force-fed during their hunger strikes in prison and the same brutal practice was used on women in the U.S.

When Lucy Burns began calling out to check on each woman's condition the warden ordered her to stop. When she continued, he had her shackled with her hands chained over her head to her cell door. Earlier he had told Denver suffragist Margaret Kessler pointedly, "We are going to stop this picketing if it costs the lives of some of your women and it will cost the lives of some of these women but we are going to stop it." He said Burns and Lewis should be thrown into solitary or lined up and shot.

The women were crammed into small cells in the men's prison and kept without food,

and Force-Feeding in Prison

water, or police matrons until the following day. There was a "sense of constant danger," Brannan reported, and the terrifying fear of assault by lawless men, whether prisoner or guard. "I was exhausted by what I had seen and been through, and spent the night in absolute terror of further attack and of what might still be in store for us," Brannan later wrote. "It seemed to me that everything had been done from the time we reached the workhouse to terrorize us, and my fear lest the extreme of outrage would be worked upon the young girls of our party became intense. It is impossible for me to describe the terror of that night."

Agony of Force-Feeding

When the government did not grant the women the rights of political prisoners they all refused to work. Sixteen began a hunger strike as a final protest against their unjust imprisonment and lengthening sentences. After several days the health of the striking women deteriorated and the government was forced to act or else allow the women to die.

On November 21 prison authorities began the painful and demeaning process of force-feeding Lewis and Burns and then several others. Elizabeth McShane, a former school principal, called it "the most revolting

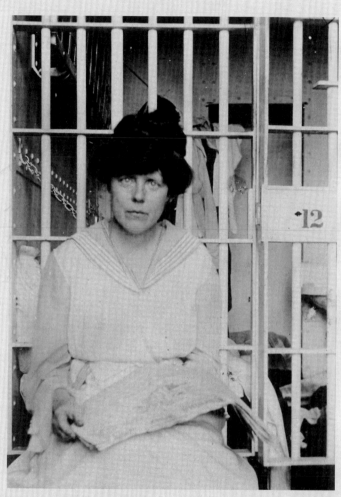

Lucy Burns was sentenced to six months in prison on November 14, having been free only a week after serving two months for her September 4 arrest. She showed understandable signs of strain (above) during her second jail term in July.

experience possible" and Lewis remembered "gasping and suffocating with the agony of it."

Burns wrote on a smuggled-out note that, although held down by five people, "I refused to open mouth. Gannon pushed the tube up left nostril. I turned and twisted my head all I could, but he managed to push it up. It hurts nose and throat very much and makes nose bleed freely. Tube drawn out covered with blood. Operation leaves one very sick. Food dumped directly into stomach feels like a ball of lead." As Sue White pointed out, force-feeding "never serves the purpose of nourishing the victims, as it brings on nausea and violent vomiting, and is but a form of punishment as a means of breaking the will of the person thus violated."

By claiming the status of political prisoners, suffragists raised the ante considerably for the government. If it recognized them as imprisoned for their beliefs it would be forced to treat other prisoners the same way, particularly those in jail for their opposition to the war.

Denying the women political prisoner status triggered work stoppages and, more seriously, hunger strikes that left the women weak, damaged, and close to death. The option of force-feeding did little to bridge the gap and its very nature caused public revulsion. The government wanted to silence the women but instead found itself on the verge of making martyrs of them.

To break the strike, prison authorities transferred Burns and Lewis to the District jail and isolated the hunger strikers. They were told "every conceivable lie," Doris Stevens reported, "in an effort to force the women to abandon their various forms of resistance," but each refused to cooperate until she had consulted with her fellow prisoners. The government, unable to end the strike, faced mass force-feedings and the unpleasant prospect of a strong public outcry in the weeks ahead. ◆

ALICE PAUL
GOT SEVEN MONTHS
BECAUSE
SHE OPPOSED A POLITICAL PARTY
WE DEMAND
THAT SHE BE TREATED AS A
POLITICAL OFFENDER

THE SUFFRAGE PRISONERS
WERE ARRESTED FOR A
POLITICAL OFFENSE.
WE DEMAND
THAT THEY BE TREATED AS
POLITICAL OFFENDERS.

TO ASK FREED
FOR WOMEN IS N
A CRIME
SUFFRAGE PRISO
SHOULD NOT BE TREA
AS CRIMINALS

Winning an Unconditional Release

THE HUNGER and work strikes, along with the abuse in the Occoquan Workhouse, continued until November 23, 1917 when counsel for the imprisoned suffragists succeeded in having the women transferred to the District jail. The weakened prisoners continued their hunger strike together with Alice Paul and the suffragists already there.

The prospect of mass force-feedings and continuing protests finally proved too much for the government. In late November, Doris Stevens reported, "the Administration was forced to capitulate. The doors of the jail were suddenly opened, and all suffrage prisoners were released." With no explanation, their "unjust and arbitrary" sentences were commuted "at the whim of the government,"

Paul noted. This mirrored the way the women had been arrested, often with no warning or reason.

Many suffragists emerged from jail in late November in what one observer called "a state of almost total collapse." Several were carried out on stretchers, their health severely affected by their prison experiences. Returning to Cameron House to recover, the women awaited signs of progress when Congress reconvened.

Above: National Woman's Party members who had originally called for political prisoner status. Lucy Burns is second from left. Right: Nina Allender's cover noted the irony of President Wilson endorsing suffrage in New York while imprisoning suffragists in the capital.

VOL. V, NO. 88
FIVE CENTS

The Suffragist

OFFICIAL WEEKLY ORGAN OF
THE NATIONAL WOMAN'S PARTY

SATURDAY, NOVEMBER 3, 1917

MR. PRESIDENT
WHAT WILL YOU
DO
FOR
WOMAN
SUFFRAGE
?

Drawn by Nina E. Allender

President Wilson Says, "Godspeed to the Cause"

Keeping the Pressure on Congress and the President

AFTER ALL the suffrage pickets had been released from jail, supporters in New York City organized a mass meeting on January 4, 1918, to keep pressure on Congress and the president. Local women (above) bundled up against the winter cold, publicized the Carnegie Hall protest which was held just days before the House of Representatives finally took up the Federal amendment.

The National Woman's Party decided to hold off further action to see if progress was forthcoming in Congress. "We hope that no more demonstrations will be necessary, that the amendment will move steadily on to passage and ratification without further suffering or sacrifice," announced Alice Paul. "But what we do depends entirely upon what the Administration does."

Moved by NAWSA lobbying and political considerations as well as the pickets,

President Wilson finally decided to support the Federal amendment. He quietly expressed his endorsement to congressmen on January 9, a day before the House vote. Paul recognized that his conversion marked a major turning point. "We knew that it and it alone would ensure our success. It means to us only one thing: victory."

During 1917 over a thousand women from across the country had joined the picket

line outside the White House. 218 women from 26 states were arrested and 97 served time in jail for "obstructing traffic." Historian Linda Ford observed that, despite its terrors, "jail created a sisterhood" which strengthened women and prepared them for what lay ahead. ◆

Above: Woman's Party supporters in New York City. Below: Leaving prison after hunger striking.

After the White House pickets were released, thousands of supporters filled the Belasco Theater in Washington D.C. to overflowing on December 6, 1917 to honor, in Alva Belmont's words, "a hundred gallant women who have endured the hardship and humiliation of imprisonment because they love liberty." Each "prisoner of freedom" was presented with a silver pin in the shape of a cell door (above). When Alice Paul's name was called, the audience rose with shouts and cheers. Paul had served five weeks of a seven month sentence and had endured, with Rose Winslow, a 22 day hunger strike. Other women had spent months in prison which severely affected their health. After the NWP's 1918 appeal (below), the arrests, convictions, and imprisonments were all ruled illegal and overturned by the District Court of Appeals.

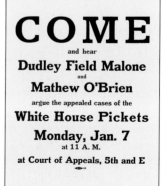

COME
and hear
Dudley Field Malone
and
Mathew O'Brien
argue the appealed cases of the
White House Pickets
Monday, Jan. 7
at 11 A.M.
at Court of Appeals, 5th and E

364

Chapter 15: 1917

Winning New York

Suffragists in New York waged a second major campaign throughout 1916 and 1917 to win the most economically powerful and politically influential state in the nation. After the 1915 defeat, groups throughout the state reorganized into the New York State Woman Suffrage Party and again won the approval of two successive state legislatures to submit the measure to the voters.

Vera Whitehouse led the state WSP, with Harriet Burton Laidlaw as vice-chair and Helen Rogers Reid as treasurer. Mary Garrett Hay again ran the WSP in New York City. Harriot Blatch was committed to war-related work but several of the new leaders were women she had originally recruited.

The war in Europe helped define the theme of the second New York campaign. Suffragists emphasized women's patriotic contributions and the logic of establishing at home the democracy America was fighting to defend abroad. Still, the suffrage drive took place in the midst of deep anxieties about the war, with citizens experiencing a vast national mobilization which demanded tremendous energy and personal sacrifice.

"The war had cut across the picturesque propaganda

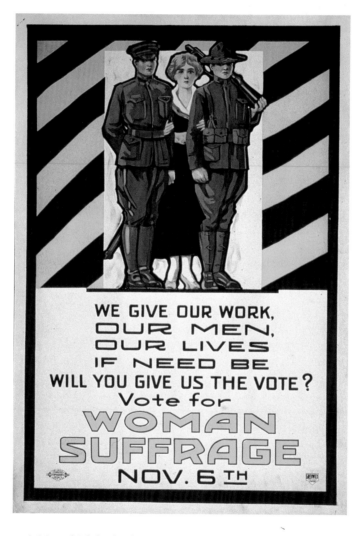

WE GIVE OUR WORK, OUR MEN, OUR LIVES IF NEED BE WILL YOU GIVE US THE VOTE? Vote for WOMAN SUFFRAGE NOV. 6TH

activities which had enlivened the 1915 campaign," noted Mary Peck, and it drew countless women from suffrage work. Gertrude Brown remembered that the suffrage campaign "seemed at its lowest ebb" during the early summer of 1917 but, "as summer waned and election day came nearer, enthusiasm again

began to flame up."

Wanting to focus their resources to insure success, NAWSA set New York as the sole campaign for 1917 although women in Maine insisted on pushing a state amendment against Carrie Catt's advice. Work continued in other states to win full or partial suffrage.

"The Woman's Hour has Struck" proclaimed this hopeful poster (facing page) from the 1917 New York campaign. Fifty years earlier women had been told to wait as it was "The Negro's Hour" and Congress enfranchised Black men without doing anything for women. During World War I, New York suffragists emphasized the themes of patriotism, solidarity, and sacrifice and tied their cause to the defense of democracy. As the campaign poster (left) suggested, suffragists literally linked arms with the war effort when they offered their services to the Federal government. The New York campaign was better organized and funded than any previous drive. But suffragists' energies were divided due to war work and there was no sense of sure victory. A flag pin (above) showed off the WSP's colors.

The Powerful Woman Suffrage Party Organizes an Intensive State Campaign

MARY GARRETT HAY led the Woman Suffrage Party in New York City, which formed the backbone of the state effort. Under Hay, the WSP had built up its own structure modeled on Tammany Hall, the powerful Democratic machine that controlled the city. Party members were organized by Assembly districts, and within every district there were election precincts, each of which had its own captain. In the city alone there were five borough leaders and 2,080 precinct captains.

Learning from their experiences in 1915, suffragists concentrated on strengthening support and weakening opposition in New York City. To that end Hay appointed numerous women connected to Tammany Hall politicians to positions in the WSP. Organizers also reached out to working families and immigrant communities, heeding Rose Schneiderman's advice that the way to the working man was through the working woman.

Above: Mary Garrett Hay (left) and Woman Suffrage Party co-workers.

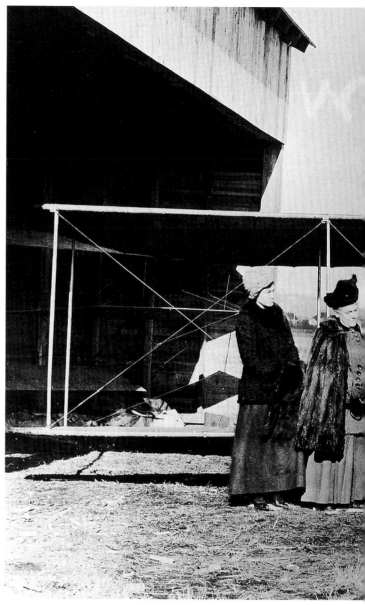

Trying to Win Upstate Voters

OUTSIDE OF the metropolitan area over 80 organizers spread out across upstate New York in 1917 and held thousands of meetings. NAWSA paid four field workers who, with countless volunteers from New York and other states, spoke at military camps, circularized voters, and prepared special literature for churches. Suffragists were especially active in Rochester, Syracuse, Buffalo, and other major cities where they advertised on billboards and street cars, and used large electric signs to flash their message at night.

The number of full suffrage states had not actually changed since 1914, but with presidential suffrage the total electoral votes women had a say in had increased from 91 to 172. New York could add another 43.

Left: Seven states passed presidential suffrage since January 1917, creating a new sense of momentum.

New York suffragists (above) used a biplane bearing the banner "Women Want Liberty Too" to "bombard" the people of Staten Island with suffrage literature on December 2, 1916. Uncle Sam (left) steered this Ship of State float which was mounted on a horse-drawn sled for an upstate winter parade. Blindfolded Justice stood at the prow. The sail displayed a popular rhyme, "For the sake of human justice let the women have the vote, for the hand that rocks the cradle will never rock the boat."

Women's War Work Strengthens Suffrage Image

Like its counterparts in other states, the New York State Woman Suffrage Party established a War Service Committee in 1917 to implement NAWSA's wartime plan. Party members sold Liberty Bonds, worked with the Red Cross and YMCA, and helped conduct a statewide military census. Suffragists also knitted garments and supplies, and planted gardens to raise food for the war effort.

"In order to do all this work and more, we have had to lay aside much of our suffrage work," reported WSP head Vera Whitehouse in August. However, "The change in sentiment in regard to women, because of the assis-

tance they have given the government at war, has been enormous."

Anxious not to lose such favorable support, the WSP publicly condemned the pick-

eting of the White House by the National Woman's Party. Carrie Catt and others felt that the picketing alienated supporters, harassed the president, and confused the

public. NAWSA and the WSP were constantly disassociating themselves from the "disloyal" NWP pickets and never objected to the government's harsh and illegal treatment of the women.

Still, similar arguments were made by all sides. Like the pickets, *The Woman Citizen* repeatedly argued that "suffrage for women is a part of that complete democracy so aptly named by Mr. Wilson as the object of this war." President Wilson did voice his support during the New York contest.

TO THE VOTERS
RESOLUTION ADOPTED BY THE NEW YORK STATE WOMAN SUFFRAGE PARTY CONFERENCE, SARATOGA, AUGUST 30th, 1917.

WHEREAS: The New York State Woman Suffrage Party, an organization with 1,000,000 enrolled women has proclaimed its patriotism and loyalty to the Government by deeds as well as by words, and has gladly sacrificed its own campaign work to give its time and effort to government service.

BE IT RESOLVED: That the New York State Woman Suffrage Party reaffirms its condemnation of the **picketing** of the White House, which tends to harrass the Government in this time of great stress.

It further urges the press and public to discriminate between the small group of **picketers** and the great body of loyal, patriotic women in New York State who while devotedly serving their Government are working for their enfranchisement, November 6th.

Vote for the Woman Suffrage Amendment—Nov. 6

WOMAN SUFFRAGE PARTY OF THE CITY OF NEW YORK
BRONX—406 East 149th Street   MANHATTAN—3 East 38th Street
BROOKLYN—342 Livingston Street   QUEENS—Guion and Jamaica Ave., Richmond Hill, L. I.
RICHMOND—115 Davis Avenue, West New Brighton, S. I.

Above: Bronx suffragists with wartime billboard.
Left: Denouncing the pickets.

A Discouraging Setback in Maine

IN 1917 Maine suffragists disregarded Carrie Catt's advice that they needed more time, money, and experienced leadership to succeed and allowed the legislature to schedule the suffrage measure for a special election on September 10. Despite the demands of the war, members of the Maine Woman Suffrage Association, led by Katharine Reed Balentine, reached out to voters house by house and farm by farm. Supporters eventually distributed one-and-a-half million leaflets, enough for ten for every voter. NAWSA supplied speakers, eight organizers, literature, and a salary for Deborah Knox Livingston of Bangor to run the campaign. She traveled over 20,000 miles in the state speaking and raising money. Anti-suffragists were also very active during the six month contest. When Maine voters defeated the suffrage bill 38,838 to 20,684, nearly two to one, New York suffragists struggled to maintain hope in the face of yet another political setback. Catt responded, "A battle has been lost. Forget it. Others lie ahead."

Winning the Support of the Working Man

TRADE UNIONISTS and settlement house workers were zealous in promoting the suffrage amendment in New York City's working class and immigrant neighborhoods in 1917. Even though the main suffrage organizations tended to be run by the city's social elite, support for the measure was strong among Jewish and other northern and eastern European immigrants, and among others who had fled to the U.S.

Mary Dreier, head of the Women's Trade Union League, served as chair of the Woman Suffrage Party's Industrial Section. She encouraged both male and female organizers and rank and file members to speak out for the suffrage amendment. The State Federation of Labor and other trade unions officially endorsed the measure. After the legislature approved the suffrage bill for the second

Why Working Women Want the Vote

MASS MEETING

Under the Auspices of the
Industrial Section of Third Campaign District
N. Y. State Woman's Suffrage Party
To Celebrate Passage Suffrage
Amendment by Legislature.

ST. ANDREWS' HALL
EAGLE AND HOWARD STS.

Tuesday Evening, April 3rd, 1917.
8 O'CLOCK

SPEAKERS:

Miss Mary Drier   Miss Melinda Scott
Miss Leonora O'Rielly   Mrs. Sarah L. La Force
Mr. John Mitchel   Mr. James L. Mac Hale

Mr. JAMES M. NOLAN, President Central Federation of Labor of Albany. N. Y., PRESIDING.

time on March 12, labor supporters met on April 3 (inset) to celebrate the victory. It was one of the last mass meetings before war was declared.

Woman suffrage was officially supported by all of the state's political parties but suffragists still had to deal with wartime challenges, major party rivalries, the liquor industry, the prohibition concerns of male voters, and the virulent opposition of anti-suffragists.

Above: A speaker from "Labor's Flying Wedge" addressed New Yorkers at an evening street meeting. Left: Leaflet from a pre-war meeting. Top right: Poster from the New York campaign.

VOTE FOR WOMAN SUFFRAGE NOV. 6TH

Proving That "A Million New York Women Want the Vote"

An enormously ambitious house-to-house canvass was the main feature of the 1917 campaign in New York. The tactic was diplomatically chosen, Mary Peck noted, because "it demanded service from every worker, did not offend sensitive patriots as more spectacular efforts would have done, and reached into individual homes as meetings never could." To answer anti-suffragist charges that most women did not want to vote, suffragists spent more than a year going door-to-door in nearly every city and town in the state. They collected the signatures of over one million women who did want to vote. Organizers climbed thousands of tenement stairs, walked country lanes, and visited the homes of the rich and poor. The result was the largest individually-signed petition ever assembled, eventually totaling 1,030,000 names, a majority of the women in the state. For comparison, there were 1,942,000 registered male voters. Suffragists then publicized their remarkable feat as widely as possible.

Right: Signing up women.

Door to door Canvas

Women in New York City (above) prepared to march in the October 27, 1917 suffrage parade carrying a sample ballot box containing some of the one million signatures of women who said they wanted to vote. Suffrage field workers crisscrossed New York state constantly during 1917 speaking and seeking endorsements as well as collecting signatures. The pace was often exhausting, with long distances to cover between meetings. Two suffrage organizers (left) caught up with their reading and mending as they rested during one trip in the shade of a makeshift tent.

A Patriotic Woman's Parade Links Suffrage with the War Effort

I N A POWERFUL SHOW of pre-election strength, a Woman's Parade of 20,000 filled New York's Fifth Avenue on October 27, 1917, led by NAWSA officers and honored guests (above) carrying American flags.

The parade dramatically reflected the impact of the war and the depth of women's involvement. Divisions of wives and mothers of servicemen marched along with women doing war related work, industrial workers, professional women, and male supporters. The parade included 40 marching bands and took three hours to pass.

The dignity and grandeur of the wartime demonstration made a powerful impression on bystanders. "The men on the sidewalks were visibly moved," Mary Peck remembered. "It was not half as long as the mammoth parade of 1915; it did not have to be. Women had taken on a value which nothing but war seems to confer on human beings in the eyes of men."

Above: Anna Howard Shaw (in black) and Carrie Catt (center) lead the 1917 parade. Right: Advertising the president's support. The flag bearer is Katrina Tiffany.

Wartime Emotions Lead to Harsher Opposition

Patriotic appeals linking equal suffrage with the war effort were not enough to silence critics. Anti-suffragists kept up their active opposition, spending tens of thousands of dollars and increasing their personal attacks after the war began. Opponents accused Carrie Catt, Anna Howard Shaw, and other suffragists of having pro-German sympathies and claimed it was disloyal and unpatriotic to work for suffrage in wartime.

Groups like the Manhood Suffrage Association Opposed to Political Suffrage for Women advertised against the initiative, characterizing woman suffrage as an "irreparable calamity." Association president Everett P. Wheeler claimed that "Rome fell because her women entered public life."

After a while "absurd sallies and misstatement of facts grew tiresome," recalled Gertrude Brown. "It was not those who labeled themselves anti-suffragists who delayed the coming of suffrage," she emphasized. "The dangerous opponents of woman suffrage, those who manipulated legislatures and engineered fraudulent elections, did not label themselves."

With such powerful yet largely invisible opposition, the election was very much in doubt. Even in the fall, when Mary Garrett Hay predicted victory, Catt confided to Maud Wood Park, "I think Molly's crazy; for she really believes we'll win, though so far as I know she is the only person who does."

Above: An emotional campaign poster showed men and women joined in the war effort. Below: An opposing trolley car sign.

Mr. Voter: There has not been a single Suffrage Victory at the polls since 1914, but

8 STRAIGHT DEFEATS

1915:
Massachusetts
New Jersey
Pennsylvania
New York

1917:
Maine

1916:
Iowa
South Dakota
West Virginia

The majority against Woman Suffrage in New York in 1915 was 194,984.
Increase it this year by **VOTING NO** on Woman Suffrage, November 6th.

WOMEN'S ANTI-SUFFRAGE ASSOCIATION
280 Madison Avenue

City Voters Put New York Over the Top

Adramatic Procession of the Petitions served as the centerpiece of the Woman's Parade in New York City on October 27, 1917. After collecting the signatures of over a million women throughout the state who wanted to vote, Woman Suffrage Party members mounted the petitions on huge pasteboards which they carried up Fifth Avenue, putting the plea of women for democracy directly in front of voters.

Each placard was carried by two women marching eight abreast while banners gave the totals in all the upstate districts. The petitions from New York City were transported in 62 ballot boxes, each one representing an Assembly district and resting on a decorated platform carried by four women. The petition section alone covered more than half a mile (left) and involved over 2,500 women.

Huge street banners (above) were hung in all the large cities before the election. Suffragists held an estimated 11,000 meetings across the state and distributed some eighteen million leaflets, posters, buttons, and novelties. A burst of newspaper advertising climaxed the final weeks with suffrage arguments appearing almost daily in over 700 morning and evening papers including many in foreign languages.

On November 6, with over 6,300 women serving as poll watchers, New York voters passed woman suffrage by a 102,353 majority, 703,129 to 600,776. Outside of New York City the measure lost by 1,510 votes but city voters more than made up the difference. Suffragists were overjoyed and felt confident that winning New York would open the way to certain victory in the U.S. Congress.

Left: Marchers display a million signatures. Above: Floats pass under a great street banner strung across Fifth Avenue.

Suffragists' "Big Victory" in New York shared the headlines (right) on November 7, 1917 with other election and war news. One factor contributing to the victory in New York City was the decision shortly before the election to keep "hands off" the measure by Tammany Hall politicians, many of whose wives and daughters had become active in the Woman Suffrage Party. Upstate workers in Cayuga county (above) posed in their office for a post-victory portrait surrounded by signs and posters from their long campaign. Banners which the local Political Equality Club carried in suffrage parades stand against the wall.

Victory at Last

ORMER NAWSA president
Anna Howard Shaw (left)
was 70 years old when she
marched for woman suffrage
for the last time during the
1917 campaign. Much of her
remaining energy went into
national service. When the
election returns began to
come in to Woman Suffrage
Party headquarters in New
York, Shaw reportedly turned
to Carrie Catt and said, "Carrie, if we win I don't think I
can stand it." When the news
of victory came just before
midnight, the waiting women
erupted with joy. Historian
Sara Graham noted, "Anna
Howard Shaw was perhaps
the most affected by the long-
awaited victory. The elderly
orator had often been called
on to address suffragists after
bitter defeats. In victory
Shaw's voice failed her, and
she sat with tears streaming
down her face." Catt called
the victory "the Gettysburg of
the woman suffrage move-
ment" that would force Congress to pass the Federal
amendment. ◆

**Left: Anna Howard Shaw
rejoices. Above: A suffrage
fan, one of many novelties
from the 1917 campaign.**

5 cents a copy
December 22, 1917

THE Woman Citizen

THE WOMAN'S JOURNAL FOUNDED 1870

Victrix

Transforming the Political Landscape

SUFFRAGISTS ACROSS the country were ecstatic that metropolitan, influential New York, with its 43 electoral votes and 43 representatives in Congress, had actually been won. National enfranchisement was finally in sight because of the tremendous energy and resources devoted to the New York campaign.

A New Strategy

In 1917 New York suffrage leaders spent more campaign funds than ever before. While in 1915 they had less than $90,000 for the entire state, two years later they raised almost $700,000. "This, at a time when the country was at war, was an achievement which can scarcely be measured. To it suffragists everywhere contributed," noted Gertrude Brown.

Woman Suffrage Party head Vera Whitehouse and treasurer Helen Rogers Reid decided to raise money the way political parties did – from wealthy men. They succeeded in convincing ten men, including Men's League stalwarts James Lees Laidlaw and Samuel Untermeyer, to give $10,000 each, and won pledges for lesser sums from many others. In addition, the first payment from the endowment left by publisher Miriam Leslie came in February 1917, adding $50,000 to the campaign fund.

The night after the election a victory meeting in the Cooper Union was "jammed to suffocation with an ecstatic multitude," according to Mary Peck. When Carrie Catt opened with the words "Fellow Citizens," the crowd went wild and it was some time before she could continue.

New York suffrage leaders in dark outfits posed before the wartime Woman's Parade. Vera Whitehouse, chair of the state Woman Suffrage Party, is in the center with vice chair Harriot Burton Laidlaw (left) and publicity chair Mrs. John Blair (right).

Then she urged the state organization to turn without pause to supporting the Federal amendment.

Following the meeting a *New York Times* editorial blasted women for "bulldozing Congress to pass the Federal Amendment at once." An unrelenting opponent, the *Times* criticized suffragists for going to Washington to lobby for their rights because it interfered with "the vital work of the nation." Failing to distinguish the moderate Woman Suffrage Party from the National Woman's Party, the paper further claimed that "it is but a more dangerous form of picketing which these sorely misguided women are about to undertake . . . . Power brings to them no sense of responsibility. They win this state only to browbeat Congress and to seek to impose suffrage on unwilling states."

That some states still harbored powerful opponents was certainly true for the same election which saw victory in New York also saw the carefully orchestrated repeal of presidential suffrage by antis in Ohio.

Prohibition Passes

The opposition, however, was dealt a decisive blow when Congress passed the prohibition amendment in December 1917, undercutting the liquor and brewery industries that were the wealthiest and best organized opponents of woman suffrage.

Maud Wood Park immediately noted a different feeling in Washington D.C. "The carrying of New York was accepted by the politically wise as the handwriting on the wall," she observed. Politicians as well as suffragists realized that a major turning point had been reached. The enfranchisement of women had become a national issue which even the war could not entirely overshadow.

In two short years suffragists had seen dramatic changes in the political landscape. With new power and renewed hope, NAWSA focused its attention on Congress to finally take up the Federal amendment. ◆

Facing page: A triumphant "Victrix" celebrated the New York victory.

Chapter 16: 1918-1919

The Dramatic Climax to the Federal Amendment

T HERE WAS a new mood in Congress when it reconvened on December 3, 1917 following the victory in New York and a year of unprecedented demonstrations by the National Woman's Party. Despite the turmoil and uncertainty of the war, enthusiasm in the House of Representatives ran so high that suffrage lobbyists had to persuade lawmakers to delay a vote so that the amendment would not be mixed up with the vote on prohibition. After passing the prohibition amendment, Congress sent it to the states to ratify. Referring the suffrage bill to the newly-staffed Woman Suffrage Committee, the House scheduled a vote for January 10, 1918.

As the war continued, several factors worked to suffragists' favor. The Federal government began to investigate the powerful German-American Alliance and uncovered the brewer's association's covert but substantive opposition to both prohibition and woman suffrage. In addition, several midwestern states moved to require full nationalization in order to vote, changing the rules that allowed male immigrants who intended to become citizens to vote immediately.

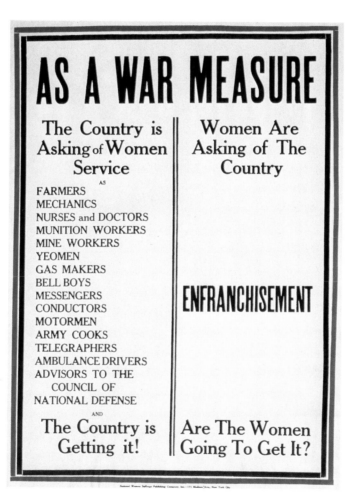

A 1917 leaflet made the case for suffrage in wartime.

Both the National Woman's Party and NAWSA called woman suffrage a war measure after congressional leaders announced they would only consider war-related legislation in 1917. President Woodrow Wilson himself adopted the argument in 1918, calling the enfranchisement of women necessary to uphold his credibility as a democratic leader. By 1918 the suffrage cause had attained a formidable new stature. Josef Keppler, Jr. captured this spirit masterfully in his cartoon (facing page) for *Puck*, "All together now! Stop her!" In a far cry from early caricatures, Keppler chose a classical figure to portray women's cause and showed her dwarfing and crushing ineffective opponents who tried to impede her progress.

The New York victory, together with presidential suffrage in a growing number of states and women's service in the war, gave the suffrage cause a new aura of respectability and promise. Political parties began to court women voters and jostled to claim credit for suffrage advances. In the midst of severe shortages associated with the war, NAWSA held its annual convention in Washington D.C. in December 1917 with a sense of impending triumph.

Maud Wood Park was asked to lead NAWSA's Congressional Committee by Carrie Catt shortly after the 1916 Atlantic City meeting which approved Catt's "Winning Plan." The Massachusetts activist responded that she was "too much a reformer and too little an opportunist" to be a good lobbyist. However, her thoroughly efficient, determined, and diplomatic efforts helped give substance to the plan proposed by Catt, and Park became one of the movement's premier legislative analysts. As head of the "Front Door Lobby" she kept a very low profile and speculated that journalists probably wondered how she kept her job. Congressmen, on the other hand, praised her unfailing tact and discretion. Park later served as the first president of the League of Women Voters, and her bequest of archival materials to Radcliffe became the core of the Schlesinger Library on the History of Women.

AN ADDRESS

to the

CONGRESS OF THE UNITED STATES

by

Carrie Chapman Catt

President of the National American Woman Suffrage Association

"SHE HAS GIVEN ME TO DEMOCRACY ; GIVE DEMOCRACY TO HER"

From The Woman Citizen

National Woman Suffrage Publishing Company, Inc.
171 Madison Avenue · · · New York, N.Y.

Demanding Democracy for Women in a Climate of War

DELEGATES TO NAWSA's annual convention in December 1917 heard what was probably Carrie Catt's most important speech, framed as a broader address to the members of Congress. *The Woman Citizen* as described it as a thorough and "absolutely conclusive argu-ment" for the Federal amendment. Calling woman suffrage inevitable, just like political parties, Catt declared, "The idea will not perish; the party which opposes it may."

The hour-and-a-half long speech was reprinted and distributed to every senator and representative. Later it was revised and sent to the members of the 48 state legislatures. The theme of democracy denied was emphasized by both NAWSA and the National Woman's Party.

Above: Carrie Catt's widely circulated 1917 speech.

NAWSA's "Front Door Lobby" Earns Respect in the Capital

NAWSA's Congressional Committee grew into a powerful presence in the capital by 1918. Nicknamed the "Front Door Lobby" by the press as a compliment for its straightforward methods, the committee organized political support and brought women from around the country to persuade their representatives to support the Federal amendment.

Between 1917 and 1919 the lobby operated out of what committee head Maud Wood Park called "a magnificent and uncomfortable mansion" in Washington D.C. which members referred to as Suffrage House. Countless workers were housed in the vast building despite its constantly chilly rooms. In the evenings the women huddled together around a heater to discuss the day's lobbying experiences and news of the war.

On June 7, 1918 members of NAWSA's "Front Door Lobby" (above) met in the capital with Honorary President Anna Howard Shaw while she was working for the Council of National Defense. The women then called on the president to thank him for encouraging swift action by the Senate. Unlike the National Woman's Party, Carrie Catt and other NAWSA leaders were convinced that Wilson was doing all in his power to get Congress to pass the suffrage measure.

Leading members of NAWSA's Front Door Lobby (above) posed in Washington D.C. on June 7, 1918 before meeting with President Wilson. In the front are chair Maud Wood Park, Anna Howard Shaw, Carrie Catt, and vice-chair Helen Gardener. In the back are Rose Young, editor of *The Woman Citizen*, Mrs. George Bass, representing Democratic women, and lobby executive secretary Ruth White.

The House of Representatives Passes Suffrage –

WITH UNPRECEDENTED congressional support, the woman suffrage amendment was finally brought to a vote in the U.S. House of Representatives on January 10, 1918.

NAWSA and National Woman's Party lobbyists, together with their congressional allies in both parties, spared no effort in making sure that all their supporters were in their seats for the vote. Representatives had been interviewed repeatedly and the women knew the exact position of each one. Suffragists were full of hope but realized they would lose if just one man wavered and changed his vote.

The measure needed a two-thirds vote to pass and, as Maud Wood Park noted, "We knew our victory hung by a thread." The bill had been defeated on January 12, 1915 by 204 to 174.

The persuasive arguments of NAWSA's Carrie Catt and Helen Gardener, together with the confrontational actions of the National Woman's Party, helped convince Woodrow Wilson to finally support the Federal amendment on January 9, just a day before the vote.

Heroic Loyalty

Excited and apprehensive, suffragists lined up early for seats in the gallery on January 10 while lobbyists made sure all representatives were pres-

"Shattering the Chain." The House vote on January 10, 1918 approving the woman suffrage amendment broke the chain of inequality in this cartoon by Harry Murphy from the *New York Journal*. On the very same day the British Parliament finally approved votes for women.

ent. The sense of history was almost palpable to those who had worked so long and so hard to see this day. "The intensity of suffragists had long ago communicated itself to many House members," Catt later wrote, "who by now were as strongly committed to the success of the measure as the heart of a suffragist could wish."

Some men went to extraordinary lengths to be present for the vote. Republican floor leader James R. Mann of Illinois left the hospital for the first time in months to weakly take his seat for the vote. Other congressmen left their sickbeds to be present. Just before the roll call, Indiana representative Henry A. Barnhart, unable to walk, was car-

ried in from the hospital on a stretcher which was set down near the Speaker's desk.

One representative, Thetus W. Sims of Tennessee, had slipped on the ice but refused to have his broken shoulder treated despite excruciating pain because it might mean he would miss the vote. He even stayed on to convince those still wavering. Most poignantly, New York congressman Frederick C. Hicks, Jr. left his wife's death bed at her insistence to cast his vote for suffrage. He then returned home for her funeral.

Jeannette Rankin opened the debate at noon and was followed by dozens of speakers both for and against the measure. At five o'clock the vote was called. Suffragists waited as each member recorded his vote exactly according to their projections. When the first roll call showed that the amendment had just barely passed, the gallery burst into cheers. After two more tense roll calls, the vote held and the chamber erupted in celebration. The bill had passed 274-136, just a single vote over the necessary two-thirds majority.

"On the floor our side was cheering wildly, and men standing below shouted their congratulation to the group of us in the front row above. . . . I had a hard time to keep back the tears," recalled Maud Wood Park.

But the U. S. Senate Refuses to Act

Leaving the gallery, the triumphant women broke into song.

Attention was immediately turned to the Senate but suffrage leaders knew that they were still ten votes short in that chamber.

Convincing Senators

Suffrage lobbyists slowly won over individual senators, calling on pressure from their home districts and the influence of friends and party leaders. As suffragists gained votes, Catt bought a new dress in preparation for a ratification tour. But lobby vice-chair Helen Gardener cautioned her, "You can't hustle the Senate," and she proved to be sadly correct. The vote had been 35 to 34 against the measure in March 1914.

In the House the measure had gained 100 more supporters since the vote in 1915, mostly from new suffrage victories. "Clearly it was state gains that carried us over the top," Park noted, emphasizing the merit of Catt's strategy. In the Senate, however, votes were hard to win. Even some senators from equal suffrage states opposed the amendment, including Senators Wadsworth from New York and Borah from Idaho. A vote was scheduled for May 1. But as the date approached Senate leaders again postponed action.

Still hoping for Senate pas-

"Blocked." After the Federal amendment passed the House its progress was blocked by the Senate, a situation clearly portrayed by this cartoon from the *Memphis Commercial Telegram*. Debate and delay consumed the first nine months of the year as the Senate refused to act.

sage yet aware of the staunch opposition, Catt drew up two plans for NAWSA. One detailed an immediate nationwide ratification drive to win the vote by 1920 while the other outlined a bold strategy to defeat four opponents in the Senate and replace them with four supporters. Catt wrote to Mary Peck, "We have plans to ratify, when and if there is something to ratify, and plans for making trou-

ble," if not. After lobbying every senator, suffragists knew that they were still two votes short.

Lobby members were in constant motion, keeping supporters in line and trying to win over others. Senate leaders repeatedly delayed the vote and NAWSA again sought President Wilson's aid. When he wrote a brief message in June urging passage, Catt complained that it was

not strong enough so Gardener told her to rewrite it herself and she would ask the president to sign it. He did. But despite pressure from all sides, the Senate recessed for the summer without taking action. A last-minute vote was blocked by a Democratic filibuster.

Nationwide Action

Catt, thoroughly disgusted, wrote in a June issue of *The Woman Citizen,* "To deny women the vote longer in any part of the country makes of our war aims a travesty and a lie. It offers vindication to the German claim that America pretends to lofty aims but they are mere talk!" But in the meantime she continued to promote Liberty Loans, in part to help keep the movement visible as the war continued. She also called for more pressure from home districts and the country as a whole, resulting in thousands of letters, telegrams, resolutions, and a new nationwide petition drive.

In addition, the National Woman's Party, after holding off all year, swung back into action. It threatened new demonstrations independent of, and not welcomed by, NAWSA to keep the cause before the public and to pressure politicians in the capital. When Congress reconvened in August 1918, both suffrage groups resumed their efforts to force a Senate vote. ◆

A New Campaign Demanding Action in the Senate Leads to New Arrests

Disregarding the hostile and repressive wartime climate, Alice Paul and the National Woman's Party organized a new series of demonstrations in the fall of 1918 to protest Senate inaction. The first took place on August 6, the birthday of the late organizer Inez Milholland Boissevain. Led by Hazel Hunkins carrying the American flag, 100 suffragists marched with tricolored banners to the Lafayette Monument, just across the street from the White House, while hundreds of curious bystanders watched.

When Dora Lewis stepped up to speak, police immediately seized and arrested her while "the great audience stood in absolute and amazed silence," remembered Doris Stevens. Suffragists "one after another came forward in an attempt to speak, but no one was allowed to continue. Wholesale arrests followed."

At their trial the defendants refused to cooperate. Paul told the court, "As a dis-enfranchised class we feel that we are not subject to the jurisdiction of this court." Nonetheless the judge sentenced 26 women to ten to fifteen days for holding a meeting without a permit and for climbing on a statue.

The women were sent to an old workhouse in the swamps near the District prison which had been abandoned as uninhabitable nine years earlier. There they demanded to be treated as political prisoners and again began a hunger strike in protest.

Police roughly broke up other demonstrations on August 12 and 14 but several suffragists still managed to speak out briefly before being arrested. "We resent the suppression of our demands," Elsie Hill shouted at one point, "but our voices will carry across the country and down through time."

Above: Speaking in front of Lafayette's statue. Right: Police arrest suffragists on August 6 in Lafayette Park.

Harsh Penalties for Protesting Senate Opposition

The miserable, dungeon-like workhouse where suffragists were imprisoned in August 1918 featured foul water and a vile, permeating odor described as "insidious and revolting." When one woman after another became violently ill, all moved their straw pallets from their damp cells to the stone floor of the hallway to escape the noxious stench. When told to return to their iron cots, they all refused as a body.

Olympia Brown, veteran suffrage leader from Wisconsin, was 84 when she joined a National Woman's Party demonstration across from the White House in 1918. Brown had become impatient with NAWSA's state-oriented petitioning and was attracted by the aggressive energy of the Congressional Union and the NWP. In Alice Paul she and others saw the single-purpose drive that had distinguished Susan B. Anthony. Brown once declared, "I belonged to this party before it was born." For years she worked in state campaigns, pressured Congress, and in 1892 founded the Federal Suffrage Association which tried to win women the right to vote for House members. Brown served on the Advisory Board of the NWP and was probably the oldest suffragist to demonstrate outside the White House. President Wilson himself bore indirect witness to her and the NWP's impact when he claimed before Congress that "the voices of the militants do not reach me." It was with the more conservative and "acceptable" NAWSA that he naturally allied himself.

Supporters outside organized vehement protests. After five days all the women were released, trembling with fever and chills and weakened by their hunger strike. When Alice Paul announced that a new demonstration would take place after the prisoners had recovered, District authorities were quick to grant a permit. But the Senate still refused to act.

Right: Refusing their cells.

A Controversial Congressional Card File Attracts Politicians' Interest

THE NATIONAL Woman's Party operated out of Cameron House, called the "Little White House," just across Lafayette Park from the president's residence. There the NWP's Legislative Committee, headed first by Anne Martin and later by Maud Younger, maintained a much-discussed Congressional Index Card File which contained regularly-updated information on each of the 581 members of Congress. In addition to their views on suffrage, the cards included as much other personal information as suffragists could obtain. The notorious card file became a source of intense interest to some politicians who speculated about "what else" was on their cards. The NWP destroyed the card file after the Federal amendment passed.

Above: Alice Paul (right) and Dora Lewis discussed the new campaign while Paul's secretary (center) took notes. Below: Updating the congressional card file.

A Dramatic Protest Chides "Words Without Action"

AFTER PRESIDENT Wilson promised that he would "do all I can" and then seemed to do nothing to get a vote scheduled in the Senate, the National Woman's Party organized another protest on

September 16, 1918. "We took these words of the president to the base of Lafayette Monument" facing the White House, recalled Doris Stevens, "and burned them in a flaming torch." Lafayette had also fought for American liberty.

Flanked by women holding the NWP's vibrant purple, white, and gold banners, Lucy Branham burned Wilson's "hollow phrases" in "protest against the action of the President and his party in delaying the liberation of American women." Supporters in the crowd cheered as she declared, "The torch which I hold symbolizes the burning indignation of the women who for years have been given words without action."

Above: Lucy Branham torches President Wilson's words. Lucy Burns is on the right.

The Senate Defeats Suffrage Again

RESPONDING TO pressure by both NAWSA and the National Woman's Party, Senate leaders reversed themselves on September 17, 1918 and scheduled a vote for October 1. As the date approached, suffragists descended on the capital hoping to see the successful climax to their long struggle with Congress. Suffrage leaders, however, knew that they were still two votes short. Hoping that President Wilson could win over the final two senators needed, Carrie Catt again asked him to intervene. He agreed to address the Senate the day before the vote, a nearly unprecedented move for a president.

On September 30, looking aged and strained by the war, Wilson told the assembled lawmakers that the nation needed "the direct and authoritative participation of women in our counsels. . . . I tell you plainly that the measure which I urge upon you is vital to the winning of the war and to the energies alike of preparation and of battle."

Maud Wood Park observed, "Perhaps if the vote had been taken immediately the result might have been different. But as soon as the President left the Chamber, opposed senators began to refute his arguments and to rattle once more the dry bones of state rights objections."

Despite all the pressure the Senate defeated the bill 34-62, two votes short of the necessary two-thirds. "Not a shred of doubt was left about the stand of any of them," Park noted. "The President's noble appeal had not changed a single vote."

Doris Stevens of the NWP observed that after five years of resistance Wilson "could not overcome with additional eloquence the opposition which he himself had so long formulated, defended, encouraged and solidified, especially when that eloquence was followed by either no action or only half-hearted efforts."

Indignant over the defeat, the NWP produced new banners like the one above to inform the public and provoke action on Capitol Hill. Suffragists also turned to an unprecedented involvement in the 1918 elections.

Above: Protesting continuing opposition in the Senate.

Picketing the Senate Brings a Violent Response

MEMBERS OF the National Woman's Party picketed the Senate following the October 1 defeat to protest its ongoing opposition to the suffrage amendment. However, each time the women approached the Capitol Building they were seized. Police ripped the banners out

of their hands and dragged them to the guard room. There the women were held without charge until after the Senate adjourned.

This went on almost daily for weeks. Small detachments of women who tried to stand with flags and lettered banners outside the Senate were assaulted and illegally detained to maintain "peace and order" on the Capitol grounds.

Not bowing to intimidation, members of the NWP announced that they would march onto the Senate floor and burn the hypocritical words of anti-suffrage members. On October 13, with senators hanging from the balcony to watch, a battalion of police blocked the line of suffragists and took them all into custody. On October 28, Alice Paul, Lucy Burns, and nineteen other women were again manhandled and held until nightfall. A few days later the women dispensed with banners and protested their illegal detentions with simple black arm bands mourning the "Death of Justice" in the Senate.

Above: Capitol police seize suffragists' banners while young men watch.

Influencing the 1918 Election

AFTER THE U.S. Senate defeated the Federal amendment on October 1, 1918, NAWSA immediately implemented its backup plan. Organized and experienced after years of work, suffragists in four states – Massachusetts, New Jersey, New Hampshire, and Delaware – joined with others working to defeat four anti-suffrage Senate candidates. "It was a colossal undertaking in view of the short time and small funds," Maud Wood Park remembered. In addition, two prominent suffragists in the west were themselves running for the Senate and four referendum campaigns were underway. The National Woman's Party for the third time went after the "party in power" by sending organizers west to work against all Democratic candidates for the Senate. Enfranchised or not, women were gaining recognition as an active and potentially powerful force in national politics.

Above: Suffragists were ready to flex their political muscles in 1918, as suggested by this editorial cartoon by Evans from *The Baltimore American*.

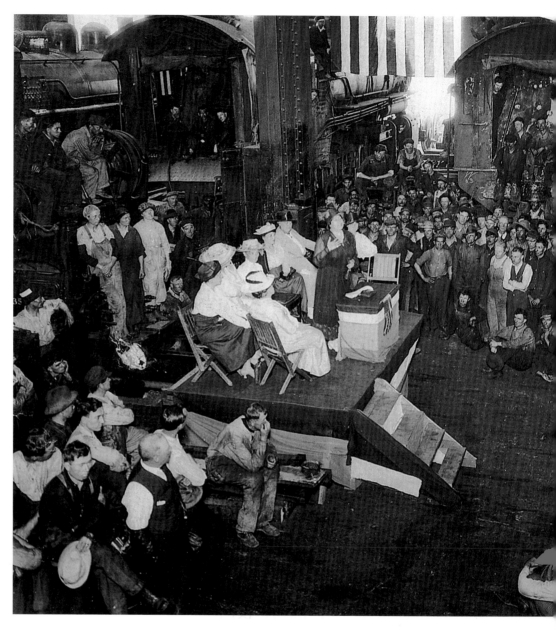

National Woman's Party organizer Margaret Whittemore (above) spoke to a packed gathering of railway workers in Pocatello, Idaho, in 1918 and asked them to pressure Republican Senator Borah to support the Federal suffrage amendment. He had promised to vote for it but went back on his word after the election. Uniformed soldiers (right) in Grand Rapids showed their support during the suffrage campaign in Michigan.

War and Epidemic Add Heartbreak to the Four Campaigns in 1918

DURING THE discouraging days of 1918 suffragists carried out campaigns in Michigan and Oklahoma, both for the third time, in South Dakota for the fifth time, and in Louisiana, the first drive in the south. Each measure had won the approval of the state legislature.

The four campaigns were waged under the most trying conditions. They strained severely the resources of both state and national organizations. Besides the burdens of the war there was also a deadly influenza epidemic which swept the country in late 1918, killing hundreds of thousands of people and leaving countless families in mourning.

While suffragists in Michigan and Oklahoma, overtaxed with war work, welcomed NAWSA's involvement, Louisiana supporters asked the association to stay away so as to not risk charges of outside agitation. Antis were still active, repeating claims that women did not want to vote and challenging the patriotism of women working for their own enfranchisement.

A key part in Carrie Catt's overall plan, state campaigns were still arduous and costly ordeals which offered no guarantee of success. After the elections were over, NAWSA field worker Nettie Rogers Shuler summarized the feelings of many organizers: "It is safe to say that all of them as they emerged from this trench warfare again questioned the advisability of trying to secure suffrage by the State route."

Above: Caring for a victim of the deadly influenza epidemic. Below: A flier from the difficult 1918 campaign in Oklahoma.

Anne Martin decided to run as an Independent candidate for the U.S. Senate from Nevada in 1918 to break new ground for women and to promote the Federal suffrage amendment. Fellow westerner Sara Bard Field described Martin as one of the "most notable and persistent leaders" of the feminist movement. The University of Nevada recognized her as a "pioneer in the triumphant struggle for women's rights." A staunch advocate of peace and responsible citizenship, Martin encouraged women to participate more actively in government. She criticized the new League of Women Voters for focusing more on education than direct political involvement by women.

Vote for
ANNE MARTIN
Independent
For
United States Senate
NOMINATED BY NEARLY TEN
THOUSAND NEVADA VOTERS

Two Leading Suffragists Run for the U.S. Senate

ANNE MARTIN, vice-chair of the National Woman's Party, declared herself a candidate for the U.S. Senate in 1918 hoping to serve the remainder of the term of a deceased Nevada senator. Leaving her NWP post she became the first woman to run for the Senate, declaring her candidacy just before Representative Jeannette Rankin of Montana announced hers. "I want to knock the fear out of the hearts of women," Martin declared. "Even if I should not win, it will never seem so strange when a woman tries it."

Both women ran without party support or significant funds but hoped that women voters in particular would support them. Both women were also subjected to innuendo and vicious personal attacks during their races.

Rankin, whose position as Representative-at-large had been eliminated, felt pressured to run for the Senate partially to disprove a rumor that she had been bribed not to by the Republicans. She came in third.

Martin was assailed for her arrests for suffrage and was criticized for being "masculine" and too old, although at 42 she was younger than most senators. Her election drive benefited enormously from the help of NWP supporters including campaign manager Mabel Vernon. After coming in third in the 1918 race with 4,603 votes out of 25,563, Martin ran again for a full term in 1920 but only garnered a few hundred more votes.

Above: Dr. Margaret Long drove Anne Martin, in the front passenger's seat, throughout Nevada during her second campaign. Below: Martin with Colorado Senator John F. Shafroth on the steps of the Senate Office Building.

YOUR VOTE should help to

DEFEAT

JOHN W. WEEKS

for United States Senator at the election November 5th

His record in Congress speaks for itself. He was,—

AGAINST the popular election of United States Senators. If Mr. Weeks' opinion had prevailed, you would not now have the opportunity to vote for or against him. (Paired against, May 13, 1912, Cong. Rec. Page 6367).

AGAINST the right of the United States to tax incomes. This was at a time when taxation of large incomes only was contemplated; without this right now, it would be impossible to finance the war. The public demand was so great that the vote stood 318 in favor and 14 against. Mr. Weeks was one of fourteen. (Voted NO, July 12, 1909, C. R. 4440).

AGAINST increasing taxation on war profits. Amendments to War Revenue Bill of 1917. (Voted NO, Sept. 1 and 4, 1917, C. R. Pages 6503, 6560 and 6570).

AGAINST the creation of the Federal Trade Commission, the body which is undermining the alleged monopoly of the Meat Packers, and which provides a prompt and inexpensive redress for victims, large and small, of unfair practices in interstate commerce. (Voted NO, Aug. 5, 1914, C. R. 13319).

AGAINST the establishment of the Shipping Board, involving the whole shipping program, which has proved so successful in getting food and troops to France. (Voted NO, Aug. 18, 1916, C. R. 12825).

AGAINST the Armor Plate Bill, thus voting to prevent the Government from establishing its own plant whereby millions of dollars could be saved which otherwise would go to the big steel corporations. (Voted NO, May 21, 1916, C. R. 4553).

AGAINST the Clayton Act, an act to strengthen the Sherman Anti-trust Law in curbing the abuses of big business while shielding from unjust attack labor and farm organizations. (Paired against, Sept. 2, 1914, C. R. 14609).

AGAINST extending government credit to farmers, Rural Credits Bill. (Paired against, C. R. 7412, May 4, 1916).

AGAINST the Equal Suffrage Amendment to the United States Constitution, in spite of the stand taken by the National Republican Committee and in spite of the President's personal appeal to the Senate to submit this measure to the Legislatures of the various States as a help in the war emergency. (Voted NO, Oct. 1, 1918, C. R. 11914).

AGAINST the extension of the Parcel Post, a measure to benefit the people and limit further the power of the Express Companies. (Voted NO, Feb. 27, 1914, C. R. 4017).

AGAINST the Prohibition Amendment to the United States Constitution. (Voted NO, August 1, 1917, C. R. 5666).

He voted:—

FOR the Shields Water Power Bill. This bill, if passed, would have turned over the public water power of the country to private interests. (Voted YES, Dec. 14, 1917, C. R. 300).

FOR the reduction of benefits of the Soldiers' and Sailors' insurance to our boys who are fighting in France. (Voted YES, Oct. 4, 1917, C. R. 7753, 8480 and 8489).

DO THESE VOTES REPRESENT YOU?

If not, vote AGAINST John W. Weeks.

It is your PATRIOTIC DUTY in these critical times to GO TO THE POLLS ON ELECTION DAY and help DEFEAT a man with a record like this.

JOHN S. CODMAN, 50 Congress St., Boston.
HENRY D. NUNN, 68 Devonshire St., Boston.
WILLIAM SHAW, Ballardvale, Mass.
HENRY D. SLEEPER, 40 Park St., Northampton, Mass.

Shortly before the 1918 election suffragists in Massachusetts prepared the flier above which was sent to voters of both parties throughout the state. Political observers called it one of the best campaign documents they had ever seen. Citing a politician's voting record was a tactic which had new power on men who now faced popular election. Until 1914 senators were selected by the state legislatures, not by the voters, and many had grown old representing powerful special interests. In fact, ten elderly senators died during the 65th Congress alone, keeping suffragists busy lining up pro-suffrage candidates to become their successors.

Suffragists Target Key Opponents in Four Senate Races

SETTING ASIDE her organization's traditional non-partisan stand in 1918, NAWSA leader Carrie Catt decided that the only way to win the necessary votes in the Senate was by defeating opponents in four Senate races. The four were John Weeks of Massachusetts, head of the Republican state machine, New Hampshire Republican George Moses, and Democrats Willard Saulsbury of Delaware and David Baird of New Jersey.

The most dramatic effort was in Massachusetts where suffragists had previously campaigned to defeat unfriendly state representatives. The Massachusetts Woman Suffrage Association and the Boston Equal Suffrage Association for Good Government formed a "Non-Partisan Committee to Defeat Weeks" and built an effective coalition of farmers, trade unionists, prohibitionists, Jews, and other constituencies. The committee prepared and sent out 370,000 copies of an impressive flier summarizing the Senator's votes on 13 critical issues and ran a last-minute advertising blitz which helped bring down the powerful anti-suffragist by 19,000 votes.

Saulsbury was also defeated in Delaware. This gave suffragists the two votes they needed. Maud Wood Park rejoiced, "Unless death or the breaking of promises intervened, we were assured of victory in the next Senate." But the current Congress sat until March and no one knew when the 66th Congress would convene.

Above: Carrie Catt (left) and Mary Garret Hay cast their ballots in New York City for the first time on November 5, 1918 after being met by a battery of cameras and reporters.

Suffragists Win Three Out of Four States

SUFFRAGISTS WAGED four difficult state campaigns in 1918 and NAWSA did what it could to supply organizers, literature, and press material. Leaving women in Louisiana to work independently as requested, NAWSA sent 18 organizers into South Dakota, Michigan, and Oklahoma and instructed state workers to collect the signatures of all the women who said they wanted to vote. Over 310,000 names were collected and then published in newspapers and on leaflets in the counties where the women lived. This proved to be a powerful factor.

South Dakota

Led by Mary Shields Pyle, and experienced after four campaigns, members of South Dakota's Universal Franchise League again appealed to farmers, businessmen, and other groups of voters. Supporters spoke at countless meetings across the state, answering questions and distributing literature. "Everywhere that voters gathered, there they were," reported Ruth Hipple, editor of the *South Dakota Messenger.* Such persistent and intensive work finally paid off when male voters approved the measure on November 6 by 20,384 votes, 49,318 to 28,934.

Michigan

In Michigan woman suffrage enjoyed the support of many prominent men and the main political parties, leading some state workers to believe that it would pass without much work on their part. A campaign plan was approved only after Carrie Catt drove home the point that women should not expect to be "rewarded" with the vote for their war work. The drive was led by Mrs. Percy J. Farrell of Detroit with the help of the WCTU.

In addition, various individual groups worked in different cities running and financing their own efforts.

Suffragists distributed 500,000 leaflets in Detroit alone, posted 13,000 posters, and advertised in one thousand streetcars. Speakers addressed workers outside automobile factories, and teachers and business women in Detroit financed a suffrage

A post card from the 1918 Louisiana campaign.

worker for several months. Supporters were overjoyed when voters finally approved the measure on November 5 by 34,506 votes, 229,790 to 195,284.

Oklahoma

The Oklahoma referendum was sought by unprepared supporters against NAWSA's advice and, after it was scheduled, state women moved that NAWSA assume complete responsibility for the campaign. The Oklahoma Woman Suffrage Association formed a fragile campaign committee headed by Mrs. Clarence Henley and NAWSA sent in an increasing number of workers together with funds and literature. The National Association eventually spent $20,000, the most it contributed to a state campaign, and referred to it as "the Oklahoma Ordeal."

NAWSA officer Nettie Rogers Shuler, who helped organize clubs throughout the state, ran the campaign for the final two months. She was joined by her daughter Marjorie, who took charge of press work. Supporters distributed one-and-a-half million leaflets and inserted over 120,000 suffrage supplements into newspapers throughout the state. Although the political parties supported the measure, the governor and highly placed state officials were opposed and did all they could to sabotage it. To carry, the amendment needed to

Suffrage supporters, in front of flag (right), spoke to men outside a Ford plant in Michigan before the 1918 election.

get a majority of the total votes cast at the election. Unmarked ballots, or "silent votes," were counted as negative.

Since the measure was printed on a separate ballot, suffragists produced tens of thousands of red, white, and blue sample ballots to show men how to vote for equal suffrage. When some polling places ran out of the official ballots, suffragists had more printed themselves to reduce the number of silent votes. On election day they watched the vote carefully, confirmed the returns, and then had them published immediately to discourage any tampering. With their vigilance and thorough organization the measure passed on November 8

by 25,428 votes, 106,909 to 81,481.

Louisiana

In Louisiana, the first southern state to hold a suffrage referendum, the measure appealed to many citizens as a better alternative than increasingly likely Federal action. Louisiana suffragists were led by a joint campaign committee including the Louisiana Woman Suffrage Association, headed by prominent New Orleans sisters Kate and Jean Gordon, and the Louisiana Woman Suffrage Party, led by Lydia Wickliffe Holmes.

Although the state association pursued state action exclusively while the WSP also supported the Federal

amendment, the two organizations united for the 1918 campaign and coordinated the efforts of over 600 volunteers. Plans for a final "whirlwind campaign," however, were dashed by bad weather and the influenza epidemic Voter turnout was low and the amendment was defeated on November 5 by 3,504 votes, 23,077 to 19,573. Still, the solid victories in three more states increased support in Washington D.C. and helped pave the way for congressional action.

The War Ends

When the war finally ended on November 11, 1918, only a few days after the elections, Carrie Catt immediately demanded women representa-

tives in the U.S. peace delegation. "If women are not heard at the peace conference now to be held, this war will not have been a war to end war," she claimed. Her hopes, however, went unrealized.

The National Woman's Party continued picketing the Senate until it recessed on November 21. Then a dozen NWP members marched from the Senate Office Building to the Capitol with a banner that read, "America enters the peace conference with unclean hands for democracy is denied to her people." Doris Stevens reported they were savagely attacked by police, who violently "dragged and pushed Alice Paul about as though personally enraged with her." ◆

Burning the President's Words

AFTER THE 1918 election, the suffrage amendment could still be taken up at any time by the Senate. Many women believed with Maud Wood Park that, since the Republicans would control the new Congress and one more senator had been won, "the Democrats would not let this last chance of credit for passing the amendment go for lack of one vote." Stubborn opponents in the Senate blocked another vote, however, and the National Woman's Party's protests continued.

In mid-December, with President Wilson in France, the NWP launched a new drive, in Doris Steven's words, "bold and offensive enough" to threaten his prestige in Europe. Suffragists announced that, on the anniversary of the Boston Tea Party, they would burn the speeches and books by the president in which he referred to "liberty," "freedom," and "democracy."

Late in the afternoon of December 16, over 300 women marched solemnly past the White House to the foot of the Lafayette monument across the street. "A slight mist added beauty to the pageant," Stevens remembered. "Half the procession carried lighted torches; the other half banners. The crowd gathered silently, somewhat awe-struck by the scene. Massed about that statue, we felt a strange strength and solidarity, we felt again that we were a part of the universal struggle for liberty."

Lighting a fire in a Grecian urn, nineteen women from across the country spoke to the gathered crowd before dropping the president's words into the flaming cauldron. "President Wilson has gone abroad to establish democracy in foreign lands when he has failed to establish democracy at home," declared Elizabeth Selden Rogers. "We burn his words on liberty today, not in malice or anger, but in a spirit of reverence for truth."

Olympia Brown, 84-years-old, told the crowd, "I have fought for liberty for 70 years and I protest the president's leaving our country with this old fight here unwon." Then she dropped Wilson's speech into the flames.

Above: Suffragists gathered in Lafayette Park in the mist.

Watchfires of Freedom Demand Action from President Wilson

WITH THE start of the new year, the National Woman's Party began a new campaign, building "watchfires of freedom" in front of the White House. The NWP believed that President Wilson could deliver the last needed vote in the Democratic-controlled Senate but was not trying hard enough. The

PRESIDENT WILSON IS DECEIVING THE WORLD
WHEN HE APPEARS AS THE PROPHET OF DEMOCRACY

PRESIDENT WILSON HAS OPPOSED THOSE WHO
DEMAND DEMOCRACY FOR THIS COUNTRY

HE IS RESPONSIBLE FOR THE DISFRANCHISEMENT
OF MILLIONS OF AMERICANS

WE IN AMERICA KNOW THIS
THE WORLD WILL FIND HIM OUT.

watchfires kept their demand before him and the public.

The first watchfire was lit on January 1, 1919, commemorating Joan of Arc who was "denied by the King after serving him." As a bell at the Little White House tolled, Dora Lewis dropped the president's recent speech into a blazing Grecian urn which contained wood from a tree in Philadelphia's Independence Square.

Soldiers and sailors in the crowd immediately rushed the women, overturned the urn, and tried to put the fire out. Over the following days the suffragists repeatedly rekindled the fire and weathered attacks by men and boys who broke the urn, scattered the fire, and ripped down their banners.

Alice Paul, Annie Arneil, and Julia Emory stood guard over the "perpetual fire" in the freezing rain throughout the first night. After four days police began arresting the women but others took their place, relighting the fires with logs soaked in kerosene. By the end of the month 29 women had been arrested. Sentenced to five days in jail, they all immediately went on hunger strikes.

Above: Suffragists tended the watchfire in front of the White House despite the winter cold.

Sue Shelton White, an officer with the Tennessee Equal Suffrage Association since 1913, left the NAWSA affiliate in 1918 to lead the state chapter of the rival National Woman's Party. A respected court reporter for ten years, "Miss Sue" championed Maud Younger's right to speak about the imprisoned pickets in late 1917 when local officials tried to deny her meeting space. Defending Younger from accusations of being "pro-German," however, triggered charges of disloyalty from Carrie Catt. White responded that if necessary "I would have to join the pickets ... not so much for equal suffrage as for freedom of speech." White, a descendant of Thomas Jefferson, was described by Lucy Branham as unusually "capable and brilliant and sincere." Frustrated with NAWSA's policy which she felt essentially wrote off the south, White embraced the NWP and played a critical role during the final ratification drive in Tennessee.

Growing Pressure Forces Another Vote in the Senate

After several weeks of watchfire demonstrations and new waves of arrests and hunger strikes, the Democratic leadership finally responded to the continuing pressure and scheduled another Senate vote on the Federal amendment for February 10, 1919. Suffragists, however, knew that they were still one vote short.

In another bold and controversial protest, the National Woman's Party announced that they would hold a cli-

mactic demonstration on the day before the Senate vote where they would burn "in effigy a portrait of President Wilson even as the Revolutionary fathers had burned a portrait of King George."

The ceremony, late in the afternoon of February 9, continued the style of beautifully staged symbolic artistry that had marked all of Alice Paul's demonstrations. In this action, a line of over one hundred women clothed in white, wearing tricolor suffrage

A Climactic National Woman's Party Protest Burns the President in Effigy

Burning the president in effigy climaxed one of the most dramatic chapters in the later suffrage movement. It was "the most difficult thing I was ever asked to do," Sue White later recalled, adding that it was only done out of "the deepest conviction." As Doris Stevens of the National Woman's Party explained, "We wanted to show our contempt for the president's inadequate support which promised so much in words and which did so little in deeds to match the words."

Caught off-guard by the speed of the action, the police immediately moved in and arrested Louisine Havemeyer and 38 other women indiscriminately, filling their patrol wagons and then commandeering automobiles for their prisoners. Just as abruptly, the arrests stopped,

police withdrew, and the remaining suffragists tended the watchfire until nightfall. Nonetheless, "The country was properly shocked," White recalled, "probably more shocked than if we had done some deed of violence."

NAWSA leaders were furious with the action and several senators condemned it when they voted against the measure the next day. As predicted, the bill was defeated by the lame duck Senate on February 10, 1919 by one vote, 63-33, while 26 women were being sentenced to five days in jail. Most of these prisoners again refused to eat until released.

Above: An "effigy" of President Wilson. Above left: A galvanized tub held the watchfire after the Grecian urn was destroyed.

sashes and carrying lettered banners, marched solemnly through a crowd of over a thousand silent spectators to the sidewalk in front of the White House. Meanwhile a bell tolled at the NWP's headquarters.

Police, as usual, had been informed beforehand of the suffragists' intentions but, Sue White noted, they had "probably expected that we would bring out a little straw man for them to pull to pieces and rescue." The actual "effigy"

was "nothing more than a small cartoon of the president," Louisine Havemeyer recalled, "making some unkept promise as usual."

After the suffragists lit their watchfire in an earthen urn and spoke at length about liberty, democracy, and freedom, a solemn Sue White took the image of the president and, calling his party autocratic for holding women "in political slavery," quickly dropped it into the fire before the police could react.

The Prison Special Tours the Country

Turning "From Prison to People," over two dozen members of the National Woman's Party toured the country during February and March 1919 aboard a chartered railroad car they called The Prison Special. The suffragists, all former prisoners, spoke to large and enthusiastic audiences across the country, relaying news of the political situation in the capital and explaining their own recent actions. Some of the women had just been released from prison and were still weak from their hunger strikes.

Lucy Burns led the tour which included NWP officers Mabel Vernon and Abby Scott Baker as well as a number of members from the south including Mary Nolan and Sue White. Alice Paul planned the route which ran through the heart of the south to the west coast and back through the mid-west to New York. When the women arrived in Charleston, South Carolina on February 16 at the start of their trans-continental trip, "thousands of people packed the auditorium and overflowed it until meetings had to be organized on street corners," White reported.

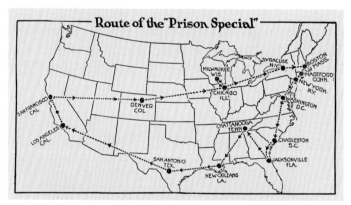

Above: Former prisoners on The Suffrage Special posed in Charleston on February 11, 1919. Louisine Havemeyer is in front, right of center, and Lucy Burns is in the back, further to the right of center. Upper right: Route of the tour. Lower right: Lucy Burns in San Francisco held a banner displaying Susan B. Anthony's favorite quote, "Resistance to Tyranny is Obedience to God."

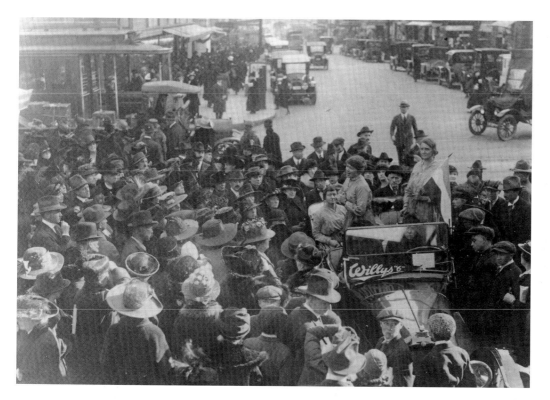

Lucy Branham (above) wore a suffrage ribbon over her prison garb when she addressed a huge New Orleans crowd on February 22, 1919 during the Prison Special tour. Branham, a 26-year-old former teacher from Baltimore, held a Ph.D. from Columbia University and followed her mother into suffrage work. Earlier she had been awarded a Carnegie hero medal for saving both a drowning girl and a male would-be rescuer. Branham had been sentenced to sixty days for picketing in 1917 and her mother (also named Lucy) was jailed for three days during the watchfire demonstrations. Suffragists in prison kept up their spirits with songs such as this, sung to the tune of "I've Been Working on the Railroad." (Zinkham was District jail warden.)

*We've been starving in the
  workhouse, all the livelong
  day,
We've been starving in the
  workhouse, just to pass the
  S.B.A. –
Don't you hear old Zinkham
  calling –
Rise up so early in the morn –
Don't you see the Senate
  moving?
Woodrow, Blow your horn.*

Activists Stir Support with Dramatic Personal Stories

SUFFRAGISTS WHO traveled on The Prison Special dressed in rough uniforms like those they wore in jail when they gave passionate accounts of their protest and prison experiences. The women captivated audiences throughout the country and won wider support for the cause. One suffragist, 44-year-old Edith Ainge, or "Aingy," from Jamestown, New York, told how she had been arrested five times and was so weakened by six weeks in jail that she lost 23 pounds. The former prisoners usually spoke in different parts of each city by day before gathering for a mass meeting at night.

Rallying support for the Federal amendment, the whirlwind tour resulted in countless letters, cables, and messages from across the country demanding Senate action. Reflecting the repressive post-war climate, there

was also a female Secret Service agent following the train to monitor the women's activity.

The tour, which Louisine Havemeyer called "a marvelous bit of publicity," helped counter the negative or inaccurate press coverage the suffrage pickets had received.

Sue White estimated the women spoke to 50,000 people before returning to New York City on March 10, 1919.

Above: Edith Ainge and Pauline Adams spoke in Los Angeles on February 27, 1919. Below: Former prisoners in San Francisco.

Bloody Protests as Congress Fails to Act

DESPITE THE February defeat in the Senate, NAWSA and the National Woman's Party kept pressuring President Wilson and the Senate to pass the Federal amendment before the 65th Congress ended on March 3, 1919.

Arrests in Boston

On February 24, with only seven days left, the NWP tried to influence Wilson in Boston when he returned from the Paris peace conference. Boldly marching right through a line of Marine guards awaiting the president's arrival, a column of banner-carrying suffragists led by organizer Katharine Morey and her mother Agnes took up positions directly in front of the president's reviewing stand. After forty-five minutes, police "politely" took nearly two dozen women into custody as the crowd watched just before Wilson arrived.

The women were joined in jail by several others who had burned the president's words on Boston Common. The prisoners refused to cooperate at their trial, many identifying themselves only as Jane Doe. Most were sentenced to eight days in jail but all were suddenly released after their fines were paid anonymously. Overflow crowds gathered a few days later when the local women were awarded NWP prison pins.

On March 4, the day after

Louise Sykes of Cambridge (top) burned President Wilson's speech on the Boston Common on February 24, 1919. Before the president arrived, suffrage pickets held their banners and stood in front of his reviewing stand (above) in what Doris Stevens called "a pageant of beauty and defiant appeal."

Congress disbanded without action, the Woman's Party organized another demonstration when Wilson spoke in New York City just before sailing back to France. One NWP banner declared, "An Autocrat At Home is a Poor Champion for Democracy Abroad."

As the line of 25 suffragists approached the heavily guarded Opera House, "a veritable battalion of policemen in close formation rushed us with unbelievable ferocity," recalled Doris Stevens. "Clubs were raised and lowered and the women beaten back with such cruelty as

none of us had ever witnessed before. The women clung to their heavy banner poles . . . but the police seized them, tore the pennants, broke the poles, some of them over our backs, trampled them underfoot, pounded us, dragged us, and in every way behaved like frantic beasts."

A Violent Assault

Soldiers and sailors joined in the attack and an enormous crowd gathered, surrounding the "suffocating melee." "Women were knocked down and trampled under foot, some of them almost unconscious, others bleeding from the hands and face," Stevens reported. Climbing to a balcony, Elsie Hill succeeded in burning part of Wilson's speech and admonishing the raging crowd still attacking the women, "Did you expect us to turn back?" she challenged them. "We never turn back . . . and we won't until democracy is won!"

The terrible night of violence proved to be one of the last confrontations in women's long struggle for liberty. The following day several servicemen came by to apologize for the actions of their fellows. With Congress adjourned, both NAWSA and the NWP kept demanding that Wilson call a special session of the new 66th Congress as soon as possible so it could finally pass the Federal amendment and send it to the states to ratify. ◆

NAWSA Flirts with a Desperate Compromise

JUST BEFORE the 65th Congress ended in March 1919, following the defeat by one vote in the Democratic Senate, Carrie Catt and others in NAWSA made moves to accommodate segregationist southern suffragists who argued that the Federal amendment would never be ratified as it was presently worded.

Together, NAWSA and congressional supporters drew up a version of the Federal amendment which altered its enforcement clause and submitted it to Congress without consulting NAWSA's members who undoubtedly would have objected. The compromise bill, of which no copy survives, only narrowly missed coming to a vote. Two senators pledged their support but a final vote was blocked by Republican opponents. It was quietly abandoned when the new Congress convened.

Southern fears proved groundless, however. Most Black women in the south would be excluded from voting for decades since the Federal government did not actively enforce the law.

Above: "Woman to the Rescue," from *The Crisis*, imagined Black women using the constitution to beat down racist laws.

Obstruction to the End

ALTHOUGH THE Federal amendment was officially endorsed by party leaders, not all politicians fell into line. In fact, New York suffragist Mary Peck reported that "the diehards went down fighting to the last." As the repeated defeats in the Senate showed, opponents tried to delay women from voting nationally as long as possible. Anti-suffragists realized that, in the early months of 1919, over forty state legislatures were in session and able to act on the amendment relatively quickly. Later in the year, many would have adjourned and suffragists would have to persuade each governor to call a special session of his legislature to consider ratification.

Opponents hoped that the added difficulty, expense, and political risk would delay woman suffrage until after the 1920 presidential election and, with luck, would tip the scales against final ratification altogether. If antis could control only 13 states, they could still block ratification. Suffrage leaders understood that prolonged delay could mean ultimate defeat and so they prepared to throw their entire strength behind immediate ratification.

Minnie Fisher Cunningham was the skilled and influential leader of the Texas Equal Suffrage Association who masterminded winning votes for women in that Democrat-controlled state. After earning a degree in pharmacy from the University of Texas, Cunningham found her calling in the political arena and at 33 was elected president of the state association in 1915. Under her enthusiastic leadership suffragists helped unseat a corrupt anti-suffrage governor, won primary suffrage, and ensured ratification of the Federal amendment. Widely respected for her energy, sound judgment, and organizational ability, Cunningham became executive secretary of the new League of Women Voters in 1920 and later ran unsuccessfully for senator.

Women are helping bring Democracy To Europe. Will you help ring the Liberty Bell for Texas women

A Final Campaign Wins Key Rights for Texas Women

LIKE MOST of the south, Texas was essentially a one-party state controlled by the Democrats. Whoever won the primary election, which chose candidates, usually won the general election.

After several defeats in the legislature, Minnie Fisher Cunningham led the Texas Equal Suffrage Association in a different direction. Working with the legislature investigating corruption in 1917, suffragists helped force the anti-suffrage governor out of office. Less than a year later, the new governor faced the risk of losing the nomination. Cunningham pragmatically suggested he back a partial suffrage bill that would allow women to vote for him in the primary election.

Convinced that he needed women's support, the governor signed the Primary Suffrage bill on March 26, 1918. Suffragists then waged a massive statewide drive, register-

ing approximately 386,000 women as voters in seventeen days, and the governor won the election handily.

When an overconfident legislature put a full suffrage measure on the May 24, 1919 ballot, state leaders turned to a reluctant NAWSA for help and a concentrated three-month drive was mounted across the state. Campaign workers spoke widely and distributed over three million flyers including small paper

> **First Aid to Patriotism: Woman Suffrage**
>
> PATRIOTISM depends on love of country and a SENSE OF RESPONSIBILITY to one's country.
>
> The responsibility in a democratic government like the United States rests with the voters.
>
> Sons inherit from mothers as well as fathers.
>
> Does the country need patriotic and responsible men?
>
> Then it must develop patriotic women with a high sense of responsibility.
>
> As long as one-half the people are denied the vote, the sense of responsibility in one-half the people will not be fully developed.
>
> WOMAN SUFFRAGE MEANS PATRIOTISM VOTES FOR WOMEN!
>
> Vote and work for the Suffrage Amendment May 24
>
> TEXAS EQUAL SUFFRAGE ASSOCIATION

Liberty Bells. Tens of thousands of men in uniform, however, were unable to vote. Anti-suffragists were active throughout the state and a controversial citizenship clause in the measure drew further opposition. It lost 166,893 to 141,773.

Eleven days later, however, Congress submitted the Federal amendment to the states and the Lone Star state ratified it in less than four weeks. Texas suffragists had grown into a powerful and influential force. For a time, Cunningham claimed, "we were the smartest group of politicians in the state."

Above: Jane McCallum (center, with floral bag), who later became Texas Secretary of State, and other women prepared to register to vote at the Austin Court House on June 26, 1918. Left: Fliers from the 1919 campaign.

Gains in Presidential Suffrage Build Pressure for the Federal Amendment

After Illinois passed presidential suffrage in 1913, legal challenges discouraged other states from taking the same action for several years. But once it was secured in 1917, it became a key strategy across the country. Carrie Catt's "Winning Plan" directed women in states where referenda were unlikely to succeed to concentrate on winning presidential suffrage. North Dakota, Nebraska, and Rhode Island passed presidential suffrage in early 1917. So did Ohio, Indiana, and Nebraska but gains in those states were challenged and later reversed.

State workers made substantial progress in the active legislative year of 1919, getting presidential suffrage bills passed in Ohio and Indiana (again), Wisconsin, Minne-

sota, Iowa, Missouri, Maine, and Tennessee. In 1920 Kentucky brought the total number of states with presidential suffrage to 13, plus Arkansas and Texas where primary suffrage essentially amounted to presidential suffrage. Together with the fifteen equal suffrage states, nearly seven million women in thirty states representing 339 electoral votes would be able to vote for president in 1920 regardless of the status of the Federal amendment.

Above: Nautically clad supporters in Wisconsin called for enfranchisement from a "rudderless" float. Left: Musical suffragists soothed a savage "Boss" in J. N. "Ding" Darling's cover illustration on an Iowa songbook.

Helen Hamilton Gardener
was the "solid and sensible"
pen name, later legally
adopted, of author Alice
Chenowith Day. After years of
travel and writing, Gardener
(on the left with Carrie Catt)
was 54 when she settled in
Washington D.C. in 1907.
As the suffrage measure
advanced in Congress, her
social contacts and influence
grew in strategic importance.
She befriended her next door
neighbor, Speaker of the
House Champ Clark, deliver-
ing southern delicacies over
the back fence and chatting
with him about suffrage
legislation. Her tact and
personal diplomacy helped
open a channel to the White
House where she met with
President Wilson more than
twenty times representing
NAWSA. Catt called her "one
of the world's wonders," and
Maud Wood Park referred to
her as "a woman of genius"
and "the Diplomatic Corps"
of the Congressional Com-
mittee. "She was as essential
to our success in Washington," Park recalled, "as Mrs.
Catt was to the country-wide
campaign."

When Both Parties Are Back of Her It's Hard to Get Anti-Slings Across

Party Support Shifts Balance Towards Suffrage

As it was up to the presi-dent to call a special ses-sion of Congress, suffragists pressured Wilson in France to act as soon as possible. After numerous trans-Atlan-tic cables, he agreed to sched-ule one for May 19, 1919.

With planks endorsing it in both the Democratic and Republican platforms and enough votes lined up in Congress, the Federal amend-ment had finally come of age. NAWSA turned its attention from individual voters to elected officials who could ac-tually pass the constitutional amendment.

The 66th Congress was no-tably supportive. "War work contributed to this change in opinion," historian Sara Graham observed, "but the aggressive campaigns waged by suffragists [against oppo-nents] in Massachusetts and Delaware were crucial fac-tors." The threat of new coali-tions and efforts by suffragists "moved the stalwarts in a way that education, entreaties and petitions never could."

Above: As Winner's cartoon suggested, major party sup-port helped shield women's cause from continuing anti-suffrage attacks.

The 66th Congress Passes the Federal Amendment

B y the spring of 1919 votes for women had become such a popular issue that politicians were rushing to jump on the bandwagon, just as Clifford Berryman envisioned in his cartoon (right), "Last Call." When the new 66th Congress convened on May 19, supporters moved quickly to have the Federal suffrage amendment called to a vote.

With smooth precision, the House Woman Suffrage Committee reported the bill onto the floor for a vote on the third day of the session. "The tense feeling that had marked our previous vote in the House was all gone," Maud Wood Park recalled. "There was no scurrying for one more vote, no sick men coming in to record their

support, no anxiety, no suspense." The House overwhelmingly passed the suffrage bill on May 21 by a vote of 304 to 89. Shocked at the

suddenness and speed of the victory, Park remembered, "For a few moments I was too stunned to realize how happy I was."

On June 4, 1919, two weeks after passage in the House, the Federal suffrage amendment came to a vote in the Senate. With passage already assured, "there was no excitement" there either, Maud Younger reported. The bill passed the Senate 65 to 30 with two votes to spare. Despite the anti-climactic quality, supporters savored the hard-fought victory. Lobbyists with the National Woman's Party (above left) posed with a key supporter on the steps of the Capitol just after the Senate vote. From the left are former Congressional Committee head Elizabeth Kent, Clara Wainwright, Senator Wesley Jones of Washington, NWP legislative chair Maud Younger, and Abby Scott Baker, the diplomatic political chair. With Congress finally won, the ratification drive began immediately and Younger voiced the growing realization that "we were in the dawn of women's political power in America." Silver pins (above) were awarded by the NWP to all women who had picketed for suffrage. The back read: "Without extinction is liberty, without retrograde is equality." Left: Jumping on the band wagon.

"Freedom has come not as a gift but as a triumph."

SUFFRAGISTS FROM NAWSA and congressional allies surrounded the Speaker of the House (above) when he signed the woman suffrage bill on June 4, 1919 while a movie camera captured the historic occasion.

From the left are national publicity head Ida Husted Harper, Harriet Taylor Upton, Front Door Lobby chair Maud Wood Park, Mary Garret Hay, Lobby vice-chair Helen Gardener, and lobby press secretary Marjorie Shuler. On the right behind House Speaker Frederick H. Gillette are supporters John E. Raker, former chair of the House Committee on Woman Suffrage, former Speaker of the House Champ Clark, House Clerk Tyler Page, and Frank W. Mondell, Republi-

can floor leader from Wyoming. No members of the National Woman's Party were invited to the brief ceremony organized by Helen Gardener, and NAWSA played up its "official recognition." Carrie Catt was in New York and Alice Paul was in Minnesota

already at work on the ratification drive. Celebrating the victory Paul declared, "Freedom has come not as a gift but as a triumph, and it is therefore a spiritual as well as a political freedom which women receive."

On June 5, flanked by Park

and Gardener, Vice-President Thomas R. Marshall (below) signed the bill passed by the Senate, sending it to the 48 states for ratification. "It was a curious fact," noted Park, "that the two men who had to sign the amendment were both anti-suffragists." The NWP remained in Washington D.C. but immediately after Senate passage NAWSA's Suffrage House was closed and its Front Door Lobby's files shipped back to New York. Suffrage leaders turned to the states with a vigorous ratification campaign. ◆

Above: Signing the suffrage bill in the House and (left) the Senate. Facing page: Justice embraced American Womanhood after Congress finally approved equal suffrage.

The Suffragist

VOL. VII. No. 24

FIVE CENTS

OFFICIAL WEEKLY ORGAN OF
THE NATIONAL WOMAN'S PARTY

SATURDAY, JUNE 21, 1919

Courtesy Philadelphia Evening Public Ledger

At Last

Chapter 17: 1919-1920

The Drive for Ratification

AFTER PASSING the U.S. Senate and House of Representatives, the Federal suffrage amendment had to be ratified by at least 36 states before it would become law. Since only seven of the 48 state legislatures were in session in June 1919, suffragists were forced to ask virtually all the other governors to call special sessions in order to ratify what would become the 19th Amendment in time for the 1920 elections. Many governors, however, were reluctant to call special sessions because of expense and political concerns.

Both Carrie Catt and Alice Paul had been preparing for the ratification drive for over a year and they each immediately mobilized their organizations to pressure politicians in every state to act quickly to approve the amendment. Suffrage leaders foresaw that ratification would be, in historian Sara Graham's words, their "most difficult political test." Many other proposed amendments had failed at the ratification stage.

Some politicians bowed to what seemed to be inevitable, like the Missouri opponent who declared, "I've played poker long enough to know when to lay down my hand." Others held fast against ratification. Anti-suffragists in the Maryland legislature not only refused to ratify the amendment but also tried to block other states from doing so. While the amendment included no time limit, suffragists were concerned that if they did not seize the present opportunity, the conservative post-war mood might delay passage indefinitely. They knew that if opponents could control only 13 states the amendment would fail.

MARYLAND Suffrage News

Entered as second-class matter at the Postoffice at Baltimore, Md., under the Act of March 3, 1879

Vol. VIII. No. 11—Weekly   BALTIMORE, MD., JUNE 14, 1919   Five Cents

UNIVERSAL SUFFRAGE

OPPOSITION

The Rising Sun

Facing page: Sunflowers graced the desk as Missouri Governor Frederick D. Gardner signed the ratification bill on July 10, 1919 surrounded by delighted suffragists. Left: A popular state periodical showed the opposition wilting under The Rising Sun of universal suffrage.

Starting the National Ratification Drive

ILLINOIS, WISCONSIN, and Michigan responded immediately to suffragists' requests and became the first states to ratify the Federal suffrage amendment on June 10, 1919. An error forced Illinois to re-ratify a week later. Ohio ratified next in a high moment of bipartisan spirit, followed by Kansas and New York where both legislatures passed the resolution unanimously.

By the end of June the first non-suffrage state, Pennsylvania, ratified under the guidance of its Republican governor despite the General Assembly being, in Carrie Catt's words, "inherently hostile to woman suffrage." Concerted efforts by suffragists in Iowa, Missouri, Massachusetts, and Texas were also successful, bringing the total in one month to eleven states representing one-half of the population of the country.

One of the last Suffrage Maps (right) showed fifteen full suffrage states, two states (Texas and Arkansas) with primary suffrage, and six states with presidential suffrage. After this leaflet was printed, seven more states passed presidential suffrage. The 30 states where women could vote for president accounted for 339 electoral votes out of 531. Suffragists had labored long and hard to build up this kind of political strength and politicians could no longer afford to ignore it.

Above: On July 1, 1919 Rhode Island suffragists staged a patriotic pageant on the steps of Providence's City Hall to celebrate Women's Independence Day, the first day women in the state could register to vote.
Right: Fifty years of effort.

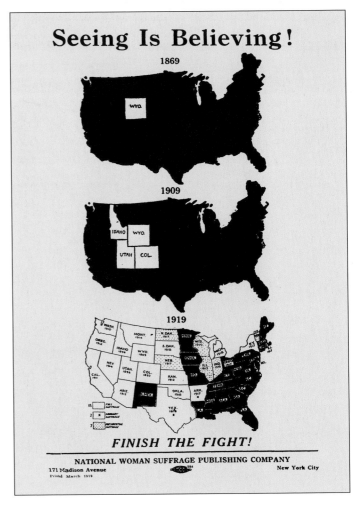

Seeing Is Believing!

1869

1909

1919

FINISH THE FIGHT!

NATIONAL WOMAN SUFFRAGE PUBLISHING COMPANY
171 Madison Avenue   New York City
Printed March 1919

Anna Howard Shaw: The Last Pioneer

IMMEDIATELY FOLLOWING her war service, veteran suffragist Anna Howard Shaw, 72, toured the country with former President Taft to build support for the League of Nations. While traveling, Shaw contracted pneumonia and returned home to Moylan, Pennsylvania, where she died on July 2, 1919 with her longtime companion Lucy Anthony by her bedside. Suffragists across the country were bereft.

Shaw was one of the last pioneers, an exceptional woman who braved ridicule and overcame prejudice to win support for women's rights in every state in the nation. She persuaded tens of thousands of men and women with her eloquence. A trained minister and doctor, she retained a common touch and personal empathy that were reminiscent of her mentor, Susan B. Anthony.

Two months before her death, Shaw had been awarded the Distinguished Service Medal for her loyal work during World War I. She had won renown, in the words of Justina Wilson of NAWSA, as "a living demonstration of the power of women and the moral force of a right idea." ◆

Above: Anna Howard Shaw at her home in Moylan, Pennsylvania. Left: Receiving the Distinguished Service Medal from the Secretary of War.

A String of Victories but the West is Slow to Act

Hoping to continue the momentum of the first month, NAWSA sent four envoys to the western states in late July 1919 to encourage the governors to call special sessions to ratify the Federal amendment. Many states where woman suffrage was well established, however, were slow to act since most suffrage organizations had been disbanded and women had been largely absorbed into the political parties.

Montana became the first western state to ratify on July 30, 1919 followed by Arkansas and Nebraska which ratified unanimously. Alabama and Georgia became the first states to defeat the amendment and the governor of Louisiana began an effort to organize 13 states to prevent ratification.

The Minnesota legislature ratified on September 8 and afterwards members broke into *The Battle Hymn of the Republic,* written so many years before by suffragist Julia Ward Howe. New Hampshire ratified at the first special session called in 29 years and Utah approved the amendment unanimously on September 30. Still, eleven full suffrage states delayed.

Carrie Catt appealed to the governors, pointing out that women now voted in virtually all the Allied, enemy, and neutral countries in Europe. She called the delay at home a "very depressing humiliation to American women." In October, having altered her ratification dress after the long delay, she took to the road to convince western governors to act.

As a result, California Governor William D. Stephens encouraged his fellow governors to ratify by Thanksgiving and on November 1, California passed the resolu-tion with only two opposed. Four days later the Maine legislature ratified but with only three votes to spare in the House. In December, North Dakota ratified the amendment and South Dakota and Colorado passed it unanimously. "The sentiment of the country is with us," Catt declared, "our duty is merely to secure its expression."

By the end of 1919, suffragists had won twenty-two states, all but four at special sessions. But the most difficult task was still ahead.

Above: To raise money for the final drive, women in Cleveland, Ohio gathered Salvage for Suffrage in March 1919. Upper right: Republican Governor Edwin P. Morrow of Kentucky signed the suffrage bill on January 6, 1920 as members of the Kentucky Equal Rights Association looked on.

Political and Legal Challenges Fight Ratification

Nettie Rogers Shuler was one of Carrie Catt's most trusted lieutenants and co-workers. Highly capable and energetic, Shuler served as president of the Western New York Federation of Women's Clubs and later joined the Woman Suffrage Party for the 1915 campaign. Chosen by Catt for NAWSA's board in 1917 she served, in historian Eleanor Flexner's words, as Catt's "alter ego" for four critical years, overseeing the New York headquarters, testifying before legislators, consulting with field workers, conducting training schools for organizers, and working for state suffrage and ratification. Shuler's only daughter Marjorie worked with her mother in Oklahoma as well as in Vermont, New Hampshire, and Tennessee where ratification was particularly difficult. The Shulers were two of NAWSA's top organizers during the final campaigns. A button (left) honored Anna Howard Shaw.

S UFFRAGISTS FACED a veritable obstacle course trying to win ratification by 36 widely differing states. In some the governor led one party while the legislature was controlled by the other, or was split. Intense local rivalries and strident political factions were disturbingly common. Conditions in each region demanded different strategies and well-informed political maneuvering. Carrie Catt remembered, "Again and again the Association had had to work its way through state situations of extreme complication."

Suffrage leaders also had to fight opposition charges that the amendment would never be approved in time for the November 1920 elections, and that calling special sessions to take immediate action was a waste of time and money. To further confuse matters, opponents filed suits which demanded that state referenda be held on the Federal amendment. NAWSA engaged Charles Evans Hughes as legal counsel and, after tense legal debate, the Supreme Court ruled on June 2, 1920 that referenda could not be used regarding amendments to the constitution.

The legal attacks themselves were used to confuse the issue as antis argued that, given such a state of "legal confusion," ratification was far from a forgone conclusion and might still be challenged successfully. As such claims circulated, supporters began to encounter evasive replies from governors and a lessening of the demand in the states for special sessions. In response, suffragists redoubled their efforts.

Jovita Idar de Juarez was a Spanish-speaking journalist, organizer, teacher, and champion of civil rights on the violent Texas/Mexico border. She exemplified politically active women in poor or minority communities for whom the vote was not the most pressing or realistic issue. Faced with widespread racial violence, she and other Hispanic women, like the early woman's rights advocates, concentrated on overcoming discrimination and winning basic rights. Idar condemned the lynching of Mexican American men and worked for decades for justice and racial pride. In 1911, when she was 26, Idar helped organize La Liga Femenil Mexicanista, the first Hispanic feminist group in the U.S. Two years later, she cofounded La Cruz Blança, similar to the Red Cross, which nursed the injured during the Mexican Revolution. Idar moved from Laredo to San Antonio in 1917 where she continued writing, teaching, and fighting discrimination. Concerns over racial prejudice were well founded. After Christia Adair of Kingsville and other Black suffragists circulated petitions in 1918, they were turned away when they went to vote because they were Black.

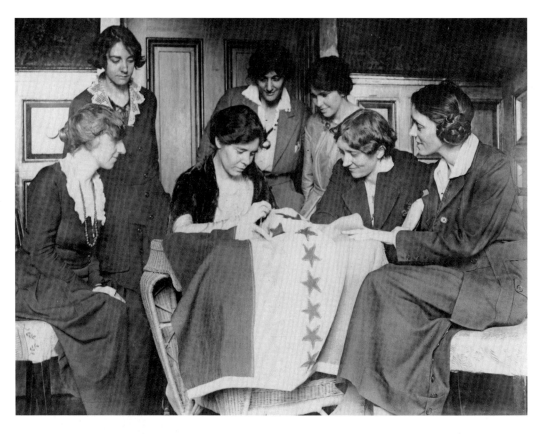

Parallel Efforts Seek Legislative Approval State By State

The National Woman's Party worked separately but simultaneously with NAWSA to win ratification in the states. As each state ratified, Alice Paul (above) added another star on the NWP's purple, white, and gold Ratification Flag.

During the first week of

1920, Rhode Island, Kansas, and Kentucky ratified and a week later Oregon approved the amendment unanimously. Indiana ratified on January 16 at a special session which the governor called only after making suffragists obtain pledges from two-thirds of the legislature to

come for a day and only consider ratification. The governor of Oklahoma made the same demand, which suffragists met, but then broke his promise.

Wyoming passed the amendment unanimously in late January, and Nevada ratified with one dissenting vote early the next month. Two more states, South Carolina and Virginia, defeated the measure in January. By early February, 28 states had ratified and 4 states had defeated it.

Above: Sewing a star on the Ratification Flag, Alice Paul was surrounded by organizers Mabel Vernon, Elizabeth Kalt, *Suffragist* editor Florence Brewer Boeckel, Anita Politzer, Sue White, and Vivian Pierce. Left: Matilda Hall Gardner appealed for funds in front of NWP headquarters.

Difficulties Increase as Suffragists Close In on the Final States

INTENSIVE LOBBYING work continued in each remaining state in 1920 as a special or regular sessions met and voted on the Federal amendment. In some western states the ratification bill was introduced by the legislature's female members and passed unanimously. New Jersey ratified after a long legislative battle on February 9. Idaho, Arizona, and New Mexico followed suit the same month. A hotly-contested drive in Oklahoma was marked by the tragic death of the secretary of the state ratification committee, Aloysius Larch-Miller. Ill with influenza, Larch-Miller literally left her sick bed to persuade her county convention to support immediate ratification in the face of the governor's indecisiveness. Her eloquent plea carried the convention. She died two days later and the flags at the state capitol were flown at half-mast in her honor. On February 28 Oklahoma became the 33rd state to ratify.

Suffragists faced a "cliffhanger" in West Virginia. A tie vote in the Senate forced supporters to hold their ground for five days against fervent anti-suffragists while an absent member raced across the country by special train to break the tie and ratify on March 10.

Slow moving Washington state finally ratified unanimously on March 22 while the Delaware legislature was also meeting. Suffragists were hoping that Delaware would become the 36th state but the legislature was in the midst of a factional fight that stretched the question out for ten excruciating weeks. Then state politicians defeated it.

The 33 White States Have Ratified

Enough of The Black States Will Soon

Suffrage Ratification Map

Above: Celebrating ratification in California on November 1, 1920. Left: As of March 6, 1920, the deep south remained solidly opposed to the Federal suffrage amendment.

Black Women Organize as Voters

REFLECTING WIDESPREAD support for woman suffrage in Black communities, local activists began efforts to prepare women to register to vote, and to overcome the opposition they knew they would face. Colored Women Voters Leagues were formed in several southern states to help both women and men qualify as voters.

After defeating more than one attempt to change the Federal amendment to apply only to white women, Black leaders supported ratification. But then they vainly sought the help of white suffragists to protect Black voting rights. In the south, enfranchisement of Black women and men would not be substantially advanced for forty years. Black voters elsewhere organized their own partisan groups such as the Colored Woman's Republican Club in New York and similar political clubs in other cities.

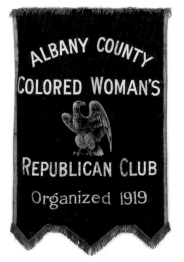

Above: Preparing to vote.
Left: Choosing parties. Right:
The anti-suffrage *Woman Patriot* claimed as late as 1919 that women voting would lead to "Race and Sex War."

Battle Drawn for the 36th State

By June 1920 the Federal amendment had been ratified by thirty-five states and defeated by eight. There were only five states left. In each, the governor needed to call a special session if a vote were to be possible. Each governor, however, refused.

Suffragists surveyed the legislatures in Florida and North Carolina and found them unfavorable, leaving only Vermont, Connecticut, and Tennessee. With strong opposition in each state, anti-suffragists remained hopeful of delaying and even preventing ratification altogether by blocking the final state needed.

In early June, feeling "it was necessary to make a stronger protest," the National Woman's Party prepared to picket the Republican National Convention in Chicago.

Above: Alice Paul (second from right) and other suffragists held a banner bearing a quotation from Susan B. Anthony before leaving for the Republican convention. **Left:** Organizers Julia Emory and Bertha Graf prepared banners and trunks of regalia for shipping to Chicago.

We protest against the continued disfranchisement of women
For which the Republican party is now responsible.
The Republican party defeated ratification in Delaware.
The Republican party is blocking ratification in Vermont.
The Republican party is blocking ratification in Connecticu'
When will the Republican party stop blocking suffrage

Picketing the 1920 Republican National Convention in Chicago

SUFFRAGISTS BROUGHT their demand for ratification to the Republican National Convention in Chicago just after their hopes were dashed by Republican-controlled Delaware. On June 8, 1920, Mabel Vernon led a long column of white-clad members of the National Woman's Party to the coliseum gates where they took up positions holding their banners and brilliant tricolor flags. "The Republican Party has the power to enfranchise women," one banner read, "When will it do so?"

On June 10, thirty women appeared carrying banners reading, "Vote Against The Republican Party As Long As It Blocks Suffrage," hoping to increase pressure on the Republican governors. In Con-

necticut, when the governor had claimed that he needed proof of an emergency to call a special session, NAWSA had organized an "Emergency

"The Last Few Buttons Are Always the Hardest"

Corps" of 48 distinguished women, one from each state, to persuade him. The women met with the reluctant governor in early May but he

claimed he was still unconvinced. In Vermont, a "silent army" of 400 women from across the state marched to the governor's office but he, too, remained unmoved.

Finally, the Democratic governor of Tennessee responded to intense lobbying, expert legal opinions, and the intervention of President Wilson and agreed to call a special session on August 9. The climax of the long struggle for woman suffrage was set for the two-party border state of Tennessee.

Facing page: Alice Paul picketed the Republican convention under the watchful eye of a security agent. Above: Suffragists demonstrating in Chicago. Left: 1920 cartoon from the *St. Louis Star*.

A Showdown on Suffrage in Tennessee:

SUFFRAGE AND anti-suffrage forces gathered in the factionalized, traditionally Democratic state of Tennessee for a showdown on the Federal woman suffrage amendment during the long sweltering summer of 1920. Suffragists were expecting the worst. NAWSA head Carrie Catt predicted that the opposition would "wage a desperate, probably unscrupulous, battle to prevent ratification in the 36th state," and that "every weak man would be set upon by powerful forces, and that every vulnerable spot in the campaign would be discovered and attacked." She did not exaggerate.

Losing Support

Organizers with both NAWSA and the National Woman's Party covered the state, visiting every legislator before the special session met in Nashville in early August. The women, hopeful at first, soon saw their support eroding as opponents and various business interests, including the powerful railroad and manufacturer's lobby, began to make their influence felt.

Marjorie Shuler had been sent to assess the situation for NAWSA and had immediately sent for Catt who came for "less than a week" on June 15 and stayed for over two months. She became the liaison officer between the governor and suffragists and "found the position most delicate and difficult." Head-

Anita Pollitzer talked with members of the Tennessee legislature in front of National Woman's Party headquarters in a Nashville storefront during the final ratification campaign.

quartered in the Hermitage Hotel, she never witnessed the actual debates in the State House as she hated the tedium and tension of events she had no control over. In addition, the "southern summer heat was merciless." Catt toured the chief cities where she held public meetings, gave newspaper interviews, and scheduled talks with political leaders as well as private conferences with suffrage workers.

Although there were welcome displays of support, Catt later wrote that she had

never seen "such a force for evil, such a nefarious lobby as labored to block the advance of suffrage in Nashville, Tennessee. In the short time I spent in Tennessee's capital, I have been called more names, been more maligned, more lied about than in the thirty previous years I worked for suffrage. I was flooded with anonymous letters, vulgar, ignorant, insane. Strange men and groups of men sprang up, men we had never met before in battle. . . . They appropriated our telegrams, tapped our telephones, listened out-

side our windows and transoms. They attacked our private and public lives."

Alice Paul stayed in Washington D.C. where she worked to bring the influence of national political forces to bear upon Tennessee lawmakers. NWP state chair Sue White opened a headquarters in Nashville and organizers Anita Pollitzer, Betty Gram, and Catherine Flanagan toured the state, surveying legislators and learning that pledged votes were steadily dropping away.

"The eyes of all America are upon us."

On August 9, Governor Albert H. Roberts opened the special session, reminding the gathered delegates of Tennessee's "pivotal position" and declaring that "the eyes of all America are upon us." The ratification resolution was introduced the next day and referred to a joint hearing. In the hours and evenings in between, to the horror of the suffragists, many representatives got wildly drunk with lobbyists representing liquor, railroad, and other interests. On August 13 the Senate passed the measure 25-4 and referred it to the House which ominously postponed the date of the vote day after day.

The suffragists' poll had a majority pledged for the bill but these men became the targets of unrelenting pressure. First, the editor of the *Nashville Banner* switched.

Waging the Last Desperate Battle

Then the Speaker of the House himself suddenly renounced his stand as a pledged supporter and became the leader of the opposition.

Suffragists made sure that national political leaders kept reminding the governor that if he allowed ratification to fail in Tennessee the Democratic Party would be held responsible by the women in the upcoming elections. Party leaders were well aware that, ratification or not, women in 30 states would be voting for president in November.

"The War of the Roses"

Anti-suffragists from around the country, particularly the south, also flocked to Nashville. Included in their ranks were two former national suffrage leaders, segregationists Laura Clay and Kate Gordon, who refused to support the Federal amendment claiming that it violated states' rights. Many antis wore a red rose as a symbol of their opposition while supporters usually displayed a yellow rose, leading one observer to label it "the war of the roses."

Members of the National Association Opposed to Woman Suffrage and the Southern Women's League for the Rejection of the Susan B. Anthony Amendment lobbied and passed out anti-ratification literature from their temporary headquarters in

Diehard states' rights supporters showed their colors outside their Anti-Ratification Headquarters in a Nashville, Tennessee, hotel room during the hot summer of 1920.

Nashville. Many southern antis insisted that voting was a right reserved for the states alone to decide. But since many states' rights advocates had supported national prohibition, suffragists could expose the inconsistency of their arguments which, not incidentally, also protected white supremacy in the south. Opponents accused suffragists of being unpatriotic "slackers" who had been concerned only with getting the franchise for themselves during the war, charges which NAWSA was forced to refute

constantly.

On August 18, with 96 legislators present, Speaker of the House Seth Walker announced that "the hour has come." Opponents were confident that they had enough votes to block ratification and moved that the bill be tabled. But when the vote tied 48-48, a second count was called and member Banks Turner changed his vote and defeated the motion so that the resolution could be voted on by the full House.

The motion to ratify was made and a voice vote began

as suffragists and anti-suffragists held their breaths. This time joining Turner in supporting woman suffrage was the youngest member of the legislature, 24-year-old Harry Burn. A well-regarded first-term Republican from a rural area, Burn had promised his mother, and suffragists, that he would vote for the amendment only if his vote was absolutely needed. When the time came, despite tremendous pressure from Walker and several of his fellow legislators, Burn held true to his promise. With his support the motion passed 49-47.

Stunned Silence

"Suffragists in the gallery sat in stunned silence," historian Sara Graham wrote, "the needed vote had miraculously appeared, the tie had been broken. Seconds later, deafening applause rained down on the young legislator as the Speaker called in vain for order."

Walker changed his vote immediately in order to move for a reconsideration later but that only guaranteed that the measure passed by a legal majority, 50-46. Opponents later tried to overturn the decision but the vote was upheld. The governor signed the resolution on August 24 and forwarded it to the U.S. Secretary of State by registered mail. With his approval, the 19th Amendment would be officially declared part of the U.S. Constitution. ◆

Tennessee Becomes "The Perfect 36th"

Pandemonium broke out when the Tennessee House of Representatives voted by the slimmest majority to ratify the Federal suffrage amendment on August 18, 1920. Supporters cheered and applauded while one legislator on the floor produced a bell and rang it steadily. Suffragists rained down yellow rose petals from the gallery as it gradually sank in that their long struggle for enfranchisement had finally been won.

The victory climaxed a remarkably successful fourteen month ratification drive encompassing every state in the Union. All but 7 of 36 states had required special sessions. Eight legislatures rejected the amendment and four had not voted on it. ◆

Above: Tallying the votes in the Tennessee Senate. **Right:** Governor Albert H. Roberts signed the ratification bill on August 24, 1920 witnessed by state officials and suffrage supporters. NAWSA vice-president Mrs. Guilford Dudley of Tennessee is on the far right.

The newspaper headline reads:

THE CHICAGO DAILY NEWS.

SPORTS ON PAGE 17 | FINAL EDITION

TWO CENTS—45TH YEAR—198. | WEDNESDAY, AUGUST 18, 1920. | ★ HOME EDITION 5 O'CLOCK

WOMEN WIN FULL U. S. VOTE

TENNESSEE RATIFIES VOTES FOR WOMEN; REJOICE IN CHICAGO

Tense Scene as 36th State O. K.'s Amendment by Narrow Margin, 49 to 47, in House; Opponents Seek Reconsideration To-Morrow.

Election Machinery Ready for New Suffragists to Cast Ballot in Illinois, Attorney-General Brundage Holds—Big Parties Prepare to Change Campaigns.

Banner headlines (above) announced the news while National Woman's Party organizers (left) congratulated members of the Tennessee legislature after the narrow victory. From the left in the back are Banks Turner, Catherine Flanagan, Anita Pollitzer, and Harry Burn in the dark suit. In the front are Thomas Simpson, Betty Gram, and Sue White. Angry anti-suffragists filed charges of bribery against Burn to punish him for changing his vote but he was cleared of any wrongdoing. On August 26, jubilant suffragists gathered at a great victory celebration in Washington D.C.

"Congratulations"

Chapter 18: 1920

Celebrating Victory

SUFFRAGE PROCLAIMED BY COLBY, WHO SIGNS AT HOME EARLY IN DAY

50 = Year Struggle Ends in Victory for Women

PROCLAMATION ENFRANCHISES WOMEN OF U. S.

NO CEREMONY IN FINAL ACTION

Secretary Felicitates Leaders; Hails New Era.

Ratification of the nineteenth amendment to the Constitution of the United States, granting suffrage to women, was proclaimed officially to-day by Secretary Colby of the State Department.

The proclamation was signed by Secretary Colby at 8 o'clock this morning at his home, when the certi-

Bainbridge Colby, Secretary of State of the United States of America.

To all to whom these presents shall come, greeting:

Know ye, that the Congress of the United States at the first session, Sixty-sixth Congress, begun at Washington on the nineteenth day of May, in the year one thousand nine hundred and nineteen, passed a resolution as follows, to wit:

Joint resolution, proposing an amendment to the Constitution extending the right of suffrage to women.

Resolved by the Senate and House of Representatives of the United States of America in Congress assembled (two-thirds of each House concurring therein), that the following article is proposed as an amendment to the Constitution, which shall be valid to all intents and purposes as part of the Constitution when ratified by the legislatures of three-fourths of the several states.

EARLY IN the morning of August 26, 1920, U.S. Secretary of State Bainbridge Colby signed the proclamation that the woman suffrage amendment had been ratified by the necessary 36 states. The 19th Amendment to the Constitution had become the law of the land.

Suffragists and supporters across the country were exultant that the "Susan B. Anthony Amendment" finally enfranchised the nation's 26 million women. Since there was no official government ceremony, only the quiet signing of a document and a public announcement, suffragists organized their own celebrations.

For many workers active in Tennessee, however, the last-minute, hyper-intense battle and its sudden finality cast an air of unreality to subsequent events. Maud Wood Park recalled that when she, Carrie Catt, and Helen Gardener learned that the proclamation had been actually signed, they were "all too stunned to make any comment." When they met with Secretary Colby in Washington D.C. to see the final declaration, "we almost had to stick pins into ourselves to realize that the simple document at which we were looking was, in reality, the long sought charter of liberty for the women of this country."

Supporters in New York City organized a last-minute "Victory Parade" on August 27, 1920 to welcome the suffrage leaders home. Veteran workers marched one last time from Pennsylvania Station to a gala reception to celebrate their hard-won national victory.

Columbia offered the nation's "Congratulations" to American women, now armed with the ballot, in Charles Dana Gibson's classic illustration for *Life* magazine (facing page). After the August 26, 1920 announcement (above left), supporters in New York met Carrie Catt with an impromptu Victory Parade (above right). Mrs. Frederick Edey carried the official NAWSA banner.

A Suffrage Victory Parade Fills New York City Streets for a Final Time

AFTER AN evening celebration in Washington D.C. on August 26, 1920 and a visit with an ailing Woodrow Wilson to express her appreciation, Carrie Catt returned home by train along with other NAWSA officials. "Her journey to New York the next day was as truly a triumphal procession as anything I ever expect to see," remembered Maud Wood Park. "At every station at which the train stopped, deputations of women, many of them smiling through tears, were waiting with their arms full of flowers for her."

A sea of well-wishers greeted the train at Pennsylvania Station in New York, including representatives of the Republican and Democratic National Committees and

New York Governor Alfred E. Smith. He congratulated the suffrage leader on "your great victory for the motherhood of America."

Mrs. John Blair of New York presented Catt with "the biggest suffrage bouquet ever

seen," made up of blue delphiniums and yellow chrysanthemums, and tied with a yellow ribbon which read: "To Mrs. Carrie Chapman Catt from the enfranchised women of the U.S."

When the 71st Regiment

Band struck up *Hail, The Conquering Hero Comes,* jubilant suffragists fell into line one more time for a final triumphal Victory Parade. State suffragists, NAWSA officers, and New York suffrage leaders escorted the returning women to an overflow reception at the Astor Gallery in the Waldorf Astoria Hotel.

Above: A suffrage honor guard marched in the Victory Parade beside the automobile carrying Carrie Catt, Harriet Taylor Upton, and other suffrage leaders. Left: Catt (with flowers) is welcomed by Mrs. John Blair, Governor Smith, and Senator Calder. On the right are Mary Garrett Hay, Mrs. Arthur Livermore, Harriet Taylor Upton, and Marjorie Shuler.

"A glorious and wonderful day"

"THIS IS a glorious and wonderful day," a triumphant Carrie Catt told well-wishers in New York City on August 27, 1920. "I have lived to realize the big, beautiful dream of my life – the enfranchisement of women." The suffrage leader was welcomed home like a conquering hero. Greeting her were veteran workers, "their cheeks flushed with excitement, their eyes bright, their heads held high," Gertrude Brown recalled. "The day was theirs. Their victory was complete."

After the parade arrived at the Waldorf Hotel reception, suffragists arose as one and greeted the NAWSA leader with a "thunder of applause." Now that women were voters, she told them, "let us remember we are no longer petitioners. We are not wards of the nation, but free and equal citizens. Let us practice the dignity of a sovereign people . . . We have proved in Tennessee that this is a government of the people, not an empire of corporations. Let us do our part to keep it a true and triumphant democracy."

At the final NAWSA convention in 1920, after other leading suffragists had been honored, Harriet Taylor Upton presented Catt with a magnificent star sapphire "Victory Brooch" paid for by the contributions from thousands of grateful citizens, young and old, across the country.

Left: Carrie Catt receives a hero's welcome in New York.

A Triumphant Nationwide Celebration

Church bells rang across the country and parades, banquets, public meetings, and memorials celebrated the suffrage victory from New York to California. Supporters in Boston held a festive victory rally in Faneuil Hall, and Philadelphia suffragists organized a mass demonstration in Independence Square where the Women's Liberty Bell was finally rung. The governor of Texas declared a state holiday and in Birmingham, Alabama, a parade of 1,500 people included decorated cars representing the 36 ratifying states.

Celebrations continued for months. "Everywhere men praised and congratulated them, and took credit for generously bestowing a gift on them," Gertrude Brown wrote, "and to their everlasting honor the women accepted the gift in the same spirit, overlooking all the weary years of waiting, the bitter ridicule, the heart breaking denials, the colossal frauds, and the many betrayals."

Facing page: Alice Paul unfurled the completed Ratification Flag. Above: Celebrating equality in New York. Left: Major Sullivan, Washington D.C. Chief of Police who sympathized with the suffragists, congratulated Paul after ratification.

The November 1920 election, the first since women were enfranchised nationally, saw eastern suffragists continuing their involvement in partisan politics. Suffrage leaders in New York campaigned to defeat long-time opponent Senator James Wadsworth (above) and in Connecticut activists threw their weight against the notoriously reactionary Senator Frank Brandegee. Both men won re-election but by substantially reduced margins. Not only did women vote in 1920 but throughout the country, women (including a number of suffragists) were also elected to local and state offices. In New Jersey two suffragists became the first women to serve in the state legislature. Eleven women had run. Anne Martin lost a second bid for the U.S. Senate from Nevada and Oklahoma elected the sole woman to Congress. Ironically, Alice M. Robertson was a conservative 66-year-old cafe owner from Muskogee who for years had been an anti-suffragist.

Women Throughout the Country Vote in the 1920 Election

WITH LESS than ten weeks between enfranchisement and the November 2, 1920 elections, NAWSA and the new League of Women Voters it had helped form ran training classes and encouraged women throughout the country to register and vote.

States where women were still disfranchised hurried to prepare, but not every state complied. Women in Georgia and Mississippi were not able to vote at all in 1920 because their legislatures refused to pass the legislation needed to register new voters in time for the election. While some Black women in the south were able to register, most were kept from voting by segregationist laws which disfranchised them. In Maine and North Dakota, suffrage campaigns which had been underway for years put the now-irrelevant state measure before voters one last time. ◆

Excited New Yorkers (above left), some with children in their arms, crowded into the polling place at Oliver and Henry Streets to sign their names on the voter rolls for the November 2, 1920 election. Three New York women (top right) voted at the 56th and Lexington Avenue polls, while in downtown Minneapolis, Minnesota (above), women lined up to vote for the first time in a national election. In Louisville, Kentucky (left) Black women registered outside the polls. While by law enfranchised, state and local requirements often kept Black and poor women as well as men from registering and voting.

Despite the suddenness, and with little preparation, women eagerly registered where they could. Carrie Catt reminded the new voters that "women have suffered agony of soul which you never can comprehend, that you and your daughters might inherit political freedom."

"It leaves its mark on

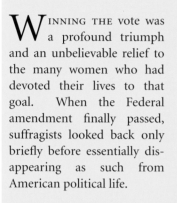WINNING THE vote was a profound triumph and an unbelievable relief to the many women who had devoted their lives to that goal. When the Federal amendment finally passed, suffragists looked back only briefly before essentially disappearing as such from American political life.

A First Step

Emphasizing the importance of their achievement, Carrie Catt told newly enfranchised women, "The vote is a power, a weapon of offense and defense . . . Use it intelligently, conscientiously, prayerfully. No soldier in the great suffrage army has labored and suffered to get a 'place' for you. Their motive has been the hope that women would aim higher than their own selfish ambitions, that they would serve the common good."

Alice Paul pointed out that winning the vote was only the first step toward achieving true equality. "Our victory cannot be a signal for rest. It is not only the symbol of the new status which women have earned, but also the tool with which they must end completely all discriminations against them in departments of life outside the political realm."

March Church Terrell recognized that "we women have now a weapon of defense which we have never possessed before. It will be a

A woman voter, Mary V. Lally, entered a New York City voting booth ready to cast her ballot in the November 1920 election, the first women throughout the country could participate in.

shame and reproach to us if we do not use it."

The suffrage struggle made its participants appreciate their democratic rights more than ever. Many suffragists took the initiative to train other women as citizens and voters. As historian Sara Graham noted, given the immensity of the sudden change in the size of the electorate, it

was surprising that there was so little effort by the government and the political parties to help women participate in public life. That task was taken up by suffragists, in part by their newly organized League of Women Voters.

Several weeks after Tennessee ratified, the Connecticut legislature finally approved the amendment,

becoming the 37th state and erasing any lingering legal doubt. Five months later, under a new governor, Vermont also ratified. It still took two years before the outstanding legal challenges were dismissed by the Supreme Court and all anti-suffrage efforts to declare the amendment invalid came to an end.

Faith in Women

That the effort itself finally succeeded was enormously liberating. "It has been a long, wearying struggle," wrote Doris Stevens, reflecting the feelings of countless women who had given years of their lives to win equal rights. "Although drudgery has persisted throughout, there have been compensatory moments of great joy and beauty. The relief that comes after a great achievement is sweet. There is no residue of bitterness. To be sure, women have often resented it deeply that so much human energy had to be expended for so simple a right. But whatever disillusionments they have experienced, they have kept their faith in women. And the winning of political power by women will have enormously elevated their status."

This faith in women and recognition of women's abilities ultimately permeated suffrage activity. That trust of women in other women, their willingness to cooperate with, work with, and follow other

one, such a struggle."

women for the sake of all, insured final victory. Suffragists "developed a sense of comradeship for each other which was half love, half admiration and all reverence," observed Inez Irwin. And ultimately, their sophisticated, concerted, and nonviolent efforts led to the passage of a constitutional amendment enfranchising half of the population.

"It is doubtful if any man, even among suffrage men, ever realized what the suffrage struggle came to mean to women before the end was allowed in America," Catt later wrote. "How much of time and patience, how much work, energy and aspiration, how much faith, how much hope, how much despair went into it. It leaves its mark on one, such a struggle. It fills the days and it rides the nights. Working, eating, drinking, sleeping, it is there.

"Not all women in all the states of the Union were in the struggle. There were some women in every state who knew nothing about it. But most women in all the states were at least on the periphery of its effort and interest when they were not in the heart of it. To them all its success became a monumental thing.

"The action of their respective legislatures in ratifying the Federal suffrage amendment was greeted by the women of every state with a vast state pride and gratifica-

Fredrikke Palmer's cartoon, "Love. Justice. Honor." suggested the flowering of women's ideals and the pure hope of the newly enfranchised.

tion because that commonwealth stood forth before the world as an upholder of the American ideal of democracy."

However, Catt continued, "To the women of ten states of the Union this pride and gratification were denied. The men of ten states left it to the generosity of the men of other states to enfranchise their own wives, mothers, sisters, daughters. One of the ten was Delaware - the only one north of the Mason and Dixon line. The other nine were Virginia, Maryland, North Carolina, South Carolina, Georgia, Alabama, Louisiana, Mississippi and Florida." Over the succeeding

decades these states eventually ratified the amendment.

Male Support

Catt did give credit to male voters and especially to the male political representatives who helped push the measure through at the end. "On the outside of politics women fought one of the strongest, bravest battles recorded in history, but to these men inside politics, some Republicans, some Democrats, and some members of minority parties, the women of the U.S. owe their enfranchisement."

By the end, however, the bitter opposition had made itself felt and suffragists were torn in their emotions. As Catt remembered, "When the final victory came women were alternatively indignant that it had been so long in coming, and amazed that it had come at all."

But the long battle had been won. In Inez Irwin's words, the final generation of suffragists, full of "the spirit of youth," had stormed the gates of political participation and "finally forced them open. They entered. And leaving behind all sinister remembrance of the battle, they turned their faces towards the morning."

When Catt bid her comrades a final farewell she addressed all the women back to the earliest pioneers when she reflected, "Ah you were heroines all — dear, blessed heroines all." ◆

Epilogue:

Suffragists After 1920

THE 20TH CENTURY was a breakthrough century for American women. The successful drive for the vote left a rich and influential heritage which inspired countless subsequent achievements. After passage of the 19th Amendment, many of the movement's participants remained active politically and had a powerful and widespread impact over the following years. Many suffrage leaders and activists in the states allied themselves with the major parties and in some cases became candidates for public office.

Age and death took their inevitable toll. Within a decade figures like Louisine Havemeyer, Olympia Brown, Mary Garrett Hay, Lila Valentine, and Crystal Eastman had passed away. Many of the veterans of the later suffrage campaigns, however, were still relatively young when the cause was finally won. They joined or led new efforts for equal rights, international peace, civic improvement, family planning, and other reforms and were active in many areas of public life.

The women's rights movement enjoyed its strongest pe-

riod of legislative influence around 1920 when politicians were still concerned that women might vote as a bloc. For a brief time, women's organizations made up one of the strongest lobbies in the nation's capital but its influence declined after 1925.

A number of former suffragists later became influential figures in state and Federal government. Many served their country in various capacities during World War II and some, including Jeannette Rankin and Florence Luscomb, remained active through the social change movements of the 1960s.

Several memoirs and biographies were written by and about individual suffragists, but in general the experiences of women carried little weight in the male world. For decades the entire women's rights movement was virtually ignored by historians, although many women recognized the importance of their own history. Particularly significant were the six-volume *History of Woman Suffrage*, completed by Ida Husted Harper, and Eleanor Flexner's book, *Century of Struggle*. After 1970 the movement drew increasing academic attention.

Fifty years after enfranchisement, the passion that drove the suffragists emerged again as a new generation of women grew aware not only of the inequality and discrimination still facing women but also of the remarkable achievements of women in the past. Therein lay the seeds of rediscovering the full story of how women won the vote and honoring anew the raw courage, strength of purpose, and remarkable accomplishments of women throughout American history.

With dignified grace, robed figures representing the early advocates of equal rights passed the torch to the legions of able women coming after them on the elegant Suffrage Memorial (above) in the Iowa State Capitol. The large bas-relief plaque, unveiled by Carrie Catt in 1936, was created by Iowa sculptor Nellie Verne Walker to pay tribute to those who helped secure the final enfranchisement of women.

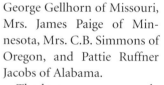

NAWSA Transforms Itself into the League of Women Voters

As THE suffrage campaign approached its successful conclusion, Carrie Catt recommended that NAWSA transform itself into a national League of Women Voters to educate women and train them to press for needed legislation.

First approved in 1919, the league was officially founded at NAWSA's final convention in February 1920. By that time many state associations had already transformed themselves into chapters of the league. After ratification, most of the others followed to form a national organization dedicated to the democratic ideals of the suffrage movement.

Members of the league's new board of directors (below) met in Chicago in February 1920. In front from the left are Maud Wood Park, the first president, Grace Wilbur Trout, chair of the Hostess Committee, and Carrie Chapman Catt, honorary president. Officers and regional directors in the back are Katherine Ludington of Connecticut, Mrs. Richard Edwards of Indiana, Della Dortch of Tennessee, Mrs. George Gellhorn of Missouri, Mrs. James Paige of Minnesota, Mrs. C.B. Simmons of Oregon, and Pattie Ruffner Jacobs of Alabama.

The league overcame early resentment within the political parties and grew into a widely respected nonpartisan organization which included hundreds of thousands of women and men throughout the country.

Above: Organizing public events like earlier suffragists, members of the League of Women Voters in Cincinnati, Ohio, used a downtown billboard to encourage voter registration during a 1926 drive. Left: Founding members of the board in Chicago.

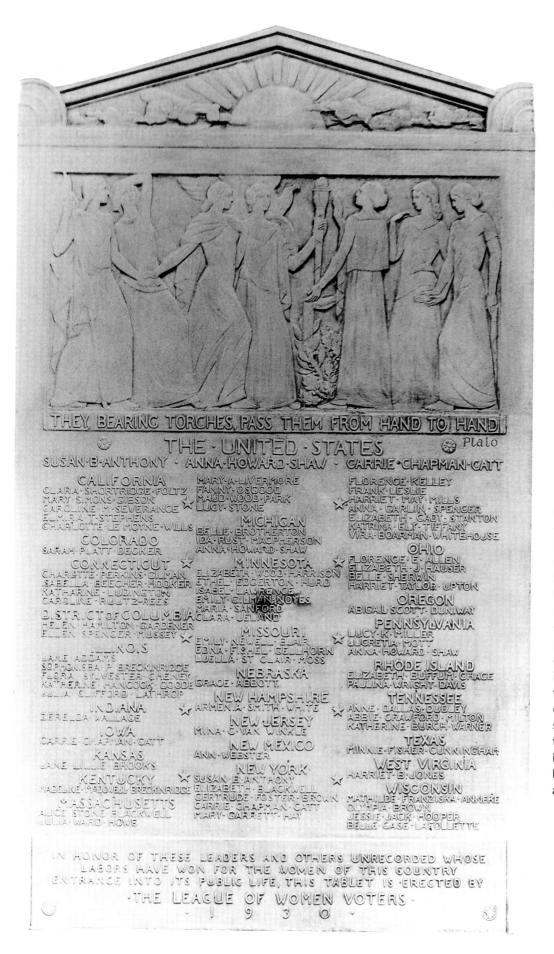

THEY BEARING TORCHES, PASS THEM FROM HAND TO HAND

THE · UNITED · STATES

SUSAN·B·ANTHONY · ANNA·HOWARD·SHAW · CARRIE·CHAPMAN·CATT

Plato

CALIFORNIA
CLARA·SHORTRIDGE·FOLTZ
MARY·SIMONS·GIBSON
CAROLINE·M·SEVERANCE
ELMIRA·T·STEPHENS
CHARLOTTE·LE·MOYNE·WILLS

COLORADO
SARAH·PLATT·DECKER

CONNECTICUT
CHARLOTTE·PERKINS·GILMAN
ISABELLA·BEECHER·HOOKER
KATHARINE·LUDINGTON
CAROLINE·RUUTZ·REES

DISTRICT OF COLUMBIA
HELEN·HAMILTON·GARDENER
ELLEN·SPENCER·MUSSEY

ILLINOIS
JANE·ADDAMS
SOPHONISBA·P·BRECKINRIDGE
FLORA·SYLVESTER·CHENEY
KATHERINE·HANCOCK·GOODE
JULIA·CLIFFORD·LATHROP

INDIANA
ZERELDA·WALLACE

IOWA
CARRIE·CHAPMAN·CATT

KANSAS
JANE·LILLIE·BROOKS

KENTUCKY
MADELINE·McDOWELL·BRECKINRIDGE

MASSACHUSETTS
ALICE·STONE·BLACKWELL
JULIA·WARD·HOWE

MARY·A·LIVERMORE
FANNY·OSGOOD
MAUD·WOOD·PARK
LUCY·STONE

MICHIGAN
BELLE·BROTHERTON
IDA·RUST·MACPHERSON
ANNA·HOWARD·SHAW

MINNESOTA
ELIZABETH·WOOD·HARRISON
ETHEL·EDGERTON·HURD
ISABEL·LAWRENCE
EMILY·GILMAN·NOYES
MARIA·SANFORD
CLARA·UELAND

MISSOURI
EMILY·NEWELL·BLAIR
EDNA·FISHEL·GELLHORN
LUELLA·ST·CLAIR·MOSS

NEBRASKA
GRACE·ABBOTT

NEW HAMPSHIRE
ARMENIA·SMITH·WHITE

NEW JERSEY
MINA·C·VAN·WINKLE

NEW MEXICO
ANN·WEBSTER

NEW YORK
SUSAN·B·ANTHONY
ELIZABETH·BLACKWELL
GERTRUDE·FOSTER·BROWN
CARRIE·CHAPMAN·CATT
MARY·GARRETT·HAY

FLORENCE·KELLEY
FRANK·LESLIE
HARRIET·MAY·MILLS
ANNA·GARLIN·SPENCER
ELIZABETH·CADY·STANTON
KATRINA·ELY·TIFFANY
VIRA·BOARMAN·WHITEHOUSE

OHIO
FLORENCE·E·ALLEN
ELIZABETH·J·HAUSER
BELLE·SHERWIN
HARRIET·TAYLOR·UPTON

OREGON
ABIGAIL·SCOTT·DUNIWAY

PENNSYLVANIA
LUCY·K·MILLER
LUCRETIA·MOTT
ANNA·HOWARD·SHAW

RHODE ISLAND
ELIZABETH·BUFFUM·CHACE
PAULINA·WRIGHT·DAVIS

TENNESSEE
ANNE·DALLAS·DUDLEY
ABBIE·CRAWFORD·MILTON
KATHERINE·BURCH·WARNER

TEXAS
MINNIE·FISHER·CUNNINGHAM

WEST VIRGINIA
HARRIET·B·JONES

WISCONSIN
MATHILDE·FRANZISKA·ANNEKE
OLYMPIA·BROWN
JESSIE·JACK·HOOPER
BELLE·CASE·LA·FOLLETTE

IN HONOR OF THESE LEADERS AND OTHERS UNRECORDED WHOSE
LABORS HAVE WON FOR THE WOMEN OF THIS COUNTRY
ENTRANCE INTO ITS PUBLIC LIFE, THIS TABLET IS ·ERECTED BY
·THE LEAGUE OF WOMEN VOTERS·
·1·9·3·0·

VOTE

BALLOT BOX

League of Women Voters

The League of Women Voters marked its tenth anniversary with a memorial plaque to the leaders of the woman suffrage movement. The bronze tablet (left), designed by Gaetano Cecere, was unveiled at league headquarters in Washington D.C. on April 15, 1931 after state chapters raised money to place each name on the memorial. Conceived to help raise a $250,000 endowment fund for the financially strapped league, the plaque naturally favored NAWSA partisans but it was still one of the only tributes that honored prominent suffragists in various states by name. Unfortunately the memorial was lost during a move to a new building. A poster (above) from the non-partisan league encouraged women to vote since so much was decided by their elected representatives in Washington. League members in state chapters were active in every election.

I WILL VOTE

Dedication
Program

Susan B. Anthony Tree

Sequoia National Park
California

June Twenty-sixth,
Nineteen Hundred Thirty-eight
Eleven-thirty a. m.

A rustic sign identified the huge Susan B. Anthony Tree (right) in California's Sequoia National Park, dedicated in 1938. The 269-foot high *Sequoia gigantea* was between 2,500 and 3,000 years old. A private effort to add Susan B. Anthony to Mt. Rushmore was eventually abandoned but she was honored on the U.S. postage stamp (below) in 1936. A Carrie Chapman Catt Center for Women and Politics was founded at Iowa State University and an Anna Howard Shaw Center was established at the Boston University School of Theology. Other forms of recognition included statues, plaques, and historic sites throughout the country.

Memorials Honor the Suffrage Pioneers

Following passage of the 19th Amendment, supporters across the country arranged for various tributes to the suffrage movement. They included the Iowa Suffrage Memorial and the Woman Suffrage Monument in the Capitol. Plaques honoring the efforts of local suffragists were dedicated in New York, Missouri, Ohio, Texas, Tennessee, and other states.

In 1980 a Women's Rights National Historical Park in Seneca Falls, New York, was approved by Congress, officially recognizing the movement as an important part of American history. The homes of suffragists such as Susan B. Anthony and Matilda Joslyn Gage in New York were designated historic sites as was the Sewall-Belmont House in Washington D.C., headquarters of the National Woman's Party. Alice Paul's birthplace, Paulsdale, in Mt. Laurel, New Jersey, was also preserved and converted into an educational and leadership development center for women and girls.

Adelaide Johnson sculpted the Woman Suffrage Monument which the National Woman's Party presented to the nation on February 15, 1921. Daughter of an Illinois farmer, Johnson was both a dedicated feminist and a passionate artist who studied sculpture in Europe and maintained a studio in Rome for 25 years. Commissioned by the NWP, she sculpted the likenesses of Elizabeth Cady Stanton, Susan B. Anthony, and Lucretia Mott emerging from an eight-ton block of Carrara marble. Each woman "could not have done her work without the other," Johnson explained. "They became the embodiment of an idea." Descendants Peggy and Hope Anthony (left) posed before the memorial on January 3, 1930. The statue was placed in the U.S. Capitol Rotunda in 1997. A commemorative U.S. postage stamp (below) recognized women's rights leaders.

A Controversial New Amendment Seeks Equal Rights for Women

Wの HITE-CLAD women with tricolor banners marched on the Capitol in 1923 to support the introduction of the Equal Rights Amendment. Alice Paul proposed the new amendment as the next necessary step after winning the ballot to overturn hundreds of discriminatory laws on the books in each of the states.

The ERA, originally called the Lucretia Mott Amendment, read simply, "Men and women shall have equal rights throughout the United States and every place subject to its jurisdiction."

The amendment, which Paul and the NWP championed for the next 50 years, called for the elimination of all unequal regulations. But since these included protective laws favoring working women, which had only recently been won against tremendous opposition, the ERA caused deep rifts between former allies.

Above: Supporting the ERA in 1923. Right: Nina Allender's illustration captured the new amendment's purpose: to unbind women from the "protective" bonds of restrictive legislation, legal discrimination, and unequal pay. Left: Promotional stamp.

Should Women Join a Party?

THE QUESTION of affiliating with a political party was one that faced a large number of women for the first time in 1920. Party officials moved quickly to appeal to the new women voters, recruiting and enlisting recognized suffrage leaders and creating new posts for women within the party structures. Some suffragists served eagerly. Others agreed with Alice Paul that the parties were "all about the same," and maintained more independent identities.

Carrie Catt urged women to find and penetrate the inner circles of party politics where the real power lay. But since the major parties had long blocked their rights, many women were wary. "The parties have welcomed women very much as the whale welcomed Jonah," National Woman's Party member Anne O'Hagen observed, "for the purpose of swallowing them whole." She defended the need for a separate women's party as "a force apart."

Republican Leaders

Predictably, however, most new voters registered with one of the two major parties and for a time several former suffragists became influential figures within their state and national parties.

Former NAWSA lobbyist Ruth Hanna McCormick of Illinois served on the Republican National Committee

(RNC) Executive Committee from 1920 to 1924 while Ohio veteran Harriet Taylor Upton was vice-chair. McCormick was elected to Congress in

Helen Todd, Rosalie Jones, and Jeanette Scheiner toured New York in support of Robert LaFollette's presidential candidacy in September 1924. The third party campaign marked a high point in the Progressive tide.

1928 and later held several important government posts, winning recognition as one of the ablest politicians in the country.

Daisy Lampkin, who led the Lucy Stone League of Black suffragists in Pittsburgh, became vice-chair of the Colored Voters Division of the RNC in 1928, and trade union leader Margaret Dreier Robins served on the RNC in 1928 but later backed the New Deal. Mary Church Terrell, Cornelia Bryce Pinchot of Pennsylvania, and Hannah J. Patterson were also active with the Republican Party.

New Jersey leader Lillian Feickert organized the Wo-

men's Republican Club which claimed a membership of 60,000 in 1922, including a majority of the state's suffragists. When she was named

vice-chair of the Republican State Committee she successfully bargained for more women in state posts and equal representation on all political committees.

Mary Garrett Hay of New York, one of the original appointees to the Republican Women's Executive Committee, resigned so that she could campaign against anti-suffrage Republican Senator Wadsworth in 1920.

Democratic Women

Many former suffragists, like Catharine Waugh McCulloch, were similarly active in the Democratic Party. Emily Newell Blair of Missouri

served on the Democratic National Committee (DNC) between 1921 and 1928, became vice-chair and its only woman officer in 1924, and was later active in the New Deal.

Pennsylvania leader Emma Guffey Miller served on the DNC from 1923 until 1970 when she died at age 92. She also chaired the National Woman's Party in the 1960s after earning the reputation of being one of the most effective women in politics between the wars. Florence Hurst Harriman of Washington D.C. co-founded the Women's National Democratic Club with Emily Blair and served for 32 years on the DNC. She was named minister to Norway in 1937.

The influence of former suffragists decreased as other less experienced and less demanding women became active in the political parties. It soon became clear that despite the tremendous transformation of the electorate, the major parties would resist significant change for as long as possible. Although "many women have entered," Emily Blair observed in 1929, "comparatively few have been able to secure place and power."

The enormous obstacles women still faced to participating on equal terms with men would take decades to overcome. And, again, the effort would be led not by parties or politicians but by women themselves. ◆

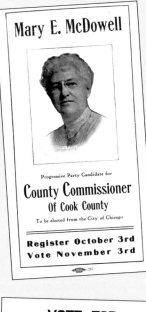

Mary E. McDowell

Progressive Party Candidate for

County Commissioner

Of Cook County

To be elected from the City of Chicago

Register October 3rd
Vote November 3rd

VOTE FOR

AGNES NESTOR

DEMOCRATIC CANDIDATE

STATE REPRESENTATIVE

6th SENATORIAL DISTRICT
PRIMARIES: APRIL 10, 1928

FOR

STATE SENATE

LAURA CLAY
Of Madison County

Democratic Candidate from the 29th District

ESTILL, JACKSON, MADISON, OWSLEY AND ROCKCASTLE COUNTIES

Settlement house director Mary E. McDowell, Illinois trade union leader Agnes Nestor, and states' rights advocate Laura Clay from Kentucky were all candidates for public office after suffrage was won.

Pioneer Women Test the

Aᴀᴛᴇʀ ʏᴇᴀʀs of campaigning at both the state and national levels, many women had developed into skilled politicians and effective legislative analysts. After enfranchisement, a good number of former suffragists in the states chose to run as candidates for public office.

Strong Showings

For some veteran activists, running for office offered a final opportunity to participate in the democratic process. Harriet Taylor Upton was 70 when she ran in the 1924 Republican primary for her father's old congressional seat. Laura Clay was 74 when she became a candidate for the Kentucky state senate in 1923, and Clara Shortridge Foltz was 81 when she entered the Republican primary for California governor in 1930.

In some cases women candidates made strong showings despite their unsuccessful attempts. Jessie Hooper carried Milwaukee when she ran as a Democrat for U.S. Senate in 1922 against fellow suffragist Robert LaFollette. The same year Belle Kearney ran for the U.S. Senate from Mississippi and won over 18,000 votes in the primary. She later served two terms in the state senate. Harriot Blatch received 82,000 votes in 1921 when she ran as the Socialist Party candidate for comptroller of the City of New York. She also

Nina Otero-Warren (left) of Santa Fe campaigned for the U.S. House of Representatives in 1922 after making sure New Mexico ratified the suffrage amendment. The widely respected Latina Republican won over 49,000 votes.

ran for the state assembly in 1922 and for the U.S. Senate in 1926, encouraging women to fully participate in and revitalize the political process. Nettie Rogers Shuler also ran for the New York state assembly.

Other former suffragists met with notable success. Edith Nourse Rogers of Massachusetts won 18 elections, serving in Congress for 35

years and championing the welfare of veterans. Attorney Gail Laughlin was elected to the Maine legislature in 1929, was re-elected twice, and then served in the state senate until 1941. Jeannette Rankin from Montana was re-elected to Congress in 1940.

Wisconsin suffragist Belle Case LaFollette, widow of the senator, could have become the first woman elected to the

Political Waters as Candidates

"How High Will She Go?" asked John T. McCutcheon's 1937 cartoon from the *Chicago Tribune* as a woman climbed the political heights towards the presidency aided by the ladder of women's votes.

Throughout the decade, thousands of women across the country ran for local and state offices and many were successful although their numbers never approached those of male candidates. One serious obstacle they nearly all faced was lack of party support.

Little Party Support

Although the Democratic and Republican parties tried to register as many women as possible as voters, they were generally unwilling to throw their weight behind women candidates. As historian Sara Graham noted, "The parties neither encouraged women to run nor supported their campaigns with adequate funds and party pressure when they did seek election."

Individual women still persisted but few succeeded in winning election to public office. In general, women voters, like male voters and the major political parties, were not immediately supportive of women candidates.

Nonetheless, women gradually made notable gains in city, county, and state elections across the country. By 1929 there were 149 women serving in 38 state legislatures and innumerable women in local government. Progress was slow, but as Illinois attorney Sophonisba Breckinridge put it, "the door had opened a little." ◆

U.S. Senate in 1925 but declined the post and helped her son win it. In 1926, Seattle club woman Bertha Knight Landes became the first woman to be elected mayor of a major city, and in 1932 Hattie Wyatt Caraway, widow of an Arkansas senator, became the first woman elected to the U.S. Senate.

Other candidates included former NAWSA officer Nellie Nugent Somerville who became the first woman elected

to the Mississippi legislature in 1923. Ida B. Wells-Barnett ran for Illinois state senate in 1930 and Texas leader Minnie Fisher Cunningham ran for U.S. Senate in 1927 and for governor in the 1940s. Susan Walker Fitzgerald was the first female Democrat to be elected to the Massachusetts House of Representatives in 1922, and Florence Luscomb narrowly lost a race for the Boston city council the same year.

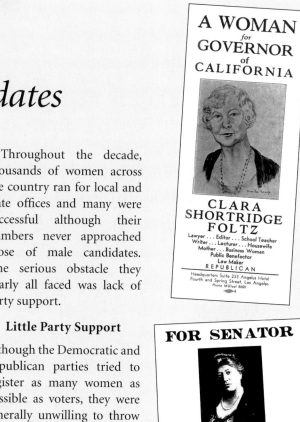

Clara Shortridge Foltz, known as "California's first woman lawyer," ran for California governor in 1930 after helping her brother become a U.S. Senator. Rhode Island suffrage leader Sara Algeo organized a statewide voter registration drive in 1919, and Jeannette Rankin returned to Congress from Montana in 1940.

Jane Addams (above) became the first American woman to win the Nobel Peace Prize in 1931. She was also the "spiritual godmother" of the League of Women Voters, which initially emphasized disarmament and international cooperation. A delegation of league members from Minnesota (upper right) brought a "Mile of Signatures" to national headquarters in Washington D.C. in support of the World Court during one petition drive in December 1923. Carrie Catt (below) led the International Woman Suffrage Alliance until 1923. She then founded the national Committee on the Cause and Cure of War which for a decade organized annual conferences. The suffrage leader was the recipient of numerous awards before her death in 1947.

CARRIE CHAPMAN CATT

Under Auspices

Omaha League
OF
Women Voters

Dec. 4th, 1923

8:00 P. M.
Fontenelle Hotel Ball Room

Subject:
"War or Peace? What Are We Going to Do About It?"

CHILD WELFARE NUMBER

THE Woman Citizen

THE WOMAN'S JOURNAL FOUNDED 1870
TEN CENTS A COPY
JANUARY 22, 1921

SOCIAL WELFARE

WAR APPROPRIATIONS

TREASURY

TWO KINDS OF DEFENSE
The Women Voters of America Don't Like the Disparity in Size, Mr. Congressman

Women Activists Call for Peace

DISTRESSED BY the terrible toll of World War I and by U.S. rejection of the League of Nations, many former suffragists turned their energies towards international peace after 1920. They helped found a number of new organizations promoting peace and civil liberties including most directly the Women's International League for Peace and Freedom, which Jane Addams led from 1919 to 1935. Other suffragists active with the WILPF included Mary Church Terrell, Anne Martin, Mabel Vernon, Emily Greene Balch, and Jeannette Rankin.

Left: Less than six months after the suffrage victory *The Woman Citizen* took aim at the disparity between war appropriations and funds available for social welfare.

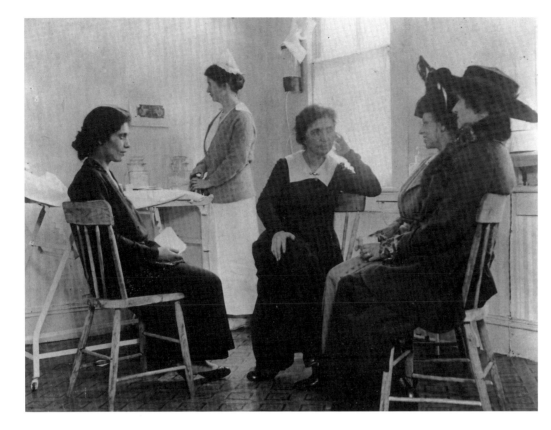

Pioneers in Family Planning

BIRTH CONTROL and family planning became primary concerns for several suffragists after 1920. Blanche Ames led the Birth Control League of Massachusetts which she had cofounded in 1916 as part of a national group headed by nurse Margaret Sanger. Mary Ware Dennett also became a prominent health educator and a rival of Sanger's because of her demand that birth control information be circulated widely, not just to doctors. Her suffrage colleague Katharine Dexter McCormick supported contraceptive research for decades. In the 1950s McCormick used her MIT education to help direct research and her family wealth to help fund the development of the birth control pill, first commercially marketed in 1960.

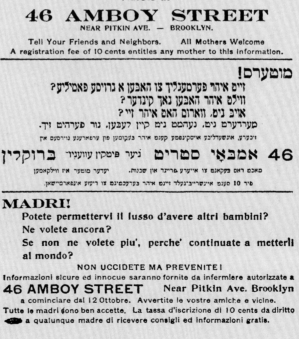

MOTHERS!
Can you afford to have a large family?
Do you want any more children?
If not, why do you have them?
DO NOT KILL, DO NOT TAKE LIFE, BUT PREVENT
Safe, Harmless Information can be obtained of trained Nurses at

46 AMBOY STREET
NEAR PITKIN AVE. — BROOKLYN.

Tell Your Friends and Neighbors.   All Mothers Welcome
A registration fee of 10 cents entitles any mother to this information.

מוטערס!
זײם איהר פערמעגליך צו האבען א גרויסע פאמיליע?
ווילם איהר האבען נאך קינדער?
אויב נים, וואָרום האם איהר זײ?
מערדערם נים, נעהמם נים קין לעבען, נור פערהים זיך.
זיכערע, אונשעדליכע אויסקינפטע קענם איהר בעקומען פון ערפארענע נוירסעם אין

46 אמבאי סטרים ניער פיטקין עוועניו **ברוקלין**
סאכם ראם בעקאנם צו אייערע פריינד און שכנות.   יעדער מומער אין ווילקאמען
פיר 10 סענם אײנשרײבניעלד זינם איהר בערעכמיגם צו דיזע אינפארמיישאן.

MADRI!
Potete permettervi il lusso d'avere altri bambini?
Ne volete ancora?
Se non ne volete piu', perche' continuate a metterli al mondo?
NON UCCIDETE MA PREVENITE!
Informazioni sicure ed innocue saranno fornite da infermiere autorizzate a
46 AMBOY STREET   Near Pitkin Ave. Brooklyn
a cominciare dal 12 Ottobre. Avvertite le vostre amiche e vicine.
Tutte le madri sono ben accette. La tassa d'iscrizione di 10 cents da diritto a qualunque madre di ricevere consigli ed informazioni gratis.

Suffragist Kitty Marion (above) bravely advertised copies of Margaret Sanger's *Birth Control Review* at a time when such information was branded "obscene." In 1915 suffragists and other women founded the National Birth Control League in response to the spread of venereal diseases, unwanted pregnancies, and deadly abortions as well as the basic need for sex education. Sanger (above left, center), a Lower East Side nurse, became a national figure the following year when she was arrested for opening a birth control clinic in New York City (above left), which a handbill (left) announced in English, Yiddish, and Italian. Sanger fought against the government's ban on the circulation of contraceptive information. By 1938 there was a national network of over 300 birth control clinics staffed mostly by female doctors. These led to the Planned Parenthood Federation of America in 1942 which expanded internationally as the issues of overpopulation and a woman's control over her own body grew in importance.

Assessing the Impact: The First Decade

Aᴛᴇʀ ᴛʜᴇʏ had won the vote, suffragists nationally concentrated on goals similar to those already set by women voters in the equal suffrage states. These included training women for citizenship, winning government protection for women and children, and pursuing equality for women in all areas.

Clear Objectives

Historian Felice Gordon studied the post-suffrage movement in New Jersey and summarized six "clearly discernable objectives" which women worked for "despite philosophical differences" throughout the 1920s.

Four objectives related to public welfare: legal protection for working women and children, more effective state and local government, improving the moral quality of life including reducing crime, vice, and alcoholism, and developing methods to prevent future wars. Two objectives addressed the broader rights of women: increasing the participation of women in politics including elected offices, and insuring true equality by eliminating all legal discrimination against women.

To varying degrees, women throughout the country pursued similar goals and many former suffragists made a significant impact both in their states and nationally.

The National Woman's Party led efforts to identify and rewrite discriminatory legislation and over the decade saw 89 equal rights

SUFFRAGE WON—FORWARD, MARCH!

"Forward, March!" directed the patriotic figure on the cover of *The Woman Citizen,* which continued after the suffrage victory as a magazine devoted to the civic interests of women.

bills passed in 23 states. Social welfare legislation also advanced nationally, led by the Women's Joint Congressional Committee which Florence Kelley and Mary Dreier organized.

Ten years after the suffrage victory, the *Newark Evening News* acknowledged what many suffragists had been predicting for years: that women's participation in politics "has not disrupted the home, destroyed the church nor undermined the pillars of the state anymore than it has purified politics, made human welfare the main concern of government or brought universal peace." Overblown fears and predictions, like other political rhetoric, faded away once the contest was over.

Backlash

As the decade matured, however, an increasingly reactionary political atmosphere saw political conservatives and equal rights opponents again challenging the patriotism of such notable women as Jane Addams and Florence Kelley (facing page) and smearing feminism in general. Women's efforts in support of peace and progressive candidates were used to justify charges of Bolshevism and un-Americanism, and a socially conservative backlash tried once again to define and "domesticate" women, this time arguing that their natural role was biologically determined.

In 1929 the country was plunged into the Great Depression and, just over a decade later, another terrible world war. It would take many years for another serious and organized women's movement to emerge. ◆

Facing page: Familiar names appeared on the notorious "Spider Web Chart" targeting progressive women which was circulated by the U.S. War Department in 1924. The controversial chart warned the public that allegedly subversive women's organizations were secretly out to "disarm America."

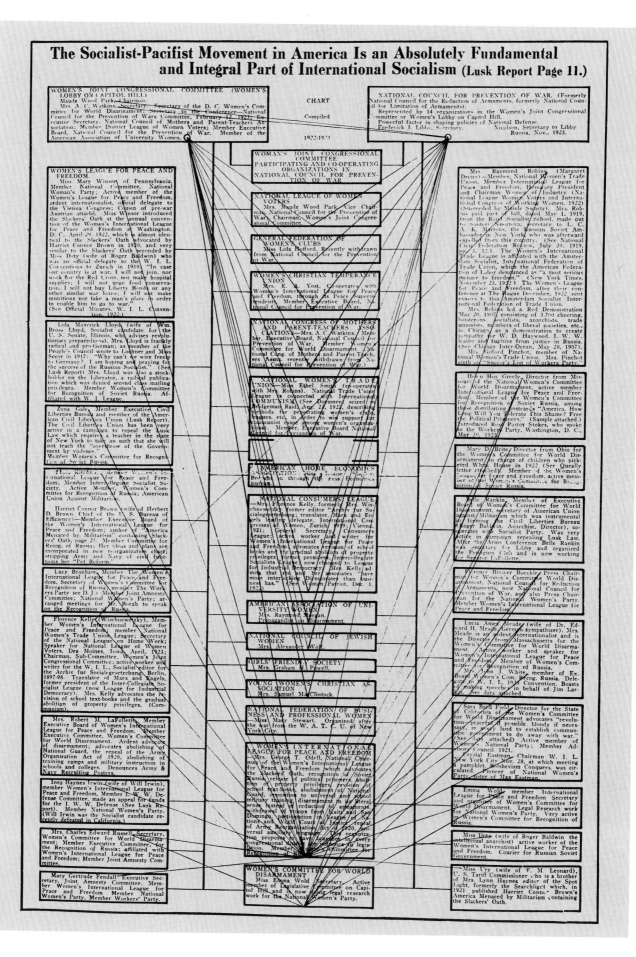

Backing the New Deal and World War II

A DECADE and a half after winning the vote, women who had been active in the suffrage campaigns became important figures in the New Deal helping the country cope with the Great Depression. Women with experience in leadership and organization were of critical importance during the mid-1930s as the country tried to survive widespread economic collapse and forge an effective plan for recovery.

Experienced Leaders

Up to that time there were only a few women in the Federal government. Helen Gardener had become the first woman appointed to the Civil Service Commission in 1920. Prominent suffrage supporters Julia Lathrop and Grace Abbott led the Federal Children's Bureau between 1912 and 1934 successively. They fought for child labor laws, supported protective legislation for working women, and promoted social welfare bills. Abbott later served as a member of the Council for Economic Security during the New Deal and helped draft the Social Security Act in 1935.

Mary Anderson, a former organizer with the Women's Trade Union League, led the Women's Bureau between 1920 and 1944 as part of the Department of Labor and became one of the most popular women in civil service. Winning the respect of both De-

mocrats and Republicans, she made sure the Federal government looked after the needs of working women.

These leading women in government were joined by a number of other former suffragists after the election of President Franklin D. Roosevelt in 1932. Bringing ideas and experiences from their previous campaigns, they became influential in shaping New Deal organizations and legislation.

Lillian Wald and her Henry

Street Settlement, along with Jane Addams and Hull House, had a particularly strong influence on the New Deal since many leading officials, both women and men, were former settlement house residents. Also important was the WTUL whose president, Rose Schneiderman, offered working women's perspective to both Franklin and Eleanor Roosevelt. Schneiderman was appointed to a Federal labor advisory board and served as secretary of the New York

State Department of Labor from 1937 to 1943.

New York suffragist Caroline Goodwin O'Day worked with Eleanor Roosevelt and Harriet May Mills of the Democratic State Committee to register women in the state in 1923. O'Day was elected to Congress in 1934 where she supported New Deal legislation during her four terms as a Representative. Another New York suffragist, Frances Perkins, became the first woman cabinet member in 1933 at age 52, serving as Secretary of Labor under FDR until 1945. She helped draft New Deal legislation, led the Department of Labor through the Depression, and then served on the Civil Service Commission from 1945 to 1953.

Presidential Advisors

Mary McLeod Bethune of Florida formed an unofficial "Black cabinet" and advised the Roosevelts during the Depression. The respected educator had led a Black voter registration drive in 1920 in Florida despite threats from the Ku Klux Klan.

Sue Shelton White of Tennessee became executive secretary of the Women's Division of the Democratic National Committee in 1930. Active with Eleanor Roosevelt in FDR's 1932 victory, White served in several New Deal posts and helped in the creation of the Social Security System.

LIFE

"DEMOCRACY: 50,000,000 VOTERS"

NOVEMBER 4, 1940 **10** CENTS
YEARLY SUBSCRIPTION $4.50

Women voters celebrated the twentieth anniversary of the 19th Amendment in 1940, just before World War II.

Women's Bureau head Mary Anderson sponsored the S.S. Anna Howard Shaw in 1943 in tribute to the late leader.

Mary Williams "Molly" Dewson of Massachusetts also led the Democratic Women's Division for a time. She helped secure jobs for women in the capital and later served on the Social Security Board. With the aid of Harriet Wiseman Elliott of North Carolina, Dewson organized Democratic women and helped popularize the New Deal. Elliott later became "the nation's #1 saleswoman" for bonds during World War II. Belle Sherwin from Ohio, the second president of the League of Women Voters, and Pattie Ruffner Jacobs of Alabama also served in Federal positions.

Another important Federal appointee was Florence Allen who was elected to the Ohio Supreme Court in 1922 and became the first woman appointed to the U.S. Court of Appeals in 1934. She was later mentioned for the U.S. Supreme Court. Nellie Tayloe Ross of Wyoming became the nation's first female governor in 1925 after her husband died. She reduced the state debt, promoted public education, and in 1933 was named the first female director of the U.S. Mint.

Many other former suffragists supported the recovery effort in the ranks of the Federal government and throughout the states. "The change from women's status in government before Roosevelt is unbelievable," Dewson happily reported.

Such hard-earned appointments and achievements as these added to women's emerging political power and provided a way for some to become involved substantively in national affairs. Finally free of the demands of constant suffrage campaigns, women who had only recently won the vote were having a formidable impact on American history.

In 1941 the second world war again mobilized American women, millions of whom put aside other concerns for national service. After the war, a conservative tide and the anti-communist "cold war" dominated the 1950s and early 1960s. ◆

"Rosie the Riveter" became a symbol of women's home front resolve and industrial involvement during World War II.

A New Women's Liberation Movement Marks the 50th Anniversary of Suffrage

FIFTY YEARS after winning the vote thousands of women again filled the streets during the Women's Strike for Equality on August 26, 1970. 50,000 women marched down Fifth Avenue in New York City. Countless others demonstrated across the country for equal opportunity, wage equity, and other issues specifically affecting women.

The demonstrations dramatically revealed the new "women's liberation" movement which had been simmering on campuses and in women's groups during the 1960s. Recognizing that their position in society was still far from equal to that of men's, women began meeting together to analyze their concerns and then organizing and demonstrating for change. The movement grew throughout the decade and activists soon turned their attention to the long-dormant Equal Rights Amendment.

Above: Women marched in Washington D.C. while Betty Friedan (below), president of the National Organization for Women, spoke to reporters in New York on August 26, 1970.

Reviving the Equal Rights Amendment

BY 1970 the Equal Rights Amendment had acquired a history remarkably similar to that of the suffrage amendment before it. Introduced in each successive Congress for nearly fifty years, it had never been voted on in the House. Finally in 1970, responding to the resurgent women's movement, Congress took up the ERA and passed it two years later.

Thirty-one of the necessary thirty-eight states ratified it by 1974 before conservative opponents organized to ensure its defeat. The final three states could not be won before the ten year deadline ran out.

The mobilization for the ERA was only one of many efforts that marked the renewed drive for equality. In nearly every area of society, from business and politics to culture, religion, and sports, the women's liberation movement fundamentally challenged traditionally male realms and forced legal and behavioral changes that furthered the goal of equal rights for women.

Alice Paul earned three law degrees during the 1920s, led the attack against gender-biased legislation in the states, and wrote the Equal Rights Amendment to end sexual discrimination nation-wide. She also founded the Inter-American Commission for Women and the World Woman's Party, working in Geneva until the start of World War II. The war would not have happened, she claimed, if women had been part of the Peace Conference at the end of the first world war. Paul devoted her life to equal rights for women. Just before the 50th anniversary of woman suffrage, she was photographed (above) viewing Adelaide Johnson's bust of Lucretia Mott at the National Woman's Party headquarters in Washington D.C.

Linking themselves with their suffrage heritage, thousands of white-clad women wearing sashes of purple, white, and gold (above) marched for the Equal Rights Amendment in Washington D.C. on August 26, 1977. Alice Paul had just died in July. The lead banner carried the wording of the amendment, which Paul revised in 1943. Opponents in Springfield, Illinois, gathered around Stop ERA leader Phyllis Schlafley (left) on June 19, 1978. Seven years earlier, Congress had approved legislation proposed by New York Representative Bella Abzug that designated August 26 as Women's Equality Day.

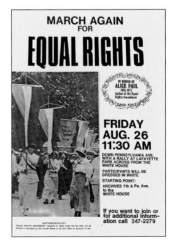

Throughout the later 20th century, women continued to expand their educational opportunities to train themselves and their daughters for new careers in business, science, and public service. But, as few women had been groomed for leadership roles, it took years for them to be accepted seriously by politicians, corporate leaders, and voters. The National Organization for Women, founded in 1966, and *Ms.* magazine, which began publishing in 1972, were particularly influential. Conventions that drew thousands of women, such as in Houston in 1977 and Beijing in 1995, reflected the feminist movement's growing influence both nationally and internationally. And, like women before them, participants emphasized that what have been referred to in the past as women's rights are in actuality basic human rights which should be universally recognized. Susan B. Anthony was honored on a U.S. silver dollar (above) in 1979, and a plaque (inset) in Seneca Falls, New York, commemorated the first woman's rights convention in 1848.

The Woman Suffrage Movement Lives On

B
Y THE START of the 21st century, what was considered "the woman's sphere" had grown to include every area of life. The influence of the women's rights movement had now reached deeply into mainstream society. Further hard-won legislation gradually addressed inequities in many fields and led to a flowering of women's accomplishments in careers and professions where they had long been excluded.

One clear example was that, although women were not allowed to become astronauts until twenty years after the American space program began, they were soon serving as captains and crew members on space shuttle flights. One voyage in 1999 included three women astronauts (above) who, in the weightlessness of space, paid tribute to their suffrage forbearers by carrying one of the National Woman's Party's tricolor banners into orbit. The symbol of the "silent sentinels" was now in the hands of women no longer demanding equal rights but busy exercising them.

They and new generations of women and men recognized that the drive for equal rights was just what the suffragists had claimed it was: a logical and necessary extension of America's ongoing quest for democracy.

Honoring the memory of the suffrage movement both reaffirms the democratic values it embodied and pays tribute to one of the most remarkable nonviolent social transformations of modern times. Suffragists did more than win their own political liberty, double the electorate, and empower American women. They also infused democracy with new life, permanently changed the fabric of American society, and did all this without resorting to threats, violence, or the taking of human life.

Harriot Stanton Blatch was justifiably proud when she wrote that American women were "the first disfranchised class in history who, unaided by any political party, won enfranchisement by its own effort alone, and achieved the victory without the shedding of a drop of human blood." It is a historical accomplishment to emulate and a lasting heritage for us all to cherish. ◆

References and Bibliography

I am listing on this page the primary books that I relied on for the text, particularly those I quoted from. Most of the information in this book can be found there. The bibliography lists other, mostly background or very specific sources. For a complete list of text references, contact the National Women's History Project or visit www.nwhp.org.

The single most useful source is the classic prepared by Elizabeth Cady Stanton and the suffrage pioneers, *The History of Woman Suffrage*. The six volumes are organized by date:

I:	1848-1861
II:	1861-1876
III:	1876-1885
IV:	1883-1900
V:	1900-1920
VI:	1900-1920

While the early volumes are useful for the early days, I particularly depended on volumes 5 and 6. Volume 5 includes reports and speeches from the National American Woman Suffrage Association's conventions, year by year, during the early 20th century. These accounts are rich with detail and information about events the previous year. Some information overlaps that in volume 6, which is organized by state. There the experiences of women in each state during the 20th century are chronicled.

Nearly all the information on the 20th century state campaigns is from volume 6. There are useful appendices, particularly in volume 5, covering men, anti-suffragists, the war, international suffrage work, and other topics. The books' focus on NAWSA, however, means that the National Woman's Party, Black suffragists, and differing points of view are rarely mentioned.

Original – and even reprint – copies of these books are hard to find, but the set is available on CD-ROM from The Bank of Wisdom.

There is no single inclusive source of information on this topic. Many relevant specifics reside only in biographies, periodicals, and the memoirs of individual suffragists. Some are listed in the bibliography. Readers are encouraged to use them to find additional resources on specific women, historic periods, and topics that interest them. Many more exist than can be listed here.

Suffrage Movement History

African American Women in the Struggle for the Vote, Rosalyn Terborg-Penn
Century of Struggle, Eleanor Flexner
Front Door Lobby, Maud Wood Park
Harriot Stanton Blatch and the Winning of Woman Suffrage, Ellen Carol DuBois
Ladies of Seneca Falls, Miriam Gurko
On Account of Sex, Gertrude Foster Brown
Cartooning for Suffrage, Alice Sheppard
The History of Woman Suffrage, Elizabeth Cady Stanton, ed.
Victory: How We Won It, National American Woman Suffrage Association
Woman Suffrage and Politics, Carrie Chapman Catt and Nettie Shuler
Woman Suffrage and the New Democracy, Sara Graham
Women Against Equality, A History of the Anti-Suffrage Movement in the United States from 1895 to 1920, Anne Benjamin

National Woman's Party

The Story of Alice Paul, Inez Haynes Irwin
Iron-Jawed Angels, Linda Ford
Jailed for Freedom, Doris Stevens
Ladies in the Streets, Marjory Nelson

Biographies, Reference Books, and Anthologies

Black Women in America, Darlene Hine, ed.
Carrie Chapman Catt, Mary Peck
Carrie Chapman Catt: A Public Life, Jacqueline Van Voris
Challenging Years, Harriot Stanton Blatch
Notable American Women, Edward James, ed.
One Woman, One Vote, Marjorie Spruill Wheeler, ed.
Susan B. Anthony, Ida Husted Harper
The Story of a Pioneer, Anna Howard Shaw
Women Together, Judith Papachristou
Women's History Sources, Andrea Hinding, ed.

Bibliography

Adams, Mildred. *The Right to Be People.* Philadelphia: J.B. Lippincott, 1967.

Addams, Jane. *The Second Twenty Years at Hull-House.* New York: Macmillan, 1930.

Alexander, Adele Logan. "Grandmother, Grandfather, W.E.B. Du Bois and Booker T. Washington." The Crisis, February 1983, pp 8-11.

Alexander, Adele Logan. "How I Discovered My Grandmother and the Truth about Black Women and the Suffrage Movement." MS Magazine, November 1983, pp 29-35.

Andersen, Kristi. *After Suffrage: Women in Partisan and Electoral Politics before the New Deal.* Chicago: University of Chicago Press, 1996.

Anderson, Bonnie S. *Joyous Greetings: The First International Women's Movement, 1830-1860.* Oxford: Oxford University Press, 2000.

Anthony, Katharine. *Susan B. Anthony, Her Personal History and Her Era.* Garden City, NY: Doubleday, 1954.

Armitage, Shelley. *Kewpies and Beyond, The World of Rose O'Neill.* Jackson: University Press of Mississippi, 1994.

Bacon, Margaret Hope. *Mothers of Feminism, The Story of Quaker Women in America.* San Francisco: Harper & Row, 1986.

Bacon, Margaret Hope. *Valiant Friend, The Life of Lucretia Mott.* New York: Walker & Co., 1980.

Baker, Jean H. *Votes for Women: The Struggle for Suffrage Revisited.* New York: Oxford University Press, 2002.

Bauer, Heidi ed. *The Privilege for Which We Struggled, Leaders of the Woman Suffrage Movement in Minnesota.* St. Paul, MN: Upper Midwest Women's History Center, 1999.

Baughman, Mary U. Foster. "The Day 'Those Creatures' Shook a City, Recollections of the Woman's Suffrage Procession, March 3, 1913." Hyattsville, MD: Shirley Baughman O'Leary, 1963. [in Alice Paul Collection, MC 399, f. 279, Schlesinger Library.]

Bausum, Ann. *With Courage and Cloth, Winning the Fight for a Woman's Right to Vote.* Washington DC: National Geographic, 2004.

Beard, Mary Ritter. *Woman as a Force in History.* New York: Macmillan, 1946.

Beeton, Beverly. *Women Vote in the West: The Woman Suffrage Movement, 1869-1896.* New York: Garland Press, 1986.

Benjamin, Anne. *A History of the Anti-Suffrage Movement in the United States from 1895 to 1920. Women Against Equality.* Lewiston, NY: Edwin Mellen Press, 1991.

Bennion, Sherilyn Cox. *Equal to the Occasion: Women Editors of the Nineteenth-Century West.* Reno and Las Vegas: University of Nevada Press, 1990.

Berson, Robin Kadison. *Marching to a Different Drummer: Unrecognized Heroes of American History* [Jovita Idar], Westport, CT: Greenwood Press, 1994, pp 150-57.

Blackwell, Alice Stone. *Lucy Stone, Pioneer of Woman's Right.* Charlottesville, VA: University Press of Virginia, 2001. Reprint ed.

Bland, Sidney R. "New Life in an Old Movement: Alice Paul and the Great Suffrage Parade of 1913 in Washington, D.C." Records of the Columbia Historical Society 48, 1971-71, pp 657-78.

Blatch, Harriot Stanton and Alma Lutz, *Challenging Years: The Memoirs of Harriot Stanton Blatch.* New York: G.P. Putnam, 1940.

Braly, John Hyde. *Memory Pictures: An Autobiography.* Los Angeles: Neuser, 1912.

Brink, Carol. *Harps in the Wind, The Story of the Singing Hutchinsons.* New York: Macmillan, 1947.

Brown, Elisabeth Potts and Susan Mosher Stuard, eds. *Witnesses for Change, Quaker Women over Three Centuries.* New Brunswick: Rutgers University Press, 1989.

Brown, Gertrude Foster. *On Account of Sex.* Unpublished manuscript. [in Sophia Smith Collection, Suffrage 10:162.]

Brown, Harriet Connor, ed. "Official Program of the Woman's Suffrage Procession." 1913 parade handout. [in Library of Congress.]

Buhle, Mari Jo, and Paul Buhle. *The Concise History of Woman Suffrage.* Urbana: University of Illinois Press, 1978.

Camhi, Jane Jerome. *Women Against Women: American Antisuffragism, 1880-1920.* New York: Carlson Publishing, 1993.

Catt, Carrie Chapman and Nettie Rogers Shuler. *Woman Suffrage and Politics, The Inner Story of the Suffrage Movement.* New York: Charles Scribner's, 1926.

Chen, Constance M. *"The Sex Side of Life," Mary Ware Dennett's Pioneering Battle for Birth Control and Sex Education.* New York: New Press, 1996.

College Equal Suffrage League of Northern California. *Winning Equal Suffrage in California.* San Francisco: Press of the James H. Barry Co., 1913.

Cook, Blanche Weisen, ed. *Crystal Eastman on Women and Revolution.* New York and London: Oxford University Press, 1978.

Coss, Clare. *Lillian D. Wald, Progressive Activist.* New York: The Feminist Press, 1989.

Cote, Charlotte. *Olympia Brown, The Battle for Equality.* Racine, WI: Mother Courage Press, 1988.

Cott, Nancy, ed. *The History of Women in the United States, Women Suffrage.* 2 Parts. University Publications, 1994.

Cott, Nancy R. *The Grounding of Modern Feminism.* New Haven: Yale University Press, 1987.

Crew, Danny O. *Suffragist Sheet Music.* Jefferson, NC: McFarland & Co., 2002.

Davis, Allen F. *American Heroine: The Life and Legend of Jane Addams.* London: Oxford University Press, 1973.

Deckard, Barbara. *The Women's Movement, Political, Socioeconomic, and Psychological Issues.* New York: Harper & Row, 1975.

Dorr, Rheta Childe. *Susan B. Anthony: The Woman Who Changed the Mind of a Nation.* New York: Frederick A. Stokes, 1928.

DuBois, Ellen Carol. *Feminism and Suffrage: The Emergence of an Independent Women's Movement in America, 1848-1869.* Ithaca: Cornell University Press, 1978.

DuBois, Ellen Carol. *Harriot Stanton Blatch and the Winning of Woman Suffrage.* New Haven: Yale University Press, 1997.

DuBois, Ellen Carol. *Woman Suffrage and Women's Rights.* New York: New York University Press, 1998.

Duniway, Abigail. *Pathbreaking: An Autobiographical History of the Equal Suffrage Movement in the Pacific Coast States.* Portland: James, Kerns and Abbott, 1914.

Duster, Alfreda M. ed. *Crusade for Justice, The Autobiography of Ida B. Wells.* Chicago, IL: University of Chicago, 1970.

Edwards, G. Thomas. *Sowing Good Seeds: The Northwest Suffrage Campaigns of Susan B. Anthony.* Portland: Oregon Historical Society Press, 1990.

Eisenbraun, Lana Dunn. *Harriet Taylor Upton's Random Recollections.* Warren, OH: Harriet Taylor Upton Association, 2004.

Faderman, Lillian. *To Believe in Women, What Lesbians Have Done for America – A History.* Boston: Houghton Mifflin, 1999.

Finnegan, Margaret. *Selling Suffrage: Consumer Culture and Votes for Women.* New York: Columbia University Press, 1999.

Flexner, Eleanor. *Century of Struggle: The Women's Rights Movement in the United States.* rev. ed., Cambridge: The Belnap Press of Harvard University Press, 1975.

Ford, Linda G. *Iron-Jawed Angels, The Suffrage Militancy of the National Woman's Party, 1912-1920.* Lanham, MD: University Press of America, 1991.

Fowler, Robert Booth. "Carrie Chapman Catt, Strategist." In Marjorie Spruill Wheeler, ed., *One Woman, One Vote: Rediscovering the Woman Suffrage Movement,* pp 295-314. Troutdale, OR: New Sage Press, 1995.

Fradin, Dennis Brindell and Judith Bloom Fradin. *Ida B. Wells, Mother of the Civil Rights Movement.* New York: Clarion, 2000.

Frost, Elizabeth, & Kathryn Cullen-DuPont. *Women's Suffrage in America, An Eyewitness History.* New York: Facts on File, 1992.

Fry, Amelia Roberts. "Across the Continent in 80 Days in a Mortorcar for Suffrage." Unpublished article, 1995. [Author's collection.]

Fry, Amelia Roberts. "Along the Suffrage Trail, From West to East for Freedom Now!" In Nancy Cott, ed., *History of Women in the United States,* Women Suffrage.

Fuller, Paul. *Laura Clay and the Woman's Rights Movement.* Lexington: University Press of Kentucky, 1975.

Gibson, Karen Bush. *Jovita Idar.* Bear, DE: Mitchell Lane Publishers, 2003.

Giddings, Paula. *When and Where I Enter: The Impact of Black Women on Race and Sex in America.* New York: Bantam Books, 1984.

Gilman, Charlotte Perkins. *The Living of Charlotte Perkins Gilman, An Autobiography.* New York: D. Appleton-Century, 1935.

Gilman, Charlotte Perkins. *Women & Economics: The Economic Factor Between Men and Women as a Factor in Social Evolution.* New York: Harper Torchbooks, 1966.

Gluck, Sherna, ed. *From Parlor to Prison: Five American Suffragists Talk About Their Lives.* New York: Vintage Books, 1976.

Goldmark, Josephine. *Impatient Crusader: Florence Kelley's Life Story.* Urbana: University of Illinois Press, 1953.

Gordon, Ann D., with Bettye Collier-Thomas. *African American Women and the Vote, 1837 -1965.* Amherst, MA: University of Massachusetts Press, 1997.

Gordon, Felice. *After Winning: The Legacy of the New Jersey Suffragists, 1920-1947.* New Brunswick, NJ: Rutgers University Press, 1986.

Graham, Sara Hunter. *Woman Suffrage and the New Democracy.* New Haven CT: Yale University Press, 1996.

Griffith, Elisabeth. *In Her Own Right: The Life of Elizabeth Cady Stanton.* New York: Oxford University Press, 1984.

Gurko, Miriam. *The Ladies of Seneca Falls: The Birth of the Woman's Rights Movement.* New York: Schocken Books, 1976.

Hall, Jacquelyn Dowd. *Revolt against Chivalry: Jessie Daniel Ames and the Women's Campaign against Lynching.* New York: Columbia University Press, 1979.

Harper, Ida Husted, ed. *History of Woman Suffrage,* Volume 6, New York: Source Book Press, 1922; Salem, NH: Ayer Co. reprint, 1985.

Harper, Ida Husted. *Life and Work of Susan B. Anthony.* (3 vol.) Indianapolis and Kansas City: Bowen-Merrill, 1899.

Harvey, Sheridan, et al, eds. *American Women, A Library of Congress Guide for the Study of Women's History and Culture in the United States.* Washington DC: Library of Congress, 2001.

Havemeyer, Louisine. "The Prison Special: Memories of a Militant." *Scribner's* Magazine, June 1922, pp 661-676.

Havemeyer, Louisine. "The Suffrage Torch: Memories of a Militant." *Scribner's* Magazine, May 1922, pp 528-539.

Hays, Elinor Rice. *Morning Star, A Biography of Lucy Stone, 1818-1893.* New York: Harcourt, Brace & World, 1961.

Hinding, Andrea. *Women's History Sources, A Guide to Archives and Manuscript Collections in the United States.* R.R. Bowker Co., 1979.

Hine, Darlene Clark, Elsa Barkley Brown, and Rosalyn Terborg-Penn, eds. *Black Women in America, An Historical Encyclopedia.* (2 vols.) Bloomington, IN: Indiana University Press, 1994.

Horowitz, Helen Lefkowitz. *The Power and Passion of M. Carey Thomas.* New York: Knopf, 1994.

Howard, Anne Bail. *The Long Campaign.* Reno: University of Nevada Press, 1985.

Howe, Julia Ward. "The Case for Woman Suffrage." Outlook 91, April 3, 1909, pp 780-88.

Humphrey, Janet G. *A Texas Suffragist, Diaries and Writings of Jane Y. McCallum.* Austin, TX: Ellen C. Temple, 1988.

Irwin, Inez Haynes. *Angels and Amazons: A Hundred Years of American Women.* Garden City, NY: Doubleday, Doran, 1933.

Irwin, Inez Haynes. *The Story of Alice Paul and the Woman's Party.* Edgewater, FL: Denlinger's Publishers, 1977.

James, Edward L., et al, eds. *Notable American Women, A Biographical Dictionary,* (4 vol.) Cambridge, MA and London: The Belknap Press of Harvard University Press, 1971-1980.

Johnson, Mary Ann, ed. *The Many Faces of Hull-House, The Photographs of Wallace Kirkland.* Urbana, IL: University of Illinois Press, 1989.

Josephson, Hannah. *Jeannette Rankin, First Lady in Congress: A Biography.* Indianapolis: Bobbs-Merrill, 1974.

Karthaus-Hunt, Beatrix. *Posters of the American Women's Suffrage Movement, 1911-1917.* Unpublished thesis. University of California, Riverside, March 1992.

Katzenstein, Caroline. *Lifting the Curtain: The State and National Woman Suffrage Campaigns in Pennsylvania as I Saw Them,* Philadelphia: Dorrance, 1955.

Kerr, Andrea Moore. *Lucy Stone, Speaking Out for Equality.* New Brunswick, NJ: Rutgers University Press, 1992.

Lasser, Carol and Marlene Deahl Merrill. *Friends & Sisters, Letters between Lucy Stone and Antoinette Brown Blackwell 1846-1893.* Urbana, IL: University of Illinois Press, 1987.

Lerner, Gerda. *The Grimke Sisters from South Carolina, Pioneers for Woman's Rights and Abolition.* New York: Schocken Books, 1971.

Lerner, Gerda. *The Woman in American History.* Menlo Park, CA: Addams-Wesley, 1971.

Lewis, David Levering. *W.E.B. DuBois: Biography of a Race, 1868-1919.* New York: Henry Holt, 1993.

Linkugel, Wil A. and Martha Solomon. *Anna Howard Shaw, Suffrage Orator and Social Reformer.* New York: Greenwood Press, 1991.

Linn, James Weber. *Jane Addams, A Biography.* New York: Greenwood Press, 1968.

Lloyd, Trevor. *Suffragettes International, The world-wide campaign for women's rights.* New York: American Heritage Press, 1971.

Logan, Adella Hunt. "Colored Women as Voters." The Crisis, September 1912, pp 24-43.

Louis, James P. "Sue Shelton White and the Woman Suffrage Movement in Tennessee, 1913-1920." Tennessee Historical Quarterly, June 1963, pp 170-90.

Lunardini, Christine. *From Equal Suffrage to Equal Rights, Alice Paul and the National Woman's Party, 1910-1928.* Lincoln, NB: toExcel Press, 2000.

Lutz, Alma. *Susan B. Anthony.* Boston: Beacon, 1959.

Mambretti, Catherine Cole. *The Battle Against the Ballot: Illinois Woman Antisuffragists.* Chicago History, Fall 1980, pp 168-77.

Man-Suffrage Association. *The Case Against Woman Suffrage, A Manual.* New York: Man-Suffrage Association. [in Sophia Smith Collection, Anti-suffrage 18:251.]

Marshall, Shirley M. Unpublished article on the 1913 suffrage parade in Washington D.C. [Author's collection.]

Maurer, Richard. *The Wright Sister, Katharine Wright and Her Famous Brothers.* Brookfield, CT: Roaring Brook Press, 2003.

Mayer, Henry. *All on Fire: William Lloyd Garrison and the Abolition of Slavery.* New York: St. Martin's Press, 1998.

McHenry, Robert. *Liberty's Women.* Springfield, MA: G. & C. Merriam Company, 1980.

Mead, Rebecca J. *How the Vote Was Won, Woman Suffrage in the Western United States, 1868-1914.* New York: New York University Press, 2004.

Melder, Keith E. *Beginnings of Sisterhood, the American Woman's Rights Movement, 1800-1850.* New York: Schocken, 1977.

Million, Joelle. *Woman's Voice, Woman's Place, Lucy Stone and the Birth of the Woman's Rights Movement.* Westport, CT: Praeger, 2003.

Moynihan, Ruth Barnes. *Rebel for Rights: Abigail Scott Duniway.* New Haven and London: Yale University Press, 1983.

National American Woman Suffrage Association. *Victory! How Women Won It. A Centennial Symposium 1840-1940.* New York: H.W. Wilson, 1940.

National Association of Colored Women's Clubs (NACWC). *A History of the Club Movement among the Colored Women of the United States of America.* Washington DC: NACWC, 1902.

Nelson, Marjory. *Ladies in the Streets: A Sociological Analysis of the National Woman's Party, 1910-1930.* State University of New York at Buffalo. Dissertation. Xerox University Microfilms, 1976.

Neu, Charles, "Olympia Brown and the Woman Suffrage Movement." Wisconsin Magazine of History, 1959-1960, pp 277-87.

Neuman, Nancy M., ed. *A Voice of Our Own, Leading American Women Celebrate the Right to Vote.* San Francisco: Jossey-Bass Publishers, 1996.

Noun, Louise R. *Strong-minded Women.* Ames: Iowa State University Press, 1969.

O'Brien, Mary Barmeyer. *Bright Star in the Big Sky, Jeannette Rankin, 1880-1973.* Helena, Montana: Falcon Press, 1995.

Papachristou, Judith. *Women Together: A History in Documents of the Women's Movement in the United States.* New York: Alfred A. Knopf, 1976.

Park, Maud Wood. *Front Door Lobby.* Boston: Beacon Press, 1960.

Peck, Mary Gray. *Carrie Chapman Catt, A Biography.* New York: H.W. Wilson, 1944.

Rakow, Lana F. and Cheris Kramarae, eds. *The Revolution in Words, Righting Women 1868-1871.* London: Routledge, 1990.

Schaffer, Ronald. "The Problem of Consciousness in the Woman Suffrage Movement: A California Perspective." Pacific Historical Review, November 1976, pp 469-93.

Schneider, Dorothy and Carl J. *American Women in the Progressive Era, 1900-1920.* New York: Anchor Books, 1993.

Scott, Anne Firor and Andrew Scott, eds. *One Half the People: The Fight for Woman Suffrage.* Philadelphia: Lippincott, 1975.

Shaw, Anna Howard. *The Story of a Pioneer.* Cleveland, OH: The Pilgrim Press, 1994 [Reprint from 1915].

Sheppard, Alice. *Cartooning for Suffrage.* Albuquerque, NM: University of New Mexico Press, 1994.

Sherr, Lynn and Jurate Kazickas. *Susan B. Anthony Slept Here; A Guide to American Women's Landmarks.* New York: Times Books, 1994.

Sherr, Lynn. *Failure is Impossible. Susan B. Anthony in Her Own Words.* New York: Times Books, 1995.

Silver, Mae, and Sue Cazaly. *The Sixth Star: Images and Memorabilia of California Women's Political History, 1868-1915.* San Francisco: Ord Street Press, 2000.

Simon, Charnan. *Jane Addams, Pioneer Social Worker.* New York: Children's Press, 1997.

Sloan, Kay. "Sexual Warfare in the Silent Cinema: Comedies and Melodramas of Woman Suffragism." In Nancy Cott, ed., *History of Women in the United States,* Women Suffrage.

Smith, Norma. *Jeannette Rankin: America's Conscience.* Helena: Montana Historical Society Press, 2002.

Sochen, June. *Herstory: A Record of the American Woman's Past.* Palo Alto, CA: Mayfield Publishing Co., 1982.

Solomon, Martha M., ed. *A Voice of Their Own: The Woman Suffrage Press, 1840-1910.* Tuscaloosa: University of Alabama Press, 1991.

Solomons, Selina. *How We Won the Vote in California: A True Story of the Campaign of 1911.* San Francisco: New Woman Publishing, 1912.

Stalcup, Brenda, ed. *Women's Suffrage.* San Diego, CA: Greenhaven Press, 2000.

Stanton, Elizabeth Cady, Susan B. Anthony, Matilda Joslyn Gage, and Ida Husted Harper, eds. *The History of Woman Suffrage.* 6 vol. 1881-1922. Reprint ed. Salem, NH: Ayer, 1985. [Also compact disc, Bank of Wisdom: Louisville, KY.]

Stanton, Elizabeth Cady. *Eighty Years and More: Reminiscences, 1813-1897.* New York: Schocken, 1988.

Stapler, Martha G., ed. *The Woman Suffrage Year Book, 1917.* New York: National Woman Suffrage Publishing Co., 1917.

Sterling, Dorothy. *Ahead of Her Time, Abby Kelley and the Politics of Antislavery.* New York: W.W. Norton, 1991.

Stern, Madeleine B. *Purple Passage: The Life of Mrs. Frank Leslie.* Norman: University of Oklahoma Press, 1953.

Stevens, Doris. *Jailed for Freedom.* New York: Boni & Liveright, 1920.

Strom, Sharon Hartman. "Leadership and Tactics in the American Woman Suffrage Movement: A New Perspective from Massachusetts." Journal of American History, September 1975, pp 296-315.

Suhl, Yuri. *Ernestine Rose and the Battle for Human Rights.* New York: Reynal & Co., 1959.

Taber, Richard W. "Sacajawea and the Suffragettes." Pacific Northwest Quarterly, January 1967, pp 7-13.

Terborg-Penn, Rosalyn. *African American Women in the Struggle for the Vote, 1850-1920.* Bloomington, IN: Indiana University Press, 1998.

Thompson, Kathleen and Hilary MacAustin. *The Face of Our Past, Images of Black Women from Colonial America to the Present.* Bloomington: Indiana University Press, 1999.

Tilly, Louise and Patricia Gurin, eds. *Women, Politics and Change.* New York: Russell Sage Foundation, 1990.

Tremain, Rose. *The Fight for Freedom for Women.* New York: Ballantine, 1973.

Van Voris, Jacqueline. *Carrie Chapman Catt: A Public Life.* New York: The Feminist Press at the City University of New York, 1996.

Wadsworth, Mrs. James W., Jr. "Case Against Suffrage." *New York Times Magazine,* September 9, 1917.

Wagner, Sally Roesch. *A Time Of Protest: Suffragists Challenge the Republic: 1870-1887.* Sacramento, CA: Spectrum Publications, 1987.

Ward, Geoffrey C., and Ken Burns. *Not for Ourselves Alone: The Story of Elizabeth Cady Stanton and Susan B. Anthony.* New York: Alfred A. Knopf, 1999.

Ward, Jean M. and Elaine A. Maveety, eds. *"Yours for Liberty" Selections from Abigail Scott Duniway's Suffrage Newspaper.* Corvallis, OR: Oregon State University Press, 2000.

Ware, Susan. *Beyond Suffrage, Women in the New Deal.* Cambridge, MA: Harvard University Press, 1981.

Washington, Margaret, ed. *Narrative of Sojourner Truth.* New York: Vintage, 1993.

Weatherford, Doris. *A History of the American Suffragist Movement.* Santa Barbara, CA: ABC-CLIO, 1998.

Weisberg, Barbara. *Susan B. Anthony, Woman Suffragist.* New York: Chelsea House, 1988.

Wheeler, Marjorie Spruill, ed. *One Woman , One Vote: Rediscovering the Woman Suffrage Movement.* Troutdale, OR: New Sage Press, 1995.

Wheeler, Marjorie Spruill. *New Women of the New South: The Leaders of the Woman Suffrage Movement in the Southern States.* New York: Oxford University Press, 1993.

Willard, Frances E., and Mary A. Livermore, eds. *A Woman of the Century: Fourteen Hundred-Seventy Biographical Sketches Accompanied by Portraits o Leading American Women in All Walks of Life.* Buffalo, NY: Charles Wells Moulton, 1893.

Wilson, Vincent, Jr. *The Book of Distinguished American Women.* Brookeville, MD: American History Research Associates, 1983.

Yee, Shirley J. *Black Women Abolitionists, A Study in Activism, 1828-1860.* Knoxville, TN: University of Tennessee Press, 1992.

Yellin, Carol Lynn, and Janann Sherman. *The Perfect 36: Tennessee Delivers Woman Suffrage.* Oak Ridge, TN: Iris Press, 1998.

Yellin, Jean Fagan. "DuBois' Crisis and Woman's Suffrage." The Massachusetts Review, Spring 1973, pp 365-75.

Young, Louise M. *In the Public Interest, The League of Women Voters, 1920-1970.* New York: Greenwood Press, 1989.

Younger, Maud. "Revelations of a Woman Lobbyist." McCall's Magazine, Sept/Oct/Nov 1919, passim.

Younger, Maud. "Taking Orders: A Day as a Waitress in a San Francisco Restaurant." Sunset Magazine, October 1908, pp 518-22.

Younger, Maud. "The Diary of an Amateur Waitress: An Industrial Problem from a Worker's Point of View." McClure's Magazine, March 1907, pp 543-52, and April 1907, pp 665-77.

British Suffrage Movement

Atkinson, Diane. *The Purple, White and Green, Suffragettes in London 1906-1914.* London: Museum of London, 1992.

Atkinson, Diane. *The Suffragettes in Pictures.* Gloucestershire: Sutton, 1996.

Crawford, Elizabeth. *The Women's Suffrage Movement, A Reference Guide 1866-1928.* London: UCL Press, 1999.

Mackenzie, Midge. *Shoulder to Shoulder.* New York: Knopf, 1975.

Pankhurst, Richard. *Sylvia Pankhurst, Artist and Crusader.* New York: Paddington Press, 1979.

Pankhurst, Sylvia. *The Suffragettes: The History of the Women's Militant Suffragette Movement 1905-1910.* New York: Sturgist Walton, 1911.

Pethick-Lawrence, Emmeline. *My Part in a Changing World.* London: Gollancz, 1938.

Raeburn, Antonia. *The Suffragette View.* Newton Abbot: David & Charles, 1976.

Tickner, Lisa. *The Spectacle of Women, Imagery of the Suffrage Campaign 1907-1914.* Chicago, IL: University of Chicago Press, 1988.

Photographic Credits

Abbreviations

HS	Historical Society
PL	Public Library
S/SF	Suffrage, Subject File
S/US	Sufrage, U.S.
SBA	Susan B. Anthony
SHS	State Historical Society
U	University

Source Abbreviations

Bancroft	Bancroft Library, University of California, Berkeley
Brown Bros.	Brown Brothers
Bryn Mawr	Bryn Mawr College, Carrie Chapman Catt Photo Albums
Denison	Denison Library, Scripps College, Claremont, CA
ECST	Coline Jenkins, Elizabeth Cady Stanton Trust
FC	Frank Corbeil, private collector
Hoover	Hoover Institution, Stanford U
Huntington	Huntington Library, San Marino, CA
LC	Library of Congress, usually Prints and Photographs Division [LC-USZ62-# is a photo order number]
LCMS	Library of Congress Manuscript Division
LCRB	Library of Congress Rare Books
LWV	League of Women Voters
Moorland	Moorland-Spingarn Research Center, Howard U
NA	National Archives
NJHS	New Jersey Historical Society
NWHP	National Women's History Project
NWP	National Woman's Party
NYHS	New-York Historical Society
NYPL	New York Public Library [Manuscript Div., or Local History/Genealogy, NY City Views]
S.I.	Smithsonian Institution
S.L.	Schlesinger Library, Radcliffe
SSC	Sophia Smith Collection
WSMP	Woman Suffrage Media Project (author's collection)

Corbis and Culver are commercial photo agencies.

The institutions and businesses credited own the rights to these images and control their use. Contact them directly if you wish to reproduce an image. Reference numbers are included for non-commercial sources.

Many stamps, pins, and campaign buttons are reproduced larger than actual size. Some images from manuscript collections, e.g. Susan B. Anthony's scrapbooks, were only available on microfilm. Dirt and marks have been removed where necessary, but no images have been electronically altered in any way.

Picture positions on each page are keyed according to **T** (top), **B** (bottom), **R** (right), and **L** (left), and various combinations. **C** is for center.

Introduction

v NJHS Moorfield Papers. *xi* S.I. 78-17195. *xii* ECST. *xiii* LC-B201-2684-2. *xiv* WSMP.

Chapter 1. 1800-1865

1 T: Historic St. Mary's, photo by Brian Doyle; S.I., shield 79-8397, pin 81-8595. **2-3** WSMP. **3 T & B:** WSMP. **4 TL:** American Antiquarian Society; **TR:** North Wind; **BR:** LCMS Stanton p. 199; **BL:** Strong Museum No. 91.1190. **5 L:** North Wind. **TR:** LC-USZ62-29201. **BR:** LC RB. **6 TL:** Chicago HS ICHi-11897; **BL:** S.I. 74-4829. **6-7** SSC No. SAAS. **7 TR:** Cleveland PL; **BR:** LC-USZ62-1951. **8 TL:** NYHS 53370; **R:** Seneca Falls HS; **B:** LCMS Stanton. **9 TR:** LC-USZ62-50821; **B:** LC-USZ62-60868. **10 TL:** S.L. A163-6-2. **10-11** LC-USZ62-2036. **11 TR:** Chicago HS ICHi-29415; **BR:** WSMP. **12 TL:** WSMP; **BL:** S.I. 79-1266. **12-13** Cleveland PL. **13 TR:** LC-USZ62-118946; **BR:** LC RB E449.A6234. **14 TL:** LC-USZ62-7843; **BL:** Seneca Falls HS #1426; **R:** SSC Flat File 2. **15 L:** Collection of Dr. Danny O. Crew; **TR:** LCMS Catt. **16 TL:** Rhode Island HS RHi (x32) 88; **BL:** LC Music Div. M1.A12V, vol. 57; **R:** SSC Garrison 74/2078. **17** LC-USZ62-

10370. **18** TL: LCMS 12880-4; **BL:** WSMP. **18-19** S.I. 73-8070; **TR:** U of Rochester 87.5. **19 BR:** FC. **20 TL:** S.L.; **R:** U of Rochester. **21 TL:** US Army Institute; **TR:** S.L. PC1 (43)-1; **B:** LC-B8184-B445.

Chapter 2. 1865-1878

22-23 Culver. **24 T:** LC-USZ62-33935; **B:** LCMS 12880-10. **25 L:** SSC S/US 12/191; **TR:** S.L. A69-4-1; **BR:** S.L. M133, Reel E9. **26 TL:** Seaver Center P.33:29E; **BL:** New Hampshire HS 3571; **R:** LC-USZ62-60909. **27** Wisc. HS WHi (x3) 34341. **28 TL:** S.L. 178-v.3-3; **BL:** Bryn Mawr Catt 0061; **R:** Harriet Beecher Stowe Center, Hartford, CT. **29 L:** WSMP; **TR:** SHS of Iowa, Des Moines, Iowa Woman Suffrage Coll.; **BR:** S.L. WRC-26a-3. **30 TL:** LC-USZ61-788; **BL:** Houston Metro. Research Center, Houston PL, M.F. Cunningham papers, Box 3, f.20; **R:** S.L. PC1 (125)-1. **31 T:** WSMP; **B:** U of Wyoming, American Heritage Center. **32** Johns Hopkins LSL Box 16, #127B. **33** LC-USZ62-2023. **34 TL:** SSC No. WRWV. **34-35** Culver. **35 TR:** Chicago HS ICHi-14322. **36 T:** S.I. 76-14008; **B:** S.L. M133, Reel E9. **37 L:** LC-USZ62-114833; **TR:** U of Rochester Anthony papers 87.5b; **BR:** LC-USZ62-60762. **38 TL:** Moorland; **TR:** WSMP; **B:** Oregon HS OrHi 37312. **39 L:** U of Illinois at Chicago Library, Stewart Coll.; **R:** LC-USZ62-102148. **40 T:** WSMP; **B:** LC RB. **41 T:** Culver; **B:** LC RB, JK1896.A6 vol 5a, p5. **42 L:** Rochester PL; **R:** LC RB, JK1896.A6 vol 5a, p101. **43 L:** U of Rochester; **TR:** S.I. 74-847; **BR:** Florentine FIlms. **44-45** Culver. **46 T:** Cleveland PL; **BL:** WSMP; **BR:** WSMP, also LC-USZ62-61022. **47 TL:** SHS of North Dakota 239-134; **TR:** Chicago HS ICHi-19639; **B:** WSMP.

Chapter 3. 1878-1900

48 LC-USZC4-4119. **49 L:** LC-USZ62-2117; **R:** FC. **50 L:** Chicago HS ICHi-29416. **50-51** LC-USZ62-60964. **51 TR:** SSC S/Anti-S; **B:** WSMP; **52 TL:** S.L. M133, Reel E28. **52-53** Wisc. HS WHi (x3) 25278. **53 TR:** FC. **54 TL:** LC-USZ62-11080; **TR:** LC-USZ62-33867; **BR:** S.I. 78-16868; **BL:** S.I. 50326. **55 L:** S.L. M133, Reel E9; **R:** S.L. M133, Reel E9. **56 TL:** Culver; **B:** SSC Garrison 73/2063. **56-57** U of Oklahoma Swearingen Coll. #108. **57 TR:** Moorland. **58-59** LC-USZ62-10864. **60 L:** NYPL/Schomberg; **R:** Brown U, Hay Library, Broadsides RB 825. **61 L:** SSC S/US 5/100; **R:** LC-USZ62-73362. **62 L:** S.L. PC1 (147a)-8. **62-63** Chicago HS ICHi-09222. **64 L:** LCMS SBA, vol 16, p157; **R:** WSMP. **65** SSC Record 2059. **66 TL:** S.L. 178-v3-12l; **TR:** SSC No. WRBA4; **BR:** SSC S/US 5/95; **BL:** LCMS-B634-4. **67** SSC No. WRSL2.

68 TL: S.L. PC1 (43)-2; **TR:** Denver PL #11407; **BR:** WSMP; **BL:** S.L. PC1 (43)-4. **69 L:** WSMP; **R:** LC RB, JK1896.A6 vol 19. **70-71** Friends Historical Library RG6, S.6/12. **72 L:** U of Chicago Library, Wells Papers, vol 5, f7, ph2; **R:** LC-USZC2-754. **73 TL:** LC-USZ62-49487; **TR:** SBA House; **B:** WSMP. **74 TL:** WSMP; **B:** WSMP. **74-75** Idaho State HS, 78-203.95. **75 TR:** S.L. PC1 (167)-1; **BR:** S.L. Foley Coll. **76 TL:** SSC Diaz 1/leaflets; **BL:** S.L. PC1 (147a)-16; **BR:** WSMP. **76-77** U of Rochester SBA Papers. **77 R:** LCMS. **78** WSMP. **79 L:** LC-USZ62-51555; **R:** LC-USZ62-84496; **B:** LC RB, E449.D16A, 13. **80 L:** U of Illinois JAMC#13; **R:** U of Illinois JAMC#137. **81 TR:** U of Illinois JAMC#384; **BR:** U of Illinois JAMC#195. **82 T:** LC-USZ62-2470; **B:** LC-USZ62-96565. **83 TL:** LC-USZ62-11202; **TR:** S.I. 79-16867; **BR:** Nebraska State HS S946-14; **BL:** LCMS SBA, vol 20, p389.

Chapter 4. 1900-1909

84 Collection of Dr. Danny O. Crew. **85 L:** SSC S/US 12/179; **TR:** S.I. 2003-24279; **BR:** WSMP. **86 TL:** U of Kentucky Libraries, Special Coll., Clay PA46M4; **B:** ECST. **86-87** Chicago HS DN-2489. **87: TR:** U of Rochester Sweet Papers; **BR:** WSMP. **88 TL:** S.L. PC 381-1-3; **BL:** S.L. P166; **R:** S.L. GR1-48. **89 TL:** LC-USZ62-30491; **BL:** Corbis; **TR:** Huntington SBA 14:37. **90** U of Rochester/SBA House Neg 90.2. **91 TL:** LC-USZ62-92859; **TR:** LC-USZ62-79903; **BR:** LC-USZ62-118873; **BL:** FC. **92 TL:** Huntington SBA 14:37; **BL:** S.I. 79-6338; **R:** LC. **93** S.L. PC1 (143)-1. **94-95** Oregon HS OrHi 59438. **95 R:** LC-USZ62-46407. **96 TL:** Huntington SBA/PC2; **TR:** Oregon HS OrHi 37240; **BR:** LCMS SBA; **BL:** FC. **97** Florida State Archives neg 10,667. **98 T:** S.L. A68-431-10; **B:** S.I. 77-4108. **99 TL:** LC-B2-21-7; **TR:** Culver; **BR:** LC-B2-2398-9; **BL:** WSMP. **100** Huntington. **101** LC-USZC4-6471. **102 TL:** FC; **BL:** LCMS Blatch 8/87. **102-103** S.L. MC399 f.251. **103 TR:** Nebraska State HS PC1427; **BR:** FC; **BL:** WSMP. **104 L:** Wayne State U, Archives of Labor and Urban Affairs. **104-105** LC-B2-26-7. **105 TR:** Bryn Mawr Catt 0016; **BR:** Huntington SBA Clippings 15:6; **BL:** FC. **106-107** LC-USZ62-23625. **107 R:** LC-B2-499-15. **108 T:** S.I. 2003-24278; **B:** S.I. 76-3037. **109 TL:** LCMS Blatch; **TR:** LC-USZ62-132966; **B:** Vassar College Libraries, Special Collections. **110** ECST. **111 TL:** LC-USZ62-98405; **TR:** LC-USZ62-68346; **B:** Huntington SBA/PC1 #58. **112 TL:** S.I. Archives deVincent Coll. 5.7A; **TR:** WSMP; **BR:** Collection of Dr. Danny O. Crew; **BL:** Collection of Dr. Danny O. Crew. **113 all postcards** WSMP; **BL pin:** S.I. 81-8600. **114 L:** S.L. PC1 (30)-1. **114-115** Brown Bros. **115 R:** LC-USZ62-28475. **116-117** WSMP. **118 TL:** LCMS NAWSA; **TR:** LCMS Catt,

Box 29; **BR:** WSMP; **BL:** Huntington SBA/PC2#16. **119 T:** LCMS Catt, Box 29; **B:** S.L. A68-371-11.

Chapter 5. 1910

120 Bancroft Keith Family Papers. **121 L:** ECST; **TR:** FC; **BR:** S.I. 2003-24279. **122 T:** Chicago HS ICHi-20157; **B:** Connecticut HS #424. **123** LCMS Catt, Box 30. **124 L:** Huntington SBA/PC2. **124-125** S.L. Page Coll., WRC-v.23a-1. **126** WSMP. **127** Culver. **128 TL:** Corbis; **BL:** WSMP; **BR:** S.I. 2003-24274. **128-129** Bryn Mawr Catt 0265. **129 TR:** U of Rochester, Unitarian Church Papers, 177-330-2; **BR:** LCMS NAWSA. **130 T:** S.L. WRC-633-10-5; **B:** S.L. P416. **131 L:** S.L. WRC-633-3; **TR:** S.L. WRC-633-23; **BR:** S.L. PC1 (66)-2. **132 TL:** S.L. A68-251f-23; **BL:** NYPL NAWSA Ms. Box 8. **132-133** S.L. A68-632f-1. **133 TR:** U of North Carolina Bjorkman Papers, #p.3070/16; **BR:** NYPL NAWSA Ms. Box 8; **BL:** S.L. PC7 (3)-1. **134 T:** Whatcom Museum of History and Art, Courtesy of Gloria Martin; **BL:** S.I. 2003-24277; **BR:** WSMP. **135 L:** Washington State HS Curtis 19943; **TR:** Oregon HS OrHi 83650; **BR:** S.L. MC392-209. **136-137** Culver [also LC-USZC2-1049].

Chapter 6. 1911

138 S.L. GR1. **139 L:** NWHP/California Historical Society; **TR:** WSMP; **BR:** S.I. 2003-24271. **140 TL:** U of Illinois JAMC#405; **BL:** WSMP; **R:** Chicago HS ICHi-03200. **141 T:** NYHS 36220-A; **B:** SSC Record 2066. **142 TL:** S.L. PC7 (4)-1; **BL:** SSC Record 2064. **142-143** SSC Record 2065. **144 T:** ECST; **B:** LCMS Blatch. **145 T:** Ishtar Films; **B:** S.I. 77-4108. **146 T:** Chicago HS ICHi-10601; **B:** Bancroft CB773. **147 TL:** CA State Library 4427-b; **TR:** Huntington SBA/CA/Clippings (1) #49; **BR:** S.I. 81-8588; **BL:** SSC S/US 12/179. **148 TL:** Huntington SBA 1:49; **BL:** S.I. 2003-24272. **148-149** San Diego HS #12107. **150 TL:** Bancroft Special Collections, Portraits; **TR:** Bancroft Special Collections, Suffrage; **B:** LCMS NWP. **151** Huntington. **152** Bancroft Keith Family Papers. **153 TL:** Huntington pf 39871; **TR:** Huntington SBA/PC2 p29; **BR:** Huntington SBA/PC2; **BL:** ECST.

Chapter 7. 1912

154-155 LC-USZ62-58971. **155 TR:** Huntington SBA 14:37; **BR:** S.I. 2003-24270. **156 TL:** LC-USZ62-112772; **BL:** LC-USZ62-43017; **R:** SSC No. WRSRN. **157 T:** LCMS Blatch 4:3; **B:** LC-USZ62-70383. **158 TL:** ECST. **158-159** NA 208-PR-14M-1. **159 TR:** Friends Historical Library RG5, S.2; **BR:** LC-USZ62-53213. **160-161** LCMS Blatch 12:12, p123. **161 TR:** LC-B2-2544-11; **BR:** LC-USZ62-10845. **162 TL:** LC-USZ62-9355; **BL:** SSC Garrison 73/2063; **R:** SSC S/US (Biog) 11/165. **163 T:** LC-B2-2774-15; **BL:** LC-B2-2684-6; **BR:** S.I. 2003-24277. **164 T:** Bryn Mawr Catt 0021; **B:** LCMS NAWSA Reel 69. **165 T:** Bryn Mawr Catt 0264; **BL:** Bryn Mawr Catt 0023; **BR:** Bryn Mawr Catt 0189. **166 TL:** ECST; **TR:** WSMP; **BR:** Wisc. HS 67285; **BL:** Huntington SBA 14:38; **Ohio pin:** S.I. 2003-24276; **Mother pin:** ECS; **Eq. Suff. pin:** S.I. 81-8586. **167 TL:** LC-D418-15; **TR:** SSC S/US 12/195; **BR:** S.I. 2003-24280; **BL:** WSMP. **168 TL:** Huntington 323 vol.1 (55); **TR:** LC-USZ62-30776; **BR:** Bowling Green State U, Center for Archival Coll., Meekison Coll; **BL:** ECST. **169** LC-USZ62-22260. **170 TL:** S.I. Institution, Anacostia Museum; **TR:** LCMS 7179; **B:** LCMS NAWSA Reel 69. **171** WSMP. **172 TL:** Minn. HS J7.11/r4, 28847; **BL:** SSC Record 2034. **172-173** Kansas SHS FK2.D4, L.56*2. **173 TR:** Huntington SBA/PC2; **BR:** WSMP. **174 L:** ECS; **R:** SSC S/SF 18/247. **175 T:** ECST; **B:** LC-USZ62-32958. **176 TL:** Wisc. HS WHi (x3)2905; **C:** S.I. 2003-24277; **BL:** Wisc. HS WHi (x3)22887; **BR:** Wisc. HS WHi (x3)2902. **176-177** Wisc. HS WHi (x3)5587. **177 TR:** Wisc. HS WHi (x3)48222; **BR:** LC-B2-3672-10; **BL:** Wisc. HS WHi (x3)5588. **178 T:** Wisc. HS WHi (x3)22433; **B:** Wisc. HS WHi (x3)35521. **179** WSMP. **180 T:** S.L. WRC-109a-1; **BL:** LC-USZ62-53516; **BR:** Denison Suffrage 1:99. **181** WSMP, *Woman Voter*, December 1912. **182 TL:** S.L. PC60-5-8; **BL:** S.L. A63-119-3. **182-183** SSC Record 2061.

Chapter 8. 1913

184-185 LC-USZC4-2996. **186 TL:** S.L. MC399 f.340; **BL:** WSMP. **186-187** LC-USZ62-53217. **187 TR:** LC-USZ62-55985; **BR:** LC-USZ62-43682. **188 T:** LC-USZ62-49123; **B:** LC-USZ62-90317. **189 T:** NYPL 1428 A3; **B:** NWP. **190 TL:** LC-USZ62-48792; **BL:** Corbis. **190-191** LC-USZ62-34030. **191 TR:** NWP; **BR:** WSMP. **192 T:** LC-USZ61-1154; **B:** S.I. 2003-24273. **193 L:** SSC No. WRM12; **R:** S.I. 76-17852. **194-195** LC-B2-2501-1A. **196 TL:** S.I. 74-7503; **TR:** LC-USZ62-35138; **CR:** SSC Garrison 73/2064; **BR:** S.L. PC7 (5)-2. **197 T:** Denver PL, Western History Dept. Suffrage 5, Max 322; **B:** LC-USZ62-58972. **198** LC-USZ62-26724. **199 T:** LC-USZ62-34031; **B:** S.L. AW 378-1-13. **200 TL:** S.L. A/W 378-1-11; **BL:** LC-USZ62-70382. **200-201** LC-USZ62-053227. **201 TR:** LC-USZ62-106069; **BR:** LC-USZ62-10852. **202 L:** LC-USZ62-112769. **202-203** LC-USZ62-10854. **203 TR:** NYPL 1427-D7; **BR:** Historic Pictures 4147. **204 TL:** LCMS Blatch 11:78; **TR:** LC-USZ62-53221; **BR:** LC-USZ62-32461; **BL:** S.I.

2003-24267. **205** S.L. M133 D7, Foley Coll. **206 T:** NYPL NAWSA Ms. Box 7; **B:** S.I. 78-17174. **207 TL:** S.I. 7506; **TR:** Moorland; **B:** NYHS 45155. **208 TL:** U of Rochester; **BL:** NYPL 1427 E5; **BR (both pins):** S.I. 2003-24270. **208-209** LCMS 12997-1. **209 TR:** U of Rochester; **BR:** SSC No. WRSPa13. **210 TL:** NYPL 1427 B2; **BL:** LCMS Blatch 12:12, p124. **210-211** NYPL 1427 E3. **212 TL:** Corbis; **BL:** WSMP; **BR:** ECST. **212-213** LCMS Blatch 12:12, p120. **213 R:** LCMS Blatch 12:12, p121. **214 L:** Huntington. **214-215** LCMS 10:10, p154. **216 T:** Bryn Mawr Catt 0126; **B:** WSMP, *Woman Voter*, July 1913. **217 T:** LCMS Blatch 8:85; **B:** S.L. MC133, Reel 7. **218 TL:** LCMS Blatch 11:11, p76; **BL:** ECST. **218-219** Corbis. **219 R:** WSMP. **220** LC Sun Coll. **221 TL:** WSMP, *Life*, 1913; **TR:** WSMP, *Life*, August 1912. **221 B:** LC-B2-2612-9. **222** LC-USZC2-1064. **223 L:** WSMP; **TR:** WSMP; **BR:** WSMP, *New York Sun*, March 31, 1913

Chapter 9. 1914

224 LC RB, JK1896.H4 vol8. **225 L:** S.I.; **TR:** S.I. 2003-24271; **BR:** S.L. AW 378-1. **226 T:** Maryland HS, Baltimore Z24.206; **B:** LCMS Blatch 10:10 p93. **227 T:** Harriet Beecher Stowe Center, Hartford, CT. Day Photo Album p.18; **B:** SSC S/US 12/182. **228 TL:** Valentine Museum L69.27.1; **BL:** Virginia State Library and Archives, Woman Suffrage Papers; **BR:** Valentine Museum x49.37.43. **228-229** Virginia State Library and Archives. **229 TR:** S.L. PC7 (3)-2; **TC:** SSC S/US 13/206; **B:** S.L. WRC-7a-15. **230-231** Minn. HS 12378. **231 TR:** Minn. HS J7.11/r6, 58797; **BR:** Minn. HS J7.11/p2, 1316. **232 TL:** Western Reserve HS LWV PG55; **BL:** Plain Dealer; **BR:** S.I. 2003-24268. **232-233** Chicago HS ICHi-09570. **233 TR:** Chicago HS ICHi-26702; **BR:** FC. **234 TL:** U of Chicago Library, Wells Papers, vol 5, F7, ph12; **BL:** LC-USZ62-33793; **R:** U of Illinois at Chicago Library, E.T. Ross Coll. **235 TL:** LC-USZ62-34032; **TR:** LC-USZ62-37933; **B:** NA 208-PM-14M-2. **236 TL:** S.L. MC83 1:5; **TR:** Brown Bros.; **BR:** Brown Bros.; **BL:** LC Sun Coll. **237 T:** LC-USZ62-24056; **B:** S.I. 2003-24275. **238 TL:** LCMS NAWSA Reel 25; **BR:** S.I. 81-8600. **238-239** S.L. MC83 1:15. **239 TR & BR:** S.L. Suff leaflets, CU file, Foley. **240** Tenn. St. Library and Archives Overall Papers. **241 T:** Missouri HS, St. Louis Groups 62; **BR:** U of Missouri, Western Historical MS Coll. - Columbia, Finley Album C3422 v.1; **BL:** ECST. **242 TL:** Plain Dealer; **B:** LC RB, SBA Coll. **242-243** Montana HS PAC-88-29. **243 TR:** Montana HS PAC-74-98.10; **BR:** FC. **244 TL & BL:** Bancroft Woman Suffrage in the West F846, p18; **BR:** S.I. 2003-24268. **244-245** Bryn Mawr Catt 0089. **245 R:** NWP. **246 T:** FC; **B:** Bryn Mawr Catt 0186. **247 L:** Denison Suffrage 2:11; **TR:**

ECST, also S.I. 2003-24280; **BR:** S.I. 81-8601. **248** Bancroft Anne Martin Papers. **249 T:** NJHS Moorfield Papers; **B:** WSMP. **250 TL:** SSC Garrison 110/v; **TR:** NYPL 1427 E7; **BR:** NYPL 1427 F1; **BL:** LCMS Blatch 11:6. **251 T:** LC-B2-3443-11; **B:** LC-USZ62-30780.

Chapter 10. 1915

252 WSMP. **253 TL:** Collection of Dr. Danny O. Crew; **B:** Johns Hopkins LSL Box 154 #164; **TR and BR pins:** S.I. 2003-24272. **254** WSMP, *Woman Voter*, October 1915. **255 T:** U of Rochester SBA Papers; **B:** Huntington SBA 14:36. **256 TL:** Huntington SBA 14:37; **TR:** HS of PA Ms 2095 #145; **BR:** HS of PA Ms 2095 #130; **BL:** Huntington SBA 14:38. **257** WSMP. **258 TL:** Denison SBA 1:62; **BL:** S.I. 2003-24272; **BR:** S.I. 81-8597. **258-259** HS of PA Ms 2095 #126. **260** LC-USZ62-7089. **261 T:** S.L. A68-432-2; **B:** Huntington SBA 14:38. **262-263** NJHS Moorfield Papers. **263 TR:** LC-USZ62-7091; **BR:** LC-USZ62-7092. **264 T:** LC-USZ62-7093; **B:** LC-USZ62-7090. **265 L:** SSC No. WRSM; **TR:** S.I. 2003-2427; **BR:** S.I. 81-8610. **266 TL:** S.L.; **TR:** Mount Holyoke College Library/Archives; **B (both):** SSC S/US 13/206. **267 T:** Corbis; **BL:** S.L. Suff Cartoons; **BR:** SSC Record 2038. **268 TL:** WSMP; **TR:** LC-USZ62-25338; **BR:** WSMP; **BL:** WSMP. **269 L:** Wisc. HS 7-202, CF67285; **R:** S.I. 2003-24274. **270 TL:** LC-USZ62-72985; **BL & BR:** S.I. 2003-24268. **270-271** NYPL NAWSA Ms. Box 7. **271 TR:** Chicago HS ICHi-29417; **Second R:** LCMS NAWSA Reel 69; **Third R:** LCMS NAWSA Reel 69; **BR:** NYPL NAWSA Ms. Box 8; **BL:** NYPL 1428 B1. **272 TL:** LC-USZ62-42635; **BL:** WSMP; **BC:** ECST; **BR:** SSC Record 2093. **272-273** Denver PL 11407. **273 TR:** S.I. 81-10205; **BR:** LC-USZ62-108198; **BL:** S.I. 81-8596. **274 TL:** ECST, also LCMS Blatch 10:153; **BL:** FC; **TR & BR:** S.I. 2003-24273. **274-275** LCMS Blatch 11:11, p106. **275 B:** LCMS Blatch 11:22. **276 TL:** Huntington 323 (1) #61; **TR:** LC-USZ62-79502; **B:** S.L. **277 T:** NWP; **B:** NWP. **278 TL:** LCMS 704711. **278-279** Chicago HS DN-065590. **279 TR:** Denison SBA 1:84; **BR:** WSMP. **280-281** WSMP. **282 TR:** Corbis; **B:** S.I. 81-8596. **282-283** Corbis. **283 TR:** LC-USZ62-50048; **BR:** LCMS Blatch 11:147. **284 TL:** S.I. Archives Warshaw Coll.; **BR:** SSC Ames 51A/600b, *Woman's Journal*, March 4, 1916; **BL pin:** S.I. 81-8596; **BR pin:** ECST. **284-285** NJHS Moorfield Papers. **285 TR:** LC-B2-3562-7; **BR:** LCMS Blatch, 11:11, p153. **286 T:** NJHS Moorfield Papers; **BL:** S.I. 2003-24280; **BR:** SSC S/SF 18/244. **287 L:** U of Rochester; **TR:** New York State Library, St. Education Dept. SC13339; **BR:** SSC S/US 17/238. **288 TL:** SSC No. WRSBr1; **BL:** Robert F. Wagner Labor Archives, NYU NP10. **288-289** NYPL NAWSA

Ms. Box 7. **289 TR:** Emory U. Special Coll., Raoul Papers; **BL:** SSC Record 2070. **290 TL:** S.I. 2003-24273. **290-291** LC-USZ62-50393. **292 TL:** LCMS Blatch 11:11, p69; **BL:** LC-USZ62-38965; **BR:** S.I. 81-8588. **292-293** LC-B2-3643-12. **293 TR:** WSMP. **294** WSMP. **295 T:** S.L. PC7 (4)-2; **B:** U of Pittsburgh 78:20 #2. **296** Johns Hopkins LSL Box 11 #44. **297 T:** Corbis; **B:** SSC Record 2068. **298-299** LC-USZC2-1183. **299 TR:** WSMP.

Chapter 11. 1916

300 Hoover US5086. **301 TL:** LCMS Catt; **TR pin:** S.I. 77-4108; **BL:** LC-B2-3868-16. **302 TL:** SSC S/US 5/95; **BL & BR:** S.I. 81-8595. **302-303 T:** S.L. MC83 1:15. **302-303 B:** Kansas SHS FK2.S5, T.56.1916x2. **303 TR:** NWP; **BR:** WSMP. **304 TL:** Huntington SBA 14:37; **BR:** FC. **304-305** Chicago HS DN-66513. **305 TR:** WSMP; **BR:** NYPL 1428 A1; **BL:** LCMS 34355-2. **306 T:** Bryn Mawr Catt 0139; **B:** S.I. 75059. **307 T:** Chicago HS DN-066509; **B:** WSMP, *Woman Voter,* June 1916. **308 B:** S.I. 81-8585. **308-309** Bryn Mawr Catt 0176. **309 TR:** NYPL 1428 A2; **BR:** SSC Flat File Y Ames. **310 T:** Brown Bros.; **B:** WSMP, *Woman Voter,* July 1916. **311** LC Lot 12362. **312 T:** NWP; **B:** NWP. **313 TL:** S.I. 76-3036; **TR:** S.L. MC399 f.277; **BR:** Vassar College Libraries, Elsie Hill Paper; **BL:** NWP. **314 TL:** S.L. MC399 f.340; **BL:** WSMP, *Suffragist,* Sept. 9, 1916; **BR:** S.I. 81-8597. **314-315** LCMS 34355-3. **315 TR:** NWP, and LCMS 605715 #13. **316 TL:** S.I. 2003-24278; **B:** SHS of Iowa, Des Moines, Iowa Suffrage Coll. **316-317** Racine County HS and Museum 802, 11:1, 14. **317 TR:** SSC Record 2062; **B:** ECST.

Chapter 12. 1917

318 WSMP, also NWP. **319 TL:** LC-B2-4112-9; **TR:** S.I. 74-7508; **B:** NWP. **320-321** LC-USZ62-10855. **322 TL:** LC-B2-4112-10; **BL:** Philadelphia Jewish Archives Center Katzenstein Papers. **322-323** LCMS-34355-4. **324 TL:** Huntington SBA Clippings 16:23; **BL:** NWP. **324-325 T:** NA 165-WW-600A-14. **324-325 B:** LC-USZ62-31799. **325 TR:** LC-USZ62-994; **BR:** SSC. **326 T:** SHS of North Dakota C-278; **B:** NWHP. **327 T:** LCMS 15404-4; **B:** S.L. MC246, f37. **328 T:** NA 165-WW-424-P-74; **B:** SSC Ames 51A/600b. **329 L:** Corbis; **TR:** LCMS NWP; **BR:** S.L. MC392 40/665.

Chapter 13. 1917 World War I

330 LC-USZC4-3310. **331 pins:** WSMP; **TL:** NA 165-WW-600A-1; **BL:** S.I. 75053. **332 TL:** WSMP, *Puck* 1915, also S.I.

65638; **TR:** S.L. A69-4-4; **B:** Ishtar Films. **333** WSMP. **334** LC-USZC4-5762. **335 T:** S.L. WRC-1110-4; **B:** WSMP. **336 TL:** SSC S 10/162; **TR:** NA 165-WW-600A-1; **BR:** Columbia U NY State WS Assoc. Box 3; **BL:** WSMP. **337 T:** Virginia State Library and Archives; **B:** S.L. A/C 672-5. **338 T:** LC-B2-4731-5; **BL:** FC; **BR:** Culver. **339 T:** Museum of NM #58117; **B:** Museum of NM #58116. **340 TL:** S.L. Suff Cartoons; **BL:** LC-B2-4429-2; **BR:** WSMP. **340-341** NA 165-WW-600-D-7. **341 TR:** NA 86-G-6T-5; **BR:** NA 86-G-5L-1.

Chapter 14. 1917

342-343 LC-USZ62-48718. **344 TL:** NA 165-WW-600A-20; **B:** S.L. MC399 18:290. **344-345** Corbis. **346 TL:** NWP; **BL:** Corbis. **346-347** Corbis. **347 R:** S.L. MC399-5. **348 TL:** SSC; **BL:** Corbis. **348-349** NA 165-WW-600A-2. **349 TR:** NWP; **BR:** NWP. **350 TL:** NA 165-WW-600A-5; **BR:** NWP. **350-351** NA 165-WW-600A-16. **352-353** LC-USZ62-48964. **353 TR:** S.I. 2003-24275. **354 TL:** LCMS NWP, also NWP; **B:** S.I. 74-7523. **354-355** NA 165-WW-600A-12. **356 TL:** NWP; **TR:** WSMP; **B:** NWP. **357** LCMS 605715-15. **358 T:** LCMS 605715-21; **B:** WSMP. **359 TL:** Wisc. HS WHi (x3) 50844; **TR:** S.I. 88-1313; **BR:** S.I. 73-8072; **BL:** WSMP, *New York Call,* August 23, 1917. **360** WSMP. **361** NWP. **362 T:** Corbis; **B:** S.L. Periodical. **363 TL:** LC-USZ62-57866; **TR:** NWP; **BR:** WSMP; **BL:** LCMS 605715-20.

Chapter 15. 1917 New York

364 Hoover US5084. **365 L:** Hoover US5085; **TR:** ECST; **BR:** S.I. 79-1011. **366 TL:** NYPL NAWSA Ms. Box 7; **BL:** WSMP. **366-367** SSC S/SF 3/73. **367 B:** NYHS. **368 T:** SSC; **B:** WSMP. **369 TL:** Bryn Mawr Catt 0270; **TR:** Hoover US5078; **B:** S.I. 78-17170. **370 L:** S.I. 81-8597; **R:** Bryn Mawr Catt 0168. **371 T:** Corbis; **B:** Bryn Mawr Catt 0260. **372-373 T:** WSMP. **372-373 B:** SSC Record 2067. **373 T:** Hoover US5074; **B:** Hoover US5076. **374-375** Corbis. **375 R:** NYHS 71085. **376 T:** Friends Historical Library; **B:** WSMP, *New York Journal* 1917. **377 L:** LC-USZ62-20177; **R:** WSMP. **378** WSMP. **379** LC-USZ62-55372.

Chapter 16. 1918-1919

380 LC-USZ62-1187. **381 L:** Hoover US5083; **R:** S.I. 2003-24270. **382 TL:** SSC No. WRPM; **BL:** S.I. 2003-24275; **R:** S.I. 81-10201. **383** NA 165-WW-600A-3. **384** SSC Record 2063. **385** WSMP, *Woman Citizen,* August 27, 1918. **386 L:** LCMS 704711. **386-387** NWP. **387 TR:** S.L. A69-4-; **B:** NWP. **388**

TL: LC-USZ62-112770; **BL:** LC-USZ62-112771. **388-389** LC-USZ62-63001. **390 TL:** S.I. 76-3072. **390-391** NWP. **392 TL:** WSMP, *Woman Voter*, January 1917. **392-393 T:** NWP. **392-393 B:** Bryn Mawr Catt 0010. **393 TR:** NA 165-WW-269B-3; **BR:** ECST. **394 TL:** Nevada HS M50; **TR:** Nevada HS M4; **BR:** NWP; **BL:** Nevada HS Bio M-67. **395 L:** S.L. M133 Reel D4; **R:** Bryn Mawr Catt 0229. **396 T:** FC; **B:** Huntington Votes for Women #35. **397** Ford Museum P.189.11. **398 L:** S.L. MC83 1:5. **398-399** NA 165-WW-600A-9. **400 TL:** S.L. A74-11-31; **B:** FC. **400-401** LC-USZ62-47284. **401 R:** S.L. A-74-12-15. **402 T:** NWP; **RC:** WSMP; **BR:** Bancroft *SF Call* negatives. **403 TL:** NWP; **TR:** NWP; **B:** Bancroft *SF Call* negatives. **404 T:** NWP; **B:** NWP. **405 L:** WSMP, *Crisis*, May 1916. **both pins:** S.I. 81-8601. **406 TL:** Austin History Center, Austin PL, E.48.7(3); **TR:** Austin History Center, Austin PL, PICA 11669; **BR:** Austin History Center, Austin PL, McCallum Papers, Part 1, FPE.4, Bx6, f3,20; **BL:** Austin History Center, Austin PL, McCallum Papers E.4B f.1#17. **407 T:** Wisc. HS WHi (x3) 18424; **B:** SHS of Iowa, Des Moines, Iowa Woman Suffrage Coll. **408 L:** Cleveland PL; **R:** WSMP. **409 TL:** NWP; **TR:** S.I. 79-8397; **B:** LC-USZ62-13209. **410 T:** Huntington SBA Clippings 3 (76f); **B:** Huntington 323, 2:9. **411** Huntington Votes for Women #56.

Chapter 17. 1919-1920

412-413 LC-USZ62-78691. **413 B:** Houston Metro. Research Center, Houston PL, MSS74, 3:23. **414 T:** Bryn Mawr Catt 0012; **B:** LCMS NAWSA Reel 68. **415 T:** S.L. PC1 (147b)-27; **B:** S.L. PC1-147-36. **416 L:** Plain Dealer; **BR:** S.I. 2003-24277. **416-417** LC-USZ62-78691. **417 TR:** LC-USZ62-132970; **BR:** S.I. 2003-24280. **418 TL:** NWHP; **TR:** S.L. A74-11-1; **B:** NWP. **419 T:** Brown Bros.; **B:** WSMP, *Woman Citizen*, March 6, 1920. **420 T:** NYPL/Schomberg SC-CN-90-0486; **BL:** S.I. 76-6420; **BR:** WSMP. **421 T:** LC-USZ62-95442; **B:** LC-USZ62-123841. **422** NWP. **423 T:** NWP; **B:** S.I. 76-2984.

424 Cleveland PL. **425** Tenn. St. Library and Archives, J. Pearson Papers, 1:13. **426 T:** Bryn Mawr Catt 0090; **B:** S.I. 76-2985. **427 T:** WSMP; **BL:** NWP; **BR:** S.I. 81-8610.

Chapter 18. 1920

428 WSMP. **429 L:** LC-USZ62-57860; **R:** Corbis. **430 T:** S.L. PC7 (6)-2; **B:** LCMS 15404-3. **431** Culver. **432** LC-USZ62-14447. **433 T:** Corbis; **B:** Vassar College Libraries, Elsie Hill Papers. **434 TL:** SSC S/US 15/224; **B:** S.I. 81-8587. **434-435** LC-USZ62-76150. **435 TR:** LC-USZ62-75334; **BR:** Minn. HS 33314 J7.11/r1; **BL:** U of Louisville CS33312C. **436** LC-B2-4549-13. **437** S.L. M133 Reel D6.

Epilogue: After 1920

438-439 SHS of Iowa, Des Moines, Iowa Woman Suffrage Coll. **440 T:** LC-USZ62-14420; **B:** LC-USZ62-46764. **441 L:** LWV; **TR:** LC-USZ62-72736; **BR:** FC. **442 TL:** Denison SBA 1:35; **BL:** WSMP; **R:** SSC SBA 2/35. **443 L:** LC-USZ62-14416; **TR:** S.I. 78-2695; **BR:** WSMP. **444 T:** Vassar College Libraries, Elsie Hill Papers; **BL:** WSMP; **BR:** WSMP. **445** Corbis. **446 TL:** U of Illinois WS Coll.; **LC:** S.I. 60659B; **BL:** U of Kentucky Libraries, Special Coll., Clay PA46M4; **R:** NM State Archives, Bergere Coll. #21252. **447 L:** Chicago HS ICHi-14104; **TR:** Huntington SBA/CA 5:63; **RC:** LCMS NAWSA Reel 25; **BR:** WSMP. **448 TL:** WSMP; **TR:** LC-USZ62-41834; **BR:** WSMP; **BL:** SSC Record 2057. **449 TL:** Cleveland PL; **TR:** Huntington Ph-WS#3998; **B:** WSMP. **450** LWV, Kalamazoo, MI. **451** S.L. *The Dearborn Independent*, March 22, 1924. **452** WSMP. **453 T:** S.L. M133 Reel E17; **B:** NWHP. **454 TL:** Corbis; **BL:** Corbis; **BR:** WSMP. **454-455** Washington Star Coll., copyright *Washington Post*, reprinted by permission of the DC Public Library. **455 TR:** Corbis; **BR:** S.I. 77-12997-25A; **BL:** Corbis. **456 TL:** WSMP; **TR:** NWHP/NASA; **BR:** Seneca Falls HS #1421; **BL:** WSMP.

Index

Edey, Mrs. Frederick, *429*
Edison, Thomas, 164
education, 18, 27, 227
Edwards, Mrs. Richard, *440*
Eliot, Charles, 57
Elliott, Harriet Wiseman, 453
Emory, Julia, 399, *421*
Empire State Campaign
    Committee, 207, 269, 272,
    275, 289, 292-93, 296
employment, 18, 335, 453
English suffragettes. *See* Great
    Britain; Pankhurst,
    Emmeline
Equal Franchise Society, 110
Equal Rights Amendment
    (ERA), 444, 454-55
equal rights legislation
    campaigns, 17-18, 28, 438,
    444, 454-55
Equal Suffrage Associations, 74,
    76, 88, 95, 130, 145, 147,
    172-73, 217, 265, 316, 400,
    406
equal suffrage countries, 309
Equal Suffrage League, 228-29,
    337
equal suffrage states, 139, 238,
    248, 261, 301, 310-11
Equality League of Self-
    Supporting Women,
    104-05, 108-10, 114,
    127-28, 156
Every Body's League, 173
Everywoman Suffrage Club of
    Black Women, 230

F

14th Amendment, 23, 33-34, 39
15th Amendment, 23, 27
Fabian Society, 104
fairs, 178, 214, 237, 241, 243
family planning, 438, 449
farmerettes, 338
fashions of suffragists, 14-17,
    121, 159, 171, 233, 303,
    308-09, 338. *See also* colors
Fawcett, Millicent Garrett, 100,
    220
Federal Children's Bureau, 452
Federal suffrage amendment,
    50, 78, 123, 177, 185,
    190-91, 202-03, 218, 225-
    27, 233, 248, 253, 261, 277,

281, 296, 301-02, 305, 308,
    311, 343, 358, 379, 383,
    438. *See also* Congress;
    Equal Rights Amendment;
    Wilson, President
    acknowledgment of
    Congressional supporters,
    437
called "Susan B. Anthony
    Amendment," 235
compromise bill, 405
Congressional votes, 225,
    253, 384, 390, 409
constitutionality of, 216
final push, 379, 381-411
first petition drive, 123
lawsuits against, 216, 417
lobbying efforts, 343, 349,
    379, 381, 383-85, 390-91
opposition to, 175, 238-39,
    405, 419, 424-25
ratification, 409-29
signing of bill, 410
states' rights issue, 235
voting rights, 33, 35, 39, 40
Feickert, Lillian F., 261, 285,
    445
feminism under attack, 450
Ferguson, Isabella Munro, *339*
Field, Sara Bard, 245, *277-79,*
    281, *305,* 312
Finland, 97
Finley, Caroline (Dr.), 336
Fitzgerald, Susan Walker, 130,
    168, 267, 447
Flagg, James Montgomery, 225,
    295
flags of the suffrage movement,
    83, 139, 153, 155, 204, 327,
    418, 432
Flanagan, Catherine, 351-*52,*
    424, 427
Flexner, Eleanor (historian), 3,
    19, 57, 87, 98, 129, 174,
    340, 417, 439
Florida, 421, 437
Foley, Margaret, 102, 130, *170,*
    229, 245
Foltz, Clara Shortridge, 145,
    446-47
force-feedings, 220, 357, 360-62
Ford, Linda (historian), 221
Forten, Margaretta, 12
Foster, Abby Kelley, *4,* 10, 13, 41
Foster, Rachel, 55, *63*

Foster, Stephen, 27, 41
Foulke, William Dudley, 65
Fowler, Robert, 235
free speech issues, 355
Freeman, Elisabeth, *163, 186*
Friedan, Betty, 454
Fremont, John C., 17
"Front Door Lobby," 383, 410
Fuller, Margaret, 11
funding, 53, 71, 179, 204, 235,
    245, 258, 267, 272, 282,
    311, 379, 418. *See also*
    philanthropists
Funk, Antoinette, 216, 235, 243,
    245, *335*
Furuhjelm, Annie, 97

G

Gage, Frances Dana, 17
Gage, Matilda Joslyn, 27, 34,
    36, 42, 43, 53, *59,* 61, *63,*
    65, 67
Gaitliss, Flora, 273
Gardener, Helen H., *188, 383-*
    84, *408, 410,* 429, 452
Gardner, Matilda Hall, 348, 418
Garrison, William Lloyd, 6, 10,
    59, 212, 229, 250
Garwood, Omar E., 213
Gellhorn, Mrs. George, 241,
    440
General Fed. of Women's
    Clubs, 80
Georgia, 213, 234
German-American Alliance,
    240, 381
Gibson, Charles Dana, 335, 429
Gillette, Frederick H., *410*
Gillmore, Inez Haynes. *See*
    Irwin, Inez
Gilman, Charlotte Perkins, *95,*
    109, 128-*29,* 245
Giovannitti, Arturo, *273*
Golden Lane, 308-09
Goodrich, Sarah Knox, *59*
Gordon, Ann (historian), 12
Gordon, Felice (historian), 450
Gordon, Kate, 94, 96, *181,* 311
Gordon, Laura De Force, 50
Gorham, Mary, *77*
Gougar, Helen M., 38, 55, *59,*
    82
Graf, Bertha, 421
Graham, Hattie, 105

Graham, Sara (historian), 87,
    413, 436, 447
Gram, Betty, 424, 427
Grant, President Ulysses S., 37
Great Britain's suffrage
    movement, 99-103, 110,
    121, 128, 220-23, 236, 241,
    360, 384. *See also*
    Pankhurst, Emmeline
Great Depression, 450, 452
Greeley, Helen Hoy, 145
Green, Julie (Dr.), 242
Greenleaf, John Brooks, 71
Gregory, Alice (Dr.), 336
Gregg, Laura, 78, 90, 96, 172
Grimke sisters (Angelina and
    Sarah), 3, 33, 229
Gripenberg, Alexandra, *63*
Grossman, Leonard J. 213
Groth, Sophia Magelsson, *63*
Grove, Mrs. George, *189*
"guerrilla warfare," 220

H

Haley, Margaret, 145-*46*
Hall, Louise, *168*
Hamilton, Alice (Dr.), 251
Hamilton, Grant E., 49
Hanna, Phil, 296
Happersett, Reese, 35
Harbert, Elizabeth Boynton, *59,*
    63
Hard, William, 273
Harland, Hester A., *76*
Harper, Frances E.W. , *13*
Harper, Ida Husted (historian),
    43, 77, 110, 121, *410,* 439
Harriman, Florence Hurst, 445
Hasbrouck, Lydia, 16
Havemeyer, Louisine, *282-83,*
    285, 312, 401-02, 438
Hay, Mary Garrett, 74, *77,* 90,
    365-66, 373, 395, *410,* 438,
    445
Hearst, Phoebe A., 304
Hemingway, Lulu, 188
Hicks, Frederick C., Jr. (Rep.),
    384
Higgins, Bertha, 234
Higginson, Thomas
    Wentworth, 28
Hill, Alberta, 109, 275
Hill, Elsie, 188, *313,* 404
Hill, Mrs. Homer M., 78